THE EMC Write-In READER

Reading Strategies and Test Practice

REDWOOD LEVEL

EMCParadigm Publishing Company

Staff Credits

Editorial

Laurie Skiba
Managing Editor

Brenda Owens
Editor

Becky Palmer
Reading Specialist

Nichola Torbett
Associate Editor

Jennifer Joline Anderson
Associate Editor

Diana Moen
Associate Editor

Mary Curfman
Editorial Consultant

Paul Spencer
Art and Photo Researcher

Design and Production

Shelley Clubb
Production Manager

Matthias Frasch
Cover Designer and
Production Specialist

Jennifer Wreisner
Text Designer

Erica Tava
Production Specialist

Lisa Beller
Production Specialist

Sharon O'Donnell
Proofreader

ISBN 0-8219-2908-9

© 2005 EMC Corporation

Published by EMC/Paradigm Publishing
875 Montreal Way
St. Paul, Minnesota 55102
www.emcp.com
E-mail: educate@emcp.com

Printed in the United States of America
10 9 8 7 6 5 4 3   XXX 10 09 08 07 06

Consultants and Contributors

Maria Callis
Reading Specialist/Department Chair
Trafalgar Middle School
Cape Coral, Florida

Shari Carlson
English/Reading Instructor
Fridley Middle School
Fridley, Minnesota

T. Carolyn Coleman
Language Arts/Reading Instructor
Gwinnett County Schools
Lawrenceville, Georgia

Dr. Edmund J. Farrell
Emeritus Professor of English Education
University of Texas at Austin
Austin, Texas

Sharon Kremer
Language Arts Instructor
Denton High School
Denton, Texas

Lisa Larnerd
English Department Chairperson
Basic High School
Henderson, Nevada

Beth Lee
Language Arts Instructor
Heritage Middle School
Longmont, Colorado

Cecilia Lewis
Language Arts Instructor
Mariner High School
Cape Coral, Florida

John Oricchio
Educational Consultant
Port Washington, New York

John Owens
Literacy Specialist
Heritage Middle School
Longmont, Colorado

Mary Spychalla
English/Reading Instructor
Valley Middle School
Apple Valley, Minnesota

Contents

UNIT 9 DEVELOPING VOCABULARY SKILLS

UNIT 10 TEST-TAKING STRATEGIES

APPENDICES

Overview of Skills

Literary Tools

Informational and Visual Media Tools

Overview of Features

The EMC Write-In Reader helps you to interact with reading selections as never before! This portable anthology guides you in using reading strategies—reading tools that help you get more meaning from what you read. Questions and tips in the margins prompt you to record your thoughts and notes as you read. Using selections from the *Literature and the Language Arts* textbook, *The EMC Write-In Reader* gives you an opportunity to complete rich reading tasks, expand your reading skills, and increase your test-taking abilities.

The EMC Write-In Reader shows you how to use reading strategies before, during, and after reading and includes activities that develop your comprehension, fluency, and vocabulary skills.

The EMC Write-In Reader helps you learn how reading strategies work, how to combine them, and how to apply them to any reading task. These eight active reading strategies help you interact with a text to create meaning.

1. Read with a Purpose
2. Connect to Prior Knowledge
3. Write Things Down
4. Make Predictions
5. Visualize
6. Use Text Organization
7. Tackle Difficult Vocabulary
8. Monitor Your Reading Progress

Detailed instruction on one reading strategy is carried through the before, during, and after stages of the reading process for each selection.

The EMC Write-In Reader offers a unique text organization, including

- an **introduction to reading** unit that defines and explains the reading process, eight active reading strategies, and fix-up ideas to use when you have trouble
- a unit focusing on **essential reading skills** and tasks evaluated on standardized tests
- a unit for each **genre,** or kind of text, with an introduction on how to apply reading strategies to that genre
- a unit on **vocabulary development** to help you unlock word meaning
- a unit on **standardized test practice** to help you prepare for state and national tests
- an appendix of **fluency activities** to build word recognition skills, silent reading fluency, and oral reading fluency
- an appendix containing a multitude of **reading strategy graphic organizers**

Become a successful, active reader with *The EMC Write-In Reader!*

How to use this book

BEFORE READING

1 **Reader's Resource** provides background information to help you **set a purpose** for reading.

2 The **Active Reading Strategy** gives you step-by-step instruction on how to use the reading strategy **before reading**.

3 A **Graphic Organizer** for each selection helps you to **visualize** and **understand text organization** as you read.

CONNECT

1 **Reader's resource**

Richard Peck notes that his books have one theme in common: that a person will never begin to grow up until he or she becomes independent from other students. Peck's stories examine characters who learn to think and act for themselves. In **"Priscilla and the Wimps,"** young people learn to deal with a gang of bullies in their school. As you read the story, think about who the hero of the story is and what you can learn from that person.

4 **Word watch**

PREVIEW VOCABULARY

bar	pun
fate	slither
laceration	subtle

5 **Reader's journal**

What have you or some of your classmates done when intimidated by a bully or gang member?

_____
_____
_____
_____

"Priscilla and the Wimps"
by Richard Peck

2 *Active* READING STRATEGY

MAKE PREDICTIONS

Before Reading ▶ MAKE PRELIMINARY PREDICTIONS

❑ Preview the story. Look at the title, the Reader's Resource, and the illustration. Think about what you know about the story.
❑ Then read the first sentence in the story. What do you think this story will be about?
❑ Place your initial prediction about the story in the cluster chart that follows. As you read, you will make additional predictions about the characters listed in the chart.

Graphic Organizer: Prediction Cluster Chart **3**

Prediction 1
Before reading: What will happen in this story?

Prediction 2
After line 28: What will happen to Monk?

"Priscilla and the Wimps"

Prediction 3
After line 48: What will happen to Melvin?

Prediction 4
After line 85: What will happen to Priscilla?

4 **WordWatch** gives you the opportunity to **preview** the vocabulary Words for Everyday Use for the selection.

5 **Reader's Journal** helps you to **connect** with what you know and to your own life.

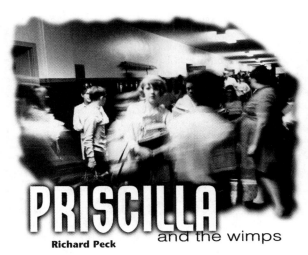

PRISCILLA and the wimps

Richard Peck

Listen, there was a time when you couldn't even go to the *rest room* around this school without a pass. And I'm not talking about those little pink tickets made out by some teacher. I'm talking about a pass that could cost anywhere up to a buck, sold by Monk Klutter.

Not that Mighty Monk ever touched money, not in public. The gang he ran, which ran the school for him, was his collection agency. They were Klutter's Kobras, a name spelled out in nailheads on six well-known black plastic windbreakers.

10   Monk's threads were more . . . <u>subtle</u>. A pile-lined suede battle jacket with lizard-skin flaps over tailored Levis and a pair of ostrich-skin boots, brassed-toed and suitable for kicking people around. One of his Kobras did nothing all day but walk a half step behind Monk, carrying a fitted bag with Monk's gym shoes, a roll of rest-room passes, a cashbox, and a switchblade that Monk gave himself manicures with at lunch over at the Kobras' table.

words for everyday use	**sub • tle** (sə' tal) *adj.,* delicate or refined. *The perfume was so <u>subtle</u> that the smell didn't overpower the room.*

During Reading ➤ 6

MAKE PREDICTIONS

❑ Follow along as your teacher reads the first six paragraphs of the story aloud. When your teacher stops, make another prediction on your chart by answering this question: What will happen to Monk?

❑ Continue reading on your own. Pause from time to time to make predictions in your chart. To help you make predictions, ask yourself questions like "What will happen next?", "What will happen to this character?", and "How will the character solve this problem?" Add your predictions to your chart as new circles.

7

NOTE THE FACTS

Who runs the narrator's school?

Monk Klutter
_____

6 **During Reading** instruction in the margin tells you how to apply the reading strategy as you read.

7 **Note the Facts** questions give you the space to **make notes** about factual information as you read (see example).

How to use this book

DURING READING

8 Think and Reflect questions deepen your understanding of what you are reading.

9 Literary Tools explain **literary techniques and concepts** and help you recognize these elements as you read.

10 Mark the Text activities ask you to **underline or highlight** information in the text to help you read actively and organize your thoughts (see example).

---

8 THINK AND REFLECT

The narrator says, "I paid up on a regular basis. And I might add: so would you." Do you think the narrator is right? What would you do in this situation? **(Extend)**

_____

_____

Literary TOOLS 9

CHARACTER. A **character** is a person or other being that takes part in the action of a literary work. Characters can be classified as *major characters* or *minor characters*. Major characters play an important role in the literary work. Minor characters play less important roles. List the characters you have encountered so far. Then circle the names of new characters you meet.

_____

_____

_____

10 MARK THE TEXT

Underline or highlight why Priscilla and Melvin are called The Odd Couple.

---

20   Speaking of lunch, there were a few cases of advanced malnutrition among the newer kids. The ones who were a little slow in handing over a cut of their lunch money and were therefore <u>barred</u> from the cafeteria. Monk ran a tight ship.

I admit it, I'm five foot five, and when the Kobras <u>slithered</u> by, with or without Monk, I shrank. And I admit this, too: I paid up on a regular basis. And I might add: so would you.

This school was old Monk's Garden of Eden. Unfortunately for him, there was a serpent in it. The reason Monk didn't recognize trouble when it was staring him in the face is that the serpent in the Kobras' Eden was a girl.

30   Practically every guy in school could show you his scars. Fang marks from Kobras, you might say. And they were all highly visible in the shower room: lumps, <u>lacerations</u>, blue bruises, you name it. But girls usually got off with a warning.

Except there was this one girl named Priscilla Roseberry. Picture a girl named Priscilla Roseberry, and you'll be light years off. Priscilla was, hands down, the largest student in our particular institution of learning. I'm not talking fat. I'm talking big. Even beautiful, in a bionic way. Priscilla wasn't inclined toward organized crime. Otherwise, she could have put together a gang that would turn Klutter's

40   Kobras into garter snakes.

Priscilla was basically a loner except she had one friend. A little guy named Melvin Detweiler. You talk about The Odd Couple. Melvin's one of the smallest guys above midget status ever seen. A really nice guy, but, you know—little. They even had lockers next to each other, in the same bank as mine. I don't know what they had going. I'm not saying this was a romance. After all, people deserve their privacy.

Priscilla was sort of above everything, if you'll pardon a

50   <u>pun</u>. And very calm, as only the very big can be. If there was anybody who didn't notice Klutter's Kobras, it was Priscilla.

---

11 words for everyday use

bar (bär) v., confine; keep out or exclude. *Because he wouldn't sit down, Chris was <u>barred</u> from riding the bus.*

slith • er (sli' thər) v., slide like a snake. *My cat was so sneaky that it <u>slithered</u> past me without my notice.*

lac • er • a • tion (la sə rā' shən) n., deeply cut wound. *His leg had many <u>lacerations</u> caused by the knife.*

pun (pən') n., humorous use of a word to suggest two or more meanings. *The comedian's <u>pun</u> made everyone laugh.*

---

11 Words for Everyday Use includes the definition and pronunciation for new vocabulary. A sample sentence demonstrates the use of the word in context.

Until one winter day after school when we were all grabbing our coats out of our lockers. And hurrying, since Klutter's Kobras made sweeps of the halls for after-school shakedowns.[1]

Anyway, up to Melvin's locker swaggers one of the Kobras. Never mind his name. Gang members don't need names. They've got group identity. He reaches down and grabs little Melvin by the neck and slams his head against 60 his locker door. The sound of skull against steel rippled all the way down the locker row, speeding the crowds on their way.

"Okay, let's see your pass," snarls the Kobra.

"A pass for what this time?" Melvin asks, probably still dazed.

"Let's call it a pass for very short people," says the Kobra, "a dwarf tax." He wheezes a little Kobra chuckle at his own wittiness. And already he's reaching for Melvin's wallet with the hand that isn't circling Melvin's windpipe. All this time, of course, Melvin and the Kobra are standing in Priscilla's 70 big shadow.

She's taking her time shoving her books into her locker and pulling on a very large-size coat. Then, quicker than the eye, she brings the side of her enormous hand down in a chop[2] that breaks the Kobra's hold on Melvin's throat. You could hear a pin drop in that hallway. Nobody'd ever laid a finger on a Kobra, let alone a hand the size of Priscilla's.

Then Priscilla, who hardly ever says anything to anybody except Melvin, says to the Kobra, "Who's your leader, wimp?"

This practically blows the Kobra away. First he's chopped 80 by a girl, and now she's acting like she doesn't know Monk Klutter, the Head Honcho of the World. He's so amazed, he tells her. "Monk Klutter."

"Never heard of him," Priscilla mentions. "Send him to see me." The Kobra just backs away from her like the whole situation is too big for him, which it is.

Pretty soon Monk himself slides up. He jerks his head once, and his Kobras slither off down the hall. He's going to handle this interesting case personally. "Who is it around here doesn't know Monk Klutter?"

---

1. **shakedowns.** Thorough and complete searches
2. **chop.** Sharp downward blow

Margin notes:

Use THE STRATEGY

MAKE PREDICTIONS. Stop after you read line 63. Make a prediction about what will happen to Melvin. Add this prediction to your chart.

FIX-UP IDEA

Connect to Prior Knowledge
If you are having trouble understanding the story, jot down thoughts that come to mind as you read such as: I don't understand this . . ., this reminds me of . . ., I like this part because . . ., I didn't guess that this would happen because. . . . Jot down your thoughts at least four times.

READ ALOUD

Read the highlighted text aloud. Then make a prediction about what will happen to Priscilla, and add it to your chart.

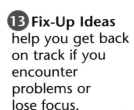

12 Use the Strategy reminds you to use the strategy to read actively.

13 Fix-Up Ideas help you get back on track if you encounter problems or lose focus.

14 Read Aloud activities in the margins help you to **build fluency** by giving you the chance to speak and listen to ideas you are trying to understand.

15 Footnotes explain references, unusual usage, and uncommon terms or words.

How to use this book

AFTER READING

16 **After Reading** activities follow up on the reading strategy and help you to summarize, synthesize, and reflect on the material you have read.

17 **Reading Skills and Test Practice** develops essential reading skills assessed on standardized tests.

18 **Think-Aloud Notes** help you organize your discussion ideas in writing.

---

16 *Reflect* O N   Y O U R   R E A D I N G

After Reading ➤ SHARE PREDICTIONS WITH A PARTNER

❑ With a partner, discuss the predictions you made. Discuss what details in the story helped you make your predictions.
❑ Share your predictions with the class. Were your predictions similar to those made by others? Which events affected everyone's predictions? How did your predictions change as you read on?

Reading Skills and Test Practice **17**

COMPARE AND CONTRAST IDEAS

Discuss with your partner how to answer the following questions that require you to compare and contrast ideas. Use the Think-Aloud Notes to write down your reasons for eliminating the incorrect answers.

_____1. The major difference between Monk at the beginning of the story and Monk at the end of the story is that at the end Monk is
   a. friendlier.
   b. an outsider.
   c. no longer a threat.
   d. a drop-out.

_____2. Melvin and Priscilla were called The Odd Couple because
   a. Melvin was small and Priscilla was tall.
   b. Melvin was rich and Priscilla was poor.
   c. Melvin was sloppy and Priscilla was neat.
   d. Melvin was smart and Priscilla was not smart.

How did using the reading strategy help you to answer the questions?

_____

_____

18

THINK-ALOUD NOTES

_____
_____
_____
_____
_____
_____
_____
_____
_____
_____
_____
_____
_____

Investigate, Inquire, and Imagine

RECALL: GATHER FACTS
1a. What does Priscilla do at the end of the story?

→ **INTERPRET: FIND MEANING**
1b. What makes Priscilla different from the other kids in the story? Is it just her size, or is there something else?

ANALYZE: TAKE THINGS APART
2a. Make a list of the actions of Monk and his Kobras.

→ **SYNTHESIZE: BRING THINGS TOGETHER**
2b. Based on your listing, summarize the main characteristics of Monk and his Kobras. How would you describe them?

EVALUATE: MAKE JUDGMENTS
3a. Do you think the humor in the story is effective? Is the ending effective? Explain.

→ **EXTEND: CONNECT IDEAS**
3b. What do you think is the lesson of this story?

Literary Tools

CHARACTER. A **character** is a person or being who takes part in the action of a story. The main character is called the *protagonist*. A character who struggles against the main character is called an *antagonist*. Characters can also be classified as *major characters* or *minor characters*. Major characters play an important role in the literary work. Minor characters play less important roles. A *one-dimensional character*, *flat character*, or *caricature* is one who exhibits a single quality or character trait. A *three-dimensional, full,* or *rounded character* is one who seems to have all the complexities of an actual human being. Use the chart below to determine what type of character each person is. One example has been done for you.

Type of Character	Narrator	Monk Klutter	Priscilla Roseberry	Melvin Detweiler
protagonist antagonist neither	✔			
major character minor character	✔			
one-dimensional character three-dimensional character	✔			

Explain why each of the characters is a one-dimensional or three-dimensional character.

19 Investigate, Inquire, and Imagine critical thinking questions further your understanding of the reading, from basic recall and interpret questions to those that ask you to analyze, synthesize, evaluate, and extend your ideas. Some questions also ask you to look at a specific point of view or a different perspective.

20 Literary Tools follows up on the literary techniques and concepts introduced during reading and asks you to apply your understanding.

How to use this book

 WordWorkshop activities apply vocabulary development concepts to the words from the selection.

WordWorkshop

VOCABULARY CARDS. A good way to help yourself learn and remember new words is to create vocabulary cards. Create a separate note card or notebook page for each word. Write the word in the center. In the top left corner write the definition. In the top right corner, write a synonym. In the bottom left corner, write a sentence using the word. In the bottom right corner, draw a picture to help you remember the word. Create your own vocabulary cards for the Words for Everyday Use for this story.

Read-Write Connection

Do you think Monk really spends a week in the locker? Explain your answer.

_____

_____

_____

_____

_____

_____

 Read-Write Connection gives you the opportunity to write about your responses to the selection.

Beyond the Reading 23

READ ABOUT PEER PRESSURE. One of the most important steps in growing up is learning to resist peer pressure, or the pressure to do what others your age expect or want you to do. Find a book in which a character faces peer pressure. Richard Peck's books all deal with this topic, as do many books by other young adult writers. Write a review of the book you have chosen. In your review, explain how the character does or does not resist peer pressure.

GO ONLINE. To find links and additional activities for this selection, visit the EMC Internet Resource Center at **emcp.com/languagearts** and click on Write-In Reader.

23 **Beyond the Reading** activities extend the ideas, topics, and themes from the selection.

UNIT 3 / READING FICTION   **71**

Unit ONE

Introduction to READING

PURPOSES OF READING

As a reader, you read for different purposes. You might **read for experience**—for insights into ideas, other people, and the world around you. You can also **read to learn**. This is the kind of reading done most often in school. When you read to learn, you may read textbooks, newspapers and newsmagazines, and visual "texts" such as art and photographs. The purpose of this type of reading is to gain knowledge. Third, you can **read for information**. When you read in this way, you are looking for specific data in sources such as reference materials, tables, databases, and diagrams.

Reading for Experience

READING LITERATURE

The most important reason to read literature is to educate your imagination. Reading literary works, which include fiction, nonfiction, poetry, and drama, will train you to think and feel in new ways. In the process of reading literary works and thinking about your own and others' responses to them, you will exercise your imagination as you encounter characters and situations that you would otherwise never know.

Reading to Learn

READING TEXTBOOKS AND NONFICTION

When you are reading to learn, you have two main goals: to expand your knowledge on a particular topic and to remember the information later. When you read to learn, you will often work with textbooks; reference books; periodicals such as newspapers, journals, and newsmagazines; and related art and photographs.

Textbooks provide a broad overview of a course of study in an objective, factual way. Other types of nonfiction works provide information about people, places, things, events, and ideas. Types of

NOTE THE FACTS

What are three purposes for reading?

_____

_____

_____

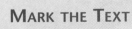

MARK THE TEXT

Underline or highlight two goals you might have when you are reading to learn.

nonfiction include histories, biographies, autobiographies, and memoirs. Periodicals such as newspapers, journals, and newsmagazines contain an enormous amount of information about current events around the world. While few people have time to read everything that appears in news periodicals, it is important to stay aware of what is going on in the world around you.

Reading for Information

READING INTERNET, REFERENCE, AND VISUAL MATERIALS

When you are reading for information, you are looking for information that answers a specific, immediate question; that helps you learn how to do something; or that helps you make a decision or draw a conclusion about something. One of the most important things for you to learn in school is how to find, process, and think about the vast amount of information available to you in online and printed reference works, graphic aids, and other visual materials.

THE READING PROCESS

The reading process begins before you actually start to read. Before reading, you begin to develop your own purpose and expectations for what you are about to read. These are related to what you already know and what you have experienced. During reading, you use your natural habits and responses to help you understand what you are reading, perhaps by adjusting your initial purpose and expectations. After reading, you think and reflect on what you have read. All readers use a reading process, even if they don't think about it. By becoming aware of this process, you can become a more effective reader. The reading process can be broken down into three stages: before reading, during reading, and after reading.

Before Reading

Have a plan for reading actively. Before you begin to read, establish a plan for reading actively by setting a purpose, previewing the material, and connecting with what you already know.

- ❏ **Set a purpose** for reading. Know why you are reading and what information you seek. Are you reading for experience or enjoyment, reading to learn, or reading for specific information?
- ❏ **Preview** the organization of the material. Glance at any visuals and think about how they add to the meaning of the text. Skim headings and introductory paragraphs.
- ❏ **Connect** with what you know. Think about how what you are reading connects to your own life and to your prior experience.

Before Reading ➤

ASK YOURSELF

- What's my purpose for reading this?
- What is this going to be about?
- How is this information organized?
- What do I already know about the topic?
- How can I apply this information to my life?

During Reading

Use reading strategies to read actively. Reading strategies are actions you can take on paper, in your head, or aloud that help you understand what you are reading. During reading, you will use reading strategies to read actively. Keep in mind that you will often use a combination of these strategies to read a single text.

- ❏ **Read aloud** to build reading fluency and give oral emphasis to ideas you are trying to understand. Hearing words aloud may help you untangle difficult ideas. Listen to your teacher read passages aloud, or read aloud by yourself or with a partner.
- ❏ **Write things down** to note your responses to what you are reading. Methods such as highlighting and marking a text, taking or making notes, and creating graphic organizers help you read actively and organize your thoughts. Underline or copy to your notebook the main points. Note unusual or interesting ideas or things you don't understand. Jot down words you need to define. Write your reactions to what you read.
- ❏ **Think and reflect** by asking questions to further your understanding of what you are reading. Asking questions helps you to pinpoint parts of the text that are confusing. You can ask questions in your head, or you may write them down.

Check your reading and use fix-up ideas. Monitor your reading comprehension by paying attention to how well you understand what you are reading. If you find yourself reading the words but not actually understanding what you are reading, get back on track by using a **fix-up idea** such as rereading, reading in shorter chunks, changing your reading rate, or trying a new reading strategy. A fix-up idea will be presented with each reading strategy accompanying the selections in this text. (For more information on fix-up ideas, see pages 14–15.)

After Reading

Reflect on your reading. After you finish reading, summarize, synthesize, and reflect on the material you have read.

- ■ **Summarize** what you have read to help identify, understand, and remember the main and supporting ideas in the text.
- ■ **Synthesize** different ideas in the material by pulling the ideas together and drawing conclusions about them. Reread any sections you don't remember clearly. Answer any questions you had.
- ■ **Extend** your reading by examining how your knowledge has grown and identifying questions you still have about the material.

During Reading

ASK YOURSELF

- ■ What is the best way to accomplish my purpose for reading?
- ■ What do I want or need to find out while I'm reading?
- ■ What is the essential information presented here?
- ■ What is the importance of what I am reading?

CHECK YOUR READING

- ■ Do I understand what I just read? Can I summarize it?
- ■ What can I do to make the meaning more clear?

After Reading

ASK YOURSELF

- ■ What did I learn from what I have read?
- ■ What is still confusing?
- ■ What do I need to remember from my reading?
- ■ What effect did this text have on my thinking?
- ■ What else do I want to know about this topic?

USING ACTIVE READING STRATEGIES

Reading actively means thinking about what you are reading as you read. A reading strategy, or plan, helps you read actively and search for meaning in what you are reading. As a reader, you are in charge of unlocking the meaning of each text you read. This book will introduce you to eight excellent strategies that develop active reading. The following strategies can be applied at each stage of the reading process: before, during, and after reading.

Active Reading Strategies

1. Read with a Purpose
2. Connect to Prior Knowledge
3. Write Things Down
4. Make Predictions
5. Visualize
6. Use Text Organization
7. Tackle Difficult Vocabulary
8. Monitor Your Reading Progress

As you become experienced with each of the reading strategies, you will be able to use two or three strategies at a time, instead of just one. By using multiple strategies, you will become a thoughtful, active, and successful reader—not only in your English language arts classes but also in other content areas, during testing situations, and beyond the classroom. You will learn which strategies work best for you and use these strategies in every reading task you encounter.

1 Read with a Purpose

Before you begin reading, think about your reason for reading the material. You might be reading from a textbook to complete a homework assignment, skimming a magazine for information about one of your hobbies, or reading a novel for your own personal enjoyment. Know why you are reading and what information you seek. Decide on your purpose for reading as clearly as you can. Be aware that your purpose may change as you read.

Read with a Purpose

Before Reading	Establish a purpose for reading
During Reading	Read with this purpose in mind
After Reading	Reflect on how the purpose affected the reading experience

THE READING PROCESS

BEFORE READING

Have a plan for reading
- ❏ Set a purpose
- ❏ Preview
- ❏ Connect

DURING READING

Use reading strategies
- ❏ Read aloud
- ❏ Write things down
- ❏ Think and reflect
- ❏ Check your reading and use fix-up ideas

AFTER READING

Reflect on your reading
- ❏ Summarize
- ❏ Synthesize
- ❏ Extend

After you determine your purpose for reading, you can choose a method of reading that fits that purpose. Scanning, skimming, and close reading are three different ways of reading.

SCANNING. When you **scan**, you look through written material quickly to locate particular information. Scanning is useful when, for example, you want to find an entry in an index or a definition in a textbook chapter. To scan, simply run your eye down the page, looking for a key word or words. When you find the key words, slow down and read carefully.

SKIMMING. When you **skim,** you glance through material quickly to get a general idea of what it is about. Skimming is an excellent way to get a quick overview of material. It is useful for previewing a chapter in a textbook, for surveying material to see if it contains information that will be useful to you, and for reviewing material for a test or essay. When skimming, look at titles, headings, and words that appear in boldface or colored type. Also read topic sentences of paragraphs, first and last paragraphs of sections, and any summaries or conclusions. In addition, glance at illustrations, photographs, charts, maps, or other graphics.

READING CLOSELY. When you **read closely**, you read slowly and carefully, looking at each sentence and taking the time to absorb its meaning before going on. Close reading is appropriate, for example, when you are reading some poems for pleasure or studying a textbook chapter for the first time. If you encounter words that you do not understand, try to figure them out from context or look them up in a dictionary. You may want to record such words in a word study notebook. The act of writing a word will help you to remember it later. When reading for school, take notes using a rough outline form or other note-taking format. Outlining the material will help you to learn it.

Setting a purpose gives you something to focus on as you read. For example, you might read the user's manual for your new phone to find out how to program speed-dial numbers. Or, you might read a mystery novel to find out which character committed the crime.

A few of the purposes you might have for reading the excerpt from *Gorillas in the Mist* by Dian Fossey in Unit 7, page 277, might be to gain knowledge about gorillas, to find out where the events took place, or to learn about how to conduct field research. Read the

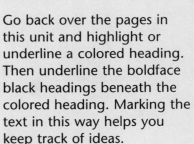

NOTE THE FACTS

What are three different ways of reading a text?

_____

_____

_____

MARK THE TEXT

Go back over the pages in this unit and highlight or underline a colored heading. Then underline the boldface black headings beneath the colored heading. Marking the text in this way helps you keep track of ideas.

following background information from the Reader's Resource for the excerpt from *Gorillas in the Mist*. When you finish reading, complete the **Think and Reflect** activity in the margin.

THINK AND REFLECT

Write a purpose for reading the excerpt from *Gorillas in the Mist*. **(Connect)**

_____

_____

_____

Dian Fossey had a lifelong interest in animals. On a trip to Africa in 1963, she briefly met the famous anthropologist Louis Leakey and became interested in mountain gorillas. When Fossey returned to the United States, she raised money to start a research program. She established the Karisoke Research Centre in Rwanda in 1967. Intense observation over thousands of hours enabled Fossey to earn the trust of the wild gorilla groups she studied. Her research helped ensure their survival. Fossey's research was cut short when she was found murdered in her cabin at Karisoke on December 26, 1985. Her murder remains unsolved.

2 Connect to Prior Knowledge

Prior knowledge is what you already know or have already experienced before reading something. Before and during reading, think about what you already know about the topic or subject matter. By connecting to your prior knowledge, you can increase your interest in and understanding of what you read. The Reader's Journal activities that come before each selection in this book provide an opportunity to connect to experiences in your own life. Information in the Reader's Resource expands your knowledge of what you are about to read.

Connect to Prior Knowledge	
Before Reading	Think about what you already know about the topic
During Reading	Use what you already know about the topic to make inferences and predictions
After Reading	Describe how the reading experience expanded your knowledge of the topic

Read the following information from the Reader's Resource for "Choosing a Dog" in Unit 8, page 310.

The Humane Society of the United States promotes humane treatment of animals and fosters respect, understanding, and compassion for all creatures. Many other organizations and shelters exist around the country to care for and protect animals. "Choosing a Dog" explains how to use these and other sources. It describes the steps you should take to pick the right dog for you.

3 Write Things Down

Writing things down helps you pay attention to the words on a page. It is an excellent way to remember important ideas. Methods such as highlighting and marking or coding a text, taking or making notes, and creating graphic organizers help you read actively and organize your thoughts.

Write Things Down	
Before Reading	Have a plan for writing things down: sticky notes, handwritten notes, highlighters, or charts to fill in
During Reading	Use a method for writing things down; ask questions; respond
After Reading	Summarize things written down

Highlighting and marking a text helps you locate key ideas. Mark important ideas, things you would like to come back to, things that are confusing, things you like or dislike, and things with which you agree or disagree. In this Write-In Reader or a book you own, you may highlight the text itself. With other books you may need to use sticky notes and bookmarks to keep track of your thoughts.

As you read, find a way to connect to what you are reading by **coding** your reactions. Use the following system to keep track of your reactions in the margins or on sticky notes. Create additional notations for reactions you have that are not listed.

THINK AND REFLECT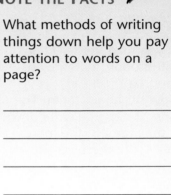

Based on what you already know about choosing a pet, what more might you learn from reading "Choosing a Dog"? **(Connect)**

_____

_____

_____

NOTE THE FACTS

What methods of writing things down help you pay attention to words on a page?

_____

_____

_____

_____

MARK THE TEXT

Underline or highlight what you should do before, during, and after reading when you use the Write Things Down strategy.

Reading TIP

Additional ways to take notes:
- outline
- make lists
- create a chart or diagram
- write down main ideas and your responses
- use a tape recorder

YES	I agree with this
NO	I disagree with this
?	I do not understand this
W	I wonder . . .
+	I like this part
−	I do not like this part
!	This is like something else I know
√	This seems important
∞	I need to come back and look at this
___	_____
___	_____

If you do not have sticky notes, keep track of your reactions in a chart like the one below.

Reading TIP

As you read the selections in this book, write down important ideas and your thoughts about them. The more things you write down in the margins, the more you will understand and remember.

Reactions Chart

Page, Column, or Line Number:	Short Note about My Reactions
page 83	Wow! It has been raining nonstop for seven years.

After reading, summarize your reactions and compare them to those of your classmates.

Here is a summary of my reactions: _I liked the outer space setting and the description of the unique weather found on another planet._

Here is how my reactions were the same as those of my classmates: _Many of my classmates liked the description of the unique weather._

Here is how my reactions were different from those of my classmates: _Some of my classmates did not like reading about unrealistic events._

Taking or making notes helps you select ideas you consider important. *Paraphrase*, or write in your own words, what you have read and put it into notes you can read later. Taking or making notes is also a quick way for you to retell what you have just read. Since you cannot write in, mark up, or highlight information in a textbook or library book, make a response bookmark like the following and use it to record your thoughts and reactions. As you read, ask yourself questions, make predictions, react to ideas, identify key points, and/or write down unfamiliar words.

MARK THE TEXT

Underline or highlight what you should record on a response bookmark.

Response Bookmark

Page #	Questions, Predictions, Reactions, Key Points, and Unfamiliar Words
83	Now I get it. The story takes place on Venus.
85	These students are mean.
85	"The biggest crime of all was that she had come here . . . from Earth." Ah, the other students are jealous.

Graphic organizers help you organize ideas as you read. For instance, if you are reading an essay that compares two authors, you might use a Venn diagram or a cluster chart to collect information about each author. If you are reading about an author's life, you may construct a time line. As you read a selection, create your own method for gathering and organizing information. You might use your own version of a common graphic organizer or invent a new way to show what the selection describes. Signal words in the text can help you construct an organizer. (See Appendix B for examples of these and other graphic organizers.)

Signal Words	Common Graphic Organizer
descriptive words: *also, for instance, for example, in the beginning, in addition, the main reason, one point*	Character Chart, page B-9 Sensory Details Chart, page B-10 Summary Chart, page B-13
sequence words: *after, as before, next, now, on, first, second, finally*	Time Line, page B-11 Story Strip, page B-11 Plot Diagram, page B-12

comparison-and-contrast words: *as well as, but, either/or, likewise, on the other hand, similarly, not only/but*	Pro and Con Chart, page B-6 Cluster Chart, page B-7 Venn Diagram, page B-7
cause-and-effect words: *as a result, because, if/then, since, therefore, this led to*	Note Taking Chart, page B-6 Cause-and-Effect Chart, page B-13 Drawing Conclusions Log, page B-14

After reading the following excerpt from "Priscilla and the Wimps" by Richard Peck, Unit 3, page 64, answer the question in the margin. Underline or highlight signal words in the excerpt that direct you to the answer.

I admit it, I'm five foot five, and when the Kobras slithered by, with or without Monk, I shrank. And I admit this, too: I paid up on a regular basis. And I might add: so would you.

This school was old Monk's Garden of Eden. Unfortunately for him, there was a serpent in it. The reason Monk didn't recognize trouble when it was staring him in the face is that the serpent in the Kobras' Eden was a girl.

4 Make Predictions

When you **make predictions** during reading, you are making guesses about what the reading is going to be about or what might happen next. Before reading, make predictions based on clues from the page and from what you already know about the topic. Continue making predictions as you read. Remember, your predictions do not have to be correct. Pause during reading to gather information that helps you make more predictions and check predictions you have already made.

Reading TIP

By learning to make predictions while you read, you become more engaged in your reading and remember more information.

Make Predictions	
Before Reading	Gather information and make preliminary predictions
During Reading	Continue making predictions
After Reading	Analyze and verify predictions

Read an excerpt from the fairy tale "Dragon, Dragon" by John Gardner, Unit 5, page 150. Look for clues that suggest what might happen next.

> There was once a king whose kingdom was plagued by a dragon. The king did not know which way to turn. The king's knights were all cowards who hid under their beds whenever the dragon came in sight, so they were of no use to the king at all. And the king's wizard could not help either because, being old, he had forgotten his magic spells. . . .
>
> Now it happened that there lived in the kingdom a wise old cobbler who had a wife and three sons. The cobbler and his family came to the king's meeting and stood way in the back by the door, for the cobbler had a feeling that since he was nobody important there had probably been some mistake, and no doubt the king had intended the meeting for everyone in the kingdom except his family and him.

Prediction Chart

Predictions	Clues	What Really Happens
One of the cobbler's sons will go after the dragon.	"The king did not know which way to turn." "The king's knights were all cowards" "the king's wizard could not help either" "a wise old cobbler" had "three sons"	

THINK AND REFLECT

Based on the clues in the excerpt, make a prediction about what might happen later in the story. Record your prediction in the first column of the chart. In the second column, tell what clues led you to make this prediction. After you read the rest of the story, you would be able to record what really happened in the story and to compare that to your original predictions. **(Predict)**

5 Visualize

Reading is more than simply sounding out words. It is an active process that requires you to use your imagination. When you **visualize,** you form a picture or an image in your mind of what the text describes. Each reader's images will be different based on his or her prior knowledge and experience. Keep in mind that there are no "right" or "wrong" visualizations.

Visualize	
Before Reading	Begin to picture what may happen
During Reading	Create mind pictures as you read
After Reading	Draw or summarize what you saw in your mind pictures

Read the following excerpt from "Eleven" by Sandra Cisneros, Unit 3, page 42. As you read, imagine what the narrator, the teacher, and the red sweater look like.

> . . . Today I wish I was one hundred and two instead of eleven because if I was one hundred and two, I'd have known what to say when Mrs. Price put the red sweater on my desk. I would've known how to tell her it wasn't mine instead of just sitting there with that look on my face and nothing coming out of my mouth.
>
> "Whose is this?" Mrs. Price says, and she holds the red sweater up in the air for all the class to see. "Whose? It's been sitting in the coatroom for a month."

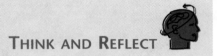

THINK AND REFLECT

Make notes or draw pictures to show the images you pictured in your mind while reading this passage. (**Visualize**)

6 Use Text Organization

Text organization refers to the different ways a text may be presented or organized. If you are aware of the ways different texts are organized, you will find it easier to understand what you read. For example, knowing about typical plot elements—the exposition, rising action, climax, falling action, and resolution—is important for understanding the events in a short story or novel. Focusing on signal words and text patterns is important for understanding nonfiction and informational text. For instance, transition words, such as *first, second, next, then,* and *finally,* might indicate that an essay is written in chronological, or time, order.

Use Text Organization

Before Reading	Preview organizational features (look over headings, pictures, format)
During Reading	Be aware of organizational features as you read
After Reading	Discuss how the text organization affected your reading experience

In this excerpt from "A Breath of Fresh Air?" by Alexandra Hanson-Harding, Unit 7, page 283, look for organizational features that help you understand the excerpt.

> ### The Culprits
> What are the two pollutants? The first is ground-level ozone; the second, something called fine particulates.
>
> Ground-level ozone is an odorless, colorless gas that is formed when sulfates react with sunlight. (Sulfates are chemicals released when coal is burned.) Ozone that occurs naturally in the upper atmosphere helps to protect Earth, but ground-level ozone, which is worse on hot days, makes it harder for people to breathe. If people inhale too much of it over time, it can damage their lungs.

7 Tackle Difficult Vocabulary

How do you deal with new or unfamiliar words as you read? Learning how to tackle difficult vocabulary on your own leads to improved reading comprehension. In some cases, you may want to identify and define new vocabulary before reading. Use context clues to guess meanings, find definitions in the dictionary, and decode words by recognizing common word parts.

Tackle Difficult Vocabulary

Before Reading	Have a plan for tackling difficult words
During Reading	Use context, word structure, footnotes, or a dictionary; ask for help
After Reading	Describe how vocabulary affected your reading experience

THINK AND REFLECT

How does Hanson-Harding help readers understand this section of her text? What organizational elements do you recognize? **(Analyze)**

_____

_____

_____

_____

Reading TIP

If you take the time to learn new words, you increase your ability to understand what you read in class and on standardized tests. One of the best ways to learn new words is to associate an image with the meaning of a new word. For instance, you might associate the word *incessant* with an image of lips that talk constantly or unceasingly because *incessant* means "continuing without interruption, unceasing." What image could you associate with the word *imperious*, meaning "commanding; marked by arrogant behavior"?

Read the following excerpt from "Ta-Na-E-Ka" by Mary Whitebird, Unit 3, page 50. As you read, record unfamiliar words in your notebook. After you finish, go back to each word you recorded. Using both context clues (words nearby that provide hints about the meaning) and word parts, unlock the meaning of each unfamiliar word. Consult a dictionary if context clues or word parts do not help.

THINK AND REFLECT

Using context and word part clues, what might *equated* mean? **(Analyze)**

_____

_____

_____

> The wisest women (generally wisdom was equated with age) often sat in tribal councils. Furthermore, most Kaw legends revolve around "Good Woman," a kind of supersquaw, a Joan of Arc of the high plains. Good Woman led Kaw warriors into battle after battle from which they always seemed to emerge victorious.

❽ Monitor Your Reading Progress

All readers occasionally have difficulty as they read. The key to reading success is being aware of these difficulties. As you read, **monitor**, or pay attention to, your progress, stopping frequently to check how well you are understanding what you are reading. If you encounter problems or lose focus, use a **fix-up idea** to regain understanding. Readers who know how to apply fix-up ideas are well on the way to reading independence. They know when they are having a problem and are able to adjust and get back on track.

USING FIX-UP IDEAS

The following **fix-up ideas** can help you "fix up" any confusion or lack of attention you experience as you read. You probably use many of these already.

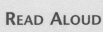

READ ALOUD

Reading fluency is your ability to read something quickly and easily. Increase your reading fluency by rereading a 100–150-word passage aloud several times. Reread the passage until you are able to read through it in less than a minute without making any mistakes. Read the passage to a partner and have your partner track your errors, or read the passage into a tape recorder, play back your recording, and keep track of your own errors. For additional fluency practice, see Appendix A.

- **Reread.** If you don't understand a sentence, paragraph, or section the first time through, go back and reread it. Each time you reread a text, you understand and remember more.

- **Read in shorter chunks.** Break a long text into shorter chunks. Read through each "chunk." Then go back and make sure you understand that section before moving on.

- **Read aloud.** If you are having trouble keeping your focus, try reading aloud to yourself. Go somewhere private and read aloud, putting emphasis and expression in your voice. Reading aloud may help you to untangle difficult text by talking your way through it.

- **Ask questions.** As you read, stop and ask yourself questions about the text. These questions help you pinpoint things that are confusing or things you want to come back to later. You can ask questions in your head, or jot them down in the margins or on a piece of paper.

- **Change your reading rate.** Your reading rate is how fast or slow you read. Good readers adjust their rate to fit the situation. Read quickly when you just need an overview or if the reading task is easy. Slow down and read carefully when a text is difficult or contains a lot of description.

- **Create a mnemonic device.** A mnemonic (ni mä′ nik) device is a memory trick that helps you memorize specific information in a text. One memory trick is to make up an acronym, or abbreviation, to help you remember items in a list. For example, the acronym *HOMES* can help you remember the names of the five great lakes, Huron, Ontario, Michigan, Erie, and Superior. Another memory trick is to create a short sentence or rhyme. For instance, if you need to remember that in the eardrum, the anvil comes before the stirrup, remember "the letter *a* comes before the letter *s*."

Monitor Your Reading Progress

Before Reading	Be aware of fix-up ideas that ease reading problems
During Reading	Use fix-up ideas
After Reading	Evaluate the fix-up ideas used

Reading TIP

As you read, use your classmates as resources to help you uncover the meaning in a selection. Working with a partner or a small group can increase your understanding of what you read.

THINK ALOUD. When you **think aloud**, you communicate your thoughts aloud to your classmates about what you are reading. Thinking aloud helps you share ideas about the text and ways in which to read it.

SHARE FIX-UP IDEAS. When you **share fix-up ideas**, you and your classmates can figure out ways to deal with difficult sections of a text.

Unit 1 READING Review

Choose and Use Reading Strategies

Before reading the excerpt below, review with a partner how to use each of these reading strategies (see pages 4–15).

1. Read with a Purpose
2. Connect to Prior Knowledge
3. Write Things Down
4. Make Predictions
5. Visualize
6. Use Text Organization
7. Tackle Difficult Vocabulary
8. Monitor Your Reading Progress

Now apply at least two reading strategies to an excerpt from Jerry Spinelli's autobiography *Night*. Use the margins and mark up the text to demonstrate how you use reading strategies to read actively. When you finish, summarize the excerpt in one sentence.

> Nighttime lent a horror not only to trains but also to garbage. Garbage had status in those days. Garbage was garbage, and trash was everything else. Garbage had a can of its own, basically an oversize metal pail with a lid. The garbage pail could be found in the back of the backyard. To lift the lid off the garbage can was to confront all the horrors of the creepiest movie: dead, rotting matter; teeming colonies of pale, slimy creeping things; and a stench that could be survived only in the smallest whiffs.

On Your Own

Apply the reading strategies you have learned in this unit to your own reading. Select a 100–150-word passage from your favorite book, magazine, or newspaper, and try one of the following activities.

FLUENTLY SPEAKING. Rehearse reading the passage aloud several times. Have a partner track your errors, or read the passage into a tape recorder, play back your recording, and keep track of your own errors. Reread the passage until you are able to read it without making any mistakes.

PICTURE THIS. As you read, create a drawing, painting, sculpture, or other visual representation of the images that come into your mind.

PUT IT IN WRITING. Write a journal entry that describes your feelings about the passage. Discuss what you like about it and why you find it interesting. Explain how the passage may relate to your own life.

Unit TWO

ESSENTIAL
READING
SKILLS

READING SKILLS

Each of the reading strategies we've discussed in Unit 1 helps you learn to think, question, and respond while you read. By using the eight active reading strategies, you will be able to demonstrate your mastery of the following reading skills:

- Identify the Author's Purpose
- Find the Main Idea
- Make Inferences
- Use Context Clues
- Analyze Text Organization
- Identify Sequence of Events
- Compare and Contrast
- Evaluate Cause and Effect
- Classify and Reorganize Information
- Distinguish Fact from Opinion
- Interpret Visual Aids
- Understand Literary Elements
- Draw Conclusions

Using these skills as you read helps you to become an independent, thoughtful, and active reader who can accomplish tasks evaluated on tests, particularly standardized tests. Standardized test practice connected to these skills follows each selection in this book.

Reading TIP

For more practice on test-taking skills, see Unit 10, Test-Taking Strategies, pages 365–378.

Identify the Author's Purpose

A writer's **purpose** is his or her aim or goal. Being able to figure out an author's purpose, or purposes, is an important reading skill. An author may write with one or more of the purposes listed in the following chart. A writer's purpose corresponds to a specific mode, or type, of writing. A writer can choose from a variety of forms while working within a mode.

Reading TIP

To **identify the author's purpose**, ask yourself

- Why did the author create this piece of writing?
- Is the author simply sharing information or trying to convince me of something?
- Is he or she writing to entertain or trying to make a point?

Purposes of Writing

Purpose	Mode	Writing Forms
to reflect	personal/ expressive writing	diary entry, personal letter, autobiography, personal essay
to entertain, to describe, to enrich, and to enlighten	imaginative/ descriptive writing	poem, character sketch, play
to tell a story, to narrate a series of events	narrative writing	short story, biography, legend, myth, history
to inform, to explain	informative/ expository writing	news article, research report, expository essay, book review
to persuade	persuasive/ argumentative writing	editorial, petition, political speech, persuasive essay

Once you identify what the author is trying to do, you can evaluate, or judge, how well the author achieved that purpose. For example, you may judge that the author of a persuasive essay made a good and convincing argument. Or, you may decide that the novel you are reading has a boring plot. In other words, the author has done a bad job of entertaining you!

Read the following lines from "The Cow of No Color" by Nina Jaffe and Steve Zeitlin, Unit 5, page 176. Think about the authors' purpose for writing a folk tale. Are the authors trying to entertain, persuade, inform, or express their feelings?

Nunyala returned to her village and sat in her hut. She thought to herself: Should I be executed because some people say I am wise as the chief? Should I lose my own life for his jealousy? Is this a wise leader's approach to justice? She had to answer the chief's impossible request, but how?

Find the Main Idea

The **main idea** is a brief statement of what you think the author wants you to know, think, or feel after reading the text. In some cases, the main idea will actually be stated. Check the first and last paragraphs for a sentence that sums up the entire passage. Usually, the author will not tell you what the main idea is, and you will have to infer it.

In general, nonfiction texts have main ideas; literary texts (poems, short stories, novels, plays, and personal essays) have themes. Sometimes, however, the term *main idea* is used to refer to the theme of a literary work, especially an essay or poem. Both deal with the central idea in a written work.

A good way to find the main or overall idea of a whole selection (or part of a selection) is to gather important details into a Main Idea Map like the one below. Use the details to determine the main or overall thought or message. This will help you to draw conclusions about the main idea when you finish reading.

Main Idea Map

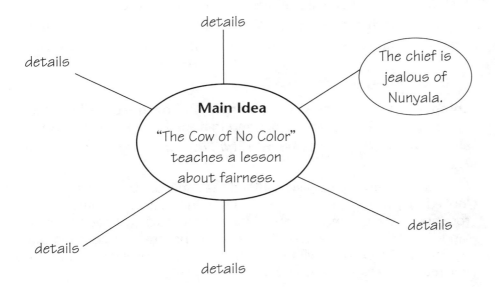

THINK AND REFLECT

Which words or phrases in the paragraph help you determine the authors' purpose? **(Infer)**

_____

_____

_____

_____

Reading TIP

To **infer the main idea,** ask yourself

- Who or what is this passage about?
- What does the author want me to know, think, feel, or do about this "who" or "what"?
- If I had to tell someone in one sentence what this passage is about, what would I say?

Reading TIP

As you make inferences, remember that each inference needs to fit with all of the clues in the text and with your prior knowledge.

Make Inferences

By paying close attention to what you read, you will be able to make inferences about what the writer is trying to communicate. **Making an inference** means putting together the clues given in the text with your own prior knowledge.

Inference Chart

Text	What I Infer
"Margot stood alone. She was a very frail girl who looked as if she had been lost in the rain for years and the rain had washed out the blue from her eyes and the red from her mouth and the yellow from her hair."	Margot is either sick or very sad.

Reading TIP

Sometimes you can determine the meaning of a word by using the context as a clue. For example, the word choice or mood of a passage in general may help you determine the meaning of a particular word.

Use Context Clues

You can often figure out the meaning of an unfamiliar word by using context clues. **Context clues** are words and phrases near a difficult word that provide hints about its meaning. The context in which a word is used may help you guess what it means without having to look it up in the dictionary.

The following table explains different kinds of context clues and includes words that signal each type of clue. Look for these words in the sentences around an unfamiliar word to see if they signal a context clue.

Context Clues

comparison clue	shows a comparison, or how the unfamiliar word is like something that might be familiar to you
signal words	*and, like, as, just as, as if, as though*

EXAMPLE

"The wind whistled, howled, whirled the snow about in *eddies*. It looked as if white imps were playing tag on the fields. A white dust rose above the ground."—from "Zlateh the Goat" by Isaac Bashevis Singer. (Since the *eddies* look like "white imps" that are "playing tag," *eddies* must refer to blowing snow that rapidly moves back and forth in circular or irregular patterns.)

contrast clue	shows that something contrasts, or differs in meaning, from something else
signal words	*but, nevertheless, on the other hand, however, although, though, in spite of*

EXAMPLE

"By the time the major leagues finally allowed him to play, in 1948, Paige should have been too old, too slow, and too beat up to get anybody out. But for a few remarkable and *flamboyant* seasons with Cleveland and St. Louis, he showed folks what they'd been missing during all those years of segregated baseball."—from "Satchel Paige" by Bill Littlefield. (*Flamboyant* must describe someone not "too old, too slow, and too beat up." It must refer to someone who can get out and show what he can do, someone "showy.")

restatement clue	uses different words to express the same idea
signal words	*that is, in other words, or, namely*

EXAMPLE

"The SCENE is the Throne Room of the Palace; a room of many doors, or, if preferred, curtain-openings; simply furnished with three *thrones* for Their Majesties and her Royal Highness the PRINCESS CAMILLA—in other words, with three handsome chairs." —from *The Ugly Duckling* by A. A. Milne. (The restatement confirms that a *throne* is another name for a "handsome chair"; the restatement also lends a bit of humor to the description of the Throne Room.)

examples clue	gives examples of other items to illustrate the meaning of something
signal words	*including, such as, for example, for instance, especially, particularly*

EXAMPLE

"It also means making sure your entry fits the contest's *theme*. If a contest asks you to tell how healthful a product is, for example, make sure that's the focus of your entry."—from "Contests!", an interview with David LaRochelle. (One example of a contest's *theme* is provided: tell how healthful a product is. This example helps you know that *theme* means "point.")

cause-and-effect clue	tells you that something happened as a result of something else
signal words	*if/then, when/then, thus, therefore, because, so, as a result of, consequently, since*

MARK THE TEXT

Underline or highlight five kinds of context clues listed on pages 20 and 21.

NOTE THE FACTS

What words signal a cause-and-effect relationship?

_____

_____

_____

'"Down the way, my three sons are to be hanged today,' she replied. " . . . They are to be killed because they killed the king's deer. Following your ways, they shot it with their *longbows* and 'twas their bad fortune that the sheriff should happen by,' she cried."—from "How Robin Hood Saved the Widow's Three Sons" by Sara Hyry. (The word *because* signals the reason why the sons are to be hanged; they shot at the king's deer. *Longbows* must be powerful enough to shoot arrows that can kill deer.)

Analyze Text Organization

Writing can be organized in different ways. To be an effective reader you need to know how to analyze how the text is organized. When you analyze something, you break it down into parts and then think about how the parts are related to each other and to the whole.

Transition words connect ideas. They indicate how a text is organized. Look for words that

- describe main points (descriptive words)
- show sequence (sequence words)
- show comparison and contrast (comparison-and-contrast words)
- show cause and effect (cause-and-effect words)

Chronological or Time Order

Events are given in the order in which they happen or should be done. Events are connected by transition words such as *first, second, next, then, furthermore,* and *finally.* Chronological order is often used to relate a narrative, as in a short story; to write a how-to article on a topic like building a bird feeder; or to describe a process, such as what happens when a volcano erupts.

Spatial or Location Order

Parts are described in order of their location in space, for example, from back to front, left to right, or top to bottom. Descriptions are connected by transition words or phrases such as *next to, beside, above, below, beyond,* and *around.* Spatial order could be used for an article that discusses a project's physical aspects, such as describing the remodeling of a kitchen, or for a descriptive passage in literature, as in establishing the setting of a science fiction story set in a space station.

Order of Importance

Details are listed from least important to most important or from most important to least important; transition phrases are used such as *more important, less important, most important,* and *least important.* For example, a speech telling voters why they should elect you class president could build from the least important reason to the most important reason.

Comparison-and-Contrast Order

Details of two subjects are presented in one of two ways. In the first method, the characteristics of one subject are presented, followed by the characteristics of the second subject. This method could be used to organize an essay that compares and contrasts two fast-food chains, and to tell why one is superior to the other.

In the second method, both subjects are compared and contrasted with regard to one quality, then with regard to a second quality, and so on. An essay organized according to this method could compare the qualities of two dogs you are considering adopting: their personalities, their size, and so forth. Ideas are connected by transition words and phrases that indicate similarities or differences, such as *likewise, similarly, in contrast, a different kind, on the other hand,* and *another difference.*

Cause-and-Effect Order

One or more causes are followed by one or more effects, or one or more effects are followed by one or more causes. Transition words and phrases that indicate cause and effect include *one cause, another effect, as a result, consequently,* and *therefore.* Cause-and-effect organization might be used for a public health announcement warning about the dangers of playing with fire or an essay discussing the outbreak of World War I and the events that led up to it.

Classification or Sorting Order

Items are classified, or grouped, in categories to show how one group is similar to or different from another. Items in the same category should share one or more characteristics. For example, Edgar Allan Poe, Agatha Christie, and Stephen King can be classified together as mystery writers. Transition words that indicate classification order are the same words that indicate comparison-and-contrast order, words such as *likewise, similarly, in contrast, a different kind,* and *another difference.*

Identify Sequence of Events

Sequence refers to the order in which things happen. When you read certain types of writing, such as a short story, a novel, a biography of a person's life, or a history book, keep track of the sequence of events. You might do this by making a time line or a sequence map.

MARK THE TEXT

Underline or highlight the six methods of text organization listed on pages 22 and 23.

NOTE THE FACTS

What are two ways to keep track of the sequence of events?

_____

_____

_____

Time Line

To make a time line, draw a line and divide it into equal parts like the one below. Label each part with a date or a time. Then add key events at the right places along the time line.

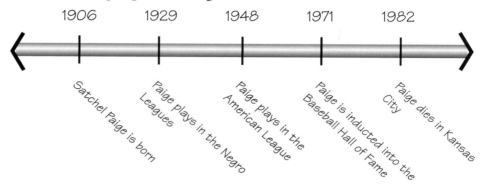

Sequence Map

In each box, draw pictures that represent key events in a selection. Then write a caption under each box that explains each event. Draw the events in the order in which they occur.

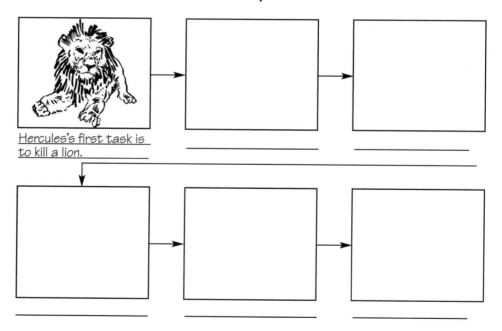

Hercules's first task is to kill a lion.

 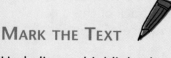
Compare and Contrast

Comparing and contrasting are closely related processes. When you **compare** one thing to another, you describe similarities between the two things; when you **contrast** two things, you describe their differences. To compare and contrast, begin by listing the features of each subject. Then go down both lists and check whether each feature is shared or not. You can also show similarities and differences in a Venn diagram. A Venn diagram uses two slightly overlapping circles. The outer part of each circle shows what aspects of two things are different from each other. The inner, or shared, part of each circle shows what aspects the two things share.

Venn Diagram

Write down ideas about Topic 1 in the first circle and ideas about Topic 2 in the second circle. The area in which the circles overlap should contain ideas common to both topics.

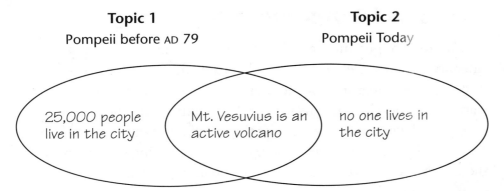

Topic 1
Pompeii before AD 79

Topic 2
Pompeii Today

25,000 people live in the city

Mt. Vesuvius is an active volcano

no one lives in the city

Evaluate Cause and Effect

When you evaluate **cause and effect**, you are looking for a logical relationship between a cause or causes and one or more effects. A writer may present one or more causes followed by one or more effects, or one or more effects followed by one or more causes. Transitional, or signal, words and phrases that indicate cause and effect include *one cause*, *another effect*, *as a result*, *because*, *since*, *consequently*, and *therefore*. As a reader, you determine whether the causes and effects in a text are reasonable. A graphic organizer like the one below will help you to recognize relationships between causes and effects.

Cause-and-Effect Chart

Keep track of what happens in a story and why in a chart like the one on page 26. Use cause-and-effect signal words to help you identify causes and their effects.

MARK THE TEXT

Underline or highlight words that signal cause and effect.

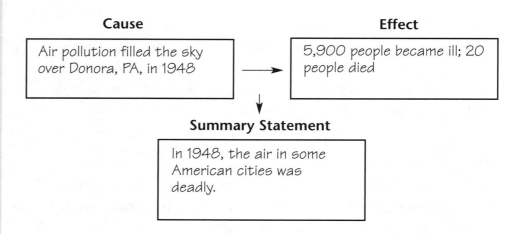

Cause		Effect
Air pollution filled the sky over Donora, PA, in 1948	→	5,900 people became ill; 20 people died

Summary Statement

In 1948, the air in some American cities was deadly.

NOTE THE FACTS

What do you do when you classify information?

_____

_____

_____

Classify and Reorganize Information

To **classify** is to put into classes or categories. Items in the same category should share one or more characteristics. A writer may group, or categorize, things to show similarities and name the categories to clarify how one group is similar to or different from another. For example, whales can be classified by their method of eating as *baleen* or *toothed*, or by their types such as *orca* or *blue*. Classifying or reorganizing the information into categories as you read increases your understanding.

The key step in classifying is choosing categories that fit your purpose. Take classification notes in a chart like the one below to help you organize separate types or groups and sort their characteristics.

Classification Chart

Category 1 Herders	Category 2 Sporting Breeds	Category 3 Hounds
Items in Category Collie Welsh corgi German shepherd	**Items in Category** Pointer Irish setter Cocker spaniel	**Items in Category** Dachshund Greyhound Basset hound
Details and Characteristics Bred to herd sheep	**Details and Characteristics** Bred to hunt birds	**Details and Characteristics** Bred to hunt animals without feathers

Distinguish Fact from Opinion

A **fact** is a statement that could be proven by direct observation or a reliable reference guide. Every statement of fact is either true or false. The following statement is an example of fact:

> Lewis Carroll published *Alice in Wonderland* in 1865. (This statement is a fact that can be proven by checking the book's publication records.)

An **opinion** is a statement that expresses an attitude or desire, not a fact about the world. One common type of opinion statement is a *value statement*. A value statement expresses an attitude toward something.

> "Jabberwocky" is Carroll's most imaginative poem. (This statement expresses an opinion that can be supported but not proved.)

Value statements often include judgment words such as the following:

attractive	honest	ugly
awesome	junk	unattractive
beautiful	kind	valuable
cheap	mean	wonderful
dishonest	nice	worthless
excellent	petty	
good	treasure	

A **policy statement** is an opinion that tells not what is but what someone believes should be. Such statements usually include words like *should, should not, ought, ought not, must,* or *must not*.

> You **should** wear a seat belt when riding in a car.
> You **must not** ignore the signs urging you to buckle up.

A **prediction** makes a statement about the future. Because the future is unpredictable, most predictions can be considered opinions.

> New research will show that seat belts should be mandatory. Automobile computers may soon be able to prevent a car from operating if the driver is not wearing a seat belt.

When evaluating a fact, ask yourself whether it can be proven through direct observation or by checking a reliable source such as a reference book or an unbiased expert. An opinion is only as good as

MARK THE TEXT

Underline or highlight the definitions of a fact and an opinion.

THINK AND REFLECT

What are three judgment words you could add to the chart on the left? **(Apply)**

_____

_____

_____

the facts that support it. When reading or listening, be critical about the statements that you encounter. It may be helpful to make a chart like the one below to help distinguish fact from opinion as you read.

Fact or Opinion Chart

Fact: Traditional beadwork is still done by Native American artisans.	**Opinion:** People should not buy imitation Native American beadwork.
Proof: Examples of this beadwork can be found in stores and museums and is worn by many tribal members when they participate in Native dances.	**Support:** Although some people may consider beadwork created in factories shoddy and cheap, others may argue that it is a fast and inexpensive way to recreate intricate Native artwork.
Fact:	**Opinion:**
Proof:	**Support:**

Interpret Visual Aids

Visual aids are charts, graphs, pictures, illustrations, photos, maps, diagrams, spreadsheets, and other materials that present information. Many writers use visual aids to present data in understandable ways. Information visually presented in tables, charts, and graphs can help you find information, see trends, discover facts, and uncover patterns.

Reading Graphics

Before Reading	■ Determine the subject of the graphic by reading the title, headings, and other textual clues.
	■ Determine how the data are organized, classified, or divided by reading the labels along rows or columns.
During Reading	■ Survey the data and look for trends by comparing columns and rows, noting changes among information fields, looking for patterns, or studying map sections.
	■ Use legends, keys, and other helpful sections in the graphic.
After Reading	■ Check footnotes or references for additional information about the data and their sources.
	■ List conclusions or summarize the data.

Pie Chart

A **pie chart** is a circle that stands for a whole group or set. The circle is divided into parts to show the divisions of the whole. When you look at a pie chart, you can see the relationships of the parts to one another and to the whole.

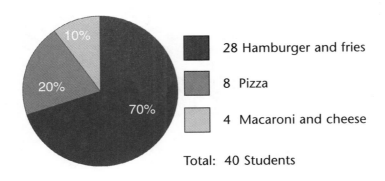

28 Hamburger and fries

8 Pizza

4 Macaroni and cheese

Total: 40 Students

FAVORITE SCHOOL LUNCH

Bar Graph

A bar graph compares amounts of something by representing the amounts as bars of different lengths. In the bar graph below, each bar represents the number of mountain gorillas counted in an official census. To read the graph, simply imagine a line drawn from the edge of the bar to the bottom of the graph. Then read the number. For example, the bar graph below shows that in 1959 approximately 450 gorillas were counted.

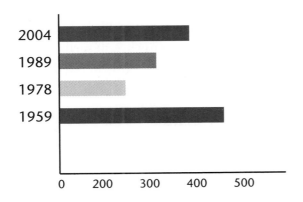

WORLD CENSUS COUNTS OF MOUNTAIN GORILLAS

NOTE THE FACTS

What percentage of students list pizza as their favorite school lunch?

_____

_____

_____

_____

NOTE THE FACTS

In what year did census takers find the fewest mountain gorillas? Approximately how many gorillas did the census takers count that year?

_____

_____

Which mountain peak on the map is closest to Delphi? When you leave Delphi, which direction would you go to reach this peak?

_____

_____

_____

Reading TIP

An author's **writing style** can affect tone and mood. For example, sentence length, sentence variety, vocabulary difficulty (the number of mono–, bi–, and polysyllabic words), and the connotation (the association a word has in addition to its literal meaning) of words help determine the tone and mood.

Map

A map is a representation, usually on a surface such as paper or a sheet of plastic, of a geographic area showing various significant features of that area.

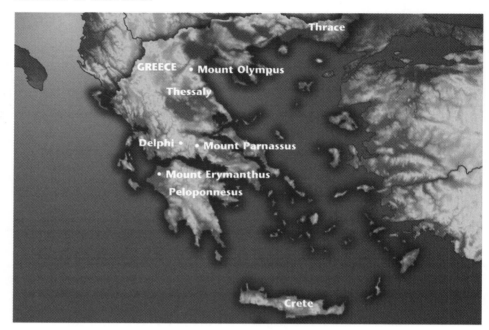

MAP OF GREECE

Understand Literary Elements

Literary elements are the terms and techniques that are used to talk about literature. When you read literature, you need to be familiar with the literary terms and reading skills listed below. These literary elements are explained in more detail in Unit 3, Reading Fiction, pages 36–38. Other literary elements are described in Units 4–7. Here are descriptions of the reading skills needed for some of the most common literary elements.

■ **RECOGNIZE MOOD AND TONE. Mood** is the atmosphere or emotion conveyed by a literary work. A writer creates mood by using concrete details to describe the setting, characters, or events. The writer can evoke in the reader an emotional response—such as fear, discomfort, longing, or anticipation—by working carefully with descriptive language and sensory details. The mood of a work might be dark, mysterious, gloomy, cheerful, inspiring, or peaceful. **Tone** is the writer's attitude toward the subject or toward the reader of a work. Examples of different tones that a work may have include familiar, ironic, playful, sarcastic, serious, and sincere.

- **UNDERSTAND POINT OF VIEW. Point of view** is the vantage point, or perspective, from which a story or narrative is told. Stories are typically written from the following points of view:

first-person point of view	narrator uses words such as *I* and *we*
second-person point of view	narrator uses *you*
third-person point of view	narrator uses words such as *he, she, it,* and *they*

- **ANALYZE CHARACTER AND CHARACTERIZATION.** A **character** is a person (or sometimes an animal) who takes part in the action of a story. **Characterization** is the literary techniques writers use to create characters and make them come alive. Writers use the following techniques to create characters:

direct description	describing the physical features, dress, and personality of the character
behavior	showing what characters say, do, or think
interaction with others	showing what other characters say or think about them
internal state	revealing the character's private thoughts and emotions

Reading TIP

A **character chart** can be used as a graphic organizer to keep track of character development as you read. See the example in Appendix B, page B-9.

- **EXAMINE PLOT DEVELOPMENT.** The plot is basically what happens in a story. A **plot** is a series of events related to a *central conflict*, or struggle. A typical plot involves the introduction of a conflict, its development, and its eventual resolution. The elements of plot include the following:

exposition	sets the tone or mood, introduces the characters and setting, and provides necessary background information
inciting incident	introduces a central conflict with or within one or more characters
rising action	develops a central conflict with or within one or more characters and develops toward a high point of intensity
climax	marks the highest point of interest or suspense in the plot at which something decisive happens
falling action	details the events that follow the climax
resolution	marks the point at which the central conflict is ended or resolved
dénouement	includes any material that follows the resolution and that ties up loose ends

Reading TIP

A graphic organizer called a **plot diagram** can be used to chart the plot of a literature selection. Refer to the example in Appendix B, page B-12.

Draw Conclusions

When you **draw conclusions,** you are gathering pieces of information and then deciding what that information means.

This passage is from Mary Mitchell's book *Dear Ms. Demeanor,* a collection of advice columns for teens.

One key idea in this excerpt is that "older folks find communicating with young people frustrating." Two supporting points—"their hearing isn't sharp" and "the person they're trying to communicate with doesn't speak clearly"—lead to the overall conclusion that the questioner needs to try an approach that doesn't rely on hearing—writing a letter.

Drawing conclusions is an essential part of reading. As you read, it may be helpful to use a graphic organizer such as a chart or log to keep track of the information you find and the conclusions you draw.

Drawing Conclusions Log

Key Idea	Supporting Points	Overall Conclusion
Older people find communicating with young people frustrating.	"their hearing isn't sharp" "the [young] person . . . doesn't speak clearly"	The questioner needs to try an approach that doesn't rely on the neighbor's ability to hear.

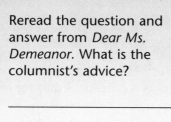

NOTE THE FACTS

Reread the question and answer from *Dear Ms. Demeanor.* What is the columnist's advice?

_____

_____

_____

NOTE THE FACTS

How can a **drawing conclusions log** help you?

_____

_____

_____

Unit 2 READING Review

Choose and Use Reading Skills

Before reading the excerpt below, review with a partner how to use each of these essential reading skills.

- Identify the Author's Purpose
- Find the Main Idea
- Make Inferences
- Use Context Clues
- Analyze Text Organization
- Identify Sequence of Events
- Compare and Contrast

- Evaluate Cause and Effect
- Classify and Reorganize Information
- Distinguish Fact from Opinion
- Interpret Visual Aids
- Understand Literary Elements
- Draw Conclusions

Read this excerpt from the short story "Joyriding" by Jim Naughton. The speaker describes what he does after school every day. As you read, note how you can use some of the reading skills discussed in this unit. After you finish reading, summarize the excerpt in two or three sentences. Then answer the questions that follow.

Peter glanced at the clock on the bookshelf. It was a quarter after four.

"Fifteen minutes to freedom," he said to himself. Fifteen minutes until he could turn off the metronome—*two, three, four*—and stop moving his fingers across the keys.

For Peter the best part of the day began at the moment he stopped practicing the piano. Beginning at four-thirty each day he had an entire hour to himself. He could read science fiction. He could play video games in the den. He just couldn't leave the house.

This had never really bothered him until the afternoon three weeks earlier when he'd seen the runner gliding up Putnam Street hill. Something about the way the older boy looked, something about the way he moved, drew Peter away from his music and out onto the porch to watch the runner race by in his maroon and gold Darden High School sweat suit.

1. When does the best part of the day begin for Peter?

   _____

   _____

2. What does this tell you about Peter?

   _____

   _____

3. What context clues help you guess the meaning of *metronome?* of *keys?*

   _____

   _____

4. What might happen next?

   _____

   _____

5. What clues in the excerpt make you think this might happen?

   _____

   _____

On Your Own

FLUENTLY SPEAKING. Select a 100–150-word passage from a book, magazine, or newspaper that you are currently reading. Working with a partner, take turns reading the passage aloud several times. Break it down into shorter sections and alternate reading paragraphs or sentences. Use the Oral Reading Skills: Repeated Reading Record in Appendix A, page A-12, to chart your progress.

PICTURE THIS. Find an article that contains data of some sort. Think about how this data can be presented using a visual aid, such as a table, chart, or graph. Do you notice any trends or patterns in the information? Draw a visual aid, such as a pie chart or bar graph, to present the information in a more understandable way.

PUT IT IN WRITING. Read a short article from a magazine or newspaper. Now go back and reread the first and last paragraphs. Write a summary of the main idea. What is it that the author wants you to know, think, feel, or do after reading this text? Is the main idea stated, or did you have to infer it?

Unit THREE

READING Fiction

FICTION

Fiction is prose writing that tells an invented or imaginary story. *Prose* is writing that uses straightforward language and differs from poetry in that it doesn't have a rhythmic pattern. Some fiction, such as the historical novel, is based on fact. Other forms of fiction, such as the fantasy tale, are highly unrealistic. Fictional works also vary in structure and length.

Forms of Fiction

The oldest form of fiction is the stories told in the oral, or folk, tradition, which include myths, legends, and fables. The most common forms of fiction are short stories, novels, and novellas.

THE SHORT STORY. A **short story** is a brief work of fiction that tells a story. It usually focuses on a single episode or scene and involves a limited number of characters. Although a short story contains all the main elements of fiction—character, setting, plot, and theme—it may not fully develop each element. The selections in this unit are examples of short stories.

THE NOVEL AND NOVELLA. A **novel** is a long work of fiction that usually has more complex elements than a short story. Its longer format allows the elements of fiction to be more fully developed. A **novella** is a work of fiction that is longer than a typical short story but shorter than a typical novel.

Other types of fiction include romances, historical fiction, and science fiction. **Romances** are tales that feature the adventures of legendary figures such as Alexander the Great and King Arthur. **Historical fiction** is partly based on actual historical events and is partly made up. **Science fiction** is imaginative literature based on scientific principles, discoveries, or laws; it often deals with the future, the distant past, or worlds other than our own.

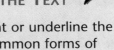

NOTE THE FACTS

What is fiction?

_____

_____

MARK THE TEXT

Highlight or underline the most common forms of fiction.

THINK AND REFLECT

Which type of fiction do you think you'd most enjoy? Why? **(Extend)**

_____

_____

_____

Elements of Fiction

CHARACTER. A **character** is a person (or sometimes an animal or thing) who takes part in the action of a story. The following are some useful terms for describing characters.

protagonist (main character)	central figure in a story
antagonist	character who struggles against the protagonist
major character	character with a significant role in the action of the story
minor character	character who plays a lesser role
one-dimensional character (flat character)	character who exhibits a single dominant quality (character trait)
three-dimensional character (full or rounded character)	character who exhibits the complexity of traits of a human being
static character	character who does not change during the course of the story
dynamic character	character who does change during the course of the story
stock character	character found again and again in different literary works

CHARACTERIZATION. **Characterization** is the use of literary techniques to create characters and make them come alive. Writers use the following techniques to create characters:

direct description	describing the physical features, dress, and personality of the character
behavior	showing what the character says or does
interaction with others	showing what other characters say or think about the character
internal state	revealing the character's private thoughts and emotions

SETTING. The **setting** of a work of fiction is the time and place in which the events take place. In fiction, setting is most often revealed by description of landscape, scenery, buildings, weather, and season. Setting reveals important information about the time period, geographical location, cultural environment, and physical conditions in which the characters live.

Reading STRATEGY REVIEW

CONNECT TO PRIOR KNOWLEDGE. Give an example of a protagonist in a book or story you have read.

_____

_____

Reading TIP

Motivation is the force that moves a character to think, feel, or behave a certain way. For example, a character may be motivated by greed, love, or friendship.

MOOD AND TONE. Mood is the atmosphere or emotion created by a literary work. A writer creates mood by using concrete details to describe the setting, characters, or events. The mood of a work might be dark, mysterious, gloomy, cheerful, inspiring, or peaceful.

Tone is the writer's attitude toward the subject or toward the reader of a work. The tone of a work may be familiar, ironic, playful, sarcastic, serious, or sincere.

POINT OF VIEW. Point of view is the vantage point from which a story is told. You need to consider point of view to understand the perspective from which the events in the story are being told. Stories are typically written from the following points of view:

first-person point of view	narrator uses words such as *I* and *we*
second-person point of view	narrator uses *you*
third-person point of view	narrator uses words such as *he, she, it,* and *they*

Most of the literature you read will be told from either the first-person or third-person point of view. In stories written from a first-person point of view, the narrator may be a participant or a witness of the action. In stories told from a third-person point of view, the narrator generally stands outside the action. In some stories, the narrator's point of view is *limited*. In this case, the narrator can reveal only his or her private, internal thoughts or those of a single character. In other stories, the narrator's point of view is *omniscient*. In such stories the narrator can reveal the private, internal thoughts of any character.

CONFLICT. A conflict is a struggle between two forces in a literary work. A plot involves the introduction, development, and eventual resolution of a conflict. A struggle that takes place between a character and some outside force is called an *external conflict*. A struggle that takes place within a character is called an *internal conflict.*

PLOT. When you read short stories or novels, it helps to know the parts of a plot. The plot is basically what happens in a story. A **plot** is a series of events related to a central conflict, or struggle. A typical plot involves the introduction of a conflict, its development, and its eventual resolution. The elements of plot include the following:

Reading TIP

Writers often work carefully with descriptive language and sensory details to create an emotional response, such as fear or longing, in the reader. Sensory details appeal to any of the five senses—sight, hearing, smell, taste, and touch.

MARK THE TEXT

Highlight or underline the explanation of what limited point of view means.

Reading TIP

In a work of fiction, the main character often takes one side of the central conflict. That character may struggle against another character, against the forces of nature, against society or how society expects him or her to live, against fate, or against some elements within himself or herself.

Which point of the plot could be called the "introduction"? (Infer)

_____

_____

exposition	sets the tone or mood, introduces the characters and setting, and provides necessary background information
inciting incident	event that introduces a central conflict
rising action	develops a central conflict and rises toward a high point of intensity
climax	the high point of interest or suspense in the plot where something decisive happens
falling action	the events that follow the climax
resolution	the point at which the central conflict is ended or resolved
dénouement	any material that follows the resolution and that ties up loose ends

Use a **plot diagram** like the one that follows to chart the plot of a literature selection.

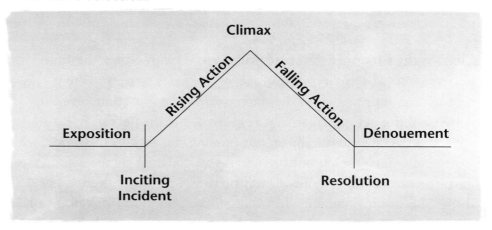

Reading TIP

Remember, plots may not follow this order exactly, but all plots center around a conflict or struggle.

Become an Active Reader

The instruction in this unit gives you an in-depth look at how to use one active reading strategy for each story. Questions and tips in the margins keep your attention focused on reading actively. White space in the margins allows you to add your own comments and strategy ideas. Brief margin notes guide your use of additional strategies. Learning how to use several strategies in combination will ensure your complete understanding of what you are reading. When you have difficulty, use fix-up ideas to correct the problem. For further information about the active reading strategies, see Unit 1, pages 4–15.

USING READING STRATEGIES WITH FICTION

Active Reading Strategy Checklists

When reading fiction, you need to be aware of the plot (or what happens), the characters, and the setting. The following checklists offer things to consider as you read fiction.

1 **READ WITH A PURPOSE.** Before reading about imagined events and characters, give yourself a purpose, or something to look for, as you read. Say to yourself
- ❏ I want to look for . . .
- ❏ I need to learn what happens to . . .
- ❏ I want to experience what it is like in . . .
- ❏ I want to understand . . .

2 **CONNECT TO PRIOR KNOWLEDGE.** Being aware of what you already know and thinking about it as you read can help you keep track of what's happening and will increase your knowledge. As you read, say to yourself
- ❏ I already know this about the story . . .
- ❏ This part of the story reminds me of . . .
- ❏ I think this part of the story is like . . .
- ❏ My experience tells me that . . .
- ❏ I like this description because . . .

3 **WRITE THINGS DOWN.** As you read short stories or novels, writing things down is very important. Possible ways to write things down include
- ❏ Underline characters' names.
- ❏ Write messages on sticky notes.
- ❏ Highlight the setting.
- ❏ Create a graphic organizer to keep track of plot elements.
- ❏ Use a code in the margin that shows how you respond to the characters, settings, or events. For instance, you can mark a description you like with a "+."

4 **MAKE PREDICTIONS.** Make predictions about characters, settings, and events in a story. Your predictions will help you think about what lies ahead. Make predictions like the following:
- ❏ I predict that this character will . . .
- ❏ The setting of this story makes me think that . . .
- ❏ I bet there will be a conflict between . . .
- ❏ This event in the story makes me guess that . . .

Reading TIP

Sometimes a purpose will be a directive from a teacher: "Compare the narrator's experience to your own life." Other times you can set your own purpose. To set a purpose, preview the title, the opening paragraphs, and instructional information for the story. Think about what you want to get out of the reading.

Reading TIP

Instead of writing down a short response, use a symbol or a short word to indicate your response. Use codes like the ones listed below.

+	I like this.
–	I don't like this.
√	This is important.
Yes	I agree with this.
No	I disagree with this.
?	I don't understand this.
!	This is like something I know.
↩	I need to come back to this later.

Reading TIP

Other tips for visualizing:
- Say to yourself, "If this were a movie, I'd see and hear . . ."
- Make quick sketches of what you imagine.
- Fill in gaps with details of your own based on experience.
- Think about how things would sound, smell, and feel if you were in the scene.

Reading TIP

Keep a vocabulary notebook as you read. Jot down new words and their meanings. After you finish reading, you can practice using the words in sentences, word sorts, and daily conversation.

FIX-UP IDEAS

- Reread
- Ask a question
- Read in shorter chunks
- Read aloud
- Retell
- Work with a partner
- Unlock difficult words
- Vary your reading rate
- Choose a new reading strategy
- Create a mnemonic device

5 **VISUALIZE.** Visualizing, or allowing the words on the page to create images in your mind, is one the most important things to do while reading fiction. Become part of the action. "See" what the author describes. Make statements like
- ❑ I imagine the setting to look like . . .
- ❑ This description of the main character makes me . . .
- ❑ I picture that this is what happens in this section . . .
- ❑ I envision myself in the action by . . .

6 **USE TEXT ORGANIZATION.** Fiction writing has a plot that you can follow. Use the plot, or the series of events, to keep track of what is happening. Say to yourself
- ❑ The exposition, or introduction, tells me . . .
- ❑ The conflict centers on . . .
- ❑ The climax, or high point of interest, occurs when . . .
- ❑ The resolution, or the outcome, of this story lets me know . . .
- ❑ Signal words like *first*, *then*, and *finally* explain . . .

7 **TACKLE DIFFICULT VOCABULARY.** Difficult words in a story can get in the way of your ability to follow the events in a work of fiction. Use aids that a text provides, consult a dictionary, or ask someone about words you do not understand. When you come across a word you do not know, say to yourself
- ❑ The context tells me that this word means . . .
- ❑ A dictionary definition provided in the story shows that the word means . . .
- ❑ My work with the word before class helps me know that the word means . . .
- ❑ A classmate said that the word means . . .
- ❑ I can skip knowing the exact meaning of this word because . . .

8 **MONITOR YOUR READING PROGRESS.** All readers encounter difficulty when they read, especially if the reading material is not self-selected. When you have to read something, take note of problems you are having and fix them. The key to reading success is knowing when you are having difficulty. To fix problems, say to yourself
- ❑ Because I do not understand this part, I will . . .
- ❑ Because I am having trouble staying interested in the story, I will . . .
- ❑ Because the words are too hard, I will . . .
- ❑ Because the story is very long, I will . . .
- ❑ Because I cannot remember what I have just read, I will . . .

How to Use Reading Strategies with Fiction

Note how a reader uses active reading strategies while reading this excerpt from "The All-American Slurp" by Lensey Namioka.

The first time our family was invited out to dinner in America, we disgraced ourselves while eating celery. We had emigrated to this country from China, and during our early days here we had a hard time with American table manners.

In China, we never ate celery raw, or any other kind of vegetable raw. We always had to disinfect the vegetables in boiling water first. When we were presented with our first relish tray, the raw celery caught us unprepared.

We had been invited to dinner by our neighbors, the Gleasons. After arriving at the house, we shook hands with our hosts and packed ourselves into a sofa. As our family of four sat stiffly in a row, my younger brother and I stole glances at our parents for a clue as to what to do next.

Mrs. Gleason offered the relish tray to Mother. The tray looked pretty, with its tiny red radishes, curly sticks of carrots, and long, slender stalks of pale green celery. "Do try some of the celery, Mrs. Lin," she said. "It's from a local farmer, and it's sweet."

VISUALIZE

I can see the family squished onto the sofa. They are sitting uncomfortably, perched on the edge of the seat.

USE TEXT ORGANIZATION

The narrator's difficulty adapting to American manners seems to be a conflict in this story.

WRITE THINGS DOWN

I'll make a Plot Diagram for this story. One thing I know from the introduction is that the main character is Chinese and has trouble adapting to American culture.

MONITOR YOUR READING PROGRESS

I'll retell what I've read so far to make sure I'm getting it: The narrator and her family, who recently came to America from China, go to a dinner party. They have some mishaps because of not understanding table manners. The first problem involves celery.

TACKLE DIFFICULT VOCABULARY

Emigrated has some similar word parts to *immigrant*, which means "someone who has come to this country from another." From word parts and context, I can guess that *emigrated* means to leave one country to come to another.

MAKE PREDICTIONS

I predict that the narrator and her family crunch too loudly with the celery.

READ WITH A PURPOSE

I want to find out how the narrator's family disgraced themselves.

CONNECT TO PRIOR KNOWLEDGE

I've been in situations where I didn't know what the proper or polite thing to do was. It's embarrassing.

Reader's resource

The preteen and teenage years can be the most challenging years in a person's life. Like the narrator in **"Eleven,"** young people begin to realize that the world is not always as simple or fair as it might have seemed. A person might blow out the candles of a birthday cake and know that he or she is another year older but not feel more mature. With each year and each birthday, a person is expected to grow farther from childhood and closer to adulthood. Growing up is a long but exciting process.

Reader's journal

When do you feel most grown up and able to handle anything? When do you feel young and unsure of yourself?

_____

_____

_____

"Eleven" by Sandra Cisneros

Active READING STRATEGY

VISUALIZE

Before Reading ➤ **COLLECT INFORMATION AND IMAGES**

❏ Preview the entire selection, including activities before, during, and after the story. Read the title and the Reader's Resource. Picture what might happen in this story.

❏ Imagine your last birthday. Was it a happy event? sad? confusing? boring? Sometimes you can use prior knowledge or your own experience to help fill in details as you visualize.

❏ Use the graphic organizer to show what you are imagining. Stop three times to draw the facial expressions of Rachel, other students in the class, and Mrs. Price. The faces should show how the characters feel at that point in the story. Use word balloons with words from the story to show what is happening.

Graphic Organizer: Visualization Chart

Sketch 1
The quote from the text that I am sketching is on page _____.

Sketch 2
The quote from the text that I am sketching is on page _____.

Sketch 3
The quote from the text that I am sketching is on page _____.

Eleven

Sandra Cisneros

During Reading

MAKE MIND MOVIES

❏ As your teacher reads the first page of "Eleven" aloud, picture what the narrator describes. Picture how things look and how the narrator feels.

❏ When your teacher reaches lines 50–51 "Because she's older and the teacher, she's right and I'm not" on page 44, begin reading on your own, but continue the mind movie you have been making.

❏ Stop three times to draw the facial expressions of Rachel, other students in the class, and Mrs. Price in your Visualization Chart.

What they don't understand about birthdays and what they never tell you is that when you're eleven, you're also ten, and nine, and eight, and seven, and six, and five, and four, and three, and two, and one. And when you wake up on your eleventh birthday, you expect to feel eleven, but you don't. You open your eyes and everything's just like yesterday, only it's today. And you don't feel eleven at all. You feel like you're still ten. And you are—underneath the year that makes you eleven.

10   Like some days you might say something stupid, and that's the part of you that's still ten. Or maybe some days you might need to sit on your mama's lap because you're scared, and that's the part of you that's five. And maybe one day when you're all grown up, maybe you will need to cry like if you're three, and that's OK. That's what I tell Mama when she's sad and needs to cry. Maybe she's feeling three.

Because the way you grow old is kind of like an onion or like the rings inside a tree trunk or like my little wooden dolls that fit one inside the other, each year inside the next one.
20   That's how being eleven years old is.

You don't feel eleven. Not right away. It takes a few days, weeks even, sometimes even months before you say Eleven when they ask you. And you don't feel smart eleven, not until you're almost twelve. That's the way it is.

Only today I wish I didn't have only eleven years rattling inside me like pennies in a tin Band-Aid box. Today I wish I was one hundred and two instead of eleven because if I was

Literary TOOLS

SIMILE. A **simile** is a comparison using *like* or *as*. What is one thing Cisneros compares growing older to in the highlighted paragraph?

_____

_____

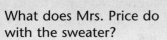
FIX-UP IDEA

Connect to What You Know
The narrator of "Eleven" describes what a bad day at school is like. If you are having trouble under-standing the story, draw an asterisk (*) or another mark next to places in the text that remind you of bad days you have heard about or experienced. Find at least three places in the story that remind you of something that has happened to you. You may mark more places if you wish.

one hundred and two, I'd have known what to say when Mrs. Price put the red sweater on my desk. I would've known how
30 to tell her it wasn't mine instead of just sitting there with that look on my face and nothing coming out of my mouth.

"Whose is this?" Mrs. Price says, and she holds the red sweater up in the air for all the class to see. "Whose? It's been sitting in the coatroom for a month."

"Not mine," says everybody. "Not me."

"It has to belong to somebody," Mrs. Price keeps saying, but nobody can remember. It's an ugly sweater with red plastic buttons and a collar and sleeves all stretched out like you could use it for a jump rope. It's maybe a thousand years
40 old, and even if it belonged to me, I wouldn't say so.

Maybe because I'm skinny, maybe because she doesn't like me, that stupid Sylvia Saldívar says, "I think it belongs to Rachel." An ugly sweater like that, all raggedy and old, but Mrs. Price believes her. Mrs. Price takes the sweater and puts it right on my desk, but when I open my mouth, nothing comes out.

"That's not, I don't, you're not . . . Not mine," I finally say in a little voice that was maybe me when I was four.

"Of course it's yours," Mrs. Price says. "I remember you
50 wearing it once." Because she's older and the teacher, she's right and I'm not.

Not mine, not mine, not mine, but Mrs. Price is already turning to page thirty-two, and math problem number four. I don't know why, but all of a sudden I'm feeling sick inside, like the part of me that's three wants to come out of my eyes, only I squeeze them shut tight and bite down on my teeth real hard and try to remember today I am eleven, eleven. Mama is making a cake for me for tonight, and when Papa comes home, everybody will sing Happy birthday, happy
60 birthday to you.

But when the sick feeling goes away and I open my eyes, the red sweater's still sitting there like a big red mountain. I move the red sweater to the corner of my desk with my ruler. I move my pencil and books and eraser as far from it as possible. I even move my chair a little to the right. Not mine, not mine, not mine.

In my head I'm thinking how long till lunchtime, how long till I can take the red sweater and throw it over the

schoolyard fence, or leave it hanging on a parking meter, or
bunch it up into a little ball and toss it in the alley. Except
when math period ends, Mrs. Price says loud and in front of
everybody, "Now, Rachel, that's enough," because she sees
I've shoved the red sweater to the tippy-tip corner of my desk
and it's hanging all over the edge like a waterfall, but I don't
care.

   "Rachel," Mrs. Price says. She says it like she's getting mad.
"You put that sweater on right now and no more nonsense."

   "But it's not—"

   "Now!" Mrs. Price says.

   This is when I wish I wasn't eleven, because all the years
inside of me—ten, nine, eight, seven, six, five, four, three,
two, and one—are pushing at the back of my eyes when I put
one arm through one sleeve of the sweater that smells like
cottage cheese, and then the other arm through the other and
stand there with my arms apart like if the sweater hurts me
and it does, all itchy and full of germs that aren't even mine.

   That's when everything I've been holding in since this
morning, since when Mrs. Price put the sweater on my desk,
finally lets go, and all of a sudden I'm crying in front of
everybody. I wish I was invisible, but I'm not. I'm eleven and
it's my birthday today and I'm crying like I'm three in front of
everybody. I put my head down on the desk and bury my face
in my stupid clown-sweater arms. My face all hot and spit
coming out of my mouth because I can't stop the little animal
noises from coming out of me, until there aren't any more
tears left in my eyes, and it's just my body shaking like when
you have the hiccups, and my whole head hurts like when you
drink milk too fast.

   But the worst part is right before the bell rings for lunch.
That stupid Phyllis Lopez, who is even dumber than Sylvia
Saldívar, says she remembers the red sweater is hers! I take it
off right away and give it to her, only Mrs. Price pretends like
everything's OK.

   Today I'm eleven. There's a cake Mama's making for
tonight, and when Papa comes home from work, we'll eat it.
There'll be candles and presents, and everybody will sing
Happy birthday, happy birthday to you, Rachel, only it's too
late.

70

80

90

100

READ ALOUD

Read the highlighted lines
aloud. What tone of voice
do you think Mrs. Price
uses? Think about how a
teacher or parent talks
when he or she is getting
angry.

_____

NOTE THE FACTS

How does Rachel react
when she puts on the
sweater?

_____

_____

_____

THINK AND REFLECT

Is Rachel's reaction to the
sweater rational? How
would you react?
(Evaluate)

_____

_____

_____

_____

_____

_____

Use THE STRATEGY

VISUALIZE. The selection ends with a vivid image. Imagine a balloon going higher and farther away. Picture it getting smaller and smaller. How does this image make you feel?

_____

_____

_____

110   I'm eleven today. I'm eleven, ten, nine, eight, seven, six, five, four, three, two, and one, but I wish I was one hundred and two. I wish I was anything but eleven, because I want today to be far away already, far away like a runaway balloon, like a tiny o in the sky, so tiny-tiny you have to close your eyes to see it. ■

Reflect ON YOUR READING

After Reading ➤ **DRAW PICTURES OF YOUR MIND MOVIES**

❑ Share the pictures from your Visualization Chart of what you "saw" or imagined. What kinds of facial expressions do the characters have in your sketches? How do you feel about Mrs. Price? Do you like her? Does Rachel like her? Do your classmates feel the same way about Mrs. Price? Why, or why not?

❑ Go back to the story and find details that help you draw conclusions about Mrs. Price. Make a list of those details here.

_____

_____

_____

_____

Reading Skills and Test Practice

EVALUATE POINT OF VIEW

Discuss with your partner how best to answer these questions about point of view. Use the Think-Aloud Notes to write down your reasons for eliminating the incorrect answers.

_____1. What might Rachel believe is the worst thing that happens to her on her birthday?
   a. Mrs. Price ignores Rachel's answers about who owns the sweater.
   b. Sylvia Saldivar tells everyone that the sweater is Rachel's.
   c. Rachel starts crying in front of everybody when she has to put on the sweater.
   d. Mrs. Price will not allow Rachel to celebrate her birthday in class.

_____2. Read this passage from the story.

   What they don't understand about birthdays and what they never tell you is that when you're eleven, you're also ten, and nine, and eight, and seven, and six, and five, and four, and three, and two, and one.

   Why does the author describe birthdays in this way?
   a. to emphasize that birthdays are important
   b. to explain how people sometimes feel younger than they are
   c. to show readers why people celebrate birthdays
   d. to tell readers how to figure out a person's age

Investigate, Inquire, and Imagine

RECALL: GATHER FACTS
1a. What does Sylvia say to Mrs. Price about the sweater? How do Mrs. Price and Rachel react?

INTERPRET: FIND MEANING
1b. Why doesn't Rachel want the sweater? How does she try to make herself feel better?

ANALYZE: TAKE THINGS APART
2a. Identify the words and actions of Mrs. Price that affect Rachel's day.

SYNTHESIZE: BRING THINGS TOGETHER
2b. Why does Mrs. Price do and say these things? Why does Rachel react the way she does?

PERSPECTIVE: LOOK AT OTHER VIEWS
3a. What do you think Rachel does after school on this day? What do you think she tells her parents about the day? How do you think her mood might change, if at all?

EMPATHY: SEE FROM INSIDE
3b. If you had been in Rachel's position, what would you have done?

Literary Tools

SIMILE. A **simile** is a comparison using *like* or *as*. Find examples of similes in "Eleven" and note them in the graphic organizer.

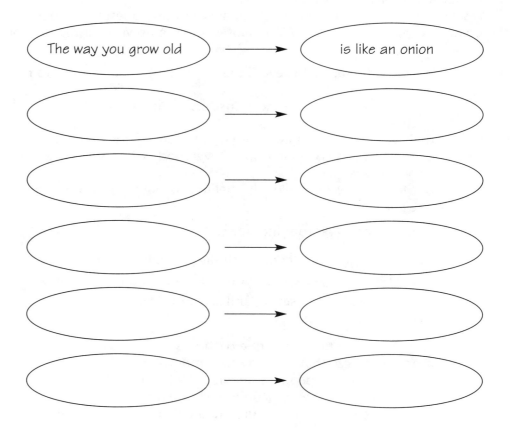

The way you grow old → is like an onion

WordWorkshop

NUMBERS COUNT. Numbers can be written numerically (11) or spelled out as words (eleven). How you decide to write a number depends on how it is being used (called "usage") and the manner in which the kind of writing you are doing usually shows numbers (called "style").

Use a hyphen to join the parts of a two-digit number over 20 when you spell it out:

   27   twenty-seven
   83   eighty-three

Don't use a hyphen for hundreds or higher:

   101   one hundred one
   614   six hundred fourteen

In "Eleven," the author wrote out all the numbers she used. Some of these numbers are written as numerals in the left column below. Translate them into words in the right column.

Numerals	Words
8	
111	
31	
1,000,000	
1,600	
98	

Read-Write Connection

Describe your last birthday and how you felt about it.

_____

_____

_____

Beyond the Reading

READ A "COMING-OF-AGE" NOVEL. In many novels, a young main character learns something that makes him or her more grown up. These are called coming-of-age novels. Find and read a coming-of-age novel. Then create a collage that shows some of the changes the character goes through on the way to becoming more adult. Be prepared to explain why you chose the images you did for your collage.

GO ONLINE. To find links and additional activities for this selection, visit the EMC Internet Resource Center at **emcp.com/languagearts** and click on Write-In Reader.

Reader's resource

"Ta-Na-E-Ka" features a Kaw Indian girl who goes through Ta-Na-E-Ka—a rite of passage for boys and girls moving into adulthood. Rites of passage, which take place in all societies, usually involve ritual activities and teachings designed to prepare young people for new roles. Rites of passage also reaffirm and honor the values of a society. The main character in this story manages to lessen the discomforts usually associated with this process by following her own instincts as well as the directions of her grandfather.

Word watch

PREVIEW VOCABULARY

anticipate	hostility
audacity	ordeal
dejected	sacred
equate	shrewd
fend	skirmish
heritage	unsightly
hospitality	virtue

Reader's journal

What traditions does your family observe? What do you think of these traditions?

_____

_____

_____

"TA-NA-E-KA"
by Mary Whitebird

Active READING STRATEGY

TACKLE DIFFICULT VOCABULARY

Before Reading ▶ **SORT VOCABULARY WORDS**

❑ In a small group, make a list of the fourteen vocabulary words and seven footnotes in "Ta-Na-E-Ka." Add an eighth term, *Kaw*, to the footnote list. Skim the story to find four more challenging words to add to your vocabulary list. Define each word and footnote.

❑ Sort the words and footnotes using one of the following methods: same parts of speech, words with similar or opposite meanings, words with prefixes and suffixes, or words that relate to each other or that can be used together. Put your categories at the top of the columns. Then write the words in the grid. When you finish using one sorting method, try one of the other methods. Make your own grid for your second sorting.

❑ Compare the two sorting methods you tried. Which method was harder to use? Why?

Graphic Organizer: Word Sort

Category _____	Category _____	Category _____

"TA-NA-E-KA"

Mary Whitebird

During Reading →

USE WHAT YOU KNOW

- ❑ Read the story, using what you have learned about words in the story to help you understand what sort of rite of passage Ta-Na-E-Ka is.
- ❑ If you forget the meaning of a word or phrase, use the definitions on your word list and at the bottom of each page.

READ ALOUD

Practice pronouncing *Ta-Na-E-Ka* [tä nä' ē kä]. Knowing how to pronounce this word will help you read the story smoothly, even if you are reading silently.

MARK THE TEXT

Highlight or underline why *eleven* was a magic word among the Kaw.

A s my birthday drew closer, I had awful nightmares about it. I was reaching the age at which all Kaw Indians had to participate in Ta-Na-E-Ka. Well, not all Kaws. Many of the younger families on the reservation were beginning to give up the old customs. But my grandfather, Amos Deer Leg, was devoted to tradition. He still wore handmade beaded moccasins instead of shoes, and kept his iron gray hair in tight braids. He could speak English, but he spoke it only with white men. With his
10 family he used a Sioux dialect.

Grandfather was one of the last living Indians (he died in 1953 when he was eighty-one) who actually fought against the U.S. Cavalry.[1] Not only did he fight, he was wounded in a <u>skirmish</u> at Rose Creek—a famous encounter in which the celebrated Kaw chief Flat Nose lost his life. At the time, my grandfather was only eleven years old.

Eleven was a magic word among the Kaws. It was the time of Ta-Na-E-Ka, the "flowering of adulthood." It was the age, my grandfather informed us hundreds of times,
20 "when a boy could prove himself to be a warrior and a girl took the first steps to womanhood."

"I don't want to be a warrior," my cousin, Roger Deer Leg, confided to me. "I'm going to become an accountant."

---

1. **U.S. Cavalry.** Early mounted troops

---

words for everyday use skir • mish (skər' mish) *n.,* minor fight in war. *My brother got hurt in a <u>skirmish</u> during WWII.*

THINK AND REFLECT

Why does the narrator
think the Kaw were the
originators of the
women's liberation
movement? (Synthesize)

_____

_____

_____

"None of the other tribes make girls go through the endurance ritual," I complained to my mother.

"It won't be as bad as you think, Mary," my mother said, ignoring my protests. "Once you've gone through it, you'll certainly never forget it. You'll be proud."

30 I even complained to my teacher, Mrs. Richardson, feeling that, as a white woman, she would side with me.

She didn't. "All of us have rituals of one kind or another," Mrs. Richardson said. "And look at it this way: how many girls have the opportunity to compete on equal terms with boys? Don't look down on your heritage."

Heritage, indeed! I had no intention of living on a reservation for the rest of my life. I was a good student. I loved school. My fantasies were about knights in armor and fair ladies in flowing gowns being saved from dragons. It never once occurred to me that being Indian was exciting.

40 But I've always thought that the Kaw were the originators of the women's liberation movement.[2] No other Indian tribe—and I've spent half a lifetime researching the subject—treated women more "equally" than the Kaw. Unlike most of the subtribes of the Sioux Nation, the Kaw allowed men and women to eat together. And hundreds of years before we were "acculturated,"[3] a Kaw woman had the right to refuse a prospective husband even if her father arranged the match.

The wisest women (generally wisdom was equated with age) often sat in tribal councils. Furthermore, most Kaw 50 legends revolve around "Good Woman," a kind of supersquaw, a Joan of Arc[4] of the high plains. Good Woman led Kaw warriors into battle after battle from which they always seemed to emerge victorious.

And girls as well as boys were required to undergo Ta-Na-E-Ka.

---

2. **women's liberation movement.** A movement for political, social, and educational equality of women with men. Its roots in America date back to 1848, but women were not granted equal rights until the 1920s.
3. **acculturated.** Adapting to or borrowing traits from another culture
4. **Joan of Arc.** French saint and national heroine who was ultimately burned at the stake for standing up for her beliefs

words for everyday use
her • i • tage (her′ ə tij) *n.,* something that is passed on to an heir; tradition. *Wearing our hair in braids is a tradition in my heritage.*
equate (ē kwāt′) *v.,* make equal. *People sometimes equate a doctor with a healer.*

The actual ceremony varied from tribe to tribe, but since the Indians' life on the plains was dedicated to survival, Ta-Na-E-Ka was a test of survival.

"Endurance is the loftiest <u>virtue</u> of the Indian," my
60   grandfather explained. "To survive, we must endure. When I was a boy, Ta-Na-E-Ka was more than the mere symbol it is now. We were painted white with the juice of a <u>sacred</u> herb and sent naked into the wilderness without so much as a knife. We couldn't return until the white had worn off. It wouldn't wash off. It took almost eighteen days, and during that time we had to stay alive, trapping food, eating insects and roots and berries, and watching out for enemies. And we did have enemies—both the white soldiers and the Omaha[5] warriors, who were always trying to capture Kaw
70   boys and girls undergoing their endurance test. It was an exciting time."

"What happened if you couldn't make it?" Roger asked. He was born only three days after I was, and we were being trained for Ta-Na-E-Ka together. I was happy to know he was frightened too.

"Many didn't return," Grandfather said. "Only the strongest and <u>shrewdest</u>. Mothers were not allowed to weep over those who didn't return. If a Kaw couldn't survive, he or she wasn't worth weeping over. It was our way."

80   "What a lot of hooey," Roger whispered. "I'd give anything to get out of it."

"I don't see how we have any choice," I replied.

Roger gave my arm a little squeeze. "Well, it's only five days."

Five days! Maybe it was better than being painted white and sent out naked for eighteen days. But not much better.

We were to be sent, barefoot and in bathing suits, into the woods. Even our very traditional parents put their foot down when Grandfather suggested we go naked. For five days we'd have to live off the land, keeping warm as best we

---

5. **Omaha.** North American Plains Indians who migrated from the Ohio valley to the Missouri and Mississippi River valleys and finally settled in Iowa

words for everyday use	**vir • tue** (vər′ chü) *n.*, particular strength or moral excellence. *A <u>virtue</u> my dad has is honesty because he never lies.* **sa • cred** (sā′ krəd) *adj.*, highly valued, important. *Saffron is a <u>sacred</u> type of spice, and it is highly valued.* **shrewd** (shrüd′) *adj.*, clever, having a high degree of common sense. *Jill, who solved the hardest riddle, is one of the <u>shrewdest</u> people I know.*

READ ALOUD

Read the highlighted paragraph aloud. Try to say the words the way the grandfather might have said them. What is the main point of Ta-Na-E-Ka? How has it changed since the grandfather's day?

_____

_____

Literary TOOLS

PLOT. The **plot** is a series of events related to a central conflict, or struggle. As you read, keep track of the main events of the story and try to determine the conflict. You could highlight important events or write a note in the margin. Another way to track events is to use a graphic organizer like the one in Literary Tools on page 62.

MARK THE TEXT

Highlight or underline what Mary and Roger have to do.

90
could, getting food where we could. It was May, but on the northernmost reaches of the Missouri River the days were still chilly and the nights were fiercely cold.

Grandfather was in charge of the month's training for Ta-Na-E-Ka. One day he caught a grasshopper and demonstrated how to pull its legs and wings off in one flick of the fingers and how to swallow it.

I felt sick, and Roger turned green. "It's a darn good thing it's 1947," I told Roger teasingly. "You'd make a terrible warrior." Roger just grimaced.

100
I knew one thing. This particular Kaw Indian girl wasn't going to swallow a grasshopper, no matter how hungry she got. And then I had an idea. Why hadn't I thought of it before? It would have saved nights of bad dreams about squooshy grasshoppers.

I headed straight for my teacher's house. "Mrs. Richardson," I said, "would you lend me five dollars?"

"Five dollars!" she exclaimed. "What for?"

"You remember the ceremony I talked about?"

"Ta-Na-E-Ka. Of course. Your parents have written me
110
and asked me to excuse you from school so you can participate in it."

"Well, I need some things for the ceremony," I replied, in a half-truth.

"I don't want to ask my parents for the money."

"It's not a crime to borrow money, Mary. But how can you pay it back?"

"I'll baby-sit for you ten times."

"That's more than fair," she said, going to her purse and handing me a crisp new five-dollar bill. I'd never had that
120
much money at once.

"I'm happy to know the money's going to be put to a good use," Mrs. Richardson said.

A few days later, the ritual began with a long speech from my grandfather about how we had reached the age of decision, how we now had to <u>fend</u> for ourselves and prove

---

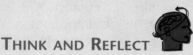

THINK AND REFLECT

Why is Mary's response a "half-truth"? Why do you think she needs the money? **(Infer)**

_____

_____

_____

---

words for everyday use	**fend** (fend') v., provide for, support. *Now that the baby bird can fly, it will have to* <u>*fend*</u> *for itself.*

that we could survive the most horrendous of <u>ordeals</u>. All the friends and relatives who had gathered at our house for dinner made jokes about their own Ta-Na-E-Ka experiences. They all advised us to fill up now, since for the

130   next five days we'd be gorging ourselves on crickets.

Neither Roger nor I was very hungry. "I'll probably laugh about this when I'm an accountant," Roger said, trembling.

"Are you trembling?" I asked.

"What do you think?"

"I'm happy to know boys tremble too," I said.

At six the next morning we kissed our parents and went off to the woods. "Which side do you want?" Roger asked. According to the rules, Roger and I would stake out "territories" in separate areas of the woods, and we weren't

140   to communicate during the entire ordeal.

"I'll go toward the river, if it's okay with you," I said.

"Sure," Roger answered. "What difference does it make?"

To me, it made a lot of difference. There was a marina a few miles up the river and there were boats moored there. At least, I hoped so. I figured that a boat was a better place to sleep than under a pile of leaves.

"Why do you keep holding your head?" Roger asked.

"Oh, nothing. Just nervous," I told him. Actually, I was afraid I'd lose the five-dollar bill, which I had tucked into

150   my hair with a bobby pin. As we came to a fork in the trail, Roger shook my hand.

"Good luck, Mary."

"*N'ko-n'ta*," I said. It was the Kaw word for courage.

The sun was shining and it was warm, but my bare feet began to hurt immediately. I spied one of the berry bushes Grandfather had told us about. "You're lucky," he had said. "The berries are ripe in the spring, and they are delicious and nourishing." They were orange and fat and I popped one into my mouth.

words for everyday use

or • deal (or dēl') *n.*, severe test or trial. *Training camp is one of many <u>ordeals</u> a soldier must go through to become an officer.*

TACKLE DIFFICULT VOCABULARY. One way to find the meaning of unfamiliar words is to use context clues. For example, if you do not know what *horrendous* means, you can guess that it means horrible or awful because it describes the word *ordeal.* Try using context clues to help you find the meaning of other unfamiliar words.

MARK THE TEXT

Underline or highlight what Mary and Roger cannot do during Ta-Na-E-Ka.

FIX-UP IDEA

Refocus
If you are having trouble understanding events in the story, try changing your focus. Read the story silently with a partner. Pretend that you are the narrator and that you are trying to help someone understand what Ta-Na-E-Ka is. When you find sections of the story that describe Ta-Na-E-Ka, read those sections aloud with your partner in the way that shows how the narrator would say them. Use facial and vocal expressions that demonstrate the narrator's feelings.

NOTE THE FACTS

What did Mary realize after she watched a rabbit, a redheaded woodpecker, and a civet cat?

_____

_____

_____

THINK AND REFLECT

Why is Mary disappointed there are no boats? **(Infer)**

_____

_____

THINK AND REFLECT

Why does Mary check the window lock in the ladies' room? **(Infer)**

_____

_____

160   *Argh!* I spat it out. It was awful and bitter, and even grasshoppers were probably better tasting, although I never intended to find out.

    I sat down to rest my feet. A rabbit hopped out from under the berry bush. He nuzzled the berry I'd spat out and ate it. He picked another one and ate that too. He liked them. He looked at me, twitching his nose. I watched a redheaded woodpecker bore into an elm tree and I caught a glimpse of a civet cat[6] waddling through some twigs. All of a sudden I realized I was no longer frightened. Ta-Na-E-Ka

170 might be more fun than I'd <u>anticipated</u>. I got up and headed toward the marina.

    "Not one boat," I said to myself <u>dejectedly</u>. But the restaurant on the shore, "Ernie's Riverside," was open. I walked in, feeling silly in my bathing suit. The man at the counter was big and tough-looking. He wore a sweat shirt with the words "Fort Sheridan, 1944," and he had only three fingers on one of his hands. He asked me what I wanted.

    "A hamburger and a milk shake," I said, holding the five-

180 dollar bill in my hand so he'd know I had money.

    "That's a pretty heavy breakfast, honey," he murmured.

    "That's what I always have for breakfast," I lied.

    "Forty-five cents," he said, bringing me the food. (Back in 1947, hamburgers were twenty-five cents and milk shakes were twenty cents.) "Delicious," I thought. "Better'n grasshoppers—and Grandfather never once mentioned that I couldn't eat hamburgers."

    While I was eating, I had a grand idea. Why not sleep in the restaurant? I went to the ladies' room and made sure

190 the window was unlocked. Then I went back outside and played along the riverbank, watching the water birds and trying to identify each one. I planned to look for a beaver dam the next day.

---

6. **civet cat.** Small spotted skunk of western North America

words for everyday use	**an • tic • i • pate** (an ti′ sə pāt) *v.,* look forward to, expect. *I've <u>anticipated</u> the coming of my birthday, and it's finally here.* **de • ject • ed** (di jek′ təd) *adj.,* be cast down in spirits, depressed. *Brett looked at the crowd of <u>dejected</u> people after he missed the touchdown pass.* **dejectedly,** *adv.*

The restaurant closed at sunset, and I watched the three-fingered man drive away. Then I climbed in the unlocked window. There was a night light on, so I didn't turn on any lights. But there was a radio on the counter. I turned it on to a music program. It was warm in the restaurant, and I was hungry. I helped myself to a glass of milk and a piece of pie, intending to keep a list of what I'd eaten, so I could leave money. I also planned to get up early, sneak out through the window, and head for the woods before the three-fingered man returned. I turned off the radio, wrapped myself in the man's apron, and, in spite of the hardness of the floor, fell asleep.

"What the heck are you doing here, kid?"

It was the man's voice.

It was morning. I'd overslept. I was scared.

"Hold it, kid. I just wanna know what you're doing here. You lost? You must be from the reservation. Your folks must be worried sick about you. Do they have a phone?"

"Yes, yes," I answered. "But don't call them."

I was shivering. The man, who told me his name was Ernie, made me a cup of hot chocolate while I explained about Ta-Na-E-Ka.

"Darndest thing I ever heard," he said, when I was through. "Lived next to the reservation all of my life and this is the first I've heard of Ta-Na-whatever-you-call-it." He looked at me, all goosebumps in my bathing suit. "Pretty silly thing to do to a kid," he muttered.

That was just what I'd been thinking for months, but when Ernie said it, I became angry. "No, it isn't silly. It's a custom of the Kaw. We've been doing this for hundreds of years. My mother and my grandfather and everybody in my family went through this ceremony. It's why the Kaw are great warriors."

"Okay, great warrior," Ernie chuckled, "suit yourself. And, if you want to stick around, it's okay with me." Ernie went to the broom closet and tossed me a bundle. "That's the lost-and-found closet," he said. "Stuff people left on boats. Maybe there's something to keep you warm."

The sweater fitted loosely, but it felt good. I felt good. And I'd found a new friend. Most important, I was surviving Ta-Na-E-Ka.

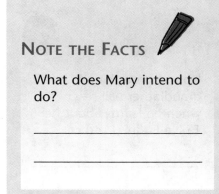

NOTE THE FACTS

What does Mary intend to do?

_____

_____

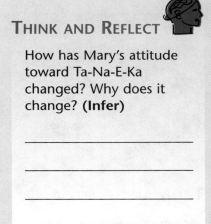

THINK AND REFLECT

How has Mary's attitude toward Ta-Na-E-Ka changed? Why does it change? **(Infer)**

_____

_____

_____

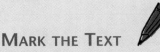

MARK THE TEXT

Highlight or underline the reasons Mary is feeling good.

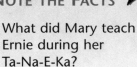
NOTE THE FACTS

What did Mary teach Ernie during her Ta-Na-E-Ka?

_____

_____

THINK AND REFLECT

What was different about Mary's and Roger's Ta-Na-E-Ka experiences? (Analyze)

_____

_____

_____

My grandfather had said the experience would be filled with adventure, and I was having my fill. And Grandfather had never said we couldn't accept hospitality.

I stayed at Ernie's Riverside for the entire period. In the mornings I went into the woods and watched the animals and picked flowers for each of the tables in Ernie's. I had never felt better. I was up early enough to watch the sun rise on the Missouri, and I went to bed after it set. I ate everything I wanted—insisting that Ernie take all my money for the food. "I'll keep this in trust[7] for you, Mary," Ernie promised, "in case you are ever desperate for five dollars."

I was sorry when the five days were over. I'd enjoyed every minute with Ernie. He taught me how to make western omelets and to make Chili Ernie Style (still one of my favorite dishes). And I told Ernie all about the legends of the Kaw. I hadn't realized I knew so much about my people.

But Ta-Na-E-Ka was over, and as I approached my house at about nine-thirty in the evening, I became nervous all over again. What if Grandfather asked me about the berries and the grasshoppers? And my feet were hardly cut. I hadn't lost a pound and my hair was combed.

"They'll be so happy to see me," I told myself hopefully, "that they won't ask too many questions."

I opened the door. My grandfather was in the front room. He was wearing the ceremonial beaded deerskin shirt which had belonged to his grandfather. "*N'g'da'ma,*" he said. "Welcome back."

I embraced my parents warmly, letting go only when I saw my cousin Roger sprawled on the couch. His eyes were red and swollen. He'd lost weight. His feet were an unsightly mass of blood and blisters, and he was moaning: "I made it, see. I made it. I'm a warrior. A warrior."

My grandfather looked at me strangely. I was clean,

240

250

260

7. **in trust.** Money that is held for future use

words for everyday use

hos • pi • ta • li • ty (häs pə ta' lə tē) *n.,* generous and pleasant treatment or reception. *The hospitality of my friend's mom was generous and friendly.*
un • sight • ly (un sīt' lē) *adj.,* not pleasing to see. *The dog's broken leg was unsightly.*

270　obviously well-fed, and radiantly healthy. My parents got the message. My uncle and aunt gazed at me with <u>hostility</u>.

Finally my grandfather asked, "What did you eat to keep you so well?"

I sucked in my breath and blurted out the truth: "Hamburgers and milk shakes."

"Hamburgers!" my grandfather growled.

"Milk shakes!" Roger moaned.

"You didn't say we *had* to eat grasshoppers," I said sheepishly.

280　"Tell us about your Ta-Na-E-Ka," my grandfather commanded.

I told them everything, from borrowing the five dollars, to Ernie's kindness, to observing the beaver.

"That's not what I trained you for," my grandfather said sadly.

I stood up. "Grandfather, I learned that Ta-Na-E-Ka is important. I didn't think so during training. I was scared stiff of it. I handled it my way. And I learned I had nothing to be afraid of. There's no reason in 1947 to eat

290　grasshoppers when you can eat a hamburger."

I was inwardly shocked at my own <u>audacity</u>. But I liked it. "Grandfather, I'll bet you never ate one of those rotten berries yourself."

Grandfather laughed! He laughed aloud! My mother and father and aunt and uncle were all dumbfounded. Grandfather never laughed. Never.

"Those berries—they are terrible," Grandfather admitted. "I could never swallow them. I found a dead deer on the first day of my Ta-Na-E-Ka—shot by a soldier, probably—

300　and he kept my belly full for the entire period of the test!"

Grandfather stopped laughing. "We should send you out again," he said.

I looked at Roger. "You're pretty smart, Mary," Roger groaned. "I'd never have thought of what you did."

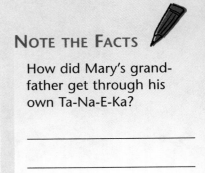

NOTE THE FACTS

What is Grandfather's first reaction when he hears about Mary's Ta-Na-E-Ka?

_____

_____

NOTE THE FACTS

How did Mary's grandfather get through his own Ta-Na-E-Ka?

_____

_____

words for everyday use	**hos • ti • li • ty** (hä stiʹ lə tē) *n.*, strong feeling of ill will toward something. *Because I lost my sister's favorite ring, she looks at me with <u>hostility</u>.* **au • da • ci • ty** (o deʹ sə tē) *n.*, excessive boldness and pride. *Kari had the <u>audacity</u> to ask her parents for money even though she was in debt to them.*

THINK AND REFLECT

What does Grandfather think about Mary's Ta-Na-E-Ka in the end? (Synthesize)

_____

_____

_____

310

"Accountants just have to be good at arithmetic," I said comfortingly. "I'm terrible at arithmetic."

Roger tried to smile, but couldn't. My grandfather called me to him. "You should have done what your cousin did. But I think you are more alert to what is happening to our people today than we are. I think you would have passed the test under any circumstances, in any time. Somehow, you know how to exist in a world that wasn't made for Indians. I don't think you're going to have any trouble surviving."

Grandfather wasn't entirely right. But I'll tell about that another time. ∎

Reflect ON YOUR READING

SUMMARIZE THE STORY EVENTS

❑ Get back together with your group from the Before Reading activity. Summarize how the narrator carried out her Ta-Na-E-Ka challenge.
❑ As a group, choose ten words and phrases from your original word list and use each in a sentence that describes something that happened in the story. Share your sentences with the class.

Reading Skills and Test Practice

ANALYZE WORDS

Discuss with your partner how to answer the following questions about words in context. Use the Think-Aloud Notes to write down your reasons for eliminating the incorrect answers.

_____1. Which pair of words or phrases has opposite meanings?
   a. ordeal, skirmish
   b. hospitality, hostility
   c. U.S. Cavalry, Joan of Arc
   d. virtue, sacred

_____2. Read this passage from the story:

   It was May, but on the northernmost reaches of the Missouri River the days were still chilly, and the nights were fiercely cold.

   What is the best meaning for the word *fiercely* as it is used in this passage?
   a. gently
   b. ferociously
   c. occasionally
   d. severely

How did using the reading strategy help you to answer the questions?

_____

_____

THINK-ALOUD NOTES

_____

_____

_____

_____

_____

_____

_____

_____

_____

_____

_____

Investigate, Inquire, and Imagine

RECALL: GATHER FACTS
1a. How did Grandfather easily endure the entire period of his Ta-Na-E-Ka test?

→ **INTERPRET: FIND MEANING**
1b. What is similar about Mary's and Grandfather's experiences of Ta-Na-E-Ka?

ANALYZE: TAKE THINGS APART
2a. Examine the events in the story that show Mary's careful honesty about money. Then make a list of the events that show her being dishonest about other matters—for example, her half-truths, lies, and sneaking actions. Rank the seriousness of her deceptions on a scale of one (least serious) to ten (most serious).

→ **SYNTHESIZE: BRING THINGS TOGETHER**
2b. What are the main causes of Mary's dishonest behavior? Why doesn't she feel guilty or uncomfortable about it?

EVALUATE: MAKE JUDGMENTS
3a. How do you think Mary will face other challenges in her life?

→ **EXTEND: CONNECT IDEAS**
3b. Tests of endurance occur throughout life in all cultures. What strategies and attitudes from the story would you choose to apply to the tests you will face? Why do you think these strategies might work?

Literary Tools

PLOT. A **plot** is a series of events related to a central conflict, or struggle. A plot usually involves the introduction of a conflict, its development, and its eventual resolution. Fill in the graphic organizer below, if you did not do so while you were reading.

Early Events	The narrator is having nightmares about participating in Ta-Na-E-Ka.
Middle Events	
Mid-to-Late Events	

What is the main conflict in "Ta-Na-E-Ka"? How is the conflict introduced? How is it resolved?

_____

_____

WordWorkshop

WORD HUNT. The "aw" sound can be spelled several different ways. Here are two sentences from the short story "Ta-Na-E-Ka." Circle the correct spelling for each word with the "aw" sound.

1. As my birthday drew closer, I had auful/awful nightmares about it.

2. It was bitter, and even grasshoppers were probably better tasting, although/olthough I never intended to find out.

Think of three words for each "aw" spelling found below. Write each word in the appropriate column. One example of each has been done for you.

a	o	aw	au
small	soggy	straw	faucet

Read-Write Connection

Imagine you participated in a rite of passage like Ta-Na-E-Ka when you turned eleven. Describe what might have happened.

_____

_____

_____

_____

Beyond the Reading

RESEARCH RITES OF PASSAGE. Rites of passage celebrate or honor the passage of an individual from one state of his or her life to another. Common rites of passage are connected to being born, becoming an adult, marrying, and dying. In small groups, brainstorm a list of rites of passage. Then do a library or Internet search to find others. As a group, choose one type of rite of passage, for example, those related to becoming an adult. Each person should choose a different rite to research and present to the class.

GO ONLINE. To find links and additional activities for this selection, visit the EMC Internet Resource Center at **emcp.com/languagearts** and click on Write-In Reader.

Reader's resource

Richard Peck notes that his books have one theme in common: that a person will never begin to grow up until he or she becomes independent from other students. Peck's stories examine characters who learn to think and act for themselves. In **"Priscilla and the Wimps,"** young people learn to deal with a gang of bullies in their school. As you read the story, think about who the hero of the story is and what you can learn from that person.

Word watch

PREVIEW VOCABULARY

bar	pun
fate	slither
laceration	subtle

Reader's journal

What have you or some of your classmates done when intimidated by a bully or gang member?

_____

_____

_____

_____

"Priscilla and the Wimps"
by Richard Peck

Active READING STRATEGY

MAKE PREDICTIONS

Before Reading ➤ **MAKE PRELIMINARY PREDICTIONS**

❏ Preview the story. Look at the title, the Reader's Resource, and the illustration. Think about what you know about the story.
❏ Then read the first sentence in the story. What do you think this story will be about?
❏ Place your initial prediction about the story in the cluster chart that follows. As you read, you will make additional predictions about the characters listed in the chart.

Graphic Organizer: Prediction Cluster Chart

Prediction 1
Before reading: What will happen in this story?

Prediction 2
After line 28: What will happen to Monk?

"Priscilla and the Wimps"

Prediction 3
After line 48: What will happen to Melvin?

Prediction 4
After line 85: What will happen to Priscilla?

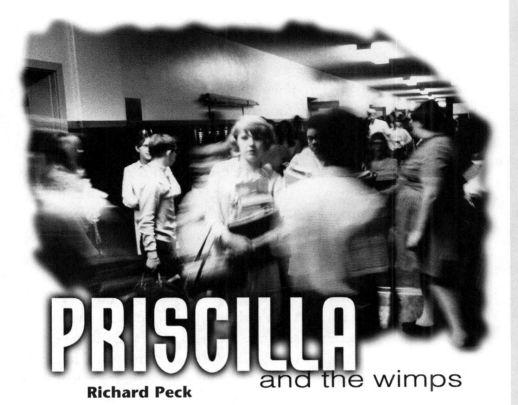

PRISCILLA and the wimps

Richard Peck

During Reading

MAKE PREDICTIONS

❑ Follow along as your teacher reads the first six paragraphs of the story aloud. When your teacher stops, make another prediction on your chart by answering this question: What will happen to Monk?

❑ Continue reading on your own. Pause from time to time to make predictions in your chart. To help you make predictions, ask yourself questions like "What will happen next?", "What will happen to this character?", and "How will the character solve this problem?" Add your predictions to your chart as new circles.

Listen, there was a time when you couldn't even go to the *rest room* around this school without a pass. And I'm not talking about those little pink tickets made out by some teacher. I'm talking about a pass that could cost anywhere up to a buck, sold by Monk Klutter.

Not that Mighty Monk ever touched money, not in public. The gang he ran, which ran the school for him, was his collection agency. They were Klutter's Kobras, a name spelled out in nailheads on six well-known black plastic windbreakers.

10   Monk's threads were more . . . <u>subtle</u>. A pile-lined suede battle jacket with lizard-skin flaps over tailored Levis and a pair of ostrich-skin boots, brassed-toed and suitable for kicking people around. One of his Kobras did nothing all day but walk a half step behind Monk, carrying a fitted bag with Monk's gym shoes, a roll of rest-room passes, a cashbox, and a switchblade that Monk gave himself manicures with at lunch over at the Kobras' table.

NOTE THE FACTS

Who runs the narrator's school?

_____

_____

words for everyday use	sub • tle (sə' təl) *adj.*, delicate or refined. *The perfume was so <u>subtle</u> that the smell didn't overpower the room.*

The narrator says, "I paid up on a regular basis. And I might add: so would you." Do you think the narrator is right? What would you do in this situation? **(Extend)**

_____

_____

Literary **TOOLS**

CHARACTER. A **character** is a person or other being that takes part in the action of a literary work. Characters can be classified as *major characters* or *minor characters.* Major characters play an important role in the literary work. Minor characters play less important roles. List the characters you have encountered so far. Then circle the names of new characters you meet.

_____

_____

_____

MARK THE TEXT

Underline or highlight why Priscilla and Melvin are called The Odd Couple.

Speaking of lunch, there were a few cases of advanced malnutrition among the newer kids. The ones who were a little
20 slow in handing over a cut of their lunch money and were therefore <u>barred</u> from the cafeteria. Monk ran a tight ship.

I admit it, I'm five foot five, and when the Kobras <u>slithered</u> by, with or without Monk, I shrank. And I admit this, too: I paid up on a regular basis. And I might add: so would you.

This school was old Monk's Garden of Eden. Unfortunately for him, there was a serpent in it. The reason Monk didn't recognize trouble when it was staring him in the face is that the serpent in the Kobras' Eden was a girl.

Practically every guy in school could show you his scars.
30 Fang marks from Kobras, you might say. And they were all highly visible in the shower room: lumps, <u>lacerations</u>, blue bruises, you name it. But girls usually got off with a warning.

Except there was this one girl named Priscilla Roseberry. Picture a girl named Priscilla Roseberry, and you'll be light years off. Priscilla was, hands down, the largest student in our particular institution of learning. I'm not talking fat. I'm talking big. Even beautiful, in a bionic way. Priscilla wasn't inclined toward organized crime. Otherwise, she could have put together a gang that would turn Klutter's
40 Kobras into garter snakes.

Priscilla was basically a loner except she had one friend. A little guy named Melvin Detweiler. You talk about The Odd Couple. Melvin's one of the smallest guys above midget status ever seen. A really nice guy, but, you know—little. They even had lockers next to each other, in the same bank as mine. I don't know what they had going. I'm not saying this was a romance. After all, people deserve their privacy.

Priscilla was sort of above everything, if you'll pardon a
50 <u>pun</u>. And very calm, as only the very big can be. If there was anybody who didn't notice Klutter's Kobras, it was Priscilla.

words for everyday use	**bar** (bär') *v.,* confine; keep out or exclude. *Because he wouldn't sit down, Chris was <u>barred</u> from riding the bus.* **slith • er** (sli' thər) *v.,* slide like a snake. *My cat was so sneaky that it <u>slithered</u> past me without my notice.* **lac • er • a • tion** (la sə rā' shən) *n.,* deeply cut wound. *His leg had many <u>lacerations</u> caused by the knife.* **pun** (pən') *n.,* humorous use of a word to suggest two or more meanings. *The comedian's <u>pun</u> made everyone laugh.*

Until one winter day after school when we were all grabbing our coats out of our lockers. And hurrying, since Klutter's Kobras made sweeps of the halls for after-school shakedowns.[1]

Anyway, up to Melvin's locker swaggers one of the Kobras. Never mind his name. Gang members don't need names. They've got group identity. He reaches down and grabs little Melvin by the neck and slams his head against

60 his locker door. The sound of skull against steel rippled all the way down the locker row, speeding the crowds on their way.

"Okay, let's see your pass," snarls the Kobra.

"A pass for what this time?" Melvin asks, probably still dazed.

"Let's call it a pass for very short people," says the Kobra, "a dwarf tax." He wheezes a little Kobra chuckle at his own wittiness. And already he's reaching for Melvin's wallet with the hand that isn't circling Melvin's windpipe. All this time, of course, Melvin and the Kobra are standing in Priscilla's

70 big shadow.

She's taking her time shoving her books into her locker and pulling on a very large-size coat. Then, quicker than the eye, she brings the side of her enormous hand down in a chop[2] that breaks the Kobra's hold on Melvin's throat. You could hear a pin drop in that hallway. Nobody'd ever laid a finger on a Kobra, let alone a hand the size of Priscilla's.

Then Priscilla, who hardly ever says anything to anybody except Melvin, says to the Kobra, "Who's your leader, wimp?"

This practically blows the Kobra away. First he's chopped

80 by a girl, and now she's acting like she doesn't know Monk Klutter, the Head Honcho of the World. He's so amazed, he tells her. "Monk Klutter."

"Never heard of him," Priscilla mentions. "Send him to see me." The Kobra just backs away from her like the whole situation is too big for him, which it is.

Pretty soon Monk himself slides up. He jerks his head once, and his Kobras slither off down the hall. He's going to handle this interesting case personally. "Who is it around here doesn't know Monk Klutter?"

---

1. **shakedowns.** Thorough and complete searches
2. **chop.** Sharp downward blow

Use **THE STRATEGY**

MAKE PREDICTIONS. Stop after you read line 63. Make a prediction about what will happen to Melvin. Add this prediction to your chart.

FIX-UP IDEA

Connect to Prior Knowledge
If you are having trouble understanding the story, jot down thoughts that come to mind as you read such as: I don't understand this . . ., this reminds me of . . ., I like this part because . . ., I didn't guess that this would happen because. . . . Jot down your thoughts at least four times.

READ ALOUD

Read the highlighted text aloud. Then make a prediction about what will happen to Priscilla, and add it to your chart.

He's standing inches from Priscilla, but since he'd have to look up at her, he doesn't. "Never heard of him," says Priscilla.

Monk's not happy with this answer, but by now he's spotted Melvin, who's grown smaller in spite of himself. Monk breaks his own rule by reaching for Melvin with his own hands. "Kid," he says, "you're going to have to educate your girl friend."

His hands never quite make it to Melvin. In a move of pure poetry Priscilla has Monk in a hammerlock.[3] His neck's popping like gunfire, and his head's bowed under the immense weight of her forearm. His suede jacket's peeling back, showing pile.

Priscilla's behind him in another easy motion. And with a single mighty thrust forward, frog-marches Monk into her own locker. It's incredible. His ostrich-skin boots click once in the air. And suddenly he's gone, neatly wedged into the locker, a perfect fit. Priscilla bangs the door shut, twirls the lock, and strolls out of school. Melvin goes with her, of course, trotting along below her shoulder. The last stragglers leave quietly.

Well, this is where <u>fate</u>, an even bigger force than Priscilla, steps in. It snows all that night, a blizzard. The whole town ices up. And school closes for a week. ■

---

3. **hammerlock.** Wrestling hold in which an opponent's arm is held bent behind his back

NOTE THE FACTS

What does Priscilla do to Monk?

_____

_____

_____

THINK AND REFLECT

Is the ending to the story realistic? Is it satisfying? Why, or why not? **(Evaluate)**

_____

_____

_____

words for everyday use

fate (fāt') *n.*, inevitable outcome or end; destiny. *It was <u>fate</u> that my best friend and I met at camp.*

Reflect ON YOUR READING

After Reading ➤ SHARE PREDICTIONS WITH A PARTNER

❑ With a partner, discuss the predictions you made. Discuss what details in the story helped you make your predictions.
❑ Share your predictions with the class. Were your predictions similar to those made by others? Which events affected everyone's predictions? How did your predictions change as you read on?

Reading Skills and Test Practice

COMPARE AND CONTRAST IDEAS

Discuss with your partner how to answer the following questions that require you to compare and contrast ideas. Use the Think-Aloud Notes to write down your reasons for eliminating the incorrect answers.

_____1. The major difference between Monk at the beginning of the story and Monk at the end of the story is that at the end Monk is
a. friendlier.
b. an outsider.
c. no longer a threat.
d. a drop-out.

_____2. Melvin and Priscilla were called The Odd Couple because
a. Melvin was small and Priscilla was tall.
b. Melvin was rich and Priscilla was poor.
c. Melvin was sloppy and Priscilla was neat.
d. Melvin was smart and Priscilla was not smart.

How did using the reading strategy help you to answer the questions?

_____

_____

THINK-ALOUD NOTES

_____

_____

_____

_____

_____

_____

_____

_____

_____

_____

_____

_____

Investigate, Inquire, and Imagine

RECALL: GATHER FACTS
1a. What does Priscilla do at the end of the story?

→ INTERPRET: FIND MEANING
1b. What makes Priscilla different from the other kids in the story? Is it just her size, or is there something else?

ANALYZE: TAKE THINGS APART
2a. Make a list of the actions of Monk and his Kobras.

→ SYNTHESIZE: BRING THINGS TOGETHER
2b. Based on your listing, summarize the main characteristics of Monk and his Kobras. How would you describe them?

EVALUATE: MAKE JUDGMENTS
3a. Do you think the humor in the story is effective? Is the ending effective? Explain.

→ EXTEND: CONNECT IDEAS
3b. What do you think is the lesson of this story?

Literary Tools

CHARACTER. A **character** is a person or being who takes part in the action of a story. The main character is called the *protagonist*. A character who struggles against the main character is called an *antagonist*. Characters can also be classified as *major characters* or *minor characters*. Major characters play an important role in the literary work. Minor characters play less important roles. A *one-dimensional character, flat character,* or *caricature* is one who exhibits a single quality or character trait. A *three-dimensional, full,* or *rounded character* is one who seems to have all the complexities of an actual human being. Use the chart below to determine what type of character each person is. One example has been done for you.

Type of Character	Narrator	Monk Klutter	Priscilla Roseberry	Melvin Detweiler
protagonist antagonist neither	✔			
major character minor character	✔			
one-dimensional character three-dimensional character	✔			

Explain why each of the characters is a one-dimensional or three-dimensional character.

WordWorkshop

VOCABULARY CARDS. A good way to help yourself learn and remember new words is to create vocabulary cards. Create a separate note card or notebook page for each word. Write the word in the center. In the top left corner write the definition. In the top right corner, write a synonym. In the bottom left corner, write a sentence using the word. In the bottom right corner, draw a picture to help you remember the word. Create your own vocabulary cards for the Words for Everyday Use for this story.

Read-Write Connection

Do you think Monk really spends a week in the locker? Explain your answer.

_____

_____

_____

_____

_____

_____

Beyond the Reading

READ ABOUT PEER PRESSURE. One of the most important steps in growing up is learning to resist peer pressure, or the pressure to do what others your age expect or want you to do. Find a book in which a character faces peer pressure. Richard Peck's books all deal with this topic, as do many books by other young adult writers. Write a review of the book you have chosen. In your review, explain how the character does or does not resist peer pressure.

GO ONLINE. To find links and additional activities for this selection, visit the EMC Internet Resource Center at **emcp.com/languagearts** and click on Write-In Reader.

Reader's resource

Like many of Isaac Bashevis Singer's stories, **"Zlateh the Goat,"** is set in a nineteenth-century *shtetl*, or small Jewish village in Poland. The story takes place during Hanukkah, an eight-day Jewish festival celebrated in December. During Hanukkah, Jewish people remember the victory of the first Jews who fought to defend their religion against a Syrian king. As you read, look at the close relationship between Zlateh the goat and Aaron, a boy in the family who owns Zlateh.

Word watch

PREVIEW VOCABULARY

cleft
eddy

Reader's journal

Have you ever had a special relationship with an animal? What can you learn about yourself through a relationship with an animal?

_____

_____

_____

_____

"Zlateh the Goat"

by Isaac Bashevis Singer

Active READING STRATEGY

MAKE PREDICTIONS

Before Reading ▶ **START A PREDICTION CHART**

❑ With a partner, preview the entire selection, including activities before, during, and after the selection. Read the title and the Reader's Resource.

❑ What do you think the story will be about? Write this prediction in the Prediction Chart that follows. In the first column, write down when you made the prediction (before reading). In the second column, write your prediction. If you learn new information as you read that makes you change a previous prediction, write it in the third column.

Graphic Organizer: Prediction Chart

When I Made Prediction	Prediction	Adjustment/Assessment of Prediction

the Goat

Isaac Bashevis Singer

MAKE MORE PREDICTIONS

❑ With your partner, take turns reading the first three paragraphs of the story aloud. Discuss what could happen next, and write a prediction in your chart. Remember to record when you made the prediction (the line number) in the first column.

❑ Continue reading the story silently. Stop occasionally to make and adjust predictions. Add your predictions to your chart.

NOTE THE FACTS

Why does Reuven plan to sell Zlateh?

_____

_____

THINK AND REFLECT

"Aaron understood what taking the goat to Feyvel meant." What does it mean? How does Aaron feel about it? **(Infer)**

_____

_____

At Hanukkah time, the road from the village to the town is usually covered with snow, but this year the winter had been a mild one. Hanukkah had almost come, yet little snow had fallen. The sun shone most of the time. The peasants complained that because of the dry weather there would be a poor harvest of winter grain. New grass sprouted, and the peasants sent their cattle out to pasture.

For Reuven, the furrier,[1] it was a bad year, and after long hesitation he decided to sell Zlateh the goat. She was old
10 and gave little milk. Feyvel, the town butcher, had offered eight gulden[2] for her. Such a sum would buy Hanukkah candles, potatoes and oil for pancakes, gifts for the children, and other holiday necessaries for the house. Reuven told his oldest boy, Aaron, to take the goat to town.

Aaron understood what taking the goat to Feyvel meant, but he had to obey his father. Leah, his mother, wiped the tears from her eyes when she heard the news. Aaron's younger sisters, Anna and Miriam, cried loudly. Aaron put on his quilted jacket and a cap with earmuffs, bound a rope
20 around Zlateh's neck, and took along two slices of bread with cheese to eat on the road. Aaron was supposed to deliver the goat by evening, spend the night at the butcher's, and return the next day with the money.

While the family said goodbye to the goat, and Aaron placed the rope around her neck, Zlateh stood as patiently and good-naturedly as ever. She licked Reuven's hand. She shook her small white beard. Zlateh trusted human beings.

---

1. **furrier.** Dealer in furs
2. **gulden.** Unit of money

FIX-UP IDEA

Use Margin Questions
If you are having trouble making predictions or deciding when to make them, stop at each margin question or activity. After answering the question, make a prediction based on your answer.

NOTE THE FACTS

How does the weather change?

_____

_____

_____

THINK AND REFLECT

How would you feel if you were Aaron? What do you think you would do? **(Empathize)**

_____

_____

_____

She knew that they always fed her and never did her any harm.

30   When Aaron brought her out on the road to town, she seemed somewhat astonished. She'd never been led in that direction before. She looked back at him questioningly, as if to say, "Where are you taking me?" But after a while she seemed to come to the conclusion that a goat shouldn't ask questions. Still, the road was different. They passed new fields, pastures, and huts with thatched roofs. Here and there a dog barked and came running after them, but Aaron chased it away with his stick.

The sun was shining when Aaron left the village.
40   Suddenly the weather changed. A large black cloud with a bluish center appeared in the east and spread itself rapidly over the sky. A cold wind blew in with it. The crows flew low, croaking. At first it looked as if it would rain, but instead it began to hail as in summer. It was early in the day, but it became dark as dusk. After a while, the hail turned to snow.

In his twelve years, Aaron had seen all kinds of weather, but he had never experienced a snow like this one. It was so dense it shut out the light of the day. In a short time their
50   path was completely covered. The wind became as cold as ice. The road to town was narrow and winding. Aaron no longer knew where he was. He could not see through the snow. The cold soon penetrated his quilted jacket.

At first Zlateh didn't seem to mind the change in weather. She too was twelve years old and knew what winter meant. But when her legs sank deeper and deeper into the snow, she began to turn her head and look at Aaron in wonderment. Her mild eyes seemed to ask, "Why are we out in such a storm?" Aaron hoped that a peasant would
60   come along with his cart, but no one passed by.

The snow grew thicker, falling to the ground in large, whirling flakes. Beneath it Aaron's boots touched the softness of a plowed field. He realized that he was no longer on the road. He had gone astray. He could no longer figure out which was east or west, which way was the village, the town. The wind whistled, howled, whirled the snow about in <u>eddies</u>. It looked as if white imps[3] were playing tag on the fields. A white dust rose above the ground. Zlateh stopped. She could walk no longer. Stubbornly she anchored her <u>cleft</u> hooves in the earth and bleated[4] as if pleading to be taken home. Icicles hung from her white beard, and her horns were glazed with frost.

Aaron did not want to admit the danger, but he knew just the same that if they did not find shelter, they would freeze to death. This was no ordinary storm. It was a mighty blizzard. The snowfall had reached his knees. His hands were numb, and he could no longer feel his toes. He choked when he breathed. His nose felt like wood, and he rubbed it with snow. Zlateh's bleating began to sound like crying. Those humans in whom she had so much confidence had dragged her into a trap. Aaron began to pray to God for himself and for the innocent animal.

Suddenly he made out the shape of a hill. He wondered what it could be. Who had piled snow into such a huge heap? He moved toward it, dragging Zlateh after him. When he came near it, he realized that it was a large haystack which the snow had blanketed.

Aaron realized immediately that they were saved. With great effort he dug his way through the snow. He was a village boy and knew what to do. When he reached the hay, he hollowed out a nest for himself and the goat. No matter how cold it may be outside, in the hay it is always warm. And hay was food for Zlateh. The moment she smelled it, she became contented and began to eat. Outside the snow continued to fall. It quickly covered the passageway Aaron had dug. But a boy and an animal need to breathe, and there was hardly any air in their hideout. Aaron bored a kind of a window through the hay and snow and carefully kept the passage clear.

---

3. **imps.** Young demons
4. **bleated.** Made the cry of a goat or sheep

words for everyday use	**eddy** (ed′ ē) *n.*, whirlwind; whirlpool. *The rocks tumbled about in the swirling <u>eddy</u> of foaming water.* **cleft** (kleft′) *adj.*, split; divided. *Sheila used the crevice in the <u>cleft</u> rock as a handhold while climbing.*

Use **THE STRATEGY**

MAKE PREDICTIONS. Read lines 73–75. What do you think will happen to Aaron? Write a prediction in your chart.

NOTE THE FACTS

What saves Aaron and Zlateh? How does it save them?

_____

_____

_____

100   Zlateh, having eaten her fill, sat down on her hind legs and seemed to have regained her confidence in man. Aaron ate his two slices of bread and cheese, but after the difficult journey he was still hungry. He looked at Zlateh and noticed her udders were full. He lay down next to her, placing himself so that when he milked her, he could squirt the milk into his mouth. It was rich and sweet. Zlateh was not accustomed to being milked that way, but she did not resist. On the contrary, she seemed eager to reward Aaron for bringing her to a shelter whose very walls, floor, and

110   ceiling were made of food.

Through the window Aaron could catch a glimpse of the chaos outside. The wind carried before it whole drifts of snow. It was completely dark, and he did not know whether night had already come or whether it was the darkness of the storm. Thank God that in the hay it was not cold. The dried hay, grass, and field flowers exuded the warmth of the summer sun. Zlateh ate frequently; she nibbled from above, below, from the left and right. Her body gave forth an animal warmth, and Aaron cuddled up to her. He had always loved Zlateh, but

120   now she was like a sister. He was alone, cut off from his family, and wanted to talk. He began to talk to Zlateh.

"Zlateh, what do you think about what has happened to us?" he asked.

"Maaaa," Zlateh answered.

"If we hadn't found this stack of hay, we would both be frozen stiff by now," Aaron said.

"Maaaa," was the goat's reply.

"If the snow keeps falling like this, we may have to stay here for days," Aaron explained.

130   "Maaaa," Zlateh bleated.

"What does 'Maaaa' mean?" Aaron asked. "You'd better speak up clearly."

"Maaaa. Maaaa," Zlateh tried.

"Well, let it be 'Maaaa' then," Aaron said patiently. "You can't speak, but I know you understand. I need you and you need me. Isn't that right?"

"Maaaa."

Aaron became sleepy. He made a pillow out of some hay, leaned his head on it, and dozed off. Zlateh too fell asleep.

140　　When Aaron opened his eyes, he didn't know whether it
was morning or night. The snow had blocked up his
window. He tried to clear it, but when he had bored
through to the length of his arm, he still hadn't reached the
outside. Luckily he had his stick with him and was able to
break through to the open air. It was still dark outside. The
snow continued to fall and the wind wailed, first with one
voice and then with many. Sometimes it had the sound of
devilish laughter. Zlateh too awoke, and when Aaron
greeted her, she answered, "Maaaa." Yes, Zlateh's language

150　　consisted of only one word, but it meant many things. Now
she was saying, "We must accept all that God gives us—
heat, cold, hunger, satisfaction, light, and darkness."

　　Aaron had awakened hungry. He had eaten up his food,
but Zlateh had plenty of milk.

　　For three days Aaron and Zlateh stayed in the haystack.
Aaron had always loved Zlateh, but in these three days he
loved her more and more. She fed him with her milk and
helped him keep warm. She comforted him with her
patience. He told her many stories, and she always cocked

160　　her ears and listened. When he patted her, she licked his
hand and his face. Then she said, "Maaaa," and he knew it
meant, I love you too.

　　The snow fell for three days, though after the first day it
was not as thick, and the wind quieted down. Sometimes
Aaron felt that there could never have been a summer, that
the snow had always fallen, ever since he could remember.
He, Aaron, never had a father or mother or sisters. He was
a snow child, born of the snow, and so was Zlateh. It was so
quiet in the hay that his ears rang in the stillness. Aaron

170　　and Zlateh slept all night and a good part of the day. As for
Aaron's dreams, they were all about warm weather. He
dreamed of green fields, trees covered with blossoms, clear
brooks, and singing birds. By the third night the snow had
stopped, but Aaron did not dare to find his way home in
the darkness. The sky became clear, and the moon shone,
casting silvery nets on the snow. Aaron dug his way out and
looked at the world. It was all white, quiet, dreaming
dreams of heavenly splendor. The stars were large and
close. The moon swam in the sky as in a sea.

THINK AND REFLECT

List the things Aaron does
for Zlateh in the haystack.
List the things Zlateh does
for Aaron. **(Analyze)**

_____

_____

_____

Use THE STRATEGY

MAKE PREDICTIONS. Read lines
163–164. What do you think
will happen to Aaron and
Zlateh? Write a prediction in
your chart.

NOTE THE FACTS

What does it look like
outside?

_____

_____

THINK AND REFLECT

What do you think Zlateh is saying in response to Aaron's question? (Infer)

_____

_____

180   On the morning of the fourth day Aaron heard the ringing of sleigh bells. The haystack was not far from the road. The peasant who drove the sleigh pointed out the way to him—not to the town and Feyvel, the butcher, but home to the village. Aaron had decided in the haystack that he would never part with Zlateh.

Aaron's family and their neighbors had searched for the boy and the goat but had found no trace of them during the storm. They feared they were lost. Aaron's mother and sisters cried for him; his father remained silent and gloomy.
190 Suddenly one of the neighbors came running to their house with the news that Aaron and Zlateh were coming up the road.

There was great joy in the family. Aaron told them how he had found the stack of hay and how Zlateh had fed him with her milk. Aaron's sisters kissed and hugged Zlateh and gave her a special treat of chopped carrots and potato peels, which Zlateh gobbled up hungrily.

Nobody ever again thought of selling Zlateh, and now that the cold weather had finally set in, the villagers needed
200 the services of Reuven, the furrier, once more. When Hanukkah came, Aaron's mother was able to fry pancakes every evening, and Zlateh got her portion too. Even though Zlateh had her own pen, she often came to the kitchen, knocking on the door with her horns to indicate that she was ready to visit; and she was always admitted. In the evening Aaron, Miriam, and Anna played dreidel. Zlateh sat near the stove watching the children and the flickering of the Hanukkah candles.

Once in a while Aaron would ask her, "Zlateh, do you
210 remember the three days we spent together?"

And Zlateh would scratch her neck with a horn, shake her white bearded head, and come out with the single sound which expressed all her thoughts, and all her love. ■

Reflect ON YOUR READING

❑ Look over your Prediction Chart. Were your predictions correct? What helped you make your predictions?
❑ Talk about your predictions with another pair of students. Did they have similar predictions?

Reading Skills and Test Practice

FIND MAIN IDEAS

READ, THINK, AND EXPLAIN. What is the lesson of the story? Use details and information from the story to support your answer.

_____

_____

_____

_____

_____

_____

_____

_____

REFLECT ON YOUR RESPONSE. Compare your response to that of your partner and talk about how the information you wrote down while reading helped form your response.

_____

_____

_____

_____

THINK-ALOUD NOTES

_____

_____

_____

_____

_____

_____

_____

_____

_____

_____

_____

Investigate, Inquire, and Imagine

RECALL: GATHER FACTS
1a. How old is Zlateh? How long has she lived with Aaron and his family?

INTERPRET: FIND MEANING
1b. How does Zlateh feel about humans? How do Aaron and his family feel about Zlateh?

ANALYZE: TAKE THINGS APART
2a. In what ways does Zlateh assist Aaron during the time they spend in the haystack? In was ways does Zlateh help Aaron?

SYNTHESIZE: BRING THINGS TOGETHER
2b. Which of the two is most responsible for saving the other's life?

PERSPECTIVE: LOOK AT OTHER VIEWS
3a. Why does Aaron become so attached to the goat during the time they spend together in the haystack?

EMPATHY: SEE FROM INSIDE
3b. If you experienced a life-threatening situation like this one and lived through it with someone, how might you feel about that person or animal afterward?

Literary Tools

SENSORY DETAILS. **Sensory details** are words and phrases that describe how things look, sound, smell, taste, or feel. Fill in the chart below with sensory details from the story. Try to fill in at least one detail for each sense.

See			
Hear			
Smell			
Taste			
Feel			

WordWorkshop

Synonyms. Synonyms are words that have the same or nearly the same meaning. For example, a synonym of the word *eddy* is *whirlpool* and a synonym of the word *cleft* is *split*. Choose five words from "Zlateh the Goat" that you would like to know. Write each word and a synonym on the lines below. You can use a dictionary or thesaurus to find synonyms.

1. Word from Story _____

   Synonym _____

2. Word from Story _____

   Synonym _____

3. Word from Story _____

   Synonym _____

4. Word from Story _____

   Synonym _____

5. Word from Story _____

   Synonym _____

Read-Write Connection

Do you think Zlateh means different things when she says "Maaaa"? Why, or why not?

_____

_____

_____

Beyond the Reading

Debate Animals' Emotions. Form two groups. One group should argue the point that animals have emotions and communicate them to humans. The other group should argue that animals do not have emotions. Each group should research their position and work together to plan arguments for their side. They should also think about what arguments their opponents might make and prepare counterarguments to these. Then the whole class should debate the issue.

Go Online. To find links and additional activities for this selection, visit the EMC Internet Resource Center at **emcp.com/languagearts** and click on Write-In Reader.

Reader's resource

Ray Bradbury's science fiction stories, including "**All Summer in a Day**," use strange new worlds and circumstances to point out problems in our own world. In "All Summer in a Day," a group of children is about to experience a rare and exciting event that only one of them has experienced before. Notice how the children treat the one person who has more knowledge than they do of what is going to happen.

Word watch

PREVIEW VOCABULARY

apparatus	savor
bear	slacken
concussion	surge
immense	tumultuous
resilient	

Reader's journal

Imagine that you are describing the sun to someone who has never seen or felt it before. How would you describe the sun? To what would you compare it?

_____

_____

_____

_____

"All Summer in a Day"
by Ray Bradbury

Active READING STRATEGY

WRITE THINGS DOWN

Before Reading ➤ **PREVIEW THE SELECTION**

❑ In a small group, read the title and the Reader's Resource.
❑ Brainstorm ideas about what you think the story is going to be about. Jot down your ideas.
❑ Review the parts of a plot on page 38. As you read this story, you will keep track of important events and place them on the Plot Diagram below.

Graphic Organizer: Plot Diagram

```
                    _____
                    _____
                    _____
                      Climax
                       /\
                      /  \
_____   Rising Action   Falling Action   _____
_____    /                        \      _____
_____   /   _____          \     _____
 Exposition  /                            \    Dénouement
                 _____
   Inciting                        Resolution
   Incident      _____

     _____          _____

     _____          _____

     _____          _____
```

All Summer in a Day

Ray Bradbury

During Reading

WRITE THINGS DOWN

❏ As you read, underline or highlight key events in the story. You can also make other kinds of notes—write answers to the margin questions, highlight interesting lines, or note your reactions to certain parts.

❏ If you come to a part that you don't understand, put a question mark in the margin or write down a question you want answered. Then work with your group to figure out the difficult section.

❏ Look for the climax, or high point, of the story. Write it down on your plot diagram. Also look for and record the resolution of the conflict.

"Ready?"

"Ready."

"Now?"

"Soon."

"Do the scientists really know? Will it happen today, will it?"

"Look, look; see for yourself!"

The children pressed to each other like so many roses, so many weeds, intermixed, peering out for a look at the hidden sun.

It rained.

It had been raining for seven years; thousands upon thousands of days compounded and filled from one end to the other with rain, with the drum and gush of water, with the sweet crystal fall of showers and the <u>concussion</u> of storms so heavy they were tidal waves come over the islands. A thousand forests had been crushed under the rain and grown up a thousand times to be crushed again. And this was the way life was forever on the planet Venus, and this was the schoolroom of the children of the rocket men and women who had come to a raining world to set up civilization and live out their lives.

NOTE THE FACTS

Where does the story take place? What is unusual about the weather there?

_____

_____

words for everyday use	**con • cus • sion** (kən kush′ ən) *n.,* strong shaking; collision. *John's head hit the cement with such force that he suffered a <u>concussion</u>.*

THINK AND REFLECT

Underline or highlight
what, according to
Margot, the other
children remember in
their dreams. What
might they really be
remembering? (Infer)

_____

_____

Literary TOOLS

SIMILE AND METAPHOR. A
simile is a comparison
using *like* or *as*. A
metaphor is a figure of
speech in which one thing
is spoken or written about
as if it were another. Reread
lines 39–43. List one simile
and one metaphor from
this passage.

_____

_____

Reading STRATEGY
REVIEW

MAKE PREDICTIONS. Review
the Active Reading
Strategy for "Zlateh the
Goat" on page 72. Try
making predictions as you
read "All Summer in a
Day." Read lines 49–53.
Predict whether the
children will see the sun.

_____

_____

"It's stopping, it's stopping!"

"Yes, yes!"

Margot stood apart from them, from these children who could never remember a time when there wasn't rain and rain and rain. They were all nine years old, and if there had been a day, seven years ago, when the sun came out for an hour and showed its face to the stunned world, they could not recall. Sometimes, at night, she heard them stir, in remembrance, and she knew they were dreaming and remembering gold or a yellow crayon or a coin large enough to buy the world with. She knew that they thought they remembered a warmness, like a blushing in the face, in the body, in the arms and legs and trembling hands. But then they always awoke to the tatting drum, the endless shaking down of clear bead necklaces upon the roof, the walk, the gardens, the forest, and their dreams were gone.

All day yesterday they had read in class about the sun. About how like a lemon it was, and how hot. And they had written small stories or essays or poems about it:

I think the sun is a flower
That blooms for just one hour.

That was Margot's poem, read in a quiet voice in the still classroom while the rain was falling outside.

"Aw, you didn't write that!" protested one of the boys.

"I did," said Margot. "I *did*."

"William!" said the teacher.

But that was yesterday. Now, the rain was <u>slackening</u>, and the children were crushed to the great thick windows.

"Where's teacher?"

"She'll be back."

"She'd better hurry; we'll miss it!"

They turned on themselves, like a feverish wheel, all tumbling spokes.

words for everyday use

slack • en (slak' ən) v., lessen; let up. "*Slacken* that rope before it snaps!" cried Petunia.

Margot stood alone. She was a very frail girl who looked as if she had been lost in the rain for years and the rain had washed out the blue from her eyes and the red from her mouth and the yellow from her hair. She was an old photograph dusted from an album, whitened away, and if she spoke at all, her voice would be a ghost. Now she stood, separate, staring at the rain and the loud, wet world beyond the huge glass.

"What're *you* looking at?" said William.

Margot said nothing.

"Speak when you're spoken to." He gave her a shove. But she did not move; rather, she let herself be moved only by him and nothing else.

They edged away from her; they would not look at her. She felt them go away. And this was because she would play no games with them in the echoing tunnels of the underground city. If they tagged her and ran, she stood blinking after them and did not follow. When the class sang songs about happiness and life and games, her lips barely moved. Only when they sang about the sun and the summer did her lips move, as she watched the drenched windows.

And then, of course, the biggest crime of all was that she had come here only five years ago from Earth, and she remembered the sun and the way the sun was and the sky was when she was four, in Ohio. And they, they had been on Venus all their lives, and they had been only two years old when last the sun came out and had long since forgotten the color and heat of it and the way that it really was. But Margot remembered.

"It's like a penny," she said, once, eyes closed.

"No, it's not!" the children cried.

"It's like a fire," she said, "in the stove."

"You're lying; you don't remember!" cried the children.

But she remembered and stood quietly apart from all of them and watched the patterning windows. And once, a month ago, she had refused to shower in the school shower rooms, had clutched her hands to her ears and over her head, screaming that the water mustn't touch her head. So after that, dimly, dimly, she sensed it; she was different, and they knew her difference and kept away.

NOTE THE FACTS

What does Margot look like?

_____

_____

_____

NOTE THE FACTS

Why do the other children dislike Margot?

_____

_____

_____

THINK AND REFLECT

Why might the other children be so bothered by Margot? (Interpret)

_____

_____

MARK THE TEXT

Underline or highlight what Margot's parents are going to do for her.

There was talk that her father and mother were taking her back to Earth next year; it seemed vital to her that they do so, though it would mean the loss of thousands of dollars to her family. And so the children hated her for all these reasons, of big and little consequence. They hated her pale, snow face,
100   her waiting silence, her thinness, and her possible future.

"Get away!" The boy gave her another push. "What're you waiting for?"

Then, for the first time, she turned and looked at him. And what she was waiting for was in her eyes.

"Well, don't wait around here!" cried the boy, savagely. "You won't see nothing!"

Her lips moved.

"Nothing!" he cried. "It was all a joke, wasn't it?" He turned to the other children. "Nothing's happening today.
110   *Is* it?"

They all blinked at him and then, understanding, laughed and shook their heads. "Nothing, nothing!"

"Oh, but," Margot whispered, her eyes helpless. "But, this is the day, the scientists predict, they say, they *know*, the sun . . ."

"All a joke!" said the boy, and seized her roughly. "Hey, everyone, let's put her in a closet before teacher comes!"

"No," said Margot, falling back.

They <u>surged</u> about her, caught her up and <u>bore</u> her,
120   protesting and then pleading and then crying, back into a tunnel, a room, a closet, where they slammed and locked the door. They stood looking at the door and saw it tremble from her beating and throwing herself against it. They heard her muffled cries. Then, smiling, they turned and went out and back down the tunnel, just as the teacher arrived.

"Ready, children?" She glanced at her watch.

"Yes!" said everyone.

"Are we all here?"

"Yes!"
130   The rain slackened still more.

THINK AND REFLECT

How do the children feel right after doing this? How can you tell? **(Infer)**

_____

_____

words for everyday use	surge (sərj') *v.*, suddenly push forward in a violent way. *The waves <u>surged</u> forward into the weakened dock.* bear (bār') *v.*, carry; transport. *The crew will <u>bear</u> the cargo to the warehouse.* **bore**, *past tense*

They crowded to the huge door.

The rain stopped.

It was as if, in the midst of a film concerning an avalanche, a tornado, a hurricane, a volcanic eruption, something had, first, gone wrong with the sound <u>apparatus</u>, thus muffling and finally cutting off all noise, all of the blasts and repercussions and thunders, and then, secondly, ripped the film from the projector and inserted in its place a peaceful tropical slide which did not move or tremor. The world ground to a standstill. The silence was so <u>immense</u> and unbelievable that you felt that your ears had been stuffed or you had lost your hearing altogether. The children put their hands to their ears. They stood apart. The door slid back, and the smell of the silent, waiting world came in to them.

The sun came out.

It was the color of flaming bronze, and it was very large. And the sky around it was a blazing blue tile color. And the jungle burned with sunlight as the children, released from their spell, rushed out, yelling, into the summertime.

"Now, don't go too far," called the teacher after them. "You've got only one hour, you know. You wouldn't want to get caught out!"

But they were running and turning their faces up to the sky and feeling the sun on their cheeks like a warm iron; they were taking off their jackets and letting the sun burn their arms.

"Oh, it's better than the sunlamps, isn't it?"

"Much, much better!"

They stopped running and stood in the great jungle that covered Venus, that grew and never stopped growing <u>tumultuously</u>, even as you watched it. It was a nest of octopuses, clustering up great arms of flesh-like weed, wavering, flowering in this brief spring. It was the color of rubber and ash, this jungle, from the many years without sun. It was the color of stones and white cheeses and ink.

140

150

160

Reading STRATEGY REVIEW

VISUALIZE. Create a picture in your head of what Venus looks like on an ordinary day, according to this story. Then notice how it is described as the sun comes out. Picture the changes and the students' reactions to them.

Use THE STRATEGY

WRITE THINGS DOWN. Remember to underline key events. What is the high point of this story? Write this event down above the word "Climax" on your Plot Diagram. After reading, you will fill in events that lead up to this high point and those that come after it.

MARK THE TEXT

Highlight or underline how long the sun will last.

words for everyday use	**ap • pa • ra • tus** (ap ə rat′ əs) *n.*, machine; instrument. *Gina knows how to fix the ship's <u>apparatus</u>.* **im • mense** (im mens′) *adj.*, very large; enormous. *The <u>immense</u> tower loomed over the island.* **tu • mul • tu • ous** (too mul′ choo əs) *adj.*, wild and disorderly. *The <u>tumultuous</u> crowd stormed the exits of the hall.* **tumultuously,** *adv.*

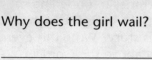
FIX-UP IDEA

Refocus
If you are having trouble identifying key events or picking out the climax, refocus your reading. Pay attention to your feelings about what is happening. Then identify the events that create those feelings. The event that creates the most intense feeling is probably the climax.

The children lay out, laughing, on the jungle mattress and heard it sigh and squeak under them, <u>resilient</u> and alive. They ran among the trees, they slipped and fell, they pushed each other, they played hide-and-seek and tag; but most of all they

170 squinted at the sun until tears ran down their faces, they put their hands up at that yellowness and that amazing blueness, and they breathed of the fresh air and listened and listened to the silence which suspended them in a blessed sea of no sound and no motion. They looked at everything and <u>savored</u> everything. Then, wildly, like animals escaped from their caves, they ran and ran in shouting circles. They ran for an hour and did not stop running.

And then—

In the midst of their running, one of the girls wailed.

180 Everyone stopped.

The girl, standing in the open, held out her hand.

"Oh, look, look," she said, trembling.

They came slowly to look at her opened palm.

In the center of it, cupped and huge, was a single raindrop. She began to cry, looking at it.

They glanced quickly at the sky.

"Oh. Oh."

A few cold drops fell on their noses and their cheeks and their mouths. The sun faded behind a stir of mist. A wind

190 blew cool around them. They turned and started to walk back toward the underground house, their hands at their sides, their smiles vanishing away.

A boom of thunder startled them, and like leaves before a new hurricane, they tumbled upon each other and ran. Lightning struck ten miles away, five miles away, a mile, a half mile. The sky darkened into midnight in a flash.

They stood in the doorway of the underground for a moment until it was raining hard. Then they closed the door and heard the gigantic sound of the rain falling in tons and

200 avalanches everywhere and forever.

"Will it be seven more years?"

---

words for everyday use

re • si • lient (ri zil′ yənt) *adj.,* flexible and springy. *The <u>resilient</u> mesh showed no sign of damage from the goat's rampage.*
sa • vor (sā′ vər) *v.,* take great pleasure in. *I <u>savored</u> every bite of the delicious meal.*

"Yes. Seven."

Then one of them gave a little cry.

"Margot!"

"What?"

"She's still in the closet where we locked her."

"Margot."

They stood as if someone had driven them, like so many stakes, into the floor.

210 They looked at each other and then looked away. They glanced out at the world that was raining now and raining and raining steadily. They could not meet each other's glances. Their faces were solemn and pale.

They looked at their hands and feet, their faces down.

"Margot."

One of the girls said, "Well . . . ?"

No one moved.

"Go on," whispered the girl.

They walked slowly down the hall in the sound of cold rain. They turned through the doorway to the room, in the sound of the storm and thunder, lightning on their faces, blue and terrible. They walked over to the closet door slowly and stood by it.

Behind the closet door was only silence.

They unlocked the door, even more slowly, and let Margot out. ■

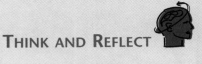

THINK AND REFLECT

What do the children realize they have done? How do they feel about their actions? **(Infer)**

_____

_____

_____

Use __THE STRATEGY__

WRITE THINGS DOWN. How is the conflict between Margot and the other children resolved? Write your answer next to "Resolution" on your Plot Diagram.

Reflect ON YOUR READING

After Reading ➤ COMPLETE A PLOT DIAGRAM

- ❏ Go back to your Before Reading group. Compare the events you listed as climax and resolution with those events listed by your group members.
- ❏ With your group, make a list of story events from those that you underlined. Talk about which part of the story these events represent and complete the Plot Diagram. Come up with one Plot Diagram for your group.
- ❏ Share your group's Plot Diagram with the class, and explain how you decided to place story events in your chart.

Reading Skills and Test Practice

EVALUATE CAUSE AND EFFECT

READ, THINK, AND EXPLAIN. Why is Margot locked in the closet? Use details and information from the story to support your answer.

_____

_____

_____

_____

_____

_____

_____

_____

REFLECT ON YOUR RESPONSE. Compare your response to that of your partner and talk about how the information you wrote down while reading helped form your response.

_____

_____

_____

_____

_____

_____

_____

_____

_____

_____

_____

_____

_____

_____

_____

Investigate, Inquire, and Imagine

RECALL: GATHER FACTS → INTERPRET: FIND MEANING
1a. What is so exciting about the day on which this story takes place? What makes Margot different from the other children?

1b. Why do the children lock Margot in the closet?

ANALYZE: TAKE THINGS APART → SYNTHESIZE: BRING THINGS TOGETHER
2a. List the reasons the children hate Margot.

2b. Before the children see the sun, they hate Margot, "for . . . reasons, of big and little consequence." After the children see the sun, they "could not meet each other's glances." How has seeing the sun changed the children?

EVALUATE: MAKE JUDGMENTS → EXTEND: CONNECT IDEAS
3a. What point do you think Ray Bradbury is trying to make in this story?

3b. How does this point apply to life on Earth? Can you think of examples of times when children you know have behaved like those in the story?

Literary Tools

SIMILE AND METAPHOR. A **simile** is a comparison using *like* or *as*. A **metaphor** is a figure of speech in which one thing is spoken or written about as if it were another. The two things compared in a simile or metaphor are called the *tenor* (the thing itself) and the *vehicle* (the thing to which it is compared). In the chart below, list the tenor and vehicle for at least five similes or metaphors from the story. Then identify what the tenor and vehicle have in common.

Tenor	Vehicle	What They Have in Common

WordWorkshop

CONTEXT CLUES. Sometimes the meaning of an unfamiliar word can be learned by studying the **context**, or the words, sentences, and paragraphs surrounding the word.

Choose three words that you don't know from "All Summer in a Day." Begin with one of the words you've selected to study. Read the sentence in which the first word is found. Guess the meaning of the word. If you still can't figure out the meaning of the word, read the sentences before and after the sentence that contains the unknown word. Once you have guessed a meaning, reread the sentence, replacing the unfamiliar word with the meaning you guessed. Does the original sentence make sense? If so, you may have solved the word puzzle. Use a dictionary to check your work.

Keep track of your word detective work below.

1. Word: _____

   Best Guess:_____

   Actual Definition: _____

2. Word: _____

   Best Guess:_____

   Actual Definition: _____

3. Word: _____

   Best Guess:_____

   Actual Definition: _____

Read-Write Connection

Imagine that you are Margot and that you have missed the one hour of sunlight that comes only once every seven years. What will you say to your parents when you get home? Why?

Beyond the Reading

RESEARCH PLANETS. In recent years, scientists have discovered information about the various planets. Select one of the planets to research. How far away is this planet from Earth? from the sun? Is it hot or cold on this planet? What have scientists discovered about its atmosphere and surface? What myths are associated with the planet you chose? Report your findings to the class.

GO ONLINE. To find links and additional activities for this selection, visit the EMC Internet Resource Center at **emcp.com/languagearts** and click on Write-In Reader.

Unit 3 READING Review

Choose and Use Reading Strategies

Before reading the selection below, review with a partner how to use each of these reading strategies.

1. Read with a Purpose
2. Connect to Prior Knowledge
3. Write Things Down
4. Make Predictions
5. Visualize
6. Use Text Organization
7. Tackle Difficult Vocabulary
8. Monitor Your Reading Progress

Now apply at least two of these reading strategies as you read the excerpt from "My Friend Flicka" by Mary O'Hara. Use the margins and mark up the text to show how you are using the reading strategies to read actively. You may find it helpful to choose a graphic organizer from Appendix B to gather information as you read the excerpt, or use the Summary Chart on page B-13 to create a graphic organizer that summarizes the excerpt.

Report cards for the second semester were sent out soon after school closed in mid-June.

Kennie's was a shock to the whole family.

"If I could have a colt all for my own," said Kennie, "I might do better."

Rob McLaughlin glared at his son. "Just as a matter of curiosity," he said, "how do you go about it to get a zero in an examination? Forty in arithmetic; seventeen in history! But a zero? Just as one man to another, what goes on in your head?"

"Yes, tell us how you do it, Ken," chirped Howard.

"Eat your breakfast, Howard," snapped his mother.

Kennie's blond head bent over his plate until his face was almost hidden. His cheeks burned.

McLaughlin finished his coffee and pushed his chair back. "You'll do an hour a day on your lessons all through the summer."

Nell McLaughlin saw Kennie wince as if something had actually hurt him.

Lessons and study in the summertime, when the long winter was just over and there weren't enough hours in the day for all the things he wanted to do!

Kennie took things hard. His eyes turned to the wide-open window with a look almost of despair.

The hill opposite the house, covered with arrow-straight jack pines, was sharply etched in the thin air of the eight-thousand-foot altitude. Where it fell away, vivid green grass ran up to meet it; and over range and upland poured the strong Wyoming sunlight that stung everything into burning color. A big jack rabbit sat under one of the pines, waving his long ears back and forth.

Ken had to look at his plate and blink back tears before he could turn to his father and say carelessly, "Can I help you in the corral with the horses this morning, Dad?"

Literary Tools

Select the best literary element on the right to complete each sentence on the left. Write the correct letter in the blank.

_____1.	The ___ of "Eleven" focuses on the narrator's conflict about feeling her age.	a. character, 66, 70
_____2.	In "Zlateh the Goat," Aaron is a(n) ____ because he is important to the action of the story.	b. major character, 66, 70 c. metaphor, 84, 91 d. minor character, 66, 70
_____3.	"The sun is like a lemon in the sky" is an example of a(n) _____.	e. plot, 53, 62 f. sensory details, 76, 80
_____4.	The sweet goat milk and the prickly hay are examples of _____.	g. simile, 43, 48, 84, 91
_____5.	Sylvia Saldivar is a(n) _____ character in "Eleven."	

WordWorkshop

UNIT 3 WORDS FOR EVERYDAY USE

anticipate, 56
apparatus, 87
audacity, 59
bar, 66
bear, 86
cleft, 75
concussion, 83
dejected, 56
eddy, 75
equate, 52
fate, 68

fend, 54
heritage, 52
hospitality, 58
hostility, 59
immense, 87
laceration, 66
ordeal, 55
pun, 66
resilient, 88
sacred, 53
savor, 88

shrewd, 53
skirmish, 51
slacken, 84
slither, 66
subtle, 65
surge, 86
tumultuous, 87
unsightly, 58
virtue, 53

WORD SORT. Choose some of the Words for Everyday Use from Unit 3. Write one word in each of the boxes below. Then write its definition and part of speech. You may refer to the page number listed to review the word. Then sort the words using one of the following methods:

- Same parts of speech
- Words with similar or opposite meanings
- Words with prefixes and suffixes
- Words that relate to each other or that can be used together
- Other sorting method: _____

Word: Definition: Part of Speech:	Word: Definition: Part of Speech:	Word: Definition: Part of Speech:
Word: Definition: Part of Speech:	Word: Definition: Part of Speech:	Word: Definition: Part of Speech:
Word: Definition: Part of Speech:	Word: Definition: Part of Speech:	Word: Definition: Part of Speech:

On Your Own

Find another short story from a collection in the library or in your classroom. Then choose one of the following projects.

FLUENTLY SPEAKING. Prepare a dramatic reading of the story. Take time to practice reading the story aloud. Use facial expressions, gestures, and shifts in tone, pitch, and volume to make your reading more interesting.

PICTURE THIS. Work with a group to illustrate the story. In your artwork, show the main events, people, objects, and themes of the story.

PUT IT IN WRITING. Write an essay comparing this story to another story you have read or one you have seen in a movie or on TV.

Unit FOUR

READING Poetry

POETRY

Defining the word *poetry* is difficult because poems take so many different forms. Poems do not have to be written down; some are chanted or sung. Some poems rhyme and have a consistent rhythm, but others do not.

Poetry differs from prose in that it packs more meaning into fewer words and often uses meter, rhyme, and rhythm more obviously. One thing that all poems have in common is that they use imaginative language carefully chosen and arranged to communicate experiences, thoughts, or emotions.

There are many different kinds of poetry. Some common kinds are listed below. The most common techniques of poetry involve imagery, shape, rhythm, and sound. Each of these techniques is also discussed below.

Forms of Poetry

NARRATIVE POETRY. A **narrative poem** is a poem that tells a story. William Stafford's "One Time" in this unit is an example of a narrative poem.

DRAMATIC POETRY. A **dramatic poem** is a poem that relies heavily on dramatic elements such as monologue (speech by a single character) or dialogue (conversation involving two or more characters). Often dramatic poems tell stories like narrative poems. "You Are Old, Father William" is a dramatic poem in this unit.

LYRIC POETRY. A **lyric poem** is a highly musical verse that expresses the emotions of a speaker. Many of the poems in this unit are lyric poems, including "Life Doesn't Frighten Me" by Maya Angelou. **Sonnets, odes, free verse, elegies, haiku**, and **imagist poems** are all forms of lyric poetry.

NOTE THE FACTS

Why is defining poetry difficult?

_____

_____

_____

MARK THE TEXT

Highlight or underline a possible similarity between narrative and dramatic poems.

Techniques of Poetry: Imagery

An **image** is language that creates a concrete representation of an object or experience. An image is also the vivid mental picture created in the reader's mind by that language. For example, in "One Time" William Stafford writes, "We were deep in the well of shadow by then." The picture created in your mind of dark shadows overtaking the people, hiding them in the dimness, is an image. When considered in a group, images are called **imagery**. Poets use colorful, vivid language and figures of speech to create imagery. A **figure of speech** is language meant to be understood imaginatively instead of literally. The following are common figures of speech:

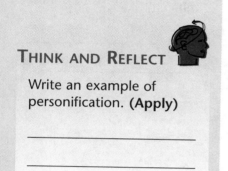

THINK AND REFLECT

Write an example of personification. **(Apply)**

_____

_____

_____

Figure of Speech	Definition	Example
metaphor	figure of speech in which one thing is written about as if it were another	"I'm the sailor and the sail"
simile	comparison using *like* or *as*	"like a thunderbolt he falls"
personification	figure of speech in which an idea, animal, or thing is described as if it were a person	"earth that is restless"

Techniques of Poetry: Shape

The shape of a poem is how it looks on the page. Poems are often divided into stanzas, or groups of lines. The following are some common types of stanzas:

Stanza Name	Number of Lines
couplet	two
triplet or tercet	three
quatrain	four
quintain	five
sestet	six
heptastich	seven
octave	eight

A **concrete poem**, or **shape poem**, is one with a shape that suggests its subject. A poem about a cloud, for example, might be written in the shape of a cloud.

Techniques of Poetry: Rhythm

The **rhythm** is the pattern of beats or stresses in a line. A regular rhythmic pattern is called a **meter**. Units of rhythm are called **feet**. A **foot** consists of some combination of weakly stressed (˘) and strongly stressed (/) syllables, as follows:

Type of Foot	Pattern	Example
iamb, or iambic foot	˘ /	˘ / afraid
trochee, or trochaic foot	/ ˘	/ ˘ freedom
anapest, or anapestic foot	˘ ˘ /	˘ ˘ / in a flash
dactyl, or dactylic foot	/ ˘ ˘	/ ˘ ˘ feverish
spondee, or spondaic foot	/ /	/ / baseball

The following terms are used to describe the number of feet in a line of poetry:

Term	# of Feet	Example
monometer	one foot	˘ / Today ˘ / We play
dimeter	two feet	/ ˘ / ˘ Following | closely
trimeter	three feet	˘ / ˘ / ˘ / God shed | His light | on thee
tetrameter	four feet	/ ˘ / ˘ / ˘ / ˘ In the | greenest | of our | valleys
pentameter	five feet	˘ / ˘ / ˘ / A vast | re pub | lic famed| ˘ / ˘ / through ev | ry clime
hexameter or Alexandrine	six feet	˘ / ˘ / ˘ / In o | ther's eyes | we see | ˘ ˘ / ˘ / ˘ / ourselves | the truth | to tell

Reading STRATEGY REVIEW

MAKE PREDICTIONS. Predict what shape the poem "The Sidewalk Racer, or On the Skateboard" will be.

_____

_____

_____

MARK THE TEXT

Underline or highlight the rhyming words in the following lines:
"You are old, Father William," the young man said,
"And your hair has become very white;
And yet you incessantly stand on your head—
Do you think, at your age, it is right?"

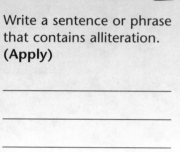

THINK AND REFLECT

Write a sentence or phrase that contains alliteration. **(Apply)**

_____

_____

_____

THINK AND REFLECT

How can you remember the difference between assonance and consonance? **(Extend)**

_____

_____

_____

Techniques of Poetry: Sound

RHYME. Rhyme is the repetition of sounds at the ends of words. _End rhyme_ is rhyme that occurs at the ends of lines. _Internal rhyme_ occurs within lines. _Sight rhyme_ occurs when two words are spelled similarly but pronounced differently. **Rhyme scheme** is a pattern of end rhymes.

ALLITERATION. Alliteration is the repetition of initial consonant sounds. The following lines from Maya Angelou's "Life Doesn't Frighten Me Now" contain two examples of alliteration: "_M_ean old _M_other Goose / _L_ions on the _l_oose."

ASSONANCE. Assonance is the repetition of vowel sounds in stressed syllables that end with different consonant sounds as in these lines from "The Springhill Disaster" by Peggy Seeger: "There's blood on the _coal_ and the miners lie / In the _roads_ that never saw sun nor sky."

CONSONANCE. In **consonance,** the ending consonant sounds match, but the preceding vowel sound does not, as in _find_ and _bound_.

ONOMATOPOEIA. Onomatopoeia is the use of words or phrases that sound like the things to which they refer, like _meow_, _buzz_, and _murmur_.

USING READING STRATEGIES WITH POETRY

Active Reading Strategy Checklists

The following checklists offer strategies for reading poetry.

❶ READ WITH A PURPOSE. Before reading a poem, give yourself a purpose, or something to look for, as you read. Sometimes a purpose will be a directive from a teacher: "Pay attention to repeated words and phrases." Other times you can set your own purpose by previewing the title, the opening lines, and other information presented with the poem. Say to yourself

- ❑ I want to look for . . .
- ❑ I want to experience . . .
- ❑ I want to enjoy . . .
- ❑ I wonder . . .
- ❑ I want to see if . . .

2 CONNECT TO PRIOR KNOWLEDGE. Being aware of what you already know and thinking about it as you read can help you keep track of what's happening and will increase your knowledge. As you read, say to yourself

- ❏ I already know this about the poem's subject matter . . .
- ❏ This part of the poem reminds me of . . .
- ❏ I think this part of the poem is like . . .
- ❏ My experience tells me that . . .
- ❏ If I were the speaker, I would feel . . .
- ❏ I associate this image with . . .

3 WRITE THINGS DOWN. As you read poetry, write down how the poem helps you "see" what is described. Possible ways to write things down include:

- ❏ Underline words and phrases that appeal to your five senses.
- ❏ Write down your questions and comments.
- ❏ Highlight figures of speech and phrases you enjoy.
- ❏ Create a graphic organizer to keep track of your responses.

4 MAKE PREDICTIONS. Before you read a poem, use information about the author, the subject matter, and the title to make a guess about what the poem may describe. As you read, confirm or deny your predictions, and make new ones based on how the poem develops. Make predictions like the following:

- ❏ The title tells me that . . .
- ❏ I predict that this poem will be about . . .
- ❏ This poet usually writes about . . .
- ❏ I think the poet will repeat . . .
- ❏ These lines in the poem make me guess that . . .

5 VISUALIZE. Visualizing, or allowing the words on the page to create images in your mind, is extremely important while reading poetry. In order to visualize the words, change your reading pace and savor the words. Allow the words to affect all of your senses. Make statements such as

- ❏ The words help me see . . .
- ❏ The words help me hear . . .
- ❏ The words help me feel . . .
- ❏ The words help me taste . . .
- ❏ The words help me smell . . .

Reading **TIP**

Remember, narrative poems tell a story. You can make a plot chart as you would for a story.

Reading **TIP**

A simple code can help you remember your reactions to a poem. You can use
!   for "This is like something I have experienced"
?   for "I don't understand this"
✓   for "This seems important"

Reading **TIP**

Try visualizing as a partner reads the poem aloud.

Reading__TIP

Sometimes the title or the shape of the poem can help you find meaning.

6 **USE TEXT ORGANIZATION.** When you read a poem, pay attention to punctuation and line breaks. Learn to chunk the lines in a poem so they make sense. Try reading all the way to the end of the sentence rather than stopping at each line break. Punctuation, rhythm, repetition, and line length offer clues that help you vary your reading rate and word emphasis. Say to yourself

- ❑ The punctuation in these lines helps me . . .
- ❑ The writer started a new stanza here because . . .
- ❑ The writer repeats this line because . . .
- ❑ The rhythm of this poem makes me think of . . .
- ❑ These short lines affect my reading speed by . . .

7 **TACKLE DIFFICULT VOCABULARY.** Difficult words in a poem can get in the way of your ability to respond to the poet's words and ideas. Use context clues that the lines provide, consult a dictionary, or ask someone about words you do not understand. When you come across a difficult word in a poem, say to yourself

Reading__TIP

If a poem has difficult vocabulary, read the poem, tackle the vocabulary you don't understand, and reread the poem.

- ❑ The lines near this word tell me that this word means . . .
- ❑ A definition provided with the poem shows that the word means . . .
- ❑ My work with the word before reading helps me know that the word means . . .
- ❑ A classmate said that the word means . . .

8 **MONITOR YOUR READING PROGRESS.** All readers encounter difficulty when they read, especially if the reading material is not self-selected. When you have to read something, take note of problems you are having and fix them. The key to reading success is knowing when you are having difficulty. To fix problems, say to yourself

Fix-Up Ideas

- ■ Reread
- ■ Read in shorter chunks
- ■ Read aloud
- ■ Ask questions
- ■ Change your reading rate
- ■ Try a different reading strategy

- ❑ Because I don't understand this part, I will . . .
- ❑ Because I'm having trouble staying connected to the ideas in the poem, I will . . .
- ❑ Because the words in the poem are too hard, I will . . .
- ❑ Because the poem is long, I will . . .
- ❑ Because I can't retell what the poem is about, I will . . .

Become an Active Reader

The instruction with the poems in this unit gives you an in-depth look at how to use one strategy for each poem. When you have difficulty, use fix-up ideas to fix a problem. For further information about the active reading strategies, see Unit 1 in this resource, pages 4–15.

How to Use Reading Strategies with Poetry

To see how readers use active reading strategies, look over the responses one reader has while reading "The Wreck of the Hesperus" by Henry Wadsworth Longfellow. As you look over the reader's responses, underline or highlight responses that demonstrate that the reader is reading actively.

READ WITH A PURPOSE

I want to find out what happens to the captain and his daughter.

MAKE PREDICTIONS

Since the poem is called "The Wreck of the Hesperus," I predict that the storm will destroy the ship.

WRITE THINGS DOWN

I'll underline details that suggest the problems to come.

It was the schooner Hesperus,
    That sailed the wintry sea;
And the skipper had taken his little daughter,
    To bear him company.

Blue were her eyes as the fairy-flax,
    Her cheeks like the dawn of day,
And her bosom white as the hawthorn buds
    That ope in the month of May.

The skipper he stood beside the helm,
    His pipe was in his mouth,
And he watched how the veering flaw did blow
    The smoke now West, now South.

Then up and spake an old Sailor,
    Had sailed the Spanish Main,
"I pray thee, put into yonder port,
    For I fear a hurricane."

VISUALIZE

I can see the daughter with her blond hair, blue eyes, and rosy cheeks.

TACKLE DIFFICULT VOCABULARY

A *flaw* is usually a defect, but that doesn't make sense here. I think from context that *flaw* means "wind."

CONNECT TO PRIOR KNOWLEDGE

A hurricane is pretty serious. I've seen some of the destruction from them.

MONITOR YOUR READING PROGRESS

I'll reread any stanzas I don't understand. I'll try reading aloud to hear the rhythm and rhyme.

USE TEXT ORGANIZATION

I'll read each stanza and paraphrase it.

"The Springhill Disaster"

by Peggy Seeger

Reader's resource

Peggy Seeger is a singer and songwriter, who comes from a family of musicians. In **"The Springhill Disaster"** she tells of a real-life mine disaster. Springhill is a town in northern Nova Scotia, Canada, with many coal mines. Like many deep mines, those of Springhill have been plagued by disaster. In 1891, 125 people died in a mining accident. In another accident in 1956, 39 people died. In 1958, part of the mine collapsed and buried miners alive; 76 people died, but some were rescued. The song you are about to read was written about the accident of 1958.

Reader's journal

In what situation would you be most frightened: atop a very tall building, in a small tight space, or lost in the pitch-black dark? Why?

_____

_____

_____

Active READING STRATEGY

MAKE PREDICTIONS

Before Reading ➤ **PREVIEW AND PREDICT**

❑ Read the Reader's Resource and think about the title.
❑ Make a prediction about what will happen in the song. Why is the song called "The Springhill Disaster"? What might the disaster be?
❑ Write your prediction in the Prediction Chart that follows.

Graphic Organizer: Prediction Chart

Stanza	Quote from Text	Prediction
Before Reading		
1		
2		
3		
4		
5		
6		
7		
8		

THE SPRINGHILL DISASTER

Peggy Seeger

During Reading

CONTINUE MAKING PREDICTIONS

❑ With a partner, take turns reading the first two stanzas aloud and make a prediction about what will happen.

❑ Then read stanzas 4, 5, and 6. What will happen to the men in the mine? Will any of them survive?

❑ Finally, read the last two stanzas, and discuss what happened to the men.

Literary TOOLS

MOOD. Mood is the feeling or emotion the writer creates in a literary work. By working carefully with descriptive language, a writer can evoke in the reader an emotional response such as fear, discomfort, longing, or anticipation. As you read, try to determine the mood of the song.

MARK THE TEXT

Underline or highlight what the earth often does in Springhill.

1

In the town of Springhill, Nova Scotia,
Down in the dark of the Cumberland Mine
There's blood on the coal and the miners lie
In the roads that never saw sun nor sky.
The roads that never saw sun nor sky.

2

In the town of Springhill, you don't sleep easy
Often the earth will tremble and roll.
When the earth is restless, miners die,
Bone and blood is the price of coal.
10   Bone and blood is the price of coal.

3

In the town of Springhill, Nova Scotia,
Late in the year of fifty-eight
Day still comes and the sun still shines
But it's dark as the grave in the Cumberland Mine.
But it's dark as the grave in the Cumberland Mine.

4

Down at the coal face, miners working
Rattle of the belt and the cutter's blade.
Rumble of rock and the walls close round
The living and the dead men two miles down.
20   The living and the dead men two miles down.

5

Twelve men lay two miles from the pitshaft
Twelve men lay in the dark and sang.
Long hot days in a miners' tomb,
It was three feet high and a hundred long.
It was three feet high and a hundred long.

THINK AND REFLECT

How might songs help the trapped miners? **(Infer)**

_____

_____

6

Three days passed and the lamps gave out
And Caleb Rushton he up and says,
"There's no more water or light or bread
So we'll live on songs and hope instead.
30   So we'll live on songs and hope instead."

7

Listen for the shouts of the bareface miners
Listen through the rubble for a rescue team,
Six hundred feet of coal and slag
Hope imprisoned in a three-foot seam.
Hope imprisoned in a three-foot seam.

READ ALOUD

Rhyme is the repetition of sounds at the ends of words. **Repetition** is more than one use of a sound, word, or group of words. Read stanza 7 aloud. Then underline the rhyming words in stanza 7 and circle examples of repetition.

8

Eight long days and some were rescued,
Leaving the dead to lie alone,
Through all their lives they dug their grave
Two miles of earth for a marking stone.
40   Two miles of earth for a marking stone. ∎

The Springhill Disaster

by Peggy Seeger

In the town of Spring- hill, Nov- a Sco- tia,
In the town of Spring- hill you don't sleep eas- y,

Down in the dark of the Cum - ber - land Mine There's
Of- ten the earth will trem-ble and roll when the

blood on the coal and the min- ers lie in the
earth is rest - less min- ers die

roads that ne-ver saw sun nor sky The
Bone and blood are the price of coal-

roads that nev- er saw sun nor sky.
Bone and blood are the price of coal.

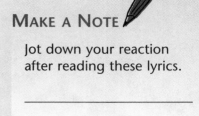

MAKE A NOTE

Jot down your reaction after reading these lyrics.

_____

_____

_____

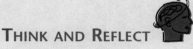

THINK AND REFLECT

If you know how to read music, look at the music on this page. Do you think the tone is appropriate for the words? (Evaluate)

_____

_____

_____

Reflect ON YOUR READING

After Reading ➤ ANALYZE YOUR PREDICTIONS

❏ Summarize the predictions in your Prediction Chart. Which of your predictions were accurate, and which ones did you have to change as you read?

❏ Discuss things that helped you make and change your predictions— prereading information, lines from the song, or what you already knew.

❏ How does making predictions affect your reading experience?

_____

_____

_____

THINK-ALOUD NOTES

_____

_____

_____

_____

_____

_____

_____

_____

_____

_____

_____

Reading Skills and Test Practice

RECOGNIZE MOOD AND TONE

Discuss with your partner how best to answer these questions about mood and tone in the song. Use the Think-Aloud Notes to write down your reasons for eliminating the incorrect answers.

_____1. The songwriter increases a feeling of sadness by
    a. repeating horrible details.
    b. discussing the miners' mangled bodies.
    c. talking about the miners' wives.
    d. not using any rhyme.

_____2. Which word best describes the mood and tone of this selection?
    a. repetitious
    b. gloomy
    c. angry
    d. upbeat

How did using the reading strategy help you to answer the questions?

_____

_____

Investigate, Inquire, and Imagine

RECALL: GATHER FACTS
1a. What does Caleb Rushton suggest that the miners do?

→ INTERPRET: FIND MEANING
1b. Why might he have made this suggestion?

ANALYZE: TAKE THINGS APART
2a. What is the fifth line of each stanza or section?

→ SYNTHESIZE: BRING THINGS TOGETHER
2b. What is similar about all eight lines? What effect does this repetition have on the mood?

EVALUATE: MAKE JUDGMENTS
3a. Do you think the title is appropriate for this selection? Why, or why not?

→ EXTEND: CONNECT IDEAS
3b. If the title of this selection were "The Springhill Rescue," how would the language in this poem be different? What do you think the mood would be like?

Literary Tools

MOOD. **Mood** is the feeling or emotion the writer creates in a literary work. Descriptive language helps create a gloomy, foreboding, frightening mood in this song. What other literary elements contribute to the mood of this song?

_____

_____

To think more about how description and mood work together, fill in the sensory detail chart that follows with details from something you recently experienced. What mood did the experience create in you?

Event:	Mood:
See	
Hear	
Smell	
Taste	
Feel	

WordWorkshop

RHYME TIME. Draw lines to connect the rhyming words below.

roll   stone

bread   sky

team   coal

alone   instead

lie   seam

Now it's your turn to create rhymes. Write a word that rhymes with each of the pairs from above.

_____ rhymes with _____ and _____.

_____ rhymes with _____ and _____.

_____ rhymes with _____ and _____.

_____ rhymes with _____ and _____.

_____ rhymes with _____ and _____.

Read-Write Connection

If you were a miner who survived the 1958 disaster, would you go back to work in the mine? Why, or why not?

_____

_____

_____

_____

_____

_____

Beyond the Reading

DISCUSS SONGS. Think about songs you know that deal with issues such as tragedy, social problems, or important events. Locate the lyrics to one of the songs you listed. Work with a group of your classmates to discuss the main idea of each song, the mood of the song, and how the song creates that mood.

GO ONLINE. To find links and additional activities for this selection, visit the EMC Internet Resource Center at **emcp.com/languagearts** and click on Write-In Reader.

"The Sidewalk Racer,
or On the Skateboard"
by Lillian Morrison

Active READING STRATEGY

USE TEXT ORGANIZATION

Before Reading → **DISCOVER WHAT A CONCRETE POEM IS**

❑ Examine the poem on the next page closely. What shape do you see? How does the shape of the poem depict something in the title?

❑ The shape of this poem makes it a **concrete poem.** How would you define *concrete poem?*

❑ The following is an example of a simple concrete poem. Using a simple word or passage, create a concrete poem of your own.

Graphic Organizer: Concrete Poem

CONNECT

Reader's resource

Skateboards have gone through many changes over time. In the early 1900s, a typical skateboard was made of roller skate wheels, a two-by-four wood plank, and a milk crate with handles—resembling a scooter. In the 1960s, the first professional skateboard was designed. Now there are skateboard parks all over the United States. The popularity of skateboarding has had its peaks and valleys. Many of the peaks are related to the fun and excitement of the sport; many of the lows are related to safety issues.

Word watch

PREVIEW VOCABULARY

asphalt   whirring
skim

Reader's journal

How does it feel to be moving really fast with the wind on your face, as on a bicycle, skis, or roller coaster?

_____

_____

_____

_____

READ ALOUD

☐ Read the poem aloud in a small group. Have each person in the group read the poem. Use the punctuation marks to guide when you pause. Don't stop at the end of a line if there is no punctuation mark there.

☐ How does the shape of the poem influence how you read the poem?

Literary TOOLS

IMAGE AND IMAGERY. An **image** is language that creates a concrete representation of an object or expression. Taken together, the images in the poem make up the poem's **imagery.** As you read, use images to help you visualize what the poem is describing.

FIX-UP IDEA

Tackle Difficult Vocabulary

If your group is having trouble reading the poem aloud, make sure that everyone in the group understands the meaning of the words at the bottom of the page. Before reading the poem, read the Words for Everyday Use aloud.

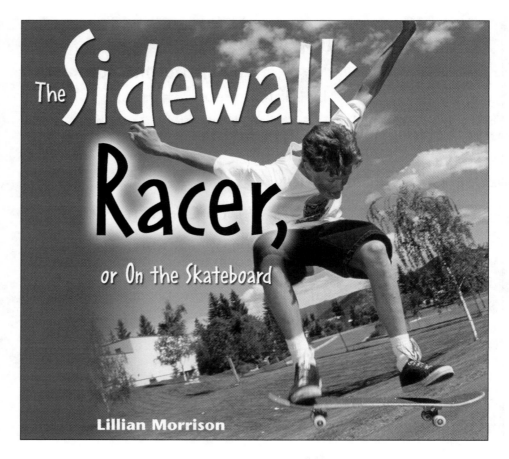

The Sidewalk Racer,
or On the Skateboard

Lillian Morrison

Skimming
 an asphalt sea
I swerve, I curve, I
sway; I speed to whirring
sound an inch above the   5
ground; I'm the sailor
and the sail, I'm the
driver and the wheel
I'm the one and only
single engine   10
human auto
mobile. ∎

words for everyday use	**skim** (skim') *v.*, glide over lightly. *Her waterskis <u>skimmed</u> the surface of the lake.* **as • phalt** (as' fôlt') *n.*, dark rocky mixture used for paving. *My dad poured new <u>asphalt</u> on our driveway.* **whir • ring** (hwur' iŋ) *adj.*, whizzing or buzzing. *The <u>whirring</u> sound of a helicopter caught my attention.*

Reflect ON YOUR READING

After Reading ➤ **WRITE A CONCRETE POEM**

❑ Discuss what the skateboarder is doing in the picture. Which lines in the poem might describe what the boy in the picture is doing?

❑ Discuss how the speaker feels about skateboarding. List in your notebook words about how the speaker feels. Then make a list of words that you would use to describe skateboarding.

❑ Make a new concrete poem about skateboarding that includes the words on your list. The shape of your skateboard poem does not have to be the same as that used in "The Sidewalk Racer, or On the Skateboard."

Reading Skills and Test Practice

RECOGNIZE ORGANIZATIONAL FEATURES

Discuss with your partner how best to answer these questions about organizational features in the poem. Use the Think-Aloud Notes to write down your reasons for eliminating the incorrect answers.

_____1. The shape of the poem lets us know that the speaker
    a. rides slowly.
    b. turns corners fast.
    c. rides in a straight line.
    d. is hurt.

_____2. The shape of the poem best describes how the speaker
    a. moves the skateboard.
    b. falls off.
    c. jumps over barriers.
    d. stops the skateboard.

How did using the reading strategy help you to answer the questions?

_____

_____

THINK-ALOUD NOTES

_____
_____
_____
_____
_____
_____
_____
_____
_____
_____
_____
_____

Investigate, Inquire, and Imagine

RECALL: GATHER FACTS
1a. What is the speaker skimming?

INTERPRET: FIND MEANING
1b. In what way does this surface suggest both skateboarding and a water sport?

ANALYZE: TAKE THINGS APART
2a. What motion words does the speaker use? What do these words have in common? What sort of motion do they describe?

SYNTHESIZE: BRING THINGS TOGETHER
2b. What do these words and phrases suggest about the speaker's feelings while skateboarding?

EVALUATE: MAKE JUDGMENTS
3a. How does the shape of this poem contribute to its meaning?

EXTEND: CONNECT IDEAS
3b. What activity causes you to feel the way this speaker feels when skateboarding?

WordWorkshop

WRITING SENTENCES. Using words in sentences that show their meaning is an excellent way to practice and learn new words. Write a sentence for each of the following Words for Everyday Use. Make sure that the meaning of the word is clear from the context of the sentence.

1. **skim**
   Sentence _____

   _____

2. **asphalt**
   Sentence _____

   _____

3. **swerve**
   Sentence _____

   _____

4. **sway**
   Sentence _____

   _____

5. **whir**
   Sentence _____

   _____

Literary Tools

IMAGE AND IMAGERY. An **image** is language that creates a concrete representation of an object or experience. Taken together, the images in a poem make up the poem's **imagery.** Describe the images you visualize as you read this poem. How does the poem's shape influence this imagery?

_____

_____

_____

_____

Read-Write Connection

What activities in your life bring you the most joy and excitement?

_____

_____

_____

_____

_____

Beyond the Reading

RESEARCH RECREATIONAL OPTIONS. Does your area have a skateboard park? Does it have other recreational areas, like basketball or tennis courts, jogging tracks, hiking trails, skating rinks, pools, or parks? Research the recreational options in your city, town, or region. Make an annotated map of your findings. The map should show where each place is located and what options it offers. If there is a recreational option you cannot find in your area that you would like to see, write a proposal saying what the option is, where it should be located, and why it would benefit your area to have it.

GO ONLINE. To find links and additional activities for this selection, visit the EMC Internet Resource Center at **emcp.com/languagearts** and click on Write-In Reader.

Reader's resource

Lewis Carroll enjoyed spending time with nieces, nephews, and the children of friends. He often told them stories, and his most famous work *Alice's Adventures in Wonderland* developed out of a story he told to Alice Liddell and some friends. **"You Are Old, Father William"** first appeared in *Alice's Adventures in Wonderland,* and **"Jabberwocky"** first appeared in the sequel, *Through the Looking Glass.* Carroll was famous for using word games and word play in his writing. "Jabberwocky" is an example of Carroll's creative use of language.

Word watch

PREVIEW VOCABULARY

airs	shun
incessant	supple
seek	

Reader's journal

Describe an imaginary creature out of your dreams or nightmares.

_____

_____

_____

_____

"Jabberwocky"
and
"You Are Old, Father William"

by Lewis Carroll

Active READING STRATEGY

TACKLE DIFFICULT VOCABULARY

Before Reading ▶ **IDENTIFY DIFFICULT WORDS**

❑ In a small group, look over the footnotes and the Words for Everyday Use for each poem. Read and discuss the meaning of each word.

❑ Draw a picture that illustrates the meaning of each word in the graphic organizer below.

Graphic Organizer: Word Sketches

shun	galumphing	supple
seek	**incessant**	**sage**
chortled	**airs**	**suet**

Jabberwocky

Lewis Carroll

TACKLE WORDS ALOUD

- ❑ In your group, read "Jabberwocky" silently first. Then read it aloud, switching speakers with each stanza.
- ❑ First get a general sense of the story told in this poem. Then try to figure out possible meanings for each stanza.
- ❑ Remember that the poem contains many nonsense words. You will have to make up meanings for the nonsense words. Use clues in the stanza to help you find meaning.

MARK THE TEXT

Highlight or underline the nonsense words in this poem.

'Twas brillig, and the slithy toves
   Did gyre and gimble in the wabe;
All mimsy were the borogoves,
   And the mome raths outgrabe.

5   "Beware the Jabberwock, my son!
   The jaws that bite, the claws that catch!
Beware the Jubjub bird, and <u>shun</u>
   The frumious Bandersnatch!"

He took his vorpal sword in hand;
10   Long time the manxome foe he <u>sought</u>—
So rested he by the Tumtum tree,
   And stood awhile in thought.

And, as in uffish thought he stood,
   The Jabberwock, with eyes of flame,
15   Came whiffling through the tulgey wood,
   And burbled as it came!

words for everyday use	
	shun (shən') *v.*, avoid on purpose. *Choua <u>shuns</u> the library, preferring to study outdoors.*
	seek (sēk') *v.*, search for. *Dan went from store to store <u>seeking</u> the perfect gift for Milla.* **sought,** *past tense*

What does the son do to
the Jabberwock?

_____

_____

_____

FIX-UP IDEA

Refocus
If you are having trouble
understanding the poem
because of the nonsense
words, try refocusing on
the words you do know.
For example, in stanza 2,
you probably understand
all the words except
Jabberwock, Jubjub, and
frumious Bandersnatch.
Using context clues, you
can determine that
Jabberwock, Jubjub bird,
and *Bandersnatch* are all
dangerous creatures.

One, two! One, two! And through and through
   The vorpal blade went snicker-snack!
He left it dead, and with its head
20   He went galumphing[1] back.

"And hast thou slain the Jabberwock?
   Come to my arms, my beamish boy!
O frabjous day! Callooh! Callay!"
   He chortled[2] in his joy.

25   'Twas brillig, and the slithy toves
   Did gyre and gimble in the wabe;
All mimsy were the borogoves,
   And the mome raths outgrabe. ∎

---

1. **galumphing.** Moving with a clumsy, heavy tread
2. **chortled.** Laughed with satisfaction

You are old, Father William

Lewis Carroll

"You are old, Father William," the young man said,
  "And your hair has become very white;
And yet you <u>incessantly</u> stand on your head—
  Do you think, at your age, it is right?"

5   "In my youth," Father William replied to his son,
  "I feared it might injure the brain;
But now that I'm perfectly sure I have none,
  Why, I do it again and again."

"You are old," said the youth, "as I mentioned before,
10   And have grown most uncommonly fat;
Yet you turned a back-somersault in at the door—
  Pray, what is the reason of that?"

---

words for everyday use

incessant (in se′ sənt) *adj.*, continuing without interruption, unceasing. *The <u>incessant</u> dripping of the faucet kept me awake.* **incessantly,** *adv.*

During Reading ➤

TACKLE WORDS ALOUD

❑ First read "You Are Old, Father William" silently. Then read it aloud with your group, taking turns reading stanzas.

❑ As you read the poem, imagine a dialogue between an old man and a young one.

MARK THE TEXT

Highlight or underline three of Father William's activities that surprise his son.

Literary TOOLS

RHYME AND RHYME SCHEME. Rhyme is the repetition of sounds at the ends of words. Patterns of rhyming words that appear at the ends of lines are called *end rhymes*. *Internal rhymes* are rhymes within a line of poetry. The pattern end of rhyme in a poem is called its **rhyme scheme**. As you read, circle rhyming words in the poem.

USE TEXT ORGANIZATION. Remember that text organization can help you understand a poem. Notice that this poem is set up like a dialogue. In the first stanza, the son talks to Father William. In the second stanza, Father William responds. Go through the poem and mark each stanza to show who is speaking; use an *S* for "son" or an *F* for "father".

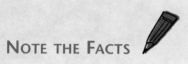

NOTE THE FACTS

What does Father William tell his son to do?

_____

_____

"In my youth," said the sage,[1] as he shook his grey locks,
    "I kept all my limbs very <u>supple</u>
By the use of this ointment—one shilling the box—
15   Allow me to sell you a couple."

"You are old," said the youth, "and your jaws are too weak
    For anything tougher than suet;[2]
Yet you finished the goose, with the bones and the beak—
20   Pray, how did you manage to do it?"

"In my youth," said his father, "I took to the law,
    And argued each case with my wife;
And the muscular strength which it gave to my jaw
    has lasted the rest of my life."

"You are old," said the youth; "one would hardly suppose
25   That your eye was as steady as ever;
Yet you balanced an eel on the end of your nose—
    What made you so awfully clever?"

"I have answered three questions, and that is enough,"
    Said his father; "don't give yourself <u>airs</u>!
30 Do you think I can listen all day to such stuff?
    Be off, or I'll kick you down stairs!" ∎

---

1. **sage.** Person known for wisdom
2. **suet.** Hard fat in beef and mutton

words for everyday use

supple (sə′ pəl) *adj.*, limber, without stiffness. *She kneaded the dough until it was <u>supple</u> enough to be formed into rolls.*
airs (ārz′) *n.*, artificial or snobby manners. *Milo sometimes puts on <u>airs</u> to hide his lack of confidence.*

Reflect ON YOUR READING

❑ Go back through each poem, and make a list of things to include in an illustration for each poem. Then have your group create an illustration for each poem.
❑ Share your illustrations with the class, discussing some of the lines you illustrated.

Reading Skills and Test Practice

IDENTIFY MOOD AND TONE

Discuss with your partner how best to answer these questions about mood and tone in the poems. Use the Think-Aloud Notes to write down your reasons for eliminating the incorrect answers.

_____1. Choose the word pair that best completes the following sentence:

The mood of "You Are Old, Father William" is _____, while the mood of "Jabberwocky" is mainly _____.

a. sincere . . . creepy
b. creepy . . . happy
c. silly . . . threatening
d. joyous . . . confused

_____2. The mood of "Jabberwocky" changes. At what point in the poem does the mood shift?
a. stanza 2
b. stanza 3
c. stanza 4
d. stanza 5

How did using the reading strategy help you to answer the questions?

_____

_____

THINK-ALOUD NOTES

_____

_____

_____

_____

_____

_____

_____

_____

_____

_____

Investigate, Inquire, and Imagine

RECALL: GATHER FACTS
1a. What does the father say in stanza 2 of "You Are Old, Father William"? What does the father say in stanza 2 of "Jabberwocky"?

INTERPRET: FIND MEANING
1b. What tone do these stanzas set?

ANALYZE: TAKE THINGS APART
2a. Identify examples in each poem of how the father communicates with his son. Then find specific examples showing how the son acts and how he communicates with his father.

SYNTHESIZE: BRING THINGS TOGETHER
2b. Develop a character description for the father and son in "You Are Old, Father William." Do the same for the father and the son in "Jabberwocky."

EVALUATE: MAKE JUDGMENTS
3a. Summarize the positive elements of the father-son relationships in both poems.

EXTEND: CONNECT IDEAS
3b. Which poem more fully describes the father-son relationship? Which father-son relationship is more believable? Which relationship is closer? Explain your answers.

Literary Tools

RHYME AND RHYME SCHEME. Rhyme is the repetition of sounds at the ends of words. Patterns of rhyming words that appear at the ends of lines are called *end rhymes*. *Internal rhymes* are rhymes within a line of poetry. The pattern of end rhymes in a poem is called its **rhyme scheme**. Use a graphic organizer like the one that follows to identify the rhyme schemes of the poems.

"You are old, Father William," the young man said,	*a*
"And your hair has become very white;	*b*
And yet you incessantly stand on your head—	*a*
Do you think, at your age, it is right?"	*b*

WordWorkshop

USING A THESAURUS. A **thesaurus** is a book that provides synonyms and antonyms of words. One way to build your vocabulary is to learn words similar in meaning to words you know. Use a thesaurus to find a synonym for each of the following words. Then use each new word in a sentence.

1. **seek**
   Synonym _____

   Sentence _____

2. **shun**
   Synonym _____

   Sentence _____

3. **supple**
   Synonym _____

   Sentence _____

4. **incessant**
   Synonym _____

   Sentence _____

5. **airs**
   Synonym _____

   Sentence _____

Read-Write Connection

When is it appropriate to question authority?

_____

_____

_____

Beyond the Reading

CREATE A GLOSSARY. Lewis Carroll used many words that seemed to have no meaning, but he created these words with logic and imagination. Create a glossary of nonsense words from "Jabberwocky." Include a definition for each word and a sentence that shows correct usage. You may wish to illustrate some words, too. Then make up a few words of your own to add to the glossary.

GO ONLINE. To find links and additional activities for this selection, visit the EMC Internet Resource Center at **emcp.com/languagearts** and click on Write-In Reader.

People have many ways of overcoming or dealing with their fears. Being able to face one's fears is the first step in overcoming them. Fear of the dark is a common fear in young children that usually disappears in time. Children often have other fears that they overcome as they grow older. Older people have fears, too. Deep-seated fears may be harder to overcome. In **"Life Doesn't Frighten Me"** Maya Angelou addresses childhood fears that have been overcome.

Reader's
journal

What situations frighten you? What do you do to overcome your fear?

_____

_____

_____

_____

_____

"Life Doesn't Frighten Me"

by Maya Angelou

Active READING STRATEGY

CONNECT TO PRIOR KNOWLEDGE

Before Reading ➤ CONNECT TO YOUR EXPERIENCE

- ❏ Look at the title of the poem. Then make a list of things that frighten you now and things that frightened you when you were younger.
- ❏ Share your thoughts about frightening things with the class. What fears are most common?
- ❏ List ways you overcame or learned to deal with your fears.
- ❏ As you read, use the graphic organizer to compare and contrast your reactions to the speaker's.

Graphic Organizer: Comparison Chart

Things Speaker Doesn't Fear	How I Feel about This Thing

"Life Doesn't Frighten Me"

Maya Angelou

Shadows on the wall
Noises down the hall
Life doesn't frighten me at all
Bad dogs barking loud
5   Big ghosts in a cloud
Life doesn't frighten me at all.

Mean old Mother Goose
Lions on the loose
They don't frighten me at all
10   Dragons breathing flame
On my counterpane
That doesn't frighten me at all.

I go boo
Make them shoo
15   I make fun
Way they run
I won't cry
So they fly
I just smile
20   They go wild
Life doesn't frighten me at all.

Tough guys in a fight
All alone at night
Life doesn't frighten me at all.

25   Panthers in the park
Strangers in the dark
No, they don't frighten me at all.

That new classroom where
Boys all pull my hair
30   (Kissy little girls
With their hair in curls)
They don't frighten me at all.

During Reading

IDENTIFY THE SPEAKER'S FEARS

- Listen as the teacher reads the poem to the class. In your Comparison Chart, write things that do not frighten the speaker.
- Write your reaction to each thing the speaker fears.
- Reread the poem on your own. Highlight things that the speaker does to overcome fears. Compare them to the ways you have tried to overcome fears.

NOTE THE FACTS

What does the speaker do to confront scary things?

_____

_____

THINK AND REFLECT

Do you think the speaker used to be afraid of these things? Why, or why not? **(Infer)**

_____

_____

Do you believe in the
speaker's magic charm?
Do you believe the rest of
what she says? **(Evaluate)**

_____

_____

_____

35 Don't show me frogs and snakes
And listen for my scream.
If I'm afraid at all
It's only in my dreams.

I've got a magic charm
That I keep up my sleeve,
I can walk the ocean floor
40 And never have to breathe.

Life doesn't frighten me at all
Not at all
Not at all.
Life doesn't frighten me at all ■

Literary TOOLS

REPETITION. Repetition is
more than one use of a
sound, word, or group of
words. What is repeated
in the last stanza?

_____

_____

_____

FIX-UP IDEA

Vary Reading Rates
Reread the poem two
more times on your own,
one time reading it faster
than normal, another time
reading it slower than
normal. Which speed
makes the most sense?

Reflect ON YOUR READING

After Reading ➤ EVALUATE THE SPEAKER'S FEARS

❑ Discuss what does not frighten the speaker in the poem. Do you think the speaker is telling the truth? Why?

_____

_____

_____

_____

Reading Skills and Test Practice

DRAW CONCLUSIONS

Discuss with your partner how best to answer these questions that require you to draw conclusions. Use the Think-Aloud Notes to write down your reasons for eliminating the incorrect answers.

_____1. Which best describes how the speaker overcomes her fears?
   a. She cries.
   b. She doesn't smile.
   c. She makes noises that frighten things away.
   d. She keeps repeating what she wants to be true.

_____2. Read these lines from the poem:

   That new classroom where
   Boys all pull my hair

   From these lines, the best guess about the speaker's age is that he or she is
   a. two years old.
   b. six years old.
   c. fourteen years old.
   d. eighteen years old.

How did using the reading strategy help you to answer the questions?

_____

_____

THINK-ALOUD
NOTES

_____

_____

_____

_____

_____

_____

_____

_____

_____

_____

Investigate, Inquire, and Imagine

RECALL: GATHER FACTS
1a. How does the speaker confront scary things?

INTERPRET: FIND MEANING
1b. How do these tactics help the speaker?

ANALYZE: TAKE THINGS APART
2a. Identify all the things in the poem that the speaker is not frightened of.

SYNTHESIZE: BRING THINGS TOGETHER
2b. How does the speaker avoid being frightened of these things? What quality or characteristic does the speaker have that allows her to feel unafraid?

EVALUATE: MAKE JUDGMENTS
3a. In making the point that life doesn't frighten her at all, the speaker mentions certain things that could be scary. What do you think about the items she mentions? Do you think this is a good representation of scary things in her life? Why, or why not?

EXTEND: CONNECT IDEAS
3b. If you were to write a poem similar to this one, what items would you use to make the point that life doesn't frighten you at all?

Literary Tools

REPETITION. **Repetition** is more than one use of a sound, word, or group of words. Repetition is used in poetry to create rhythmic effects. It is also used to emphasize ideas. How does repetition affect the rhythm of this poem? What ideas are repeated? How does repeating these ideas create a particular mood?

_____

_____

_____

_____

WordWorkshop

BRAINSTORMING. In the left column, list five people, places, things, or ideas that frighten you. In the right column, brainstorm vivid words to describe the things that frighten you. Use a thesaurus to help you add to your list.

Scary Things	Descriptive Words and Phrases

Read-Write Connection

What fears about life do you have that you don't show?

_____

_____

_____

_____

_____

Beyond the Reading

FIGHT FEARS. Write a children's story to help a young child overcome a common fear, such as fear of the dark or a monster under the bed. Choose a fear mentioned in the poem, or think of something you were afraid of when you were younger. Think about ways to overcome this fear or to show that there is nothing to fear. Write and illustrate a story to teach this lesson.

GO ONLINE. To find links and additional activities for this selection, visit the EMC Internet Resource Center at **emcp.com/languagearts** and click on Write-In Reader.

Reader's resource

Blindness and vision impairment affect more than a million people in the United States. People who are legally blind may have no vision, tunnel vision, or extremely blurred vision, or they may see just light or shadows. People who are blind may use canes or dogs to help them travel from place to place. They may use other tools to help them with other daily activities. In **"One Time,"** the narrator meets his friend's blind sister. William Stafford's ability to absorb and reflect on human nature and on the world around him makes his poems easy for readers to connect with.

Reader's journal

If you lost one of your senses, how might you use those you still had differently?

_____

_____

_____

_____

"One Time"
by William Stafford

Active READING STRATEGY

VISUALIZE

Before Reading ➤ **PREVIEW THE POEM**

❑ Read the Reader's Resource and answer the Reader's Journal question.
❑ Look at the background image on page 131.
❑ What do you think the poem will be about? Begin to visualize a scene.
❑ **Sensory details** are words and phrases that describe how things look, sound, smell, taste, or feel. Look for sensory details to help you visualize.
❑ As you read, fill in sensory details from the poem in the graphic organizer below. Add other sensory details from your visualization. Put a star next to the details from the poem itself.

Graphic Organizer: Sensory Details Chart

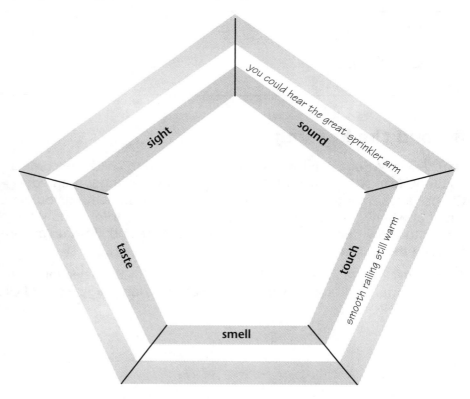

sight

sound — you could hear the great sprinkler arm

touch — smooth railing still warm

taste

smell

One time

William Stafford

When evening had flowed between houses
and paused on the schoolground, I met
Hilary's blind little sister following
the gray smooth railing still warm from the sun
with her hand; and she stood by the edge
holding her face upward waiting
while the last light found her cheek
and her hair, and then on over the trees.

You could hear the great sprinkler arm
of water find and then leave the pavement,
and pigeons telling each other their dreams
or the dreams they would have. We were
deep in the well of shadow by then, and I
held out my hand, saying, "Tina, it's me—
Hilary says I should tell you it's dark,
and, oh, Tina, it is. Together now—"

And I reached, our hands touched,
and we found our way home. ∎

During Reading

MAKE A MIND MOVIE

❑ As your teacher reads the first stanza, close your eyes, and make a mind movie. What do you think of as each line is read? For instance, when your teacher reads, "When evening had flowed between houses," picture what evening looks like. What would it sound like? How would it smell? Who would be there?

❑ Continue reading on your own. Keep making a mind movie as you read. Use as many senses as possible in your mind movie.

THINK AND REFLECT

What is happening to the daylight? **(Infer)**

_____

_____

FIX-UP IDEA

Reread
If you are having difficulty making a mind movie with your eyes closed, keep your eyes open and draw pictures of what is occurring in the poem. Reread the poem if necessary to complete your drawings.

Reflect ON YOUR READING

❑ Summarize what the evening was like for the speaker and Tina. Include in your graphic organizer sensory details for as many of the five senses as you can find.

❑ Discuss your response with a partner. Talk about other sensory details you included in your mind movie.

Reading Skills and Test Practice

DRAW CONCLUSIONS

Discuss with your partner how best to answer these questions that require you to draw conclusions. Use the Think-Aloud Notes to write down your reasons for eliminating the incorrect answers.

_____1. When the speaker says he heard "pigeons telling each other their dreams," he means he
  a. knows what the pigeons are saying.
  b. thinks that the pigeons are too noisy.
  c. assumed that the pigeons were communicating.
  d. was curious about what the pigeons were saying.

_____2. How does Tina experience a sunset?
  a. Someone has to tell her about it.
  b. She feels it on her face.
  c. She hears the sounds change.
  d. She smells nighttime fires.

How did using the reading strategy help you to answer the questions?

_____

_____

THINK-ALOUD NOTES

Investigate, Inquire, and Imagine

RECALL: GATHER FACTS
1a. What is Tina doing when the speaker finds her?

→ INTERPRET: FIND MEANING
1b. Why do you think she is doing this?

ANALYZE: TAKE THINGS APART
2a. Note the words and phrases in this poem that reveal the passing of time.

→ SYNTHESIZE: BRING THINGS TOGETHER
2b. By the last lines of the poem, what challenge does the speaker face?

EVALUATE: MAKE JUDGMENTS
3a. How does Stafford create a unique image of a sunset in this poem?

→ EXTEND: CONNECT IDEAS
3b. What sensory details would you focus on if you were creating a unique image of a sunset?

Literary Tools

SENSORY DETAILS. **Sensory details** are words and phrases that describe how things look, sound, smell, taste, or feel. Review the sensory details you put in your graphic organizer. How are sensory details important in this poem? Explain your answer.

_____

_____

_____

_____

_____

_____

WordWorkshop

WORDSTORMING. Wordstorming is the brainstorming of words. When you wordstorm, your goal is to think of as many words as you can related to a particular topic. With a small group create a list of words related to darkness. Try to think of unusual words that other groups won't include.

_____

_____

_____

_____

_____

Read-Write Connection

What mood does this poem create? Draw a picture of Tina, showing how she feels.

_____

_____

Beyond the Reading

TELL A STORY. "One Time" is a narrative poem—a poem that tells a story. Write a story that expands upon the poem. For example, you may describe the speaker in more detail, explain why he is meeting Tina, or tell what happens when they get home. When you are done, share your story with a small group of classmates.

GO ONLINE. To find links and additional activities for this selection, visit the EMC Internet Resource Center at **emcp.com/languagearts** and click on Write-In Reader.

Unit 4 READING Review

Choose and Use Reading Strategies

Before reading the poem below, review and discuss with a partner how to use reading strategies with poetry.

1. Read with a Purpose
2. Connect to Prior Knowledge
3. Write Things Down
4. Make Predictions
5. Visualize
6. Use Text Organization
7. Tackle Difficult Vocabulary
8. Monitor Your Reading Progress

Now apply at least two of these reading strategies as you read the excerpt from "The Eagle: A Fragment" by Alfred, Lord Tennyson. Use the margins and mark up the text to show how you are using the reading strategies to read actively.

> He clasps the crag with crooked hands;
> Close to the sun in lonely lands,
> Ringed with the azure world, he stands.
>
> The wrinkled sea beneath him crawls:
> He watches from the mountain walls,
> And like a thunderbolt he falls.

Literary Tools

Select the best literary element on the right to complete each sentence on the left. Write the correct letter in the blank.

_____ 1._____ helps emphasize ideas by stating them more than once.

_____ 2.The ___ of "Jabberwocky" is *abab.*

_____ 3.The ___ of "The Springhill Disaster" is somber.

_____ 4.___ of sailing and automobiles helps the reader picture the action in "The Sidewalk Racer, or On the Skateboard."

_____ 5.The line "O frabjous day! Callooh! Callay!" contains an example of ____.

_____ 6.The line "the gray smooth railing still warm from the sun" contains ____.

a. end rhyme, 100, 119, 122

b. imagery, 98, 112, 114

c. internal rhyme, 100, 119, 122

d. mood, 105, 109

e. repetition, 106, 126, 128

f. rhyme scheme, 100, 119, 122

g. sensory details, 130, 133

WordWorkshop

UNIT 4 WORDS FOR EVERYDAY USE

airs, 120	seek, 117	supple, 120
asphalt, 112	shun, 117	whirring, 112
incessant, 119	skim, 112	

SENTENCE COMPLETION. Find the word that completes each sentence below to identify seven vocabulary words from this unit. Fill in the blanks with the letters of the word that is being suggested. When you are done, you should be able to identify another vocabulary word vertically.

1. Watch the bird ___ across the water before it takes off.
   __ __ | __ | __

2. People sometimes ___ others who are different.
   __ __ __ | __

3. I hope you find what you ___.
    C
   __ | __ | __ __

4. The clay was soft and ___, making it easy to mold.
    S
   __ | __ __ __ __ __ __

5. Pretentious people often put on ___.
   __ | __ __ __

6. The ___ of the fan kept me up last night.
   __ __ __ __ __ | __ | __

7. Sand or another soft surface is better than ___ for a playground.
   __ __ __ __ __ __ | __

On Your Own

FLUENTLY SPEAKING. Work with a partner to prepare a dramatic reading of one of the poems in this unit. Pay attention to the rhythm of the poem and to techniques of sound, such as rhyme, repetition, and alliteration.

PICTURE THIS. Choose an image from one of the poems in this unit. Create a drawing, painting, or other visual representation of the image.

PUT IT IN WRITING. Try writing your own poem. It could be a narrative poem that tells a story or a lyric poem that expresses emotions. In either case, try to use vivid images and techniques of sound in your poem.

Unit FIVE

READING Folk Literature

FOLK LITERATURE

Human beings are storytelling creatures. Long before people invented writing, they were telling stories about the lives of their gods and heroes. The best of their stories were passed by word of mouth from generation to generation, from folk to folk. These early stories were told in the form of poems, songs, and what we would now call prose tales.

Stories, poems, and songs passed by word of mouth from person to person are important elements of a group's culture. Eventually, many of these verbally transmitted stories, poems, and songs were written down. **Folk literature** is the written versions of these stories, poems, and songs. Folk literature is full of literary devices that helped storytellers remember the stories. These devices include the use of repetition, common phrases such as "once upon a time" and "they lived happily ever after," and familiar characters and events. Some common types of folk literature are defined below.

Types of Folk Literature

MYTHS. **Myths** are stories that explain objects or events in the natural world as resulting from the action of some supernatural force or entity, most often a god. Every early culture around the globe has produced myths. In this unit, you will read "The Twelve Labors of Hercules," a Greek myth.

FOLK TALES. **Folk tales** are brief stories passed by word of mouth from generation to generation in a particular culture. "The Cow of No Color" in this unit is a folk tale from Africa. **Fairy tales** are folk tales that contain supernatural beings, such as fairies, dragons, ogres, and animals with human qualities. One example is "Dragon, Dragon" from this unit. **Tall tales** are colorful stories that depict the exaggerated wild adventures of North American folk heroes. Many of these heroes and stories revolve around the American frontier and the Wild West.

NOTE THE FACTS

What is folk literature?

_____

_____

_____

MARK THE TEXT

Highlight or underline eight types of folk literature. Start here and continue on the next page.

_____

_____

_____

PARABLES. **Parables** are very brief stories told to teach a moral lesson. Some of the most famous parables are those told by Jesus in the Bible.

FABLES. **Fables** are brief stories, often with animal characters, told to express a moral. Famous fables include those of Æsop and Jean de La Fontaine.

FOLK SONGS. **Folk songs** are traditional or composed songs typically made up of stanzas, a refrain, and a simple melody. They express commonly shared ideas or feelings and may be narrative (telling a story) or lyrical (expressing an emotion). Traditional folk songs are anonymous songs that have been transmitted orally.

LEGENDS. **Legends** are stories that have been passed down through time. These stories are often believed to be based on history but without evidence that the events occurred. In this unit, you will read a legend about "How Robin Hood Saved the Widow's Three Sons."

USING READING STRATEGIES WITH FOLK LITERATURE

Active Reading Strategy Checklists

In the stories, poems, and songs that are a part of folk literature, storytellers want to entertain their audiences and to pass along cultural ideas and beliefs. The following checklists offer strategies for reading folk literature.

1 READ WITH A PURPOSE. Give yourself a purpose, or something to look for, as you read. Often, you can set a purpose for reading by previewing the title, the opening lines, and the instructional information. Other times, a teacher may set your purpose: "Pay attention to the beliefs that contributed to each superstition in the article." To read with a purpose, say to yourself

❑ I want to look for . . .
❑ I will keep track of . . .
❑ I want to find out what happens to . . .
❑ I want to understand how . . .
❑ The message of this selection is . . .

Reading TIP

One purpose for reading fairy tales is to understand the fears and desires of people who lived long ago.

2 CONNECT TO PRIOR KNOWLEDGE. Connect to what you already know about a particular culture and its storytelling traditions. To connect to prior knowledge, say to yourself

- ❑ I know that this type of folk literature has . . .
- ❑ The events in this selection remind me of . . .
- ❑ Something similar I've read is . . .
- ❑ I like this part of the selection because . . .

3 WRITE THINGS DOWN. Create a written record of the cultural ideas and beliefs that a storyteller passes along. To keep a written record

- ❑ Underline characters' names.
- ❑ Write down your thoughts about the storyteller's ideas and beliefs.
- ❑ Highlight the most exciting, funniest, or most interesting parts of the tale.
- ❑ Create a graphic organizer to keep track of the sequence of events.
- ❑ Use a code to respond to what happens.

4 MAKE PREDICTIONS. Use information about the title and subject matter to guess what a folk literature selection will be about. Confirm or deny your predictions, and make new ones based on what you learn. To make predictions, say to yourself

- ❑ The title tells me that the selection will be about . . .
- ❑ I predict that this character will . . .
- ❑ Tales from this cultural tradition usually . . .
- ❑ The conflict between the characters will be resolved by . . .
- ❑ I think the selection will end with . . .

5 VISUALIZE. Visualizing, or allowing the words on the page to create images in your mind, helps you understand a storyteller's account. In order to visualize what happens in a folk literature selection, imagine that you are the storyteller. Read the words in your head with the type of expression and feeling that the storyteller might use with an audience. Make statements such as

- ❑ I imagine the characters sound like . . .
- ❑ My sketch of what happens includes . . .
- ❑ I picture this sequence of events . . .
- ❑ I envision the characters as . . .

Reading **TIP**

Instead of writing down a short response, use a symbol or a short word to indicate your response. Use codes like the ones listed below.

+	I like this.
–	I don't like this.
√	This is important.
Yes	I agree with this.
No	I disagree with this.
?	I don't understand this.
!	This is like something I know.
↫	I need to come back to this later.

Reading **TIP**

Sketching story events helps you remember and understand them.

6 **USE TEXT ORGANIZATION.** When you read folk literature, pay attention to transition or signal words such as *first*, *if/then*, and *on the other hand*. These words identify important ideas and text patterns. Stop occasionally to retell what you have read. Say to yourself

- ❏ What happens first is . . .
- ❏ There is a conflict between . . .
- ❏ The high point of interest is . . .
- ❏ I can summarize this section by . . .
- ❏ The message of this selection is that . . .

7 **TACKLE DIFFICULT VOCABULARY.** Difficult words can hinder your ability to understand folk literature. Use context, consult a dictionary, or ask someone about words you do not understand. When you come across a difficult word, say to yourself

- ❏ The words around the difficult word tell me it must mean . . .
- ❏ A dictionary definition shows that the word means . . .
- ❏ My work with the word before reading helps me know that the word means . . .
- ❏ A classmate said that the word means . . .

8 **MONITOR YOUR READING PROGRESS.** All readers encounter difficulty when they read, especially if they are reading assigned material and not something they have chosen on their own. When you are assigned to read folk literature, note the problems you are having and fix them. The key to reading success is knowing when you are having difficulty. To fix problems, say to yourself

- ❏ Because I don't understand this part, I will . . .
- ❏ Because I'm having trouble staying connected, I will . . .
- ❏ Because the words are hard, I will . . .
- ❏ Because this selection is long, I will . . .
- ❏ Because I can't retell what this section was about, I will . . .

Become an Active Reader

The instruction with the folk literature in this unit gives you an in-depth look at how to use one strategy with each folk literature selection. Learn how to combine several strategies to ensure your complete understanding of what you are reading. Use fix-up ideas to fix problems. For further information about the active reading strategies, including the fix-up ideas, see Unit 1, pages 4–15.

Reading **TIP**

You don't need to understand every word perfectly to understand folk literature. Before stopping to look up a word, ask yourself whether you understand enough from the context to keep reading.

FIX-UP IDEAS

- ■ Reread
- ■ Ask a question
- ■ Read in shorter chunks
- ■ Read aloud
- ■ Retell
- ■ Work with a partner
- ■ Unlock difficult words
- ■ Vary your reading rate
- ■ Choose a new reading strategy
- ■ Create a mnemonic device

How to Use Reading Strategies with Folk Literature

Use the following excerpts to discover how you might use reading strategies as you read folk literature.

Excerpt 1. Note how a reader uses active reading strategies while reading this excerpt from "Dragon, Dragon" by John Gardner.

VISUALIZE
Picturing the knights under their beds helps me appreciate the humor in this story.

CONNECT TO PRIOR KNOWLEDGE
I know that stories about dragons and kingdoms are often fairy tales.

There was once a king whose kingdom was plagued by a dragon. The king did not know which way to turn. The king's knights were all cowards who hid under their beds whenever the dragon came in sight, so they were of no use to the king at all. And the king's wizard could not help either because, being old, he had forgotten his magic spells. Nor could the wizard look up the spells that had slipped his mind, for he had unfortunately misplaced his wizard's book many years before. The king was at his wit's end.

READ WITH A PURPOSE
I want to find out how the king gets rid of the dragon.

USE TEXT ORGANIZATION
Understanding the usual structure of a fairy tale might help me follow this story.

Excerpt 2. Note how a reader uses active reading strategies while reading this excerpt from "The Twelve Labors of Hercules," retold by Walker Brents.

TACKLE DIFFICULT VOCABULARY
Consciousness must mean "thoughts" because in the next sentence Hercules's thoughts become scrambled.

MAKE A PREDICTION
I predict that Hera will have something to do with Hercules performing twelve labors.

The goddess Hera hated Hercules from the moment of his birth. In his infancy she sent two giant serpents to kill him as he slept, but Hercules strangled them instead. His parents rushed into the room to find the baby shaking the dead bodies of the snakes as if they were rattles. This was an early indication of his great strength, but this strength was not always used well.

Once Hera sent madness and insanity into the consciousness of Hercules. His thoughts became scrambled. Under the delusion[1] that he was at war, he mistook his nephews and nieces for enemies, and killed them. When the madness passed and he saw what he had done he was overwhelmed with grief and guilt.

---
1. **delusion.** Ongoing false belief

MONITOR YOUR READING PROGRESS
I can reread the sections with difficult vocabulary after checking the meanings of the unfamiliar words.

WRITE THINGS DOWN
I can use a time line to keep track of important events.

Reader's **resource**

A **legend** is a story that has been passed down through time and that might have some basis in history. **"How Robin Hood Saved the Widow's Three Sons"** is a popular legend. Robin Hood is best known as the leader of a band of merry men, including Little John, Friar Tuck, and Will Scarlet. This band of outlaws roamed Sherwood Forest in Nottingham, England. Robin and his followers were said to "steal from the rich and give to the poor." They challenged an unfair system of government and tried to help the less fortunate, who had few rights in the England of their time. There are many stories about Robin Hood, and historians debate whether he was a real person or a fictional hero.

Word watch

PREVIEW VOCABULARY

earnest
ponder

Reader's **journal**

What would you do if a friend was accused of doing something that he or she did not do?

"How Robin Hood Saved the Widow's Three Sons"
by Sara Hyry

Active READING STRATEGY

CONNECT TO PRIOR KNOWLEDGE

Before Reading ➤ **BUILD BACKGROUND KNOWLEDGE**

❑ As a class, discuss what you already know about Robin Hood.
❑ Read the background information in the Reader's Resource and compare it to the class discussion.
❑ Preview the Action/Motivation Chart below. As you read, you will use this chart to record the heroic actions of Robin Hood. Next to each action, you will write his motivation, or reason, for acting as he does. Use your prior knowledge about Robin Hood's goals to help you determine his motivation.

Graphic Organizer: Action/Motivation Chart

Action	Motivation

How Robin Hood Saved the Widow's Three Sons

Sara Hyry

One fine morning, Robin Hood was walking down a lane toward Nottingham town. He was dressed in the colors of green and brown. A fine figure he made as he wandered down. But as he continued, he heard a terrible wailing. Turning a corner, he found a widow weeping.

"What, pray tell, is troubling you?" Robin asked the woman. He knew her well, for he had often dined at her

10   hearth with her sons, who were counted among his followers.

"Down the way, my three sons are to be hanged today," she replied.

"What have they done to deserve such a punishment? Have they stolen? Have they killed a priest? Have they burned down a church?"

"No, none of those have they done. They are to be killed because they killed the king's deer. Following your ways, they shot it with their longbows[1] and 'twas their bad

20   fortune that the sheriff should happen by," she cried.

"That's no crime as I see it," said Robin. "You have told me just in time. If they are to be hanged today, I must be along quickly now." And he hurried off, towards the site of gallows. As he walked, he <u>pondered</u> how to save the widow's sons.

"I need some sort of disguise, to get me in to the town without the sheriff knowing," he thought. At that moment,

---

1. **longbows.** Bows used to shoot arrows. Robin Hood was an expert marksman with this weapon.

| words for everyday use | **pon • der** (pän' dər) v., think hard upon something. *Horace <u>pondered</u> carefully before making his next move.* |

During Reading →

GATHER INFORMATION

❑ With your teacher, discuss the meanings of these archaic words and expressions: *pray tell, 'twas, 'tis, for shame, dare not, halt.*

❑ Follow along as your teacher reads the first page of the story aloud. Notice the words and phrases from the list above. Write down one action and one motivation in your Action/Motivation Chart.

❑ Read the rest of the story on your own. Be sure to fill in your graphic organizer as you read.

MARK THE TEXT

Underline or highlight why the three men will be killed.

Use THE STRATEGY

CONNECT TO PRIOR KNOWLEDGE. What action does Robin Hood take after speaking with the widow, and why? Record your answers on your graphic organizer. How does this action relate to what you know about Robin Hood?

_____

_____

he happened upon an old man dressed in rags, a palmer[2] back from his journey to the Holy Land. "What news have you?" Robin asked the man.

30 "There's to be a hanging today—three hangings to be exact. And a shame it is. For the three who are to be hanged are no villains, I say."

"Why then are they to be hanged?" asked Robin.

"The sheriff finds killing the king's deer to be a crime. He wishes to make an example, for he is charged with stopping the hunting of the king's beasts. Yet, he sees nothing wrong with the likes of me and the likes of the three going hungry for want of meat, when a bit of venison would be a treat."

Robin looked at the man shrewdly. "Thank you for the
40 news, good man. And for your troubles, I propose a trade. I will give you my clothes and thirty silver coins in exchange for your clothes. What say you?"

"Don't poke fun at an old man, who has but little in this life," he protested.

"I am in <u>earnest</u>. Come, come, I haven't all day," urged Robin. "I'll give you these pieces of gold for your hat and your cloak, and your tattered old breaches."

"'Tis not a fair trade," thought the man, "but it will do me a world of good." So he did not protest when Robin
50 plucked the hat from his head and placed it on his own. Robin dressed himself in the patched breeches and the threadbare cloak. He tucked his arrows under his clothes, unstrung his bow and leaned upon it as a staff. He had his disguise, and he thought, perhaps, a plan.

Robin continued down the road, looking for all the world like the worn, old palmer he pretended to be. He reached the town and found that quite a crowd had gathered in the square. He asked some of those near him what all the hubbub was about.

60 "The sheriff is to hang three men today."

NOTE THE FACTS

What disguise does Robin wear when he goes to save the three men? Where does he get it?

_____

_____

2. **palmer.** Person who has made a pilgrimage to Jerusalem, often wearing a palm leaf as a sign of his or her religious journey

words for everyday use   ear • nest (ər′ nest) adj., serious, not joking. _We all laughed until we realized Ling was <u>earnest</u> when she told us she wanted to be a rock star._

"For what crime?" asked Robin.

"For poaching on the king's land," came the reply.

"And this is a spectacle for all the town to see. Does nobody protest such action? For shame!" Robin cried.

"We dare not protest the sheriff, for he would have our heads as well. Besides, the fellows did break the law. And there's the sheriff now."

Robin caught sight of the sheriff and began to move through the crowd. He neared the gallows and approached the sheriff. "What price do you pay your hangman today?" Robin asked. "Might you permit this old man to do the job?"

"Clothes of the hanged, of course, and by the looks of it you could use them," said the sheriff with a laugh. "Plus sixpence, two pence per man—the usual hangman's price. The job is yours if you do it right quick."

"Allow me first to take the last confessions of the men; they should not die without that."

"Very well, but be speedy, old man," said the sheriff impatiently.

"And mind you if I string up my bow that I might end their misery once they begin to swing from the ropes?"

"Fine, but again I say be quick about it."

So Robin prepared his bow and approached the widow's sons. The prisoners were bound at the hands with the nooses ready round their necks. Robin leaned in to the first man, as though to hear his confession and give him absolution.[3] But what he said was this: "Stand still, my good man, as I cut your hands free. When I throw off my cloak, pull the noose from your neck and run quickly to the forest."

To each man in turn Robin did the same. Then turning from the last, he faced the crowd and the sheriff and shouted, "I'm no hangman, nor do I wish to be!" He pulled a horn from under his rags and blew it long and loud. Then with a flourish, he tossed off his cloak. At this sign, the three men pulled the nooses from their necks and scrambled for the forest.

---

3. **absolution.** Forgiveness of sins

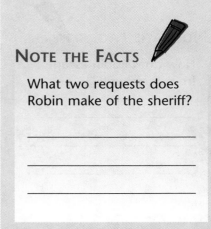

NOTE THE FACTS

What two requests does Robin make of the sheriff?

_____

_____

_____

Use THE STRATEGY

CONNECT TO PRIOR KNOWLEDGE. Given what you know about Robin Hood, why does he make these two requests? What is he planning? In your chart, write down the answer as his motivation for the action of speaking to the sheriff.

NOTE THE FACTS

How does Robin escape from the sheriff?

_____

_____

_____

"After them," ordered the sheriff.

100   "Halt!" shouted Robin. He had an arrow ready on his bow. "The first man to approach will have my arrow for a souvenir. And any who have seen me shoot know I can hit my mark."

"Yet, even you cannot shoot all at once," laughed the sheriff. "I have you now, Robin Hood." But at that moment, a hundred men in green streamed into the square, for Robin's men had heard the blast of his horn.

"Stop them," the sheriff shouted into the confusion. But the sheriff's men could not stop the men in green. Robin

110   leapt down into the crowd. He and his men let off a shower of arrows as they edged backward out of the town. They disappeared into the forest, as the widow's sons had done before them.

And that is how Robin saved three of his men from wrongly losing their lives. ■

Reflect ON YOUR READING

After Reading ➤ REVIEW WHAT YOU WROTE

❑ Look back over your graphic organizer. You should have written down at least three actions and motivations. If you haven't, review the story and margin questions to find additional actions.
❑ Discuss your graphic organizer with a partner. Did you consider the same actions heroic? How did you differ in opinion as to Robin's motivations?
❑ What does "hero" mean to you personally? Write a paragraph expressing your opinion.

Reading Skills and Test Practice

DRAW CONCLUSIONS

Discuss with a partner how best to answer the following questions that ask you to draw conclusions. Use the Think-Aloud Notes to write down your reasons for eliminating the incorrect answers.

_____1. What is the best evidence that the people support Robin Hood?
    a. He was able to buy the palmer's clothes.
    b. He easily got the job of hanging man.
    c. A hundred men in green came into the square.
    d. He was able to bring his bow and arrow to the hanging.

_____2. Read this sentence from the folk tale.

Robin leaned in to the first man, as though to hear his confession and give him absolution.

This sentence means that Robin is trying to
    a. make it look as if he forgiving the man's sins.
    b. get close and cut the ropes on the man's hands.
    c. kill the men to end their misery.
    d. remove the man's noose from his neck.

How did using the reading strategy help you to answer the questions?

_____

_____

THINK-ALOUD NOTES

_____

_____

_____

_____

_____

_____

_____

_____

_____

_____

_____

Investigate, Inquire, and Imagine

RECALL: GATHER FACTS
1a. What crime have the widow's three sons committed? What punishment are they to receive?

→ INTERPRET: FIND MEANING
1b. Does the punishment fit the crime? Explain your answer.

ANALYZE: TAKE THINGS APART
2a. Analyze the reactions Robin Hood receives when he asks about the fate of the three men. What do people think of this punishment?

→ SYNTHESIZE: BRING THINGS TOGETHER
2b. What do the punishment and people's reactions to it tell you about the sheriff and his power?

EVALUATE: MAKE JUDGMENTS
3a. Evaluate the relationship between Robin Hood and his men. What is each willing to do for the other?

→ EXTEND: CONNECT IDEAS
3b. Identify one or more relationships outside of the story that are similar to that of Robin Hood and his men. Explain why you think the relationships are similar.

Literary Tools

ORAL TRADITION. An **oral tradition** is a body of works that are passed by word of mouth over generations. Stories of Robin Hood have circulated for hundreds of years. No one is certain whether Robin Hood was a real person, but he might have been. These types of stories are called *legends*. Why do you think Robin Hood is a popular legendary figure?

_____

_____

_____

_____

_____

WordWorkshop

SYNONYMS. **Synonyms** are words that have the same or similar meanings. For each of the vocabulary words below, write a synonym. For some vocabulary words you may need to use more than one word or a contraction.

1. earnest: _____

2. 'twas: _____

3. ponder: _____

4. 'tis: _____

5. halt: _____

Read-Write Connection

If you were one of the three men, what would you say to Robin the next time you saw him?

_____

_____

_____

_____

Beyond the Reading

READ OTHER LEGENDS. There are many legends about Robin Hood and his men. Find other stories to read and enjoy. After you have met some of the other characters of the legends and read more about Robin's heroic deeds, write your own story about Robin Hood and his merry men.

GO ONLINE. To find links and additional activities for this selection, visit the EMC Internet Resource Center at **emcp.com/languagearts** and click on Write-In Reader.

Reader's resource

A **fairy tale** is a type of European folk tale containing supernatural events and imaginary creatures such as magicians, ogres, dragons, elves, or leprechauns. Most fairy tales deal with people who have magical experiences. Often they are affected by charms, potions, or spells. Although fairy tales are often told to entertain children, many were written for adults. Today, some psychologists use fairy tales to interpret and examine deep fears and desires. John Gardner, the author of **"Dragon, Dragon,"** often pokes fun at old-fashioned fairy tales.

Word watch

PREVIEW VOCABULARY

crane	plague
lunge	ravage

Reader's journal

What is the best way to slay a dragon?

_____

_____

_____

_____

_____

"Dragon, Dragon"
by John Gardner

Active READING STRATEGY

MAKE PREDICTIONS

Before Reading ▶ **MAKE YOUR FIRST PREDICTION**

❑ Read the title and skim each page of this selection, reading any text that catches your eye.

❑ Read the Reader's Resource and respond to the Reader's Journal question.

❑ Preview the Prediction Chart below. A prediction is a guess about something that will happen in the future. In the left column of the chart, you will write down predictions about what you think will happen in this story. In the right column, you will record where you are in the text when you make each prediction.

❑ Think about what you know about fairy tales and what you learned from the Reader's Resource. Consider what you know about this selection so far. Then make a prediction about what will happen in the story. Write that prediction in the left column of the Prediction Chart. In the right column, write "before reading."

Graphic Organizer: Prediction Chart

Prediction	Stopping Point

Dragon, Dragon

John Gardner

During Reading

COMPLETE THE PREDICTION CHART

❑ Listen as your teacher reads lines 1–110 aloud. When your teacher stops reading, write in your chart a new prediction about what will happen.

❑ Read to the big "N" on page 155. Write down a prediction about what will happen next. Then finish the story, stopping at least one more time to make a prediction.

There was once a king whose kingdom was <u>plagued</u> by a dragon. The king did not know which way to turn. The king's knights were all cowards who hid under their beds whenever the dragon came in sight, so they were of no use to the king at all. And the king's wizard could not help either because, being old, he had forgotten his magic spells. Nor could the wizard look up the spells that had slipped his mind, for he had unfortunately misplaced his wizard's book many years before. The king was at his wit's end.

10   Every time there was a full moon the dragon came out of his lair and <u>ravaged</u> the countryside. He frightened maidens and stopped up chimneys and broke store windows and set people's clocks back and made dogs bark until no one could hear himself think.

    He tipped over fences and robbed graves and put frogs in people's drinking water and tore the last chapters out of novels and changed house numbers around so that people crawled into bed with their neighbors' wives.

    He stole spark plugs out of people's cars and put 20   firecrackers in people's cigars and stole the clappers from all the church bells and sprung every bear trap for miles around so the bears could wander wherever they pleased.

    And to top it all off, he changed around all the roads in

NOTE THE FACTS

Why are the king's knights of no use to the king at all?

_____

_____

_____

Reading **STRATEGY REVIEW**

CONNECT TO PRIOR KNOWLEDGE. Consider what you know about dragons. How is this dragon's way of "ravaging" the kingdom unusual? What kind of tone, or attitude, does this behavior create? Is it serious or humorous? heavy or lighthearted?

_____

_____

words for everyday use	**plague** (plāg′) v., cause to suffer from disease or disaster. *Locusts <u>plagued</u> our wheat last year.* **rav • age** (rav′ ij) v., wreak havoc on. *The bear <u>ravaged</u> our garbage bins every weekend.*

the kingdom so that people could not get anywhere except by starting out in the wrong direction.

"That," said the king in a fury, "is enough!" And he called a meeting of everyone in the kingdom.

Now it happened that there lived in the kingdom a wise old cobbler who had a wife and three sons. The cobbler

30 and his family came to the king's meeting and stood way in back by the door, for the cobbler had a feeling that since he was nobody important there had probably been some mistake, and no doubt the king had intended the meeting for everyone in the kingdom except his family and him.

"Ladies and gentlemen," said the king when everyone was present, "I've put up with that dragon as long as I can. He has got to be stopped."

All the people whispered amongst themselves, and the king smiled, pleased with the impression he had made.

40 But the wise cobbler said gloomily, "It's all very well to talk about it—but how are you going to do it?"

And now all the people smiled and winked as if to say, "Well, King, he's got you there!"

The king frowned.

"It's not that His Majesty hasn't tried," the queen spoke up loyally.

"Yes," said the king, "I've told my knights again and again that they ought to slay that dragon. But I can't *force* them to go. I'm not a tyrant."

50 "Why doesn't the wizard say a magic spell?" asked the cobbler.

"He's done the best he can," said the king.

The wizard blushed and everyone looked embarrassed. "I used to do all sorts of spells and chants when I was younger," the wizard explained. "But I've lost my spell book, and I begin to fear I'm losing my memory too. For instance, I've been trying for days to recall one spell I used to do. I forget, just now, what the deuce it was for. It went something like—

60 *Bimble,*
Wimble,
Cha, Cha
CHOOMPF!"

Suddenly, to everyone's surprise, the queen turned into a rosebush.

"Oh dear," said the wizard.

"Now you've done it," groaned the king.

"Poor Mother," said the princess.

"I don't know what can have happened," the wizard said
nervously, "but don't worry, I'll have her changed back in a
jiffy." He shut his eyes and racked his brain for a spell that
would change her back.

But the king said quickly, "You'd better leave well enough
alone. If you change her into a rattlesnake we'll have to
chop off her head."

Meanwhile the cobbler stood with his hands in his pockets,
sighing at the waste of time. "About the dragon . . ." he
began.

"Oh yes," said the king. "I'll tell you what I'll do. I'll give
the princess' hand in marriage to anyone who can make the
dragon stop."

"It's not enough," said the cobbler. "She's a nice enough
girl, you understand. But how would an ordinary person
support her? Also, what about those of us that are already
married?"

"In that case," said the king, "I'll offer the princess' hand
or half the kingdom or both—whichever is most
convenient."

The cobbler scratched his chin and considered it.

"It's not enough," he said at last. "It's a good enough
kingdom, you understand, but it's too much responsibility."

"Take it or leave it," the king said.

"I'll leave it," said the cobbler. And he shrugged and went
home.

But the cobbler's eldest son thought the bargain was a
good one, for the princess was very beautiful and he liked
the idea of having half the kingdom to run as he pleased. So
he said to the king, "I'll accept those terms, Your Majesty.
By tomorrow morning the dragon will be slain."

"Bless you!" cried the king.

"Hooray, hooray, hooray!" cried all the people, throwing
their hats in the air.

The cobbler's eldest son beamed with pride, and the
second eldest looked at him enviously. The youngest son

NOTE THE FACTS

What does the king offer
to anyone who can make
the dragon stop? Who
accepts this offer?

_____

_____

_____

said timidly, "Excuse me, Your Majesty, but don't you think the queen looks a little unwell? If I were you I think I'd water her."

"Good heavens," cried the king, glancing at the queen who had been changed into a rosebush, "I'm glad you mentioned it!"

110

Now the cobbler's eldest son was very clever and was known far and wide for how quickly he could multiply fractions in his head. He was perfectly sure he could slay the dragon by somehow or other playing a trick on him, and he didn't feel that he needed his wise old father's advice. But he thought it was only polite to ask, and so he went to his father, who was working as usual at his cobbler's bench, and said, "Well, Father, I'm off to slay the dragon. Have you any advice to give me?"

120

The cobbler thought a moment and replied, "When and if you come to the dragon's lair, recite the following poem.

Dragon, dragon, how do you do? I've come from the king to murder you.

Say it very loudly and firmly and the dragon will fall, God willing, at your feet."

"How curious!" said the eldest son. And he thought to himself, "The old man is not as wise as I thought. If I say something like that to the dragon, he will eat me up in an instant. The way to kill a dragon is to out-fox him." And

130

keeping his opinion to himself, the eldest son set forth on his quest.

When he came at last to the dragon's lair, which was a cave, the eldest son slyly disguised himself as a peddler and knocked on the door and called out, "Hello there!"

"There's nobody home!" roared a voice.

The voice was as loud as an earthquake, and the eldest son's knees knocked together in terror.

"I don't come to trouble you," the eldest son said meekly. "I merely thought you might be interested in looking at

140

some of our brushes. Or if you'd prefer," he added quickly, "I could leave our catalogue with you and I could drop by again, say, early next week."

READ ALOUD

Read lines 120–131 aloud. Speak the lines as you imagine the characters and narrator would speak them.

THINK AND REFLECT

How good do you think the cobbler's advice is? **(Evaluate)** Do you think his son will follow his advice? **(Extend)**

_____

_____

_____

"I don't want any brushes," the voice roared, "and I especially don't want any brushes next week."

"Oh," said the eldest son. By now his knees were knocking together so badly that he had to sit down.

Suddenly a great shadow fell over him, and the eldest son looked up. It was the dragon. The eldest son drew his sword, but the dragon <u>lunged</u> and swallowed him in a single gulp, sword and all, and the eldest son found himself in the dark of the dragon's belly. "What a fool I was not to listen to my wise old father!" thought the eldest son. And he began to weep bitterly.

"Well," sighed the king the next morning, "I see the dragon has not been slain yet."

"I'm just as glad, personally," said the princess, sprinkling the queen. "I would have had to marry that eldest son, and he had warts."

150

Now the cobbler's middle son decided it was his turn to try. The middle son was very strong and was known far and wide for being able to lift up the corner of a church. He felt perfectly sure he could slay the dragon by simply laying into him, but he thought it would be only polite to ask his father's advice. So he went to his father and said to him, "Well, Father, I'm off to slay the dragon. Have you any advice for me?"

The cobbler told the middle son exactly what he'd told the eldest.

"When and if you come to the dragon's lair, recite the following poem.

170

Dragon, dragon, how do you do? I've come from the king to murder you.

Say it very loudly and firmly, and the dragon will fall, God willing, at your feet."

"What an odd thing to say," thought the middle son.

160

words
for
everyday
use

lunge (lunj′) *v.*, thrust or lean forward suddenly. *The baserunner <u>lunged</u> toward home plate.*

FIX-UP IDEA

Ask a Question
If you have trouble making predictions, write down a question that you have about the story instead. Ask your teacher or a friend your question. Then try again to make a prediction.

Use THE STRATEGY

MAKE PREDICTIONS. How successful do you think the middle son will be with the dragon? Write your answer in the Prediction Chart.

"The old man is not as wise as I thought. You have to take these dragons by surprise." But he kept his opinion to himself and set forth.

When he came in sight of the dragon's lair, the middle son spurred his horse to a gallop and thundered into the entrance swinging his sword with all his might.

But the dragon had seen him while he was still a long way off, and being very clever, the dragon had crawled up on top of the door so that when the son came charging in he went under the dragon and on to the back of the cave and slammed into the wall. Then the dragon chuckled and got down off the door, taking his time, and strolled back to where the man and the horse lay unconscious from the terrific blow. Opening his mouth as if for a yawn, the dragon swallowed the middle son in a single gulp and put the horse in the freezer to eat another day.

"What a fool I was not to listen to my wise old father," thought the middle son when he came to in the dragon's belly. And he too began to weep bitterly.

That night there was a full moon, and the dragon ravaged the countryside so terribly that several families moved to another kingdom.

"Well," sighed the king in the morning, "still no luck in this dragon business, I see."

"I'm just as glad, myself," said the princess, moving her mother, pot and all, to the window where the sun could get at her. "The cobbler's middle son was a kind of humpback."

Now the cobbler's youngest son saw that his turn had come. He was very upset and nervous, and he wished he had never been born. He was not clever, like his eldest brother, and he was not strong, like his second eldest brother. He was a decent, honest boy who always minded his elders.

He borrowed a suit of armor from a friend of his who was a knight, and when the youngest son put the armor on it was so heavy he could hardly walk. From another knight he borrowed a sword, and that was so heavy that the only way the youngest son could get it to the dragon's lair was to drag it along behind his horse like a plow.

When everything was in readiness, the youngest son went for a last conversation with his father.

Use **THE STRATEGY**

MAKE PREDICTIONS. What advice do you think the cobbler will give his youngest son? Write your answer in your Prediction Chart.

"Father, have you any advice to give me?" he asked.

"Only this," said the cobbler. "When and if you come to the dragon's lair, recite the following poem.

220

Dragon, dragon, how do you do? I've come from the king to murder you.

Say it very loudly and firmly, and the dragon will fall, God willing, at your feet."

"Are you certain?" asked the youngest son uneasily.

"As certain as one can ever be in these matters," said the wise old cobbler.

And so the youngest son set forth on his quest. He traveled over hill and dale and at last came to the dragon's cave.

230

The dragon, who had seen the cobbler's youngest son while he was still a long way off, was seated up above the door, inside the cave, waiting and smiling to himself. But minutes passed and no one came thundering in. The dragon frowned, puzzled, and was tempted to peek out. However, reflecting that patience seldom goes unrewarded, the dragon kept his head up out of sight and went on waiting. At last, when he could stand it no longer, the dragon <u>craned</u> his neck and looked. There at the entrance of the cave stood a trembling young man in a suit of armor twice his size, struggling with a sword so heavy he could lift

240

only one end of it at a time. At sight of the dragon, the cobbler's youngest son began to tremble so violently that his armor rattled like a house caving in. He heaved with all his might at the sword and got the handle up level with his chest, but even now the point was down in the dirt. As loudly and firmly as he could manage, the youngest son cried—

Dragon, dragon, how do you do?
I've come from the king to murder you!

DRAW A PICTURE

words for everyday use	**crane** (krān') *v.*, stretch (the neck) toward an object of attention. *Sylvia <u>craned</u> her neck to see the horses in the parade.*

250 "What?" cried the dragon, flabbergasted. "You? _You?_ Murder _Me???_" All at once he began to laugh, pointing at the little cobbler's son. "_He he he ho ha!_" he roared, shaking all over, and tears filled his eyes. "_He he he ho ho ho ha ha!_" laughed the dragon. He was laughing so hard he had to hang onto his sides, and he fell off the door and landed on his back, still laughing, kicking his legs helplessly, rolling from side to side, laughing and laughing and laughing.

The cobbler's son was annoyed. "I _do_ come from the king to murder you," he said. "A person doesn't like to be laughed at for a thing like that."

260 "_He he he!_" wailed the dragon, almost sobbing, gasping for breath. "Of course not, poor dear boy! But really, _he he_, the _idea_ of it, _ha ha ha!_ And that simply _ridiculous poem!_" Tears streamed from the dragon's eyes and he lay on his back perfectly helpless with laughter.

"It's a good poem," said the cobbler's youngest son loyally. "My father made it up." And growing angrier he shouted, "I want you to stop that laughing, or I'll—I'll—" But the dragon could not stop for the life of him. And suddenly, in a terrific rage, the cobbler's son began flopping

270 the sword end over end in the direction of the dragon. Sweat ran off the youngest son's forehead, but he labored on, blistering mad, and at last, with one supreme heave, he had the sword standing on its handle a foot from the dragon's throat. Of its own weight the sword fell, slicing the dragon's head off.

"_He he ho huk_," went the dragon—and then he lay dead.

The two older brothers crawled out and thanked their younger brother for saving their lives. "We have learned our lesson," they said.

280 Then the three brothers gathered all the treasures from the dragon's cave and tied them to the back end of the youngest brother's horse, and tied the dragon's head on behind the treasures, and started home. "I'm glad I listened to my father," the youngest son thought. "Now I'll be the richest man in the kingdom."

There were hand-carved picture frames and silver spoons and boxes of jewels and chests of money and silver compasses and maps telling where there were more treasures buried when these ran out. There was also a

290 curious old book with a picture of an owl on the cover, and inside, poems and odd sentences and recipes that seemed to make no sense.

When they reached the king's castle the people all leaped for joy to see that the dragon was dead, and the princess ran out and kissed the youngest brother on the forehead, for secretly she had hoped it would be him.

"Well," said the king, "which half of the kingdom do you want?"

300 "My wizard's book!" exclaimed the wizard. "He's found my wizard's book!" He opened the book and ran his finger along under the words and then said in a loud voice, "Glmuzk, shkzmlp, blam!"

Instantly the queen stood before them in her natural shape, except she was soaking wet from being sprinkled too often. She glared at the king.

"Oh dear," said the king, hurrying toward the door. ■

WHAT DO YOU
WONDER?

_____

_____

_____

Reflect ON YOUR READING

❑ Put a check mark next to each prediction you made that turned out to be correct.

❑ What clues in the fairy tale helped you make predictions? Think about what you already knew about fairy tales before you read this story. How did that knowledge help you guess what would happen?

_____

_____

Reading Skills and Test Practice

COMPARE AND CONTRAST

READ, THINK, AND EXPLAIN. Discuss with a partner how best to answer the following questions about comparing and contrasting. Use the Think-Aloud Notes to write down your ideas before drafting your answers.

1. Compare the two older brothers to the youngest brother. How is the youngest son different? Use details from the story in your answer.

_____

_____

_____

_____

2. Compare and contrast the dragon's behavior in this fairy tale to the behavior of other dragons you've heard about. Use details from the story in your answer.

_____

_____

_____

_____

REFLECT ON YOUR RESPONSE. How did using the reading strategy help you to answer the questions?

_____

_____

THINK-ALOUD NOTES

_____
_____
_____
_____
_____
_____
_____
_____
_____
_____
_____
_____

Investigate, Inquire, and Imagine

RECALL: GATHER FACTS
1a. How does the cobbler react to the king's offer to the person who can stop the dragon?

INTERPRET: FIND MEANING
1b. Why do you think the cobbler reacts this way while his sons decide to accept the offer? Why doesn't the cobbler follow his own advice and kill the dragon? What does this tell you about the cobbler?

ANALYZE: TAKE THINGS APART
2a. Compare and contrast the characters in this story to the same kinds of characters in traditional fairy tales. How are the knights in this tale different from the knights in traditional tales? How is the wizard different? the dragon?

SYNTHESIZE: BRING THINGS TOGETHER
2b. Why do you think Gardner has decided to present his characters this way? How is this related to who eventually kills the dragon?

EVALUATE: MAKE JUDGMENTS
3a. Examine reasons why the cobbler's two older sons refuse to follow their father's advice. What kind of people do you think they are? How is the youngest son different from his brothers?

EXTEND: CONNECT IDEAS
3b. What point might the author be trying to make by having the two oldest sons disobey their father? What do you think the two oldest sons said to their father when they got home?

Literary Tools

CHARACTERIZATION. Characterization is the act of creating or describing a character. Writers use three major techniques to create a character: they show what a character says, does, and thinks; they show what other characters say about him or her; and they describe the character's appearance, clothing, and personality. In the graphic organizer below, write down words that describe each of the characters in this story.

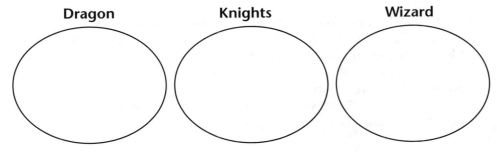

Dragon   **Knights**   **Wizard**

What details does the author give to describe the youngest son of the cobbler? In what way is this son an unusual hero?

WordWorkshop

SPELLING AND PRONUNCIATION. Sometimes studying a list of similar words can help you improve your spelling. Review the following list of words from "Dragon, Dragon":

change	dragon
challenge	plague
courage	disguise
lunge	flabbergasted
ravage	catalogue

1. With what sound does each word in the first column end? How is this sound spelled?

2. List three additional words that end in this same sound.

3. How is *plague* pronounced? How is the *g* sound in the rest of the words from the second column pronounced?

4. Use these examples to write down a spelling rule about how to spell the two *g* sounds.

5. List three additional words that could be added to the second column above.

Read-Write Connection

Would this story have been different if the cobbler had had three daughters rather than three sons? Why, or why not?

_____

_____

_____

Beyond the Reading

DISCOVER FAIRY TALE PATTERNS. Read at least five more fairy tales. Then create a chart of fairy tale characteristics. Start by listing elements shared by at least three of the six fairy tales you have read. For example, maybe four of the tales featured members of a royal family. Maybe three tales started with the words "Once upon a time." List as many shared elements as you can. Then write a paragraph describing common features of fairy tales. Use details from your reading to support your ideas.

GO ONLINE. To find links and additional activities for this selection, visit the EMC Internet Resource Center at **emcp.com/languagearts** and click on Write-In Reader.

"The Twelve Labors of Hercules"

by Walker Brents

Active READING STRATEGY

TACKLE DIFFICULT VOCABULARY

Before Reading ➤ **PREVIEW VOCABULARY WORDS**

❑ Read the Reader's Resource and respond to the Reader's Journal question.

❑ With your class, review ways to unlock the meaning of words you don't know. Talk about how and when to use word parts, context clues, and the dictionary.

❑ In the Word Association Chart below, write each vocabulary word that appears in the WordWatch section to the right. (If you run out of room, copy the chart onto your own paper.) Then, in the next column, write down anything you know about the word already. For example, you might remember having heard the word in a particular context, or you might recognize one of the word parts.

❑ Read the definition and contextual sentence for each word. Record the definition in the third column. As you read, you will use the last column to record details about the context in which the word appears.

Graphic Organizer: Word Association Chart

Word	Prior Associations	Definition	New Associations

CONNECT

Reader's resource

"The Twelve Labors of Hercules" is a myth, or story that explains objects or events in the natural world. This myth comes from ancient Greece. Around 1200 BC, the Greeks developed a system of beliefs in a group of gods and goddesses called the Olympians. Stories about these gods and goddesses were first written down around 500 BC. One of the stories has to do with a half-god named Herakles, who is often called by his Roman name, Hercules. Herakles was the son of Zeus and a human named Alcmena. Hera, the wife of Zeus, was jealous of Alcmena. As you will see, that jealousy has a big effect on Hercules's life.

Word watch

PREVIEW VOCABULARY

assent	foliage
composure	iridescent
confluence	lair
dank	protrude
derange	remorse
divert	semblance
expiate	serene

Reader's journal

Think of a time when you did something that you later regretted. What did you do to make up for your mistake?

NOTE THE FACTS

What drives Hercules to visit the oracle? What advice does he get there?

_____

_____

_____

The Twelve Labors of HERCULES

Walker Brents

The goddess Hera hated Hercules from the moment of his birth. In his infancy she sent two giant serpents to kill him as he slept, but Hercules strangled them instead. His parents rushed into the room to find the baby shaking the dead bodies of the snakes as if they were rattles. This was an early indication of his great strength, but this strength was not always used well.

Once Hera sent madness and insanity into the consciousness of Hercules. His thoughts became scrambled. Under the delusion[1] that he was at war, he mistook his nephews and nieces for enemies, and killed them. When the madness passed and he saw what he had done he was overwhelmed with grief and guilt. Terrible <u>remorse</u> drove him to the oracle[2] of the god Apollo at Delphi, and he asked the priestesses there what he could do to <u>expiate</u> his terrible deed. They told him, "Go to King Eurystheus, and undertake the labors he will put upon you."

Hercules went to Tiryns, the land ruled by King Eurystheus.

10

---

1. **delusion.** Lasting false belief
2. **oracle.** Shrine where a god shares knowledge

words for everyday use	re • morse (ri mors') *n.*, gnawing distress over guilt. *Marta felt growing <u>remorse</u> over having lied to her mother.* ex • pi • ate (ek' spē āt) *v.*, make amends for. *Gina hoped the peace offering would <u>expiate</u> her wrongdoings.*

He stood before the throne. Eurystheus said to him, "Go to
20 Nemea, where a fierce lion terrorizes the people. No weapon
can pierce through its terrible skin. Kill this lion, remove its
skin, carry it here and show it to me." Eurystheus was shrewd,
calculating, cunning, and cowardly. Each task he was to set
before Hercules was designed to be impossible, but the
determination of Hercules was to overcome the impossible.
He followed the lion's tracks to a deep dark cave hidden in a
hillside. He saw the bones strewn at the cave's entrance, and
entered in. In such a darkness he could not see his hand before
his face, the <u>dank</u> air was filled with the smell of blood. The
30 lion had just killed, and had carried its prey to this place which
was its very den. Hercules leapt upon the lion and wrestled
with it. His tremendous club and sharp knife were of no use,
for the lion's hide was too thick. Hercules grasped the lion's
neck with his hands, and held it against the cave wall until the
lion's thrashings ceased, and it was dead. Then he dragged the
lion into the light of day, skinning it with one of its own claws.
He draped the skin over his shoulders, its head over his head
like a helmet, and hurried back to the palace of King
Eurystheus, who saw him approach from a distance and was so
40 frightened at the sight that he hid in a giant olive jar. He sent
his servants to Hercules to tell him of the next task. "Go to
the swamp of Lerna and defeat the hydra,[3] who lives at the
<u>confluence</u> of the three springs."

Hercules and one of his surviving nephews, Iolaus, found
the monster in the depths of the swamp, at the confluence of
three springs. Hercules shot his arrows at the monster so as
to anger it enough to attack, and come close enough for him
to fight it with his oaken club. The monster had nine heads,
and came toward them screaming with rage, belching great
50 gouts[4] of poison bloody mud. Hercules began to knock off
the creature's heads, but saw that three heads grew back from
where one was knocked off! Iolaus lit the branch of a tree

---

3. **hydra.** Serpent monster with regrowable heads
4. **gouts.** Masses of fluid

<table>
<tr><td>words
for
everyday
use</td><td>dank (daŋk') adj., unpleasantly moist. The <u>dank</u>, dark basement smelled like mildew.
con • flu • ence (kän' flü əns) n., a coming together or gathering. The meeting
resulted in a confluence of ideas about how the organization's research should
continue.</td></tr>
</table>

As you read this selection,
underline or highlight each of
the twelve tasks Eurystheus
assigns Hercules.

Reading STRATEGY
REVIEW

VISUALIZE. Picture what
Hercules looks like as he
heads back to King
Eurystheus's castle. Why is
the king frightened by the
sight of Hercules?

_____

_____

with fire, and held this torch against the neck-stubs where Hercules knocked the heads off. The burnt blood prevented the heads from growing back. With this the tide of the battle turned. The creature was weakening. Finally, Hercules tore off the central head, the primary one. He carried it away and buried it in the ground with a great rock over it, so that it could not rejoin the body and come alive again. Then

60   Hercules dipped his arrow points in the poison blood of the hydra, which lay in pools all around, so as to make them deadly.

Other labors followed, and they took Hercules far and wide. In the forest of Ceryneia he chased a deer with golden antlers for an entire year, caught it and carried it alive to King Eurystheus, then returned to Ceryneia and let the deer go. Earlier, he had gone to the land of King Augeias, who kept a stable filled with thousands upon thousands of cattle, which had never been cleaned. Eurystheus, gleefully imagining

70   Hercules carrying baskets and baskets of dung, had ordered him to clean those stables. But Hercules <u>diverted</u> the course of two rivers and sent them through the stables so that they were entirely cleaned in one day.

On Mount Erymanthus there lived a great boar. Searching amid the lower slopes of this mountain Hercules met an old friend of his, Pholos the centaur,[5] who lived in a village of centaurs. Hercules shared a meal with his friend, but accidentally spilled a drop or two of wine upon the ground. The smell of the wine drove the centaurs insane, and they

80   attacked Hercules, who responded with a volley of arrows tipped with the hydra's poison blood. Many were killed. Pholos was burying their bodies when an arrow came loose from one of them, fell down and pierced the flesh near his hoof. The poison entered his veins and killed him. By this time, Hercules was on the upper part of the mountain hunting for the boar but when he heard of his friend's death

---

5. **centaur.** Creature that is half man and half horse

words for everyday use

di • vert (dī vərt′) v., turn from one course to another. *Father <u>diverted</u> the conversation from football to homework.*

he returned to the centaur village and in great sadness helped
with the funeral. But he had made enemies with some of the
centaurs, and one of them, Nessus, swore revenge. Hercules
90 returned to the hunt for the boar and chased it into deep
snowdrifts, where he caught it. After that he went to the land
of Thrace and fought against Diomedes, killing him and his
man-eating horses.

Another labor brought Hercules to the marshes of
Stymphalus. Somewhere in these vast marshes there lived
grotesque vicious birds that shot their feathers like arrows
into people. Then they tore the people into pieces and
carried their chunks of flesh away into the marshes where
they devoured them. No one could get to the place from
100 which they came. Hercules came very close to their <u>lair</u>, but
not close enough. The <u>foliage</u> was so thick not even he could
hack through it with his sword, so that his forward motion
was stopped, and he sat upon the ground in despair. Here an
ally came to him, the goddess Athena. She helped him. She
caused a set of brazen cymbals to appear upon the ground
next to his feet, and spoke these words into his consciousness:
"Strike the cymbals together. The sound of their brassy
clashing will startle the birds from their branches and nests.
They will fly into the air and become targets for your
110 arrows." Hercules followed her instructions. As fast as the
birds flew up his arrows pierced them. Most were killed and
those who lived flew away and never returned.

He came to Themiscyra, where the river Thermodon
flowed into the sea, in a place of many cliffs and rocky hiding
places. This was the land of the Amazons, woman-warriors,
whose queen, Hippolyte, had a sword-belt made of bronze
and <u>iridescent</u> glass, given to her by the god of war, Ares.
Hercules was to take this belt from them. Expecting a battle,
he was surprised when Hippolyte gave it to him freely, but
120 outside their meeting place, the goddess Hera filled the
minds of the Amazons with rumors of war, so that as

| words for everyday use | **lair** (lār') *n.*, resting place. *The boy accidentally wandered up to the bear's <u>lair</u>.*
fo • li • age (fō' lē ij) *n.*, leaves, flowers, and branches. *Mrs. Simms trimmed the <u>foliage</u> in her yard with a hedge clipper.*
ir • i • des • cent (ir ə des' ənt) *adj.*, showing a play of colors that produces rainbow effects. *The <u>iridescent</u> bubbles floated upward.* |

Literary **TOOLS**

CHRONOLOGICAL ORDER. Events arranged in the order of the time when they happened are said to be in **chronological order**. As you read, underline or highlight the tasks Hercules completes for Eurystheus. Also mark other events that seem important.

FIX-UP IDEA

Retell
If you are having trouble understanding this selection because of the vocabulary or other difficulty considerations, try stopping after each paragraph and retelling what just happened. Work with your partner to fill in the details until you can retell the paragraph accurately and thoroughly. Then move on to the next paragraph.

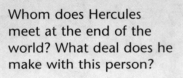

THINK AND REFLECT

How does Hera's behavior here relate to her behavior at the beginning of this myth? How do the arrows Hercules uses link this part of the story to another episode in the story? **(Synthesize)**

_____

_____

_____

NOTE THE FACTS

Whom does Hercules meet at the end of the world? What deal does he make with this person?

_____

_____

THINK AND REFLECT

How is the name of the person Hercules meets related to a common word in the English language? **(Extend)** If you were Hercules, would you trust Atlas to deliver the apples? Why, or why not? **(Evaluate)**

_____

_____

Hercules left he was suddenly attacked by battalions of Amazons. Once more his poison arrows did their deadly work, and, with the belt, he made his escape.

In Crete he carried away the bull Poseidon gave to King Minos. On the island of Erytheia, he killed Geryon, a giant man-monster with one head and three bodies, and his two-headed dog, Orthrus. He took the herd of cattle they guarded—cattle whose hides were red as the rays of the

130 setting sun. Helios the sun-god caused a floating golden cup to appear in the sea, and Hercules drove the bull of Crete and the red cattle onto this cup and floated back to Tiryns.

"Your next to last task requires that you find the garden beyond the world. There, in the Garden of the Hesperides, grow the golden apples upon the branches of a tree guarded by the serpent that never sleeps. Bring back those apples." Hercules had no sooner heard these orders than he was off. At the world's edge he met Atlas, the giant who holds up the sky. "The three sisters who live there are my own daughters.

140 Let me bring back the apples. I am the only one they will let have them. But you must hold up the sky while I am gone." So Atlas said as he waited for Hercules to climb atop the high mountain preparatory to taking upon himself the burden of the sky. Once the load was transferred, Hercules stood with the sky upon his back, watching Atlas stride away, already waist-deep in the ocean that encircles the world. Some few moments, hours, days, or months later Atlas returned, holding a branch with three golden apples. "Let me take the apples back to Eurystheus. You go on

150 holding up the sky, for I am tired of it." Atlas was getting ready to go when Hercules said, "Friend, let me do just one thing before you're off. That lion's skin lying there—I carry it with me wherever I go. It would make a good pad to cushion my shoulders against this mighty burden. Kindly take up the sky again for a moment as I gather it up. Then you can return the load to me." Atlas agreed to do so, but once the sky was returned to his keeping Hercules took the branch and walked away, ignoring Atlas' angry cries for him to return.

160 The final labor required Hercules to go down to the world of the dead and bring back Cerberus, the fierce three-headed dog. The gods Hermes and Athena met him at the river

between the two worlds and helped him. He carried Cerberus back to Tiryns and showed it to King Eurystheus. The three heads barked at him and bared their teeth, and Eurystheus died of fright.

Hercules had many other adventures besides these twelve labors. He did many terrible things and many wonderful things. His earthly father was Amphitryon, but his father in the skies was Zeus. As time went on, the events in his life brought that to clear realization. Hercules was returning from the land of Calydonia with his bride Deianeira when they were faced with a rain-swollen raging river. Hercules was unconcerned about his own ability to swim across this river, but how Deianeira would cross was another matter. Just then the centaur Nessus approached them. He spoke to them very courteously: "Ah Hercules, I congratulate your marriage. Do you remember me? I am Nessus. I was there in the village at Mount Erymanthos that awful day. It is a wonder your deadly arrows did not kill me, though I was wounded. I apologize on behalf of all us centaurs, for our <u>deranged</u> behavior then. Please allow me to carry Deianeira across this river. I am a most excellent swimmer." Hercules <u>assented</u> to this, and as Nessus clattered down into the water, with Deianeira on his back, he threw his bow and arrows across the water, and vaulted in. Reaching the other side he was startled by cries. He turned and saw Nessus farther down the riverbank crossing onto land, attempting to carry Deianeira away. "Nessus," he uttered as he placed an arrow against the bowstring and drew it back, "haven't you felt enough of the hydra's poison?" With that he let the arrow fly. It pierced Nessus' back as he fled and the point <u>protruded</u> through his chest. Coughing up blood he tumbled to the ground as Deianeira, an experienced rider, rolled free. He staggered up again but lost his footing and fell down the riverbank into the shallow waters, gasping and choking. With his dying words he requested that Deianeira take a few drops of his blood spilled onto the sand and save it. "Let my death keep your

170

180

190

words for everyday use

de • range (di rānj′) v., disturb. *The speaker tried to <u>derange</u> the audience with taunts and threats.* **deranged,** adj.
as • sent (ə sent′) v., agree. *My mother <u>assented</u> to the increase of my allowance.*
pro • trude (prō trüd′) v., stick out. *Cyrano's nose <u>protruded</u> at least six inches from the rest of his face.*

THINK AND REFLECT

What do you think will happen with Hercules's best robe? (Extend)

_____

_____

_____

Use THE STRATEGY

TACKLE DIFFICULT VOCABULARY. Remember to note in your Word Association Chart some key words that will remind you of the scene in which you found the word *semblance*.

200 love strong. Take this blood and rub it into anything your husband wears. My blood is charmed. It will renew his love whenever and wherever he puts such clothes on as have been touched with this blood." He died just before Hercules arrived upon the scene. Deianeira told him nothing about what had been said. Little did either one know of the actual reasons behind Nessus' bequest.[6]

Years later, Hercules went to a distant land and conquered it. He sent a message back home after the final battle was won. "Send me my best robe to wear for the sacrifices I will make to the gods, in gratitude for our victory here." Among 210 the captives that had earlier arrived was a woman, Iole, whose love, once long before, Hercules had tried to win. When Deianeira saw her she was reminded of that time, and began to worry. She resolved to put the blood-charm of Nessus into the robe she would send him. She gave it to the messenger, who carried it to Hercules, waiting upon a high mountain to begin the ceremony.

It was just a few moments after Hercules had donned[7] the robe and begun the sacrifice that the true nature of the charm revealed itself. A terrible burning began to spread through his 220 limbs all the way into his heart. The hydra's blood had returned to the one who had sent it out on so many arrows before. He clutched at the robe to pull it off, but it stuck fast in some places and in others great chunks of skin clung to it as it was torn free, revealing his bones. He screamed in rage and pain, stumbling through the forest, farther up the mountain. At the summit, a <u>semblance</u> of calm came to him, and he began to build his own funeral pyre.[8] When it was finished he commanded someone among those around him to set it alight. No one would. Hercules offered a shepherd's son 230 passing by, Philoctetes, his bow and arrows if he would ignite the pyre. Philoctetes agreed to, and Hercules climbed to its

---

6. **bequest.** Item given by will to another
7. **donned.** Put on
8. **pyre.** Place for burial fire

words for everyday use

sem • blance (sem' bləns) *n.,* appearance, likeness. *Amid the hubbub, the school production showed a <u>semblance</u> of control and calm.*

very top, placed upon it the skin of the Nemean Lion as a blanket, and the oaken club as a pillow, and laid himself down there in a state of <u>serene</u> <u>composure</u>. The torch was lit and handed to Philoctetes, who put it to the bier,[9] which was soon engulfed. As the flames did their work, the earthly form of Hercules disintegrated, but his godly form became more clear. The skies opened up and a chariot came down and took him away. In the heavens, Hera reconciled herself to him, and 240 he took his place amid the company of the gods.

---

9. **bier.** Coffin stand

What happens to Hercules after his death?

_____

_____

words for everyday use

se • rene (sə rēn') *adj.*, calm. *I looked out at the calm beauty of the <u>serene</u> lake.*
com • po • sure (kəm pō' zhər) *n.*, self-controlled mind or appearance. *Horace maintained his <u>composure</u> throughout the stressful day.*

Reflect ON YOUR READING

❑ Review your list of words. With your partner, brainstorm some other situations in which you might use each word. Jot some notes about each situation in the "New Associations" column of your chart.

❑ Use the new words in sentences that describe things that happened in the myth. Illustrate your sentences. Then share the illustrations and sentences with the class.

Reading Skills and Test Practice

ANALYZE WORDS

Discuss with a partner how to analyze the words in the following questions. Use the Think-Aloud Notes to write down your reasons for eliminating the incorrect answers.

_____1. What does the word *engulfed* mean in this sentence?

The torch was lit and handed to Philoctetes, who put it to the bier, which was soon engulfed.

a. betrayed
b. taken away
c. drowned
d. consumed

_____2. Which two words from the myth are most nearly opposite in meaning?
a. deranged, serene
b. serene, composure
c. lair, dank
d. iridescent, foliage

How did using the reading strategy help you to answer the questions?

_____

_____

Investigate, Inquire, and Imagine

RECALL: GATHER FACTS
1a. Why does Hercules go to Tiryns to see King Eurystheus?

→ **INTERPRET: FIND MEANING**
1b. Why does King Eurystheus give orders that are difficult to carry out?

ANALYZE: TAKE THINGS APART
2a. List the twelve labors of Hercules. Then number them according to which you think is most difficult.

→ **SYNTHESIZE: BRING THINGS TOGETHER**
2b. How do you think Hercules feels after accomplishing the twelve labors? How do his actions in life work against him at the end of the story?

EVALUATE: MAKE JUDGMENTS
3a. Who do you think is responsible for Hercules's death—Nessus, Deianeira, Hercules, Hera, or Eurystheus? Explain your answer.

→ **EXTEND: CONNECT IDEAS**
3b. Describe in your own words what kind of mythological figure Hercules is. How would such a person do in today's world?

Literary Tools

CHRONOLOGICAL ORDER. Events arranged in order of the time when they happened are said to be in **chronological order**. This method of organization is used in most stories, whether they are fiction or nonfiction. Use the time line below to put the key events of this myth in chronological order.

Is the chronological order of the twelve labors of any real importance? Which events in the story must be presented in chronological order so that the story makes sense?

_____

_____

_____

_____

WordWorkshop

ANTONYMS. The **antonym** of a word is a word with the opposite meaning. Draw a line from each of the words on the left to the word that is its antonym on the right. If you wish, you may use a dictionary or thesaurus.

assent	arid
cunning	daft
dank	dissent
divert	dull
iridescent	focus
protrude	giddy
serene	sink

Read-Write Connection

If the story of Hercules's twelve labors were set in modern America rather than in ancient Greece, what tasks might the hero be given? Write a list of twelve labors for a modern-day Hercules.

_____   _____

_____   _____

_____   _____

_____   _____

_____   _____

_____

Beyond the Reading

INVESTIGATE GREEK GODS. Research a Greek god or goddess using the Internet or books. Find descriptions of the god's actions, physical appearance, and relationships to other gods. Look for pictures of the god. What stories did he or she play a part in? With what historic events was he or she involved? Prepare a report for your class, including pictures, descriptions, and stories.

GO ONLINE. To find links and additional activities for this selection, visit the EMC Internet Resource Center at **emcp.com/languagearts** and click on Write-In Reader.

"THE COW OF NO COLOR"

by Nina Jaffe and Steve Zeitlin

Active READING STRATEGY

READ WITH A PURPOSE

Before Reading ▶ **PREVIEW**

❑ Read the Reader's Resource. Discuss what a justice tale is.

❑ Your purpose for reading this story will be to determine the aim of the storyteller. A writer or speaker's **aim** is his or her purpose. People may write or speak in order to inform; to tell a story; to reflect; to share a perspective by using art (like fiction or poetry) to entertain, enrich, or enlighten; or to persuade readers or listeners to respond in some way.

❑ Preview the Author's Purpose Chart below. Use what you already know about this story to predict what the storyteller's purpose is for telling it. Write your prediction in the Before Reading section of the chart.

Graphic Organizer: Author's Purpose Chart

Before Reading
Predict the author's purpose by previewing the kind of writing used.

During Reading
Gather ideas that the author communicates to readers.

After Reading
Summarize the ideas the author communicates. Explain how these ideas help fulfill the author's purpose.

CONNECT

Reader's resource

Ghana is a country in Africa. In Ghana, as in many African countries, storytelling is an important part of the culture. It is a way of entertaining and also of passing on history, values, and family traditions. **"The Cow of No Color"** is a type of African folk tale called a **justice tale**. In these tales, a villain is taught a lesson, and the reader is asked to think about what is truly fair in a given situation. Author Nina Jaffe and folklorist Steve Zeitlin have collected such tales in a book called *The Cow of No Color: Riddle Stories and Justice Tales from Around the World.*

Word watch

PREVIEW VOCABULARY

ponder

Reader's journal

Describe a time in your life when you felt you were being asked to do something impossible. How did you feel? What did you do?

_____

_____

_____

_____

GATHER INFORMATION

❑ Read the folk tale silently. As you read, use the chart to take notes about what you think the purpose of the story is. Who is the villain in the story? How is he or she taught a lesson?

❑ Listen as your teacher reads the story aloud. Fill in any additional notes in your chart.

NOTE THE FACTS

How does the chief feel toward the wise woman?

_____

_____

MARK THE TEXT

Underline or highlight the restrictions the chief places on the kind of cow Nunyala should bring him.

THE COW OF NO COLOR

Nina Jaffe and Steve Zeitlin

Once among the Ewe people[1] of Ghana[2] there lived a wise woman named Nunyala. For miles around, people would come to her asking for advice, and she always found a way to help them. Her fame spread till it reached the ears of the chief, who became very jealous. He called her to the palace, and when she appeared, he said to her, through his spokesman:

"I hear you are Nunyala, the wise woman."

"That may be, and that may not be," she replied. "It is
10 what some people say."

"If you are so wise," said the chief, "surely I can ask you to do one simple thing for me."

"If it is simple or not," she replied, "I will do my best."

"All you have to do to prove how wise you are," the chief said to her, "is to bring me a cow."

Nunyala thought to herself: "A cow. That is not difficult. My village is full of cows."

And she was just about to leave when the chief added, "Now listen well. Yes, I wish you to bring me a cow. But
20 this cow cannot be black, and it cannot be white. It cannot

---

1. **Ewe people.** People of southeastern Ghana who make up 13 percent of its total population
2. **Ghana.** West African country (formerly known as Gold Coast) with its southern border along the Gulf of Guinea

be brown, or yellow, or spotted, or striped. In fact, this cow cannot be of any color at all! Bring me a cow of no color in three days' time—or you will be executed[3] without delay!"

Nunyala returned to her village and sat in her hut. She thought to herself: Should I be executed because some people say I am wise as the chief? Should I lose my own life for his jealousy? Is this a wise leader's approach to justice? She had to answer the chief's impossible request, but how?

Nunyala sat and thought for three days and three nights, and at the end of that time, she sent a child from her village to the chief with a message. The chief sat on his stool,[4] waiting to hear what the child had to say. These were his words: "O Chief, Nunyala, the wise woman of our village, has sent me to repeat these words to you. This is her message. She has said, 'I have your cow of no color. It is in my house. You can come and take it.

"'But don't come in the morning. Don't come in the evening. Don't come at dawn. Don't come at twilight. Don't come at midnight. Don't come any time. You can have your cow of no color—at no time at all!'"

The boy turned and left the palace, while the chief sat speechless on his stool, to <u>ponder</u> the words of Nunyala, wise woman of the Ewe. ■

30

40

---

3. **executed.** Put to death
4. **stool.** Seat used in southern Ghana as a symbol of a chief's authority and power

NOTE THE FACTS

When may the chief pick up the cow of no color?

_____

_____

FIX-UP IDEA

Write Things Down
If you are having trouble taking notes, try writing down the story events in order of occurrence.

Reflect ON YOUR READING

After Reading ▶ IDENTIFY THE PURPOSE

❑ Review the notes you took in the Author's Purpose Chart.
❑ Work with a partner to determine the storyteller's purpose for telling this tale. What is the reader supposed to learn? Write your answer in the After Reading section of the Author's Purpose Chart.

Reading Skills and Test Practice

ANALYZE THE AUTHOR'S PURPOSE

Discuss with a partner how best to answer the following questions about main ideas. Use the Think-Aloud Notes to write down your reasons for eliminating the incorrect answers.

____1. The storyteller wants the reader to think that the chief is
  a. dull and boring.
  b. intelligent and resourceful.
  c. insecure and foolish.
  d. wise and all-knowing.

____2. With which statement would the storyteller most likely agree?
  a. Take good care of animals.
  b. Never let your jealousy rule your behavior.
  c. You do not have to get along with bad leaders.
  d. Leaders are always wise.

How did using the reading strategy help you to answer the questions?

_____

_____

_____

THINK-ALOUD
NOTES

_____
_____
_____
_____
_____
_____
_____
_____
_____
_____
_____

Investigate, Inquire, and Imagine

RECALL: GATHER FACTS → INTERPRET: FIND MEANING

1a. When Nunyala appears before the chief, by what means does he speak to her? How does she deliver her response to him?

1b. Why might the chief and Nunyala each have spoken to each other in these ways?

ANALYZE: TAKE THINGS APART → SYNTHESIZE: BRING THINGS TOGETHER

2a. Compare and contrast Nunyala and the chief.

2b. How does Nunyala demonstrate her wisdom? Why is her response wise?

EVALUATE: MAKE JUDGMENTS → EXTEND: CONNECT IDEAS

3a. Do you think the chief in this story is an effective leader? Why, or why not?

3b. What ideas about fairness and justice did you learn from this story? Describe how you could apply these ideas when you encounter unfair situations in the future.

Literary Tools

AIM. A writer's **aim** is his or her purpose, or goal. People may write or speak with the following aims:

❑   to inform (expository/informative writing)
❑   to tell a story, either true or invented, about an event or sequence of events (narrative writing)
❑   to reflect (personal/expressive writing)
❑   to share a perspective by using an artistic medium—such as fiction or poetry—to entertain, enrich, or enlighten (imaginative writing)
❑   to persuade readers or listeners to respond in some way, such as to agree with a position, change a view on an issue, reach an agreement, or perform an action (persuasive/argumentative writing)

Check the box next to the main aim of "The Cow of No Color." Explain in one or two sentences how the story achieves that aim.

_____

_____

_____

_____

WordWorkshop

SEMANTIC FAMILIES. A semantic family is a set of words related by meaning. In small groups, take ten minutes to brainstorm words related to the concept of justice. Consider words that contain the word roots *jus* and *jur*, both of which mean "just." Then think of as many other words about justice, the law, and fairness as you can. Try to think of words that other groups won't think of.

_____   _____

_____   _____

_____   _____

_____   _____

_____   _____

_____   _____

_____   _____

Read-Write Connection

How would you have responded to the chief? Would you have tried to meet his challenge?

_____

_____

_____

_____

_____

Beyond the Reading

READ AFRICAN FOLKLORE. Use books and the Internet to find and read at least five African folktales. Make a list of the values taught through these tales. Then use this list to write a paragraph about some of the values that seem to be important to African cultures.

GO ONLINE. To find links and additional activities for this selection, visit the EMC Internet Resource Center at **emcp.com/languagearts** and click on Write-In Reader.

"Don't Step on a Crack"

by Lila Perl

Active READING STRATEGY

WRITE THINGS DOWN

Before Reading ▶ **PREVIEW THE ARTICLE**

❏ Read the Reader's Resource and respond to the Reader's Journal question.

❏ Help your teacher make a list of superstitions and omens. Do you believe in any of these? Why, or why not? Discuss these questions with your class.

❏ Use the Cause and Effect Chart below to keep track of superstitions discussed in the article. Write the superstition in the first circle. Then write a possible source for that superstition in the second circle. One example has been done for you. You can add more circles to the chart to record other details about each superstition.

Graphic Organizer: Cause and Effect Chart

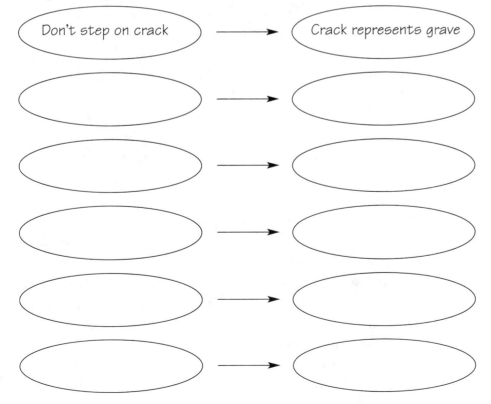

Don't step on crack ⟶ Crack represents grave

CONNECT

Reader's resource

An **oral tradition** consists of works, ideas, or customs of a culture, passed by word of mouth from generation to generation. In addition to folk tales, myths, legends, parables, and other stories, superstitions have long been a part of the oral tradition. Many of the things people today do to ensure good luck or avoid bad luck date back to the Middle Ages (about 500 to 1350). Omens, or signs of things to come, are one kind of superstition. In **"Don't Step on a Crack,"** author Lila Perl explains where many common superstitions might come from.

Reader's journal

What signs mean good luck to you? Which mean bad luck?

_____

_____

_____

_____

_____

_____

_____

KEEP TRACK OF
INFORMATION

❑ Listen as your teacher
reads the first five
paragraphs aloud. Fill in
the second row of your
Cause and Effect Chart.

❑ Take turns with a partner
to read the rest of the
selection, one paragraph
at a time. In your chart,
write down each
superstition and at least
one possible source for it.

Use THE STRATEGY

WRITE THINGS DOWN. What is
one possible source of the
connection between stepping
in a hole and breaking a sugar
bowl? Note your answer in
your Cause and Effect Chart.

Lila Perl

Step on a crack, break your mother's back.
Step in a hole, break your mother's sugar bowl.

Have you ever walked along the sidewalk being very careful not to step on the cracks in the paving? Perhaps the old rhyme above came to mind. Experts who study folklore and folk sayings think that the "crack" represents an opening in the earth that leads to a grave. The "hole" is the grave itself.

Nobody really knows why stepping on a crack should bring bad luck to one's mother rather than some other person. Even worse, the broken back is often interpreted to
10   mean death. And the broken sugar bowl is definitely a bad omen.

From quite early times, it was the custom of some peoples to bury their dead with articles of crockery. But first they would "kill" the "spirit" that lived in the bowl or plate. They did so either by driving an opening through its center or smashing the entire piece to bits. This ancient practice may well be the reason for the connection between a "hole," or grave, and a broken sugar bowl.

Most of us, of course, don't believe in the superstitious
20   rhyme about avoiding cracks and holes. If it were true, we

would all become motherless orphans at a very tender age. Similarly, we say that if we step on an ant, it will rain (possibly as a punishment for having killed an innocent creature). But if every ant or beetle crushed underfoot caused even a drizzle, the Earth would have been flooded eons ago.

One of the real hazards of trying to avoid cracks, holes, and crawling insects when we venture forth is that we may stumble.

30 Stumbling or tripping is supposed to be a dangerous sign. Stumbling as we leave the house is said to be caused by evil spirits who live on our doorstep. Some people think it is a warning not to go any further. We can try, though, to change our luck by doing and saying the following:

I turn myself three times about,
And thus I put bad luck to rout.

That *should* take care of the demons lurking in our
40 doorways. But not always. One reason given for the old custom of the groom carrying his bride across the threshold of their new home is to keep her from tripping. Such an accident would invite bad luck at the very start of their life together. No one, though, ever seems to have given a thought as to what might happen if the heavily burdened groom were to trip!

Sometimes another reason is offered for the bride's being carried over the threshold. It goes way back to the days of "bride capture," when a wife-to-be was stolen from an
50 enemy and carried into the cave or hut of her captor. She was his property from then on.

When it comes to stumbling, theater people are probably the most superstitious of all. Some actors believe that to trip as one walks onto the stage is lucky because it gets the evil happening out of the way. Others say it is a bad sign that will be followed by the actor's missing a cue or forgetting a line.

But stage people never disagree about the danger of wishing one another "good luck" just before they face an
60 audience. They feel these words are a sure invitation for mischievous forces to do their worst. So instead, they say

NOTE THE FACTS

What superstition involves ants?

_____

_____

_____

MARK THE TEXT

Underline or highlight one reason for the custom of carrying a bride across the threshold.

READ ALOUD

Read lines 52–66 aloud. The German phrase, "*Hals und Beinbruch,*" in line 65 is pronounced [häls unt bīnbruk]. Why do German opera singers say this to each other? Why might they choose this particular phrase?

_____

_____

_____

just the opposite: "Break a leg." In the German theater, especially at the opera, performers go a step further. As they are about to set foot on the stage, they tell one another, *"Hals und Beinbruch,"* or 'Break your neck *and* legs!"

In recent times there has been a new theory about stumbling. Human-behavior specialists say it is caused by something in ourselves that does not *want* to go forward. So, if you stumble out of the house some morning on your way to school or work, don't blame the wicked sprites on your doorstep. Your mind may be simply telling your body that it wishes it would go back to bed.

70

Once you *are* out and about, you may encounter even more hazards—for instance, a tall ladder leaning against the side of a building. Few of us will boldly walk under a ladder, for we've always heard that this is bad luck. But why? There is, naturally, the danger that a can of paint, a heavy tool, or some other object may fall on our heads. But there's a less obvious reason for this superstition.

80

In and of themselves, ladders are considered lucky symbols. The ancient Egyptians often placed small ladders in the tombs of their loved ones to help the souls of the dead "climb" heavenward in the afterlife. But a leaning ladder, or even an open stepladder, that forms a triangle with the ground is another matter. The three sides are said to represent the basic family unit, the very means by which life goes on. In the Christian faith, Joseph, Mary, and Jesus are called the "holy family." The much older religion of ancient Egypt had several holy families composed of father, mother, and child. Probably the best known was that of the god Osiris, the goddess Isis, and their son Horus.

90

So, walking under a ladder is said to bring bad luck because passing through the triangle violates the unity of the family. However, if you should unthinkingly find yourself under a ladder, you can still try to save yourself by crossing your fingers or by spitting three times between the rungs. On the other hand, if you decide to go *around* the ladder, be careful when walking out into the traffic. You don't want to invite some other calamity!

100

FIX-UP IDEA

Refocus
If you have trouble identifying a possible source for one of the superstitions, refocus your reading. Read a single paragraph. Then discuss with a partner what the main ideas of that paragraph are. Try to express the important ideas from the paragraph in one or two short sentences. Then determine whether one of those ideas is the source of the superstition.

On a really "unlucky" day, you might not only stumble over your doorstep and walk under a ladder, but a black cat might also cross your path.

Cats were not always thought to be unlucky. The ancient Egyptians worshiped the cat and even had a goddess named Bast who was the patroness of cats. It's quite easy to understand the Egyptian fondness for cats. They were not only house pets, they also hunted and killed the rats and mice that would otherwise have overrun the storehouses in which the Egyptians kept their grain. Cats were often honored in ancient Egypt by being mummified after they died. Thus their bodies were preserved just like those of Egypt's kings and other important people.

In parts of Europe, however, by the time of the Middle Ages, people began to believe that witches could change themselves into cats. So the black cat became a spooky symbol of Halloween. And all black cats came to be feared as witches in disguise!

There are many myths about cats that have probably led to our thinking of them as supernatural creatures. It isn't true, though, that cats can see in complete darkness or that they have nine lives. They do, however, have good coordination and a flexible spine, so they are less likely to hurt themselves in falls and other accidents.

There doesn't seem to be much we can do to counteract the bad omen of seeing a black cat. But it may be a comfort to know that in England black cats are considered lucky, and *white* cats are feared. Some people think this is because of the mummified cats that British archeologists found in ancient Egyptian tombs and brought back to England. All of the "lucky" Egyptian cats were black, as a result of the drying-out process used to make mummies. This left the British with only white cats to worry about!

Certain objects that we are likely to handle almost every day, both inside and outside our houses, are also said to have the power to bring us bad luck. Who hasn't heard that breaking a mirror can lead to seven years of misfortune?

Although breakable glass mirrors probably weren't widely known until around the 1300s, people have long feared having their image shattered. The very first "mirrors" were

110

120

130

140

NOTE THE FACTS

How did black cats become a bad omen?

_____

_____

_____

Literary TOOLS

TONE. Tone is a writer's or speaker's attitude toward the subject or the reader. For example, a writer might use a lighthearted tone when writing about something happy or funny, and a heavier one when writing about something sad. How would you describe the tone of this article?

_____

_____

NOTE THE FACTS

What were the first mirrors?

_____

_____

_____

THINK AND REFLECT

Why might having one's reflection broken up have meant bad luck? **(Interpret)**

_____

_____

_____

NOTE THE FACTS

What danger do mirrors supposedly present for babies?

_____

_____

_____

quiet pools of water. People looked into them, saw their reflection, and believed they were seeing their soul, or life force. If an enemy came by and threw a stone in the pool, the reflection broke up. This meant an evil fate was in store. If the soul was taken away completely, the person would die.

With the increased use of glass mirrors, many new superstitions came along. Some people believed that all mirrors had to be covered in a house where a death had 150 taken place. Otherwise, the soul of the dead person might be caught in the mirror and would not find its way to heaven. A different reason for covering the mirrors was to prevent the mourners from seeing their haggard and tear-stained faces. If they did, they might be tempted to stop weeping for their dead before the mourning period was up.

Some say that a baby should never be held up to a mirror during the first year of its life. Infancy is a time of great danger and the child's soul might be captured by the angel of death or by an evil spirit. The worst fear of all among 160 superstitious people is that they will look into a mirror and not see any reflection at all. This is a sure sign that death is very near.

What about the "seven years of bad luck" said to follow the breaking of a mirror? This superstition probably has something to do with the so-called magical properties of the number seven. One long-held belief is that the cells of the body renew themselves completely every seven years. So, at the end of that period, we are not the same person we were at the beginning. Therefore, we cannot be affected 170 any longer by the "curse" of the broken mirror.

Unfortunately, there is no truth to the seven-year theory about our body cells. There may be another explanation, though, for the penalty we are said to pay for breaking a mirror. When glass mirrors first appeared they were so costly that it might well have taken seven years to save enough money to replace a broken one! ■

Reflect ON YOUR READING

❑ Review your Cause and Effect Chart. Think about the things you learned from this selection.

❑ On the lines below or on your own paper, write a summary of the article for someone who has not read it.

_____

_____

_____

_____

Reading Skills and Test Practice

DETERMINE CAUSE AND EFFECT

Discuss with a partner how best to answer the following questions about cause and effect. Use the Think-Aloud Notes to write down your reasons for eliminating the incorrect answers.

_____1. Read this sentence from the story.

> One of the real hazards of trying to avoid cracks, holes, and crawling insects when we venture forth is that we may stumble.

This sentence tells readers that following superstitions
a. is a normal thing to do.
b. can cause you harm.
c. can keep you out of danger.
d. is not important.

_____2. Black cats are probably considered lucky in England because in England
a. there are more black cats.
b. there are fewer black cats.
c. black mummified cats were highly valued.
d. mummies are an important symbol of Halloween.

How did using the reading strategy help you to answer the questions?

_____

_____

THINK-ALOUD NOTES

_____

_____

_____

_____

_____

_____

_____

_____

_____

_____

_____

_____

Investigate, Inquire, and Imagine

RECALL: GATHER FACTS
1a. What do the three sides of a triangle represent?

INTERPRET: FIND MEANING
1b. How is this meaning related to the superstition about walking under a ladder? Why can you save yourself by crossing your fingers or spitting three times?

ANALYZE: TAKE THINGS APART
2a. How many of the superstitions mentioned deal with bad luck? How many deal with good luck?

SYNTHESIZE: BRING THINGS TOGETHER
2b. What is the purpose of superstitions? Why do people act according to them?

EVALUATE: MAKE JUDGMENTS
3a. Are there good reasons to believe in superstitions? Why, or why not?

EXTEND: CONNECT IDEAS
3b. Have you ever acted in a certain way to avoid bad luck or to bring on good luck? Explain your answer.

Literary Tools

TONE. **Tone** is a writer's or speaker's attitude toward the subject or the reader. For example, a writer might use a lighthearted tone when writing about something happy or funny, and a heavier one when writing about something sad. How does the author of this selection feel about superstitions?

_____

_____

How can you tell?

_____

_____

WordWorkshop

SYNONYMS AND ANTONYMS. Words that have the same or nearly the same meanings are called **synonyms**. **Antonyms** are words with opposite meanings. Write one synonym and one antonym for each word from the selection. Line numbers are included so that you can determine the meaning of the word from context. You may also use a dictionary or thesaurus to help you.

1. superstitious (line 19): _____

2. tender (line 21): _____

3. violate (line 94): _____

4. calamity (line 100): _____

5. counteract (line 125): _____

Read-Write Connection

Think of a superstition that was not included in this selection. Make up a possible origin for this superstitious belief. Later, research its real origin and compare it to your guess.

_____

_____

_____

Beyond the Reading

READ URBAN LEGENDS. New ideas about how to avoid danger are still being developed and spread throughout American culture. One place that happens is in urban legends—exaggerated or made-up stories that are told as true and spread widely, often over e-mail. Locate and read an urban legend by searching the Internet or finding a printed collection. Then share the urban legend you found with your class. Discuss why such stories are so popular and how you can evaluate the truthfulness of such stories when you receive them by e-mail.

GO ONLINE. To find links and additional activities for this selection, visit the EMC Internet Resource Center at **emcp.com/languagearts** and click on Write-In Reader.

Unit 5 READING Review

Choose and Use Reading Strategies

Before reading an excerpt from "The Singing, Springing Lark" by Jacob and Wilhelm Grimm, review with a partner how to use reading strategies with folk literature.

1. Read with a Purpose
2. Connect to Prior Knowledge
3. Write Things Down
4. Make Predictions
5. Visualize
6. Use Text Organization
7. Tackle Difficult Vocabulary
8. Monitor Your Reading Progress

Next, apply at least two of these reading strategies as you read the excerpt below. Use the margins and mark up the text to show how you are using the reading strategies to read actively. You may find it helpful to choose a graphic organizer from Appendix B to gather information as you read the excerpt, or use the Summary Chart on page B-13 to create a graphic organizer that summarizes the excerpt.

Once upon a time there was a man who was about to go on a long journey, and right before his departure he asked his three daughters what he should bring back to them. The oldest wanted pearls, the second, diamonds, but the third said, "Dear Father, I'd like to have a singing, springing lark."

"All right," said the father. "If I can get one, you shall have it."

So he kissed all three daughters good-bye and went on his way. When the time came for his return journey, he had purchased pearls and diamonds for the two oldest, but even though he had looked all over, he had not been able to find the singing, springing lark for his youngest daughter. He was particularly sorry about that because she was his favorite. In the meantime, his way took him through a forest, in the middle of which he discovered a magnificent castle. Near the castle was a tree, and way on top of this tree he saw a lark singing and springing about.

"Well, you've come just at the right time," he said, quite pleased, and he ordered his servant to climb the tree and catch the little bird. But when the servant went over to the tree, a lion jumped out from under it, shook himself, and roared so ferociously that the leaves on the trees trembled.

"If anyone tries to steal my singing, springing lark," he cried, "I'll eat him up."

WordWorkshop

Unit 5 Words for Everyday Use

assent, 169
composure, 171
confluence, 165
crane, 157
dank, 165
derange, 169
divert, 166

earnest, 144
expiate, 164
foliage, 167
iridescent, 167
lair, 167
lunge, 155
plague, 151

ponder, 143, 177
protrude, 169
ravage, 151
remorse, 164
semblance, 170
serene, 171

Context Clues. Choose the word that best completes each of the contextual sentences.

_____1. The tornado ___ the town, toppling trees and ripping roofs off many of the downtown buildings.
  a. protruded
  b. ravaged
  c. expiated
  d. lunged

_____2. The troll retreated into his ___ under the bridge to sleep.
  a. lair
  b. semblance
  c. plague
  d. composure

_____3. The basement is dark and ___ from the moisture that has seeped in over the years.
  a. serene
  b. dank
  c. earnest
  d. iridescent

_____4. It has been six months since Kurt injured his ankle, but it still ___ him when it rains.
  a. assents
  b. deranges
  c. diverts
  d. plagues

_____5. The coach got so excited by the big win that it took him awhile to regain his ___.
  a. composure
  b. foliage
  c. remorse
  d. semblance

Literary Tools

Select the best literary element on the right to complete each sentence on the left. Write the correct letter in the blank.

___ 1. To narrate events in the order in which they occurred is to use ___.

___ 2. The ___ of Robin Hood is accomplished by showing what he says and does, what others think and say about him, and how he looks.

___ 3. The ___ of "Dragon, Dragon" is lighthearted and playful.

___ 4. The ___ of many stories is to share a perspective using an artistic medium in order to enrich, enlighten, or entertain.

___ 5. Stories and beliefs passed down by word of mouth over many generations make up the ___.

a. aim, 179.

b. characterization, 152, 161

c. chronological order, 167, 173

d. oral tradition, 148

e. tone, 185, 188

On Your Own

FLUENTLY SPEAKING. Find a fairy tale, legend, myth, or other work from the oral tradition, and practice reading it aloud. Once you can read it smoothly and without errors, make a tape recording of the story. Use your voice to convey what is happening in the story and how the characters feel.

PICTURE THIS. Choose a character from a folk tale, myth, fairy tale, or legend. Think about what kind of dwelling place would be most fitting for this character. Draw a diagram of the character's home, labeling the placement of important possessions. Be prepared to explain to the class why this is an appropriate home for your character.

PUT IT IN WRITING. Choose a character from a familiar folk tale, myth, fairy tale, or legend. Then imagine that that character were alive today. Write a story about how the character would deal with twenty-first century life.

Unit SIX

READING Drama

DRAMA

A **drama,** or *play*, is a story told through characters played by actors. Early groups of people around the world acted out ritual scenes related to hunting, warfare, or religion. From these, drama arose. Western drama as we know it first began in ancient Greece.

Elements of Drama

THE PLAYWRIGHT AND THE SCRIPT. The author of a play is the **playwright.** A playwright has limited control in deciding how his or her work is presented. Producers, directors, set designers, and actors all interpret a playwright's work and present their interpretations to the audience.

A **script** is the written text from which a drama is produced. Scripts are made up of stage directions and dialogue. Scripts may be divided into long parts called acts and short parts called scenes. In this unit, you will read *The Ugly Duckling*, a one-act play written by A. A. Milne and based on the fairy tale by Hans Christian Andersen.

STAGE DIRECTIONS. **Stage directions** are notes included in a play to describe how something should look, sound, or be performed. Stage directions can describe lighting, costumes, music, sound effects, or other elements of a play. They can also describe entrances and exits, gestures, tone of voice, or other elements related to the acting of a play. Stage directions sometimes provide historical or background information. In stage directions, the parts of the stage are described from the actors' point of view, as shown in the diagram on the next page. As you read the selection from the play, pay attention to the suggestions the playwright has given for the set, the lighting, and props.

MARK THE TEXT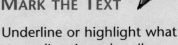

Underline or highlight what stage directions describe.

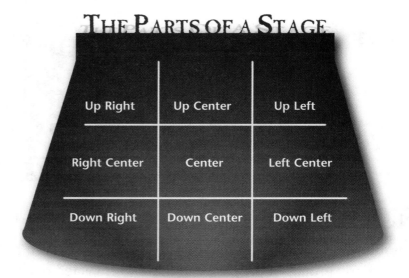

Up Right	Up Center	Up Left
Right Center	Center	Left Center
Down Right	Down Center	Down Left

Reading STRATEGY REVIEW

VISUALIZE. Using the Parts of a Stage diagram, mark where characters would go if stage directions told them to *cross down center.*

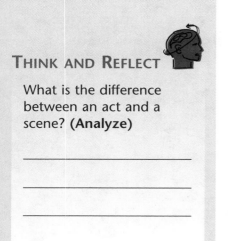

THINK AND REFLECT

What is the difference between an act and a scene? **(Analyze)**

_____

_____

_____

DIALOGUE. The speech of the actors in a play is called **dialogue.** A speech given by one character is called a **monologue.** In a play, dialogue appears after the names of characters.

ACTS AND SCENES. An **act** is a major part of a play. One-act, three-act, and five-act plays are all common. A **scene** is a short section of a literary work, one that happens in a single place and time. There may be any number of scenes in each act, and the number of scenes may vary from act to act.

SPECTACLE. The **spectacle** includes all the elements of the drama that are presented to the audience's senses. The set, props, special effects, lighting, and costumes are all part of the spectacle.

USING READING STRATEGIES WITH DRAMA

Active Reading Strategy Checklists

When reading drama, be aware of the plot (what happens), the setting, the characters, the dialogue (what the characters say), and the stage directions (how the characters say their lines and the actions they take onstage). The following checklists offer things to consider as you read drama.

1 Read with a Purpose. Before reading drama, give yourself a purpose, or something to look for, as you read. Sometimes your teacher will give you a purpose: "As you read the play, consider why A. A. Milne chose to name his play after the fairy tale." Other times you can set your own purpose by previewing the opening lines and instructional information. Say to yourself

- ❑ I want to look for . . .
- ❑ I need to learn what happens to . . .
- ❑ I want to experience how . . .
- ❑ I want to understand why . . .
- ❑ I want to figure out what causes . . .

2 **CONNECT TO PRIOR KNOWLEDGE.** Being aware of what you already know and thinking about it as you read can help you understand the characters and events. As you read, say to yourself

- ❑ The setting is a lot like . . .
- ❑ What happens here is similar to what happens in . . .
- ❑ This character is like . . .
- ❑ The ending reminds me of . . .
- ❑ I like this description because . . .

3 **WRITE THINGS DOWN.** As you read drama, write down important ideas that the author is sharing with readers. Possible ways to write things down include

- ❑ Underline important information in the stage directions.
- ❑ Write down things you want to remember about how the characters might say their lines.
- ❑ Highlight lines you want to read aloud.
- ❑ Create a graphic organizer to keep track of people and events.
- ❑ Use a code in the margin that shows how you respond to the action.

4 **MAKE PREDICTIONS.** As you read drama, use information in the stage directions and the dialogue to make guesses about what will happen next. Make predictions like the following:

- ❑ The title makes me predict that . . .
- ❑ The stage directions make me think that . . .
- ❑ I think the selection will end with . . .
- ❑ I think there will be a conflict between . . .
- ❑ The dialogue makes me guess that . . .

Reading **TIP**

Become an actor! Practice reading parts of the play aloud using a voice that expresses what the characters feel.

USE A CODE

Here's a way to code the text.
- \+ I like this
- – I don't like this
- √ This is important
- Yes I agree with this
- No I disagree with this
- ? I don't understand this
- W I wonder . . .
- ! This is like something I know
- ﹏ I need to come back to this later

Create additional code marks to note other reactions you have.

VISUALIZE. Visualizing, or allowing the words on the page to create images in your mind, helps you understand the action and how the characters may say their lines. In order to visualize the setting, the characters, and the action, make statements such as

- ❏ The setting and props . . .
- ❏ This character speaks . . .
- ❏ This character's movements are . . .
- ❏ This character wears . . .
- ❏ Over the course of the play, this character's behavior . . .
- ❏ The words help me see, hear, feel, smell, taste . . .

6 **USE TEXT ORGANIZATION.** When you read drama, pay attention to the dialogue, the characters, and the action. Learn to stop occasionally and retell what you have read. Say to yourself

- ❏ The stage directions help me pay attention to . . .
- ❏ The exposition, or introduction, is about . . .
- ❏ The central conflict centers on . . .
- ❏ The climax, or high point of interest, occurs when . . .
- ❏ The resolution, or the outcome, of the play is that . . .
- ❏ My summary of this scene is . . .

7 **TACKLE DIFFICULT VOCABULARY.** Difficult words in drama can get in the way of your ability to understand the characters and events. Use context, consult a dictionary, or ask someone about words you do not understand. When you come across a difficult word in a drama, say to yourself

- ❏ The lines near this word tell me that this word means . . .
- ❏ A dictionary definition shows that the word means . . .
- ❏ My work with the word before reading helps me know that the word means . . .
- ❏ A classmate said that the word means . . .
- ❏ This word is pronounced . . .

Reading TIP

Sketch what the stage looks like and where the characters are on the stage. The sketch will help you picture the action.

Reading TIP

Insert synonyms for difficult words into the dialogue as you read. If you are unsure about a synonym that will work, ask a classmate about the synonym he or she would use.

8 MONITOR YOUR READING PROGRESS. All readers encounter difficulty when they read, especially if the reading material is not self-selected. When you have to read something, note problems you are having and fix them. The key to reading success is knowing when you are having difficulty. To fix problems, say to yourself

- ❏ Because I don't understand this part, I will . . .
- ❏ Because I'm having trouble staying connected to what I'm reading, I will . . .
- ❏ Because the words in the play are too hard, I will . . .
- ❏ Because the play is long, I will . . .
- ❏ Because I can't retell what happened here, I will . . .

Become an Active Reader

The instruction with the drama selections in this unit gives you an in-depth look at how to use one strategy. Brief margin notes guide your use of additional strategies. Using one active reading strategy will greatly increase your reading success and enjoyment. Use the white space in the margins to add your own comments and strategy ideas. Learn how to use several strategies in combination to ensure your complete understanding of what you are reading. When you have difficulty, try a fix-up idea. For further information about the active reading strategies, see Unit 1, pages 4–15

FIX-UP IDEAS

- ■ Reread
- ■ Ask a question
- ■ Read in shorter chunks
- ■ Read aloud
- ■ Retell
- ■ Work with a partner
- ■ Unlock difficult words
- ■ Vary your reading rate
- ■ Choose a new reading strategy
- ■ Create a mnemonic device

How to Use Reading Strategies with Drama

Note how a reader uses active reading strategies while reading this excerpt from *The Ugly Duckling*.

CONNECT TO PRIOR KNOWLEDGE

The title refers to the fairy tale "The Ugly Duckling." I know that the duckling in that story turns out not to be ugly at all.

MAKE PREDICTIONS

I predict that Princess Camilla turns out to be beautiful, just like the ugly duckling did.

WRITE THINGS DOWN

I can highlight things the King says that reveal what kind of person he is. These lines make me wonder if he is judgmental. I'll see if his other statements confirm this.

CHANCELLOR.   As Your Majesty is aware, the young Prince Simon arrives today to seek Her Royal Highness's hand in marriage. He has been traveling in distant lands and, as I understand, has not—er—has not—

KING.   You mean he hasn't heard anything.

CHANCELLOR.   It is a little difficult to put this <u>tactfully</u>, Your Majesty.

KING.   Do your best, and I will tell you afterwards how you got on.

CHANCELLOR.   Let me put it this way. The Prince Simon will naturally assume that Her Royal Highness has the customary—so customary as to be, in my own poor opinion, slightly monotonous—has what one might call the inevitable—so inevitable as to be, in my opinion again, almost mechanical—will assume, that she has the, as *I* think of it, faultily faultless, icily regular, splendidly—

KING.   What you are trying to say in the fewest words possible is that my daughter is not beautiful.

CHANCELLOR.   Her beauty is certainly elusive,[1] Your Majesty.

KING.   It is. It has eluded you, it has eluded me, it has eluded everybody who has seen her. It even eluded the Court Painter. His last words were, "Well, I did my best." His successor is now painting the view across the water-meadows from the West Turret. He says that his doctor has advised him to keep to landscape.

CHANCELLOR.   It is unfortunate, Your Majesty, but there it is. One just cannot understand how it can have occurred.

---

1. **elusive.** Not easily seen or understood

MONITOR YOUR READING PROGRESS

This part is difficult. I will read on to see if what comes afterward will help me understand. If not, I will reread these lines more slowly.

TACKLE DIFFICULT VOCABULARY

The footnote tells me that *elusive* means "not easily seen or understood." I can use that definition and the context to guess that *eluded* means "managed not to be seen."

READ WITH A PURPOSE

I want to find out how Prince Simon reacts to meeting Princess Camilla.

USE TEXT ORGANIZATION

The capitalized names tell me who is speaking.

VISUALIZE

I can picture the King and Chancellor on stage, talking to each other.

THE UGLY DUCKLING

by A. A. Milne

Active READING STRATEGY

READ WITH A PURPOSE

Before Reading ➤ UNDERSTAND YOUR PURPOSE

❑ Read the Reader's Resource.

❑ Discuss what you know about the fairy tale called "The Ugly Duckling." Who is the main character of the fairy tale? How does this character change during the story? What causes this change?

❑ Preview the selection by looking at the picture on page 201 and previewing the list of characters. How will this play differ from the fairy tale?

❑ Discuss with your class what expectations you have about royal figures—kings, queens, princes, and princesses—who appear in fairy tales and other stories. How do you expect them to look? What qualities do you assume they will have? How do you imagine they should act?

❑ As you read, your purpose will be to gather information about the characters in the play by noticing Milne's use of characterization. **Characterization** is the literary techniques writers use to create characters and make them come alive. Writers use the following techniques to create characters:

direct description	describing the physical features, dress, and personality of the characters
behavior	showing what characters say, do, or think
interaction with others	showing what other characters say or think about them

❑ Use the Characterization Chart on the next page to record details about several of the characters.

CONNECT

Reader's resource

British author A. A., Milne is best known for creating the characters in the Winnie the Pooh stories, but he also wrote several plays. The one-act play *The Ugly Duckling* is named after a fairy tale. Fairy tales often take place in medieval settings and feature magical changes or events. Most of them were originally passed down through the oral tradition, although this one was written by Hans Christian Andersen. The ugly duckling in the original story suffers greatly for looking different than the other ducklings. Finally, he joins a group of swans, assuming they will kill him for his hideous appearance. When he lowers his head in anticipation of their attack, he sees his reflection and finds that he has grown to be a beautiful, graceful swan just like them. As you read, think about why A. A. Milne chose this name for his play.

Reader's journal

Which is more important to you—outer or inner beauty? Give some reasons for your answer.

_____

_____

_____

Graphic Organizer: Characterization Chart

Character	Character's Appearance, Dress, and Personality	What Character Does, Says, or Thinks	What Other Characters Say or Think
King			
Princess Camilla			
Dulcibella			
Prince Simon			

THE UGLY DUCKLING

A. A. Milne

CHARACTERS

THE KING
THE QUEEN
THE PRINCESS CAMILLA
THE CHANCELLOR[1]
DULCIBELLA
PRINCE SIMON
CARLO

(*The* SCENE *is the Throne Room of the Palace; a room of many doors, or, if preferred, curtain-openings: simply furnished with three thrones for Their Majesties[2] and Her Royal Highness[3] the* PRINCESS CAMILLA—*in other words, with three handsome chairs. At each side is a long seat: reserved, as it might be, for His Majesty's Council (if any), but useful, as today, for other purposes. The* KING *is asleep on his throne with a handkerchief over his face. He is a king of any country from any storybook, in whatever costume you please. But he should be wearing his crown.*)

10   **A VOICE.** (*Announcing*) His Excellency[4] the Chancellor! (*The* CHANCELLOR, *an elderly man in hornrimmed spectacles, enters, bowing. The* KING *wakes up with a start and removes the handkerchief from his face.*)

---

1. **Chancellor.** Official secretary or nobleman of the king
2. *Their Majesties.* Titles used when speaking of kings and queens
3. *Her Royal Highness.* Term used when referring to a ruler, especially royalty
4. **His Excellency.** Title of honor given to a man in an important position

During Reading

READ WITH A PURPOSE

- Listen as volunteers read the beginning of the play aloud. Jot down things that you learn about each of the characters in your Characterization Chart.
- Read the rest of the play silently on your own. Continue to write down telling things the characters say, do, or think; things other characters say about them; and details about their appearance, dress, and personality.

NOTE THE FACTS

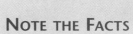

What is the King doing just before the Chancellor enters?

_____

_____

KING. (*With simple dignity*) I was thinking.

CHANCELLOR. (*Bowing*) Never, Your Majesty, was greater need for thought than now.

KING. That's what I was thinking. (*He struggles into a more dignified position.*) Well, what is it? More trouble?

CHANCELLOR. What we might call the old trouble, Your
20 Majesty.

KING. It's what I was saying last night to the Queen. "Uneasy lies the head that wears a crown,"[5] was how I put it.

CHANCELLOR. A profound and original thought, which may well go down to posterity.

KING. You mean it may go down well with posterity. I hope so. Remind me to tell you some time of another little thing I said to Her Majesty: something about a fierce light beating on a throne.[6] Posterity would like that, too. Well,
30 what is it?

CHANCELLOR. It is in the matter of Her Royal Highness's wedding.

KING. Oh . . . yes.

CHANCELLOR. As Your Majesty is aware, the young Prince Simon arrives today to seek Her Royal Highness's hand in marriage. He has been traveling in distant lands and, as I understand, has not—er—has not—

KING. You mean he hasn't heard anything.

CHANCELLOR. It is a little difficult to put this tactfully,
40 Your Majesty.

KING. Do your best, and I will tell you afterwards how you got on.

CHANCELLOR. Let me put it this way. The Prince Simon will naturally assume that Her Royal Highness has the customary—so customary as to be, in my own poor

---

5. **"Uneasy lies the head . . . crown."** From William Shakespeare's play *King Henry IV*
6. **something about a fierce light beating on a throne.** From a quotation by the poet Alfred, Lord Tennyson

words for everyday use	**dig • ni • fied** (dig′ nə fīd) *adj.*, showing nobility. *Jackson had a <u>dignified</u> look as he sat in his tuxedo.* **pos • ter • i • ty** (päs ter′ə tē) *n.*, future generations. *We will save pictures and mementos for <u>posterity</u>.* **tact • ful** (takt′ fəl) *adj.*, having or showing good sense of what to say and do. *Gina answered the sensitive question with a <u>tactful</u> response.* **tactfully,** *adv.*

opinion, slightly monotonous—has what one might call the <u>inevitable</u>—so inevitable as to be, in my opinion again, almost mechanical—will assume, that she has the, as *I* think of it, faultily faultless, icily regular, splendidly—

50   **KING.**   What you are trying to say in the fewest words possible is that my daughter is not beautiful.

CHANCELLOR.   Her beauty is certainly <u>elusive</u>, Your Majesty.

KING.   It is. It has eluded you, it has eluded me, it has eluded everybody who has seen her. It even eluded the Court Painter. His last words were, "Well, I did my best." His successor is now painting the view across the water-meadows from the West Turret. He says that his doctor has advised him to keep to landscape.

60   **CHANCELLOR.**   It is unfortunate, Your Majesty, but there it is. One just cannot understand how it can have occurred.

KING.   You don't think she takes after *me*, at all? You don't detect a likeness?

CHANCELLOR.   Most certainly not, Your Majesty.

KING.   Good. . . . Your predecessor did.

CHANCELLOR.   I have often wondered what happened to my predecessor.

KING.   Well, now you know. (*There is a short silence.*)

CHANCELLOR.   Looking at the bright side, although Her
70   Royal Highness is not, strictly speaking, beautiful—

KING.   Not, truthfully speaking, beautiful—

CHANCELLOR.   Yet she has great beauty of character.

KING.   My dear Chancellor, we are not considering Her Royal Highness's character, but her chances of getting married. You observe that there is a distinction.

CHANCELLOR.   Yes, Your Majesty.

KING.   Look at it from the <u>suitor's</u> point of view. If a girl is beautiful, it is easy to assume that she has, tucked away inside her, an equally beautiful character. But it is
80   impossible to assume that an unattractive girl, however elevated in character, has, tucked away inside her, an

---

words for everyday use

in • ev • i • ta • ble (in ev′i tə bəl) *adj.,* unavoidable. *Getting wet is <u>inevitable</u> when wind blows the rain.*

e • lu • sive (ē lōō′siv) *adj.,* not easily seen or understood. *The <u>elusive</u> wolf has only been spotted twice.*

suit • or (süt′ər) *n.,* man who is seeking a romantic relationship with a woman. *In that old movie, the <u>suitor</u> brought the young woman a bouquet of daisies.*

NOTE THE FACTS

What is the Chancellor trying to say?

_____

_____

_____

THINK AND REFLECT

What happened to the last Chancellor, and why? **(Infer)**

_____

_____

_____

Think about what this tells you about the King, and jot down your answer in the Characterization Chart.

_____

_____

_____

THINK AND REFLECT

Why might the Queen ask about the Prince's eyes? (Infer)

_____

_____

_____

equally beautiful face. That is, so to speak, not where you want it—tucked away.

CHANCELLOR. Quite so, Your Majesty.

KING. This doesn't, of course, <u>alter</u> the fact that the Princess Camilla is quite the nicest person in the Kingdom.

CHANCELLOR. (*Enthusiastically*) She is indeed, Your Majesty. (*Hurriedly*) With the exception, I need hardly say, of Your Majesty—and Her Majesty.

90 **KING.** Your exceptions are tolerated for their loyalty and <u>condemned</u> for their extreme fatuity.[7]

CHANCELLOR. Thank you, Your Majesty.

KING. As an adjective for your King, the word "nice" is ill-chosen. As an adjective for Her Majesty, it is— ill-chosen. (*At which moment* HER MAJESTY *comes in. The* KING *rises. The* CHANCELLOR *puts himself at right angles.*)

QUEEN. (*Briskly*) Ah. Talking about Camilla? (*She sits down.*)

KING. (*Returning to his throne*) As always, my dear, you are
100 right.

QUEEN. (*To* CHANCELLOR) This fellow, Simon—What's he like?

CHANCELLOR. Nobody has seen him, Your Majesty.

QUEEN. How old is he?

CHANCELLOR. Five-and-twenty, I understand.

QUEEN. In twenty-five years he must have been seen by somebody.

KING. (*To the* CHANCELLOR) Just a fleeting glimpse.

CHANCELLOR. I meant, Your Majesty, that no detailed
110 report of him has reached this country, save that he has the usual personal advantages and qualities expected of a Prince, and has been traveling in distant and dangerous lands.

QUEEN. Ah! Nothing gone wrong with his eyes? Sunstroke or anything?

---

7. **fatuity.** Stupidity

words for everyday use	**al • ter** (ôl´tər) v., change. *The waves will <u>alter</u> the shape of the sand castle.* **con • demn** (kən dem´) v., disapprove of. *My club chooses to <u>condemn</u> all acts of vandalism in the neighborhood.*

CHANCELLOR. Not that I am aware of, Your Majesty. At the same time, as I was venturing to say to His Majesty, Her Royal Highness's character and disposition are so outstandingly—

120 **QUEEN.** Stuff and nonsense. You remember what happened when we had the Tournament of Love last year.

CHANCELLOR. I was not myself present, Your Majesty. I had not then the honor of—I was abroad, and never heard the full story.

QUEEN. No; it was the other fool. They all rode up to Camilla to pay their <u>homage</u>—it was the first time they had seen her. The heralds blew their trumpets, and announced that she would marry whichever Prince was left master of the field when all but one had been unhorsed.[8] The

130 trumpets were blown again, they charged enthusiastically into the fight, and—(*The* KING *looks <u>nonchalantly</u> at the ceiling and whistles a few bars.*)—don't do that.

KING. I'm sorry, my dear.

QUEEN. (*To* CHANCELLOR) And what happened? They all simultaneously fell off their horses and <u>assumed</u> a posture of defeat.

KING. One of them was not quite so quick as the others. I was very quick. I proclaimed him the victor.

QUEEN. At the Feast of Betrothal[9] held that night—

140 **KING.** We were all very quick.

QUEEN. The Chancellor announced that by the laws of the country the successful suitor had to pass a further test. He had to give the correct answer to a riddle.

CHANCELLOR. Such undoubtedly is the fact, Your Majesty.

KING. There are times for announcing facts, and times for looking at things in a broad-minded way. Please remember that, Chancellor.

---

8. **unhorsed.** Thrown from a horse
9. **Betrothal.** Engagement or promise to marry

words for everyday use

hom • age (häm´ij) *n.,* something done to show honor or respect. *We would like to pay <u>homage</u> to volunteers in the community.*
non • cha • lant (nän´shə länt) *adj.,* unconcerned or uninterested. *Because Fatima was an enthusiastic football fan, she could not understand why her brother was <u>nonchalant</u> about the outcome of the game.* **nonchalantly,** *adv.*
as • sume (ə soom´) *v.,* take on. *I would like the children to <u>assume</u> more household responsibilities.*

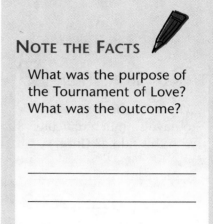

NOTE THE FACTS

What was the purpose of the Tournament of Love? What was the outcome?

_____

_____

_____

FIX-UP IDEA

Use Margin Questions
If you are having trouble identifying information about the characters, refocus on answering the margin questions. Then, after you have answered a question, ask yourself if the answer leads you to new information about a character. If so, record that information in your chart.

MARK THE TEXT

Underline or highlight the riddle and its answer.

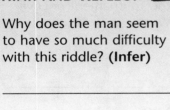

THINK AND REFLECT

Why does the man seem to have so much difficulty with this riddle? **(Infer)**

_____

_____

_____

Reading STRATEGY
                REVIEW

TACKLE DIFFICULT VOCABULARY.
When you encounter an underlined vocabulary word, read to the end of the sentence to get the gist of the meaning. Then check the definition at the bottom of the page. Reread the sentence, substituting the meaning for the underlined word. Try this process with lines 175–177.

CHANCELLOR.   Yes, Your Majesty.

QUEEN.   I invented the riddle myself. Quite an easy one.

150   What is it which has four legs and barks like a dog? The answer is, "A dog."

KING.   (*To* CHANCELLOR) You see that?

CHANCELLOR.   Yes, Your Majesty.

KING.   It isn't difficult.

QUEEN.   He, however, seemed to find it so. He said an eagle. Then he said a serpent; a very high mountain with slippery sides; two peacocks; a moonlight night; the day after tomorrow—

KING.   Nobody could accuse him of not trying.

160   **QUEEN.**   *I* did.

KING.   I *should* have said that nobody could fail to recognize in his attitude an appearance of <u>doggedness</u>.

QUEEN.   Finally he said "Death." I nudged the King—

KING.   Accepting the word "nudge" for the moment, I rubbed my ankle with one hand, clapped him on the shoulder with the other, and congratulated him on the correct answer. He disappeared under the table, and, personally, I never saw him again.

QUEEN.   His body was found in the moat[10] next morning.

170   **CHANCELLOR.**   But what was he doing in the moat, Your Majesty?

KING.   Bobbing about. Try not to ask needless questions.

CHANCELLOR.   It all seems so strange.

QUEEN.   What does?

CHANCELLOR.   That Her Royal Highness, alone of all the Princesses one has ever heard of, should lack that <u>invariable</u> <u>attribute</u> of Royalty, supreme beauty.

QUEEN.   (*To the* KING) That was your Great-Aunt Malkin. She came to the christening. You know what she said.

---

10. **moat.** Ditch dug around a castle and filled with water, used to protect against invaders

words for everyday use

dog • ged • ness (dôg´id nes) *n.*, stubbornness. *It is difficult to argue with my sister because of her <u>doggedness</u>.*

in • var • i • a • ble (in ver´ē ə bəl) *adj.*, constant. *Extremely hot temperatures are <u>invariable</u> in most countries near the equator.*

at • tri • bute (a´ trib yüt) *n.*, quality or characteristic. *Herman's sense of honesty was his finest <u>attribute</u>.*

180   **KING.**   It was <u>cryptic</u>. Great-Aunt Malkin's besetting weakness. She came to *my* christening—she was one hundred and one then, and that was fifty-one years ago. (*To* CHANCELLOR) How old would that make her?

    CHANCELLOR.   One hundred and fifty-two, Your Majesty.

    KING.   (*After thought*) About that, yes. She promised me that when I grew up I should have all the happiness which my wife deserved. It struck me at the time—well, when I say "at the time," I was only a week old—but it did strike me as soon as anything could strike me—I mean of that

190   nature—well, work it out for yourself, Chancellor. It opens up a most interesting field of speculation. Though naturally I have not liked to go into it at all deeply with Her Majesty.

    QUEEN.   I never heard anything less cryptic. She was wishing you extreme happiness.

    KING.   I don't think she was *wishing* me anything. However.

    CHANCELLOR.   (*To the* QUEEN) But what, Your Majesty, did she wish Her Royal Highness?

    QUEEN.   Her other godmother—on my side—had promised her the dazzling beauty for which all the women

200   in my family are famous—(*She pauses, and the* KING *snaps his fingers <u>surreptitiously</u> in the direction of the* CHANCELLOR.)

    CHANCELLOR.   (*Hurriedly*) Indeed, yes, Your Majesty. (*The* KING *relaxes.*)

    QUEEN.   And Great-Aunt Malkin said—(*To the* KING)— what were the words?

    KING.   I give you with this kiss
        A wedding-day surprise.
        Where ignorance is bliss
        'Tis folly to be wise.

210   I thought the last two lines rather neat. But what it *meant*—

    QUEEN.   We can all see what it meant. She was given beauty—and where is it? Great-Aunt Malkin took it away from her. The wedding-day surprise is that there will never be a wedding day.

    KING.   Young men being what they are, my dear, it would be

Reading **TIP**

Sometimes, something you read won't make sense right away, but after you learn more, you will understand it. Remember Great-Aunt Malkin's mysterious words to Camilla at her christening. They will come up again later.

NOTE THE FACTS

What does the Queen think Camilla's wedding day surprise is?

_____

_____

words for everyday use	**cryp • tic** (krip´tik) *adj.*, having hidden or mysterious meaning. *Frank was bothered by the <u>cryptic</u> message left on his answering machine.* **sur • rep • ti • tious** (sər´əp tish´əs) *adj.*, secret, sneaky. *Marvin's <u>surreptitious</u> eating of the cookies was not discovered until two days later.* **surreptitiously,** *adv.*

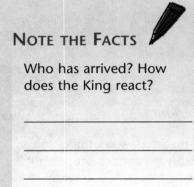

Use THE STRATEGY

READ WITH A PURPOSE. Add what you learn about Camilla's appearance to your Characterization Chart.

NOTE THE FACTS

Who has arrived? How does the King react?

_____

_____

_____

much more surprising if there *were* a wedding day. So how—

(*The* PRINCESS *comes in. She is young, happy, healthy, but not beautiful. Or let us say that by some trick of make-up or arrangement of hair she seems plain to us: unlike the* PRINCESS *of the*
220 *storybooks.*)

PRINCESS. (*To the* KING) Hallo, darling! (*Seeing the others*) Oh, I say! Affairs of state? Sorry.

KING. (*Holding out his hand*) Don't go, Camilla. (*She takes his hand.*)

CHANCELLOR. Shall I withdraw, Your Majesty?

QUEEN. You are aware, Camilla, that Prince Simon arrives today?

PRINCESS. He has arrived. They're just letting down the drawbridge.

230 **KING.** (*Jumping up*) Arrived! I must—

PRINCESS. Darling, you know what the drawbridge is like. It takes at *least* half an hour to let it down.

KING. (*Sitting down*) It wants oil. (*To the* CHANCELLOR) Have *you* been grudging it oil?

PRINCESS. It wants a new drawbridge, darling.

CHANCELLOR. Have I Your Majesty's permission—

KING. Yes, yes. (*The* CHANCELLOR *bows and goes out.*)

QUEEN. You've told him, of course? It's the only chance.

KING. Er—no. I was just going to, when—

240 **QUEEN.** Then I'd better. (*She goes to the door.*) You can explain to the girl; I'll have her sent to you. You've told Camilla?

KING. Er—no. I was just going to, when—

QUEEN. Then you'd better tell her now.

KING. My dear, are you sure—

QUEEN. It's the only chance left. (*Dramatically to heaven*) My daughter! (*She goes out. There is a little silence when she is gone.*)

KING. Camilla, I want to talk seriously to you about
250 marriage.

PRINCESS. Yes, father.

words for everyday use	**grudge** (gruj´) *v.*, not give willingly. *The company owner grudged bonuses and raises to even hard-working employees.*

KING. It is time that you learnt some of the facts of life.

PRINCESS. Yes, father.

KING. Now the great fact about marriage is that once you're married you live happy ever after. All our history books <u>affirm</u> this.

PRINCESS. And your own experience too, darling.

KING. (*With dignity*) Let us confine ourselves to history for the moment.

260   **PRINCESS.** Yes, father.

KING. Of course, there *may* be an exception here and there, which, as it were, proves the rule; just as—oh, well, never mind.

PRINCESS. (*Smiling*) Go on, darling. You were going to say that an exception here and there proves the rule that all princesses are beautiful.

KING. Well—leave that for the moment. The point is that it doesn't matter *how* you marry, or *who* you marry, as long as you *get* married. Because you'll be happy ever after in

270   any case. Do you follow me so far?

PRINCESS. Yes, father.

KING. Well, your mother and I have a little plan—

PRINCESS. Was that it, going out of the door just now?

KING. Er—yes. It concerns your waitingmaid.[11]

PRINCESS. Darling, I have several.

KING. Only one that leaps to the eye, so to speak. The one with the—well, with everything.

PRINCESS. Dulcibella?

KING. That's the one. It is our little plan that at the first

280   meeting she should pass herself off as the Princess—a harmless <u>ruse</u>, of which you will find frequent record in the history books—and allure Prince Simon to his—that is to say, bring him up to the—in other words, the wedding will take place immediately afterwards, and as quietly as possible—well, naturally in view of the fact that your Aunt Malkin is one hundred and fifty-two; and since you will be

---

11. **waitingmaid.** Person whose job is to assist a queen or princess

words for everyday use	af • firm (ə furm´) *v.*, prove. *The way the defendant averted his eyes served only to <u>affirm</u> his guilt from the prosecutor's point of view.* ruse (rōōz´) *v.*, trick. *Queen Fatima knew that the enemy's apparent surrender was merely a <u>ruse</u> to draw her own troops out into the open.*

Literary TOOLS

DIALOGUE. The speech of actors in a play is called **dialogue**. Most of the information in a play is given in the dialogue. What do you learn about Camilla by the fact that she calls her father "Darling"? What does the King reveal about his marriage in lines 258–259 and lines 261–263? Record your answers in your Characterization Chart.

NOTE THE FACTS

What plan have the King and Queen made?

_____

_____

_____

_____

wearing the family bridal veil—which is no doubt how the custom arose—the surprise after the ceremony will be his. Are you following me at all? Your attention seems to be
290   wandering.

PRINCESS. I was wondering why you needed to tell me.

KING. Just a <u>precautionary</u> measure, in case you happened to meet the Prince or his attendant before the ceremony; in which case, of course, you would pass yourself off as the maid—

PRINCESS. A harmless ruse, of which, also, you will find frequent record in the history books.

KING. Exactly. But the occasion need not arise.

A VOICE. (*Announcing*) The woman Dulcibella!

300   **KING.** Ah! (*To the* PRINCESS) Now, Camilla, if you will just <u>retire</u> to your own apartments, I will come to you there when we are ready for the actual ceremony. (*He leads her out as he is talking; and as he returns calls out.*) Come in, my dear! (DULCIBELLA *comes in. She is beautiful, but dumb.*) Now don't be frightened, there is nothing to be frightened about. Has Her Majesty told you what you have to do?

DULCIBELLA. Y-yes, Your Majesty.

KING. Well now, let's see how well you can do it. You are sitting here, we will say. (*He leads her to a seat.*) Now
310   imagine that I am Prince Simon. (*He curls his moustache and puts his stomach in. She giggles.*) You are the beautiful Princess Camilla whom he has never seen. (*She giggles again.*) This is a serious moment in your life, and you will find that a giggle will not be helpful. (*He goes to the door.*) I am announced: "His Royal Highness Prince Simon!" That's me being announced. Remember what I said about giggling. You should have a far-away look upon the face. (*She does her best.*) Farther away than that. (*She tries again.*) No, that's too far. You are sitting there, thinking beautiful
320   thoughts—in maiden <u>meditation</u>, fancy-free, as I remember saying to Her Majesty once . . . speaking of somebody else . . . fancy-free, but with the mouth definitely shut—that's

| words for everyday use | **pre • cau • tion • ar • y** (prē kô´shən ar ē) *adj.,* safety. *Many car companies are installing air bags in their vehicles as <u>precautionary</u> devices.*
re • tire (ri tīr´) *v.,* go away. *The servant said that since he was no longer needed, he would like to <u>retire</u> for the evening.*
med • i • ta • tion (med ə tā´ shən) *n.,* deep and continued thought. *Pamela spent hours in <u>meditation</u> before deciding whether to have an operation or not.* |

better. I advance and fall upon one knee. (*He does so.*) You extend your hand graciously—*graciously*; you're not trying to push him in the face—that's better, and I raise it to my lips—so—and I kiss it—(*He kisses it warmly.*)—no, perhaps not so <u>ardently</u> as that, more like this (*He kisses it again.*), and I say, "Your Royal Highness, this is the most—er— Your Royal Highness, I shall ever be—no—Your Royal

330   Highness, it is the proudest—" Well, the point is that he will say it, and it will be something complimentary, and then he will take your hand in both of his, and press it to his heart. (*He does so.*) And then—what do you say?

DULCIBELLA.   Coo!

KING.   No, *not* Coo.

DULCIBELLA.   Never had anyone do *that* to me before.

KING.   That also strikes the wrong note. What you want to say is, "Oh, Prince Simon!" . . . Say it.

DULCIBELLA.   (*Loudly*) Oh, Prince Simon!

340   **KING.**   No, no. You don't need to shout until he has said "What?" two or three times. Always consider the possibility that he *isn't* deaf. Softly, and giving the words a dying fall, letting them play around his head like a flight of doves.

DULCIBELLA.   (*Still a little overloud*) O-o-o-o-h, Prinsimon!

KING.   Keep the idea in your mind of a flight of *doves* rather than a flight of panic-stricken elephants, and you will be all right. Now I'm going to get up and you must, as it were, <u>waft</u> me into a seat by your side. (*She starts wafting.*)

350   *Not* rescuing a drowning man, that's another idea altogether, useful at times, but at the moment <u>inappropriate</u>. Wafting. Prince Simon will put the necessary muscles into play—all you require to do is to indicate by a gracious movement of the hand the seat you require him to take. Now! (*He gets up, a little stiffly, and sits next to her.*) That was better. Well, here we are. Now, I think you give me a look: something, let us say, half-way between a worshipful

Reading **STRATEGY REVIEW**

VISUALIZE. Picture the interaction between the King and Dulcibella as you read. Notice how you can tell what she does by how he responds to her. If you are having trouble understanding what is happening, work with a partner to act out lines 308–333.

READ ALOUD

With a partner, read the highlighted text aloud. Try to say the words the way the characters would say them. The stage directions will help you. What does this interaction tell you about Dulcibella? Record your answer in your Characterization Chart.

attitude and wild <u>abandonment</u>, with an undertone of regal dignity, touched, as it were, with good comradeship. Now try

360   that. (*She gives him a vacant look of bewilderment.*) Frankly, that didn't quite get it. There was just a little something missing. An absence, as it were, of all the qualities I asked for, and in their place an odd resemblance to an unsatisfied fish. Let us try to get at it another way. Dulcibella, have you a young man of your own?

DULCIBELLA.   (*Eagerly, seizing his hand*) Oo, yes, he's ever so smart, he's an archer, well not as you might say a real archer, he works in the armory, but old Bottlenose, *you* know who I mean, the Captain of the Guard, says the very

370   next man they ever has to shoot, my Eg shall take his place, knowing Father and how it is with Eg and me, and me being maid to Her Royal Highness and can't marry me till he's a real soldier, but ever so loving, and funny like, the things he says, I said to him once, "Eg," I said—

KING.   (*Getting up*) I rather fancy, Dulcibella, that if you think of Eg all the time, *say* as little as possible, and, when thinking of Eg, see that the mouth is not more than partially open, you will do very well. I will show you where you are to sit and wait for His Royal Highness. (*He leads her*

380   *out. On the way he is saying*) Now remember—*waft—waft—* not *hoick.*[12] (PRINCE SIMON *wanders in from the back unannounced. He is a very ordinary-looking young man in rather dusty clothes. He gives a deep sigh of relief as he sinks into the* KING's *throne. . . .* CAMILLA, *a new and strangely beautiful* CAMILLA, *comes in.*)

PRINCESS.   (*Surprised*) Well!

PRINCE.   Oh, hallo!

PRINCESS.   Ought you?

PRINCE.   (*Getting up*) Do sit down, won't you?

390   **PRINCESS.**   Who are you, and how did you get here?

PRINCE.   Well, that's rather a long story. Couldn't we sit

---

12. *hoick.* Hunter's call

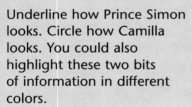

NOTE THE FACTS

Who is Eg?

_____

_____

MARK THE TEXT

Underline how Prince Simon looks. Circle how Camilla looks. You could also highlight these two bits of information in different colors.

down? You could sit here if you liked, but it isn't very comfortable.

PRINCESS. That is the King's Throne.

PRINCE. Oh, is that what it is?

PRINCESS. Thrones are not meant to be comfortable.

PRINCE. Well, I don't know if they're meant to be, but they certainly aren't.

PRINCESS. Why were you sitting on the King's Throne, and who are you?

PRINCE. My name is Carlo.

PRINCESS. Mine is Dulcibella.

PRINCE. Good. And now couldn't we sit down?

PRINCESS. (*Sitting down on the long seat to the left of the throne, and, as it were, wafting him to a place next to her*) You may sit here, if you like. Why are you so tired? (*He sits down.*)

PRINCE. I've been taking very <u>strenuous</u> exercise.

PRINCESS. Is that part of the long story?

PRINCE. It is.

PRINCESS. (*Settling herself*) I love stories.

PRINCE. This isn't a story really. You see, I'm attendant on Prince Simon who is visiting here.

PRINCESS. Oh? I'm attendant on Her Royal Highness.

PRINCE. Then you know what he's here for.

PRINCESS. Yes.

PRINCE. She's very beautiful, I hear.

PRINCESS. Did you hear that? Where have you been lately?

PRINCE. Traveling in distant lands—with Prince Simon.

PRINCESS. Ah! All the same, I don't understand. Is Prince Simon in the Palace now? The drawbridge *can't* be down yet!

PRINCE. I don't suppose it is. *And* what a noise it makes coming down!

PRINCESS. Isn't it terrible?

PRINCE. I couldn't stand it any more. I just had to get away. That's why I'm here.

PRINCESS. But how?

words for everyday use

stren • u • ous (stren′ yü əs) *adj.*, requiring hard work and energy. *Rocco was out of shape, and swimming just a few laps had become* <u>strenuous</u> *for him.*

400

410

420

NOTE THE FACTS

How do the Prince and Princess introduce themselves to each other?

_____

_____

_____

THINK AND REFLECT

Who is Carlo? **(Infer)** Is he really speaking? **(Predict)**

_____

_____

_____

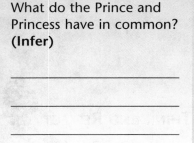

THINK AND REFLECT

What do the Prince and Princess have in common? (Infer)

_____

_____

_____

Use THE STRATEGY

READ WITH A PURPOSE. Reread lines 456–459. What do these lines tell you about the Princess's personality? Record your answer in your chart.

PRINCE.   Well, there's only one way, isn't there? That beech tree, and then a swing and a grab for the battlements, and don't ask me to remember it all—(*He shudders.*)

430

PRINCESS.   You mean you came across the moat by that beech tree?

PRINCE.   Yes. I got so tired of hanging about.

PRINCESS.   But it's terribly dangerous!

PRINCE.   That's why I'm so exhausted. Nervous shock. (*He lies back and breathes loudly.*)

PRINCESS.   Of course, it's different for *me*.

PRINCE.   (*Sitting up*) Say that again. I must have got it wrong.

PRINCESS.   It's different for me, because I'm used to it. Besides, I'm so much lighter.

440

PRINCE.   You don't mean that *you*—

PRINCESS.   Oh yes, often.

PRINCE.   And I thought I was a brave man! At least, I didn't until five minutes ago, and now I don't again.

PRINCESS.   Oh, but you are! And I think it's wonderful to do it straight off the first time.

PRINCE.   Well, *you* did.

PRINCESS.   Oh no, not the first time. When I was a child.

PRINCE.   You mean that you crashed?

450

PRINCESS.   Well, you only fall into the moat.

PRINCE.   Only! Can you *swim?*

PRINCESS.   Of course.

PRINCE.   So you swam to the castle walls, and yelled for help, and they fished you out and walloped you. And next day you tried again. Well, if *that* isn't pluck—

PRINCESS.   Of course I didn't. I swam back, and did it at once; I mean I tried again at once. It wasn't until the third time that I actually did it. You see, I was afraid I might lose my nerve.

460

PRINCE.   Afraid she might lose her nerve!

PRINCESS.   There's a way of getting over from this side, too; a tree grows out from the wall and you jump into another tree—I don't think it's quite so easy.

words
for
everyday
use

pluck (pluk′) *n.,* courage and strength. *The boxer showed a lot of pluck by continuing to fight even after his opponent had knocked him down.*

PRINCE. Not quite so easy. Good. You must show me.

PRINCESS. Oh, I will.

PRINCE. Perhaps it might be as well if you taught me how to swim first. I've often heard about swimming but never—

PRINCESS. You can't swim?

PRINCE. No. Don't look so surprised. There are a lot of other things which I can't do. I'll tell you about them as soon as you have a couple of years to spare.

PRINCESS. You can't swim and yet you crossed by the beech tree! And you're *ever* so much heavier than I am! Now who's brave?

PRINCE. (*Getting up*) You keep talking about how light you are. I must see if there's anything to it. Stand up! (*She stands obediently and he picks her up.*) You're right, Dulcibella. I could hold you here forever. (*Looking at her*) You're very lovely. Do you know how lovely you are?

PRINCESS. Yes. (*She laughs suddenly and happily.*)

PRINCE. Why do you laugh?

PRINCESS. Aren't you tired of holding me?

PRINCE. Frankly, yes. I <u>exaggerated</u> when I said I could hold you forever. When you've been hanging by the arms for ten minutes over a very deep moat, wondering if it's too late to learn how to swim—(*He puts her down.*)—what I meant was that I should *like* to hold you forever. Why did you laugh?

PRINCESS. Oh, well, it was a little private joke of mine.

PRINCE. If it comes to that, I've got a private joke too. Let's exchange them.

PRINCESS. Mine's very private. One other woman in the whole world knows, and that's all.

PRINCE. Mine's just as private. One other man knows, and that's all.

PRINCESS. What fun. I love secrets. . . . Well, here's mine. When I was born, one of my godmothers promised that I should be very beautiful.

PRINCE. How right she was.

words for everyday use

ex • ag • ger • ate (eg zaj´ər āt) *v.*, make something seem greater than it really is. *No one believed Luther when he said he owned twenty rare pets because they knew he loved to <u>exaggerate</u>.*

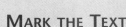

MARK THE TEXT

Underline the compliment the Prince pays Camilla. Circle her response.

PRINCESS.   But the other one said this:
　　　　　　I give you with this kiss
　　　　　　A wedding-day surprise.
　　　　　　Where ignorance is bliss
　　　　　　'Tis folly to be wise.
And nobody knew what it meant. And I grew up very plain.
And then, when I was about ten, I met my godmother in
the forest one day. It was my tenth birthday. Nobody knows
this—except you.

PRINCE.   Except us.

510 **PRINCESS.**   Except us. And she told me what her gift
meant. It meant that I *was* beautiful—but everybody else
was to go on being ignorant, and thinking me plain, until
my wedding day. Because, she said, she didn't want me to
grow up spoiled and willful and <u>vain</u>, as I should have done
if everybody had always been saying how beautiful I was;
and the best thing in the world, she said, was to be quite
sure of yourself, but not to expect admiration from other
people. So ever since then my mirror has told me I'm
beautiful, and everybody else thinks me ugly, and I get a lot
520 of fun out of it.

PRINCE.   Well, seeing that Dulcibella is the result, I can
only say that your godmother was very, very wise.

PRINCESS.   And now tell me *your* secret.

PRINCE.   It isn't such a pretty one. You see, Prince Simon
was going to woo Princess Camilla, and he'd heard that she
was beautiful and haughty and <u>imperious</u>—all *you* would
have been if your godmother hadn't been so wise. And
being a very ordinary-looking fellow himself, he was afraid
she wouldn't think much of him, so he suggested to one of
530 his attendants, a man called Carlo, of extremely attractive
appearance, that *he* should pretend to be the Prince, and
win the Princess's hand; and then at the last moment they
would change places—

PRINCESS.   How would they do that?

NOTE THE FACTS

What does the god-mother's gift mean?

_____

_____

_____

THINK AND REFLECT

What misunderstanding does the Prince's secret reveal? **(Infer)** How are the situations of the Prince and Princess similar? **(Analyze)**

_____

_____

---

words for everyday use

vain (vān) *adj.*, being too concerned with one's own looks or possessions. *We did not compliment Reggie on his new wardrobe because he was too <u>vain</u> already.*
im • per • i • ous (im pēr´ē yus) *adj.*, commanding; marked by arrogant assurance. *Sheila's <u>imperious</u> behavior caused others to shy away from her.*

PRINCE. The Prince was going to have been married in full armor—with his visor[13] down.

PRINCESS. (*Laughing happily*) Oh, what fun!

PRINCE. Neat, isn't it?

PRINCESS. (*Laughing*) Oh, very . . . very . . . very.

540 **PRINCE.** Neat, but not so terribly *funny*. Why do you keep laughing?

PRINCESS. Well, that's another secret.

PRINCE. If it comes to that, *I've* got another one up my sleeve. Shall we exchange again?

PRINCESS. All right. You go first this time.

PRINCE. Very well. . . . I am not Carlo. (*Standing up and speaking dramatically*) I am Simon!—ow! (*He sits down and rubs his leg violently.*)

PRINCESS. (*Alarmed*) What is it?

550 **PRINCE.** Cramp. (*In a mild voice, still rubbing*) I was saying that I was Prince Simon.

PRINCESS. Shall I rub it for you? (*She rubs.*)

PRINCE. (*Still hopefully*) I am Simon.

PRINCESS. Is that better?

PRINCE. (*Despairingly*) I am Simon.

PRINCESS. I know.

PRINCE. How did you know?

PRINCESS. Well, you told me.

PRINCE. But oughtn't you to <u>swoon</u> or something?

560 **PRINCESS.** Why? History records many similar ruses.

PRINCE. (*Amazed*) Is that so? I've never read history. I thought I was being profoundly original.

PRINCESS. Oh, no! Now I'll tell you *my* secret. For reasons very much like your own, the Princess Camilla, who is held to be extremely plain, feared to meet Prince Simon. Is the drawbridge down yet?

PRINCE. Do your people give a faint, surprised cheer every time it gets down?

---

13. **visor.** In a suit of armor, a movable part of the helmet that can be lowered to cover the face

words for everyday use

swoon (swōōn′) *v.*, faint; feel powerful emotion. *Frank will <u>swoon</u> when he gets a visit from his hero.*

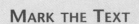

MARK THE TEXT

Underline or highlight the second secret the Prince reveals.

WHAT DO YOU WONDER?

_____

_____

_____

_____

PRINCESS. Naturally.

570 **PRINCE.** Then it came down about three minutes ago.

PRINCESS. Ah! Then at this very moment your man Carlo is declaring his passionate love for my maid, Dulcibella. That, I think, is funny. (*So does the* PRINCE. *He laughs heartily*.) Dulcibella, by the way, is in love with a man she calls Eg, so I hope Carlo isn't getting carried away.

PRINCE. Carlo is married to a girl he calls "the little woman," so Eg has nothing to fear.

PRINCESS. By the way, I don't know if you heard, but I said, or as good as said, that I am the Princess Camilla.

580 **PRINCE.** I wasn't surprised. History, of which I read a great deal, records many similar ruses.

PRINCESS. (*Laughing*) Simon!

PRINCE. (*Laughing*) Camilla! (*He stands up.*) May I try holding you again? (*She nods. He takes her in his arms and kisses her.*) Sweetheart!

PRINCESS. You see, when you lifted me up before, you said, "You're very lovely," and my godmother said that the first person to whom I would seem lovely was the man I should marry; so I knew then that you were Simon and I

590 should marry you.

PRINCE. I knew directly I saw you that I should marry you, even if you were Dulcibella. By the way, which of you *am* I marrying?

PRINCESS. When she lifts her veil, it will be Camilla. (*Voices are heard outside.*) Until then it will be Dulcibella.

PRINCE. (*In a whisper*) Then good-bye, Camilla, until you lift your veil.

PRINCESS. Good-bye, Simon, until you raise your visor. (*The* KING *and* QUEEN *come in arm-in-arm, followed by* CARLO

600 *and* DULCIBELLA *also arm-in-arm. The* CHANCELLOR *precedes them, walking backwards, at a loyal angle.*)

PRINCE. (*Supporting the* CHANCELLOR *as an accident seems inevitable*) Careful! (*The* CHANCELLOR *turns indignantly round.*)

KING. Who and what is this? More accurately who and what are all these?

CARLO. My attendant, Carlo, Your Majesty. He will, with Your Majesty's permission, prepare me for the ceremony. (*The* PRINCE *bows.*)

KING. Of course, of course!

NOTE THE FACTS

When did the Princess realize on her own who the Prince was? Why did she realize this?

_____

_____

_____

610 **QUEEN.**   (*To* DULCIBELLA) Your maid, Dulcibella, is it not, my love? (DULCIBELLA *nods violently.*) I thought so. (*To* CARLO) She will prepare Her Royal Highness. (*The* PRINCESS *curtsies.*)

KING.   Ah, yes. Yes. *Most* important.

PRINCESS.   (*Curtsying*) I beg pardon, Your Majesty, if I've done wrong, but I found the gentleman wandering—

KING.   (*Crossing to her*) Quite right, my dear, quite right. (*He pinches her cheek, and takes advantage of this kingly gesture to say in a loud whisper*) We've pulled it off! (*They sit down;*
620 *the* KING *and* QUEEN *on their thrones,* DULCIBELLA *on the* PRINCESS's *throne.* CARLO *stands behind* DULCIBELLA, *the* CHANCELLOR *on the right of the* QUEEN, *and the* PRINCE *and* PRINCESS *behind the long seat on the left.*)

CHANCELLOR.   (*Consulting documents*) H'r'm! Have I Your Majesty's authority to put the final test to His Royal Highness?

QUEEN.   (*Whispering to* KING) Is this safe?

KING.   (*Whispering*) Perfectly, my dear. I told him the answer a minute ago. (*Over his shoulder to* CARLO) Don't forget, *Dog*. (*Aloud*) Proceed, Your Excellency. It is my
630 desire that the affairs of my country should ever be conducted in a strictly constitutional manner.

CHANCELLOR.   (*Oratorically*) By the constitution of the country, a suitor to Her Royal Highness's hand cannot be deemed successful until he has given the correct answer to a riddle. (*Conversationally*) The last suitor answered incorrectly, and thus failed to win his bride.

KING.   By a coincidence he fell into the moat.

CHANCELLOR.   (*To* CARLO) I have now to ask Your Royal
640 Highness if you are prepared for the <u>ordeal</u>?

CARLO.   (*Cheerfully*) Absolutely.

CHANCELLOR.   I may mention, as a matter, possibly, of some slight historical interest to our visitor, that by the constitution of the country the same riddle is not allowed to be asked on two successive occasions.

KING.   (*Startled*) What's that?

---

words for everyday use

or • deal (ôr dēl´) *n.*, difficult experience. *Benedict considered sitting quietly for twenty minutes to be the most difficult <u>ordeal</u> imaginable.*

THINK AND REFLECT

Why is Carlo so confident that he is ready for the ordeal? **(Infer)** How does what the Chancellor says next threaten the success of the marriage? **(Interpret)**

CHANCELLOR. This one, it is interesting to recall, was <u>propounded</u> exactly a century ago, and we must take it as a

650   fortunate <u>omen</u> that it was well and truly solved.

KING. (*To* QUEEN) I may want my sword directly.

CHANCELLOR. The riddle is this. What is it which has four legs and mews like a cat?

CARLO. (*Promptly*) A dog.

KING. (*Still more promptly*) Bravo, bravo! (*He claps loudly and nudges the* QUEEN, *who claps too.*)

CHANCELLOR. (*Peering at his documents*) According to the records of the occasion to which I referred, the correct answer would seem to be—

660   **PRINCESS.** (*To* PRINCE) Say something, quick!

CHANCELLOR. —not dog, but—

PRINCE. Your Majesty, have I permission to speak? Naturally His Royal Highness could not think of justifying himself on such an occasion, but I think that with Your Majesty's gracious permission, I could—

KING. Certainly, certainly.

PRINCE. In our country, we have an animal to which we have given the name "dog," or, in the local dialect of the more mountainous districts, "doggie." It sits by the fireside

670   and purrs.

CARLO. That's right. It purrs like anything.

PRINCE. When it needs milk, which is its <u>staple</u> food, it mews.

CARLO. (*Enthusiastically*) Mews like nobody's business.

PRINCE. It also has four legs.

CARLO. One at each corner.

PRINCE. In some countries, I understand, this animal is called a "cat." In one distant country to which His Royal Highness and I penetrated, it was called by the very curious

680   name of "hippopotamus."

CARLO. That's right. (*To the* PRINCE) Do you remember that ginger-colored hippopotamus which used to climb on to my shoulder and lick my ear?

words for everyday use

pro • pound (prə pound´) v., propose. *The city council chose the occasion of the big parade to <u>propound</u> its new zoning policies.*

o • men (ō´mən) n., sign of a future event. *The black clouds that Gertrude saw before she left for school seemed to her a bad <u>omen</u> for a test day.*

sta • ple (stā´pəl) adj., most important. *In many countries, rice is the <u>staple</u> crop.*

PRINCE. I shall never forget it, sir. (*To the* KING) So you see, Your Majesty—

KING. Thank you. I think that makes it perfectly clear. (*Firmly to the* CHANCELLOR) You are about to agree?

CHANCELLOR. Undoubtedly, Your Majesty. May I be the first to congratulate His Royal Highness on solving the

690 riddle so accurately?

KING. You may be the first to see that all is in order for an immediate wedding.

CHANCELLOR. Thank you, Your Majesty. (*He bows and withdraws. The* KING *rises, as do the* QUEEN *and* DULCIBELLA.)

KING. (*To* CARLO) Doubtless, Prince Simon, you will wish to retire and prepare yourself for the ceremony.

CARLO. Thank you, sir.

PRINCE. Have I Your Majesty's permission to attend His Royal Highness? It is the custom of his country for Princes

700 of the royal blood to be married in full armor, a matter which requires a certain adjustment—

KING. Of course, of course. (CARLO *bows to the* KING *and* QUEEN *and goes out. As the* PRINCE *is about to follow, the* KING *stops him.*) Young man, you have a quality of quickness which I admire. It is my pleasure to reward it in any way which commends itself to you.

PRINCE. Your Majesty is ever gracious. May I ask for my reward *after* the ceremony? (*He catches the eye of the* PRINCESS, *and they give each other a secret smile.*)

710 **KING.** Certainly. (*The* PRINCE *bows and goes out. To* DULCIBELLA) Now, young woman, make yourself scarce. You've done your work excellently, and we will see that you and your—what was his name?

DULCIBELLA. Eg, Your Majesty.

KING. —that you and your Eg are not forgotten.

DULCIBELLA. Coo! (*She curtsies and goes out.*)

PRINCESS. (*Calling*) Wait for me, Dulcibella!

KING. (*To* QUEEN) Well, my dear, we may congratulate ourselves. As I remember saying to somebody once, "You

720 have not lost a daughter, you have gained a son." How does he strike you?

QUEEN. Stupid.

KING. They made a very handsome pair, I thought, he and Dulcibella.

Use **THE STRATEGY**

READ WITH A PURPOSE. What does the King say he admires in the Prince? Record your answer in the Characterization Chart.

QUEEN. Both stupid.

KING. I said nothing about stupidity. What I *said* was that they were both extremely handsome. That is the important thing. (*Struck by a sudden idea*) Or isn't it?

QUEEN. What do *you* think of Prince Simon, Camilla?

730 **PRINCESS.** I adore him. We shall be so happy together.

KING. Well, of course you will. I told you so. Happy ever after.

QUEEN. Run along now and get ready.

PRINCESS. Yes, mother. (*She throws a kiss to them and goes out.*)

KING. (*Anxiously*) My dear, have we been wrong about Camilla all this time? It seemed to me that she wasn't looking *quite* so plain as usual just now. Did *you* notice anything?

740 **QUEEN.** (*Carelessly*) Just the excitement of the marriage.

KING. (*Relieved*) Ah, yes, that would account for it. ∎

THINK AND REFLECT

Is the Queen right about the reason for the change in Camilla? Why, or why not? **(Evaluate)**

_____

_____

_____

Reflect ON YOUR READING

❑ Compare your Characterization Chart with that of a partner. Think of a word or short phrase that you would use to describe each character listed in the chart. Then highlight or underline the details from the chart that support that description.

❑ Choose one of the characters, and write a paragraph describing that character. Begin with a topic sentence that includes your brief description. Then support that topic sentence with the details you highlighted or underlined.

Reading Skills and Test Practice

DRAW CONCLUSIONS

READ, THINK, AND EXPLAIN. Discuss with a partner how best to answer the following questions that require you to draw conclusions. Use the Think-Aloud Notes to write down your ideas before drafting your answers.

1. Which character from this play is the "ugly duckling"? How is he or she like the fairy tale character?

_____

_____

_____

_____

_____

2. What does Great-Aunt Malkin think about the effects of beauty?

_____

_____

_____

_____

REFLECT ON YOUR RESPONSE. How did using the reading strategy help you to answer the questions?

_____

_____

THINK-ALOUD
NOTES

_____

_____

_____

_____

_____

_____

_____

_____

_____

_____

Investigate, Inquire, and Imagine

RECALL: GATHER FACTS
1a. What happened at the Tournament of Love last year?

→ **INTERPRET: FIND MEANING**
1b. Why did this happen? Now, knowing what you know about Camilla's appearance, what does this say about the men who competed in the tournament?

ANALYZE: TAKE THINGS APART
2a. What attitudes are presented in this play about outer beauty? about inner beauty? Focus your response on the attitudes of the Chancellor, the King, the Queen, Great-Aunt Malkin, the Princess herself, and Prince Simon.

→ **SYNTHESIZE: BRING THINGS TOGETHER**
2b. What do you think is this play's theme about beauty and judging others using a single standard of beauty?

EVALUATE: MAKE JUDGMENTS
3a. The King says that "once you're married you live happily ever after." Explain whether this is true for the King and Queen. How happy do they seem together? How can you tell?

→ **EXTEND: CONNECT IDEAS**
3b. Based on what you have learned about Princess Camilla, Prince Simon, and how they get along, explain how you think their marriage will compare with the King and Queen's.

Literary Tools

DIALOGUE. The speech of actors in a play is called **dialogue.** In *The Ugly Duckling,* the reader learns about the characters and plot largely through the dialogue. Find two places in the play where you learn important information through the words characters speak to each other.

Lines _____ What I Learned _____

_____

Lines _____ What I Learned _____

_____

The humor in the play is also conveyed through dialogue. Find two examples of humorous dialogue.

Lines _____ Why This Is Funny_____

_____

Lines _____ Why This Is Funny_____

_____

WordWorkshop

VOCABULARY CHARADES. Acting out vocabulary words in a game of charades will help you remember the words more easily. **Charades** is a game in which players use silent cues to help other players guess a word or phrase. To begin, divide the class in half. Write each of the vocabulary words on a slip of paper. Fold the slips in half, and put them in a central container. Flip a coin to determine which side of the class goes first. A player from the first team should draw a slip of paper from the container. This player's task is to get the rest of his or her team to guess the correct word using only gestures and facial expressions. If the team guesses correctly, they get a point. If they don't guess the correct word in 45 seconds, the other team has 15 seconds to guess and win the point. Play continues with a representative from the second team drawing a word.

Read-Write Connection

Do you think Great-Aunt Malkin's gift to Camilla was a good idea? Why, or why not? How might Camilla's life have been different if her beauty had not been hidden?

_____

_____

_____

_____

_____

_____

Beyond the Reading

PREPARE A DRAMATIC MONOLOGUE. In this selection, you learned how to determine character traits from dialogue. A **monologue** is a speech given by one character, and it too can give you a sense of who a character is. Find a collection of dramatic monologues at the library. Select one, and prepare to perform it for the class. Try to figure out what the character is like, and deliver the lines in the way that character would speak them.

GO ONLINE. To find links and additional activities for this selection, visit the EMC Internet Resource Center at **emcp.com/languagearts** and click on Write-In Reader.

Unit 6 READING Review

Choose and Use Reading Strategies

Before reading an excerpt from the screenplay *In the Fog* by Milton Geiger, review with a partner how to use reading strategies with drama.

1. Read with a Purpose
2. Connect to Prior Knowledge
3. Write Things Down
4. Make Predictions
5. Visualize
6. Use Text Organization
7. Tackle Difficult Vocabulary
8. Monitor Your Reading Progress

Next, apply at least two of these reading strategies as you read the screenplay excerpt below. A **screenplay** is the written version of a television program or film. As the excerpt begins, the doctor has gotten lost driving in thick, eerie fog. He has just stopped and gotten out of his car to study a road sign when his flashlight goes out. Use the margins and mark up the text to show how you are using reading strategies to read actively. You may find it helpful to choose a graphic organizer from Appendix B to gather information as you read the excerpt, or use the Summary Chart on page B-13 to create a graphic organizer that summarizes the excerpt.

> **DOCTOR.** Darn! *(He fumbles with the flashlight in the gloom. Then a voice is raised to him from off-scene.)*
>
> **EBEN.** *(Off-scene, strangely)* Turn around, mister . . . *(The DOCTOR turns sharply to stare off-scene. His face is lit by a bobbing light from off-scene.)*
>
> **ZEKE.** *(Off-scene)* You don't have to be afraid, mister . . .
>
> *(CUT TO: What DOCTOR sees. Two men are slowly approaching out of the fog, grotesque in the distorting gloom. One carries a lantern below his knees. The other holds a heavy rifle of dim manufacture. Their features are utterly indistinct as they approach and the rifleman holds up his gun with quiet threat.)*
>
> *(CUT TO: Group shot, angling past DOCTOR'S shoulder, at their faces.)*
>
> **EBEN.** You don't have to be afraid.
>
> **DOCTOR.** *(More indignant than afraid)* So you say! Who are you, man?
>
> **EBEN.** We don't aim to hurt you none.

> **DOCTOR.** That's reassuring. I'd like to know just what you mean by this? This gun business! Who *are* you?
>
> **ZEKE.** *(Mildly)* What's your trade, mister?
>
> **DOCTOR.** I . . . I'm a doctor. Why?
>
> **ZEKE.** *(to EBEN)* Doctor.
>
> **EBEN.** *(Nods; then to DOCTOR)* Yer the man we want.

WordWorkshop

UNIT 6 WORDS FOR EVERYDAY USE

abandonment, 212	grudge, 208	precautionary, 210
affirm, 209	homage, 205	propound, 220
alter, 204	imperious, 216	retire, 210
ardent, 211	inappropriate, 211	ruse, 209
assume, 205	inevitable, 202	staple, 220
attribute, 206	invariable, 206	strenuous, 213
condemn, 204	meditation, 210	suitor, 202
cryptic, 207	nonchalant, 205	surreptitious, 207
dignified, 202	omen, 220	swoon, 217
doggedness, 206	ordeal, 219	tactful, 202
elusive, 202	pluck, 214	vain, 216
exaggerate, 215	posterity, 202	waft, 211

CATEGORIZE VOCABULARY WORDS. Categorizing vocabulary words, or sorting them into groups based on shared characteristics, can help you create associations among words that will help you remember them. On your own paper, make a five-column chart. Label the columns with the headings below. Then determine which words from the list above fit in each category. You can include a word in more than one category, but you should be prepared to explain how it fits in each.

❑ Words describing ways of moving

❑ Words suitable for royalty or other people in high positions

❑ Words about love

❑ Words about what you say or how you say it

❑ Other category _____

Literary Tools

Select the best literary element on the right to complete each sentence on the left. Write the correct letter in the blank.

___ 1. ___ are notes included in a play to describe how something should look, sound, or be performed.

___ 2. A(n) ___ is a major section of a play. There are often one, three, or five of these in a dramatic work.

___ 3. A. A. Milne is the ___ who wrote *The Ugly Duckling*.

___ 4. The words characters say to each other can be called ___.

___ 5. The written version of a play is called its ___.

___ 6. A short part of a play that happens in a single time and place is called a(n) ___.

___ 7. In a(n) ___, a story is told through characters played by actors.

___ 8. A speech given by one character is called a(n) ___.

___ 9. The act of creating a character is called ___.

___10. Sets, props, special effects, lighting, and costumes are all elements presented to the audience's senses; these elements combined are called the ___.

a. act, 194

b. characterization, 199

c. dialogue, 194, 209, 224

d. drama, 193

e. monologue, 194, 225

f. playwright, 193

g. scene, 194

h. script, 193

i. spectacle, 194

j. stage directions, 193, 204

On Your Own

Find a scene from a play that you like by looking through drama anthologies, screenplays, and scripts in the library. Then choose one of the following activities.

FLUENTLY SPEAKING. Work with a small group or partner to do a dramatic reading of one scene. Introduce the scene with background information that will help your audience understand what the scene is about. Practice your lines until you and the other actors can present the play smoothly and with appropriate feeling.

PICTURE THIS. Adapt the scene you have chosen into a comic strip or short comic book. As you sketch the characters, use their gestures, body language, and facial expressions to show how they are feeling about the events and the other characters. Use word bubbles to show what they are saying or thinking.

PUT IT IN WRITING. Pick one of the characters from the scene you have chosen. Write a dramatic monologue in which the character shares his or her thoughts and feelings about what happened in the scene.

Unit SEVEN

READING Nonfiction

NONFICTION

Nonfiction is writing about real people, places, things, and events. It also may present an author's thoughts and ideas. Forms of nonfiction writing include articles, autobiographies, biographies, documentary writings, essays, histories, how-to writings, memoirs, and speeches.

Forms of Nonfiction

ARTICLE. An **article** is a brief work of nonfiction on a specific topic. You can find articles in encyclopedias, newspapers, and magazines.

AUTOBIOGRAPHY. An **autobiography** is the story of a person's life told by that person. Consequently, autobiographies are told from the first-person point of view. In this unit, the excerpt from *Geronimo's Story of His Life* is an example of an autobiography.

BIOGRAPHY. A **biography** is the story of a person's life told by another person. Although biographies are told from a third-person point of view, autobiographical excerpts such as **letters**, **diaries**, and **journals** may be included. Bill Littlefield's story about the life of Satchel Paige is an example of a biography.

DOCUMENTARY WRITING. **Documentary writing** is writing that records an event or subject in accurate detail. In this unit, the excerpt from Dian Fossey's *Gorillas in the Mist* is an example of documentary writing.

ESSAY. An **essay**, originally meaning "a trial or attempt," is a short nonfiction work that explores a single subject and is typically a more lasting work than an article. Among the many types of essays are personal and expository essays. A **personal**, or **expressive**, **essay**

MARK THE TEXT

Underline or highlight the forms of nonfiction writing.

NOTE THE FACTS

How is a biography different from an autobiography?

_____

_____

_____

CONNECT TO PRIOR
KNOWLEDGE. What types of histories have you read in social studies class?

_____

_____

_____

_____

THINK AND REFLECT

Write another example of how-to writing. **(Apply)**

_____

_____

_____

Reading TIP

Nonfiction work can have more than one purpose. For example, in a speech about the Americans with Disabilities Act, actor Christopher Reeve entertains, informs, and persuades the audience to take action.

deals with the life or interests of the writer. Personal essays are often, but not always, written in the first person. An **expository essay** features the developed ideas of the writer on a certain topic, usually expressing an author's opinion. "Pompeii" by Robert Silverberg is an example of an expository essay.

HISTORY. A **history** is an account of past events. To write their histories, writers may use **speeches, sermons, contracts, deeds, constitutions, laws, political tracts**, and other types of public records.

HOW-TO WRITING. How-to writing is writing that explains a procedure or strategy. A manual that explains how to operate a DVD player is an example of how-to writing.

MEMOIR. A **memoir** is a nonfiction narration that tells a story autobiographically or biographically. Memoirs are based on a person's experiences and reactions to events.

SPEECH. A **speech** is a public address that was originally delivered orally.

Purposes and Methods of Writing in Nonfiction

PURPOSE. A writer's **purpose**, or aim, is a writer's reason for writing. The following chart classifies modes, or categories, of prose writing by purpose.

Modes and Purposes of Writing		
Mode	**Purpose**	**Writing Forms**
personal/ expressive writing	to reflect	diary entry, memoir, personal letter, autobiography, personal essay
imaginative/ descriptive writing	to entertain, to describe, to enrich, and to enlighten	poem, character sketch, play, short story
narrative writing	to tell a story, to narrate a series of events	short story, biography, legend, myth, history
informative/ expository writing	to inform, to explain	news article, research report, expository essay, book review
persuasive/ argumentative writing	to persuade	editorial, petition, political speech, persuasive essay

Types of Nonfiction Writing

In order to write effectively, a writer can choose to organize a piece of writing in different ways. The following chart describes types of writing that are commonly used in nonfiction, as well as how they are organized.

Type of Writing	Description
narration	Narrative writing tells a story or describes events. It may use chronological, or time, order.
dialogue	Dialogue reveals people's actual speech, which is set off with quotation marks.
description	Descriptive writing tells how things look, sound, smell, taste, or feel, often using spatial order.
exposition	Expository writing presents facts or opinions and is sometimes organized in one of these ways: ■ **Analysis** breaks something into its parts and shows how the parts are related. ■ **Classification** places subjects into categories according to what they have in common. ■ **Comparison-and-contrast order** presents similarities as it compares two things and differences as it contrasts them. ■ **How-to writing** presents the steps in a process or directions on how to do something.

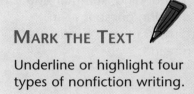

MARK THE TEXT

Underline or highlight four types of nonfiction writing.

Active Reading Strategy Checklists

When reading nonfiction, it is important to know that the author is telling you about true events. The following checklists offer things to consider when reading nonfiction selections.

1 READ WITH A PURPOSE. Before reading nonfiction, give yourself a purpose, or something to look for, as you read. Sometimes a purpose will be a directive from a teacher: "Find out how Satchel Paige experienced and reacted to racism." Other times you can set your own purpose by previewing the title, the opening lines, and instructional information. Say to yourself

- ❑ This selection will be about . . .
- ❑ I will keep track of . . .
- ❑ The author wants readers to know . . .
- ❑ The author wrote this to . . .

2 CONNECT TO PRIOR KNOWLEDGE. Being aware of what you already know and calling it to mind as you read can help you understand a writer's views. As you read, say to yourself

- ❑ I already know this about the author's ideas . . .
- ❑ These things in the selection are similar to something I have experienced . . .
- ❑ Something similar I've read is . . .
- ❑ I agree with this because . . .

3 WRITE THINGS DOWN. As you read nonfiction, write down or mark important points that the author makes. Possible ways to keep a written record include

- ❑ Underline the author's key ideas.
- ❑ Write down your thoughts about the author's ideas.
- ❑ Highlight the author's main points and supporting details.
- ❑ Create a graphic organizer to keep track of ideas.
- ❑ Use a code to respond to the author's ideas.

Reading TIP

Nonfiction reading can be challenging. As you read, make sure you are "getting it" by responding, summarizing, and asking questions—in writing or in your head—as you read.

Reading TIP

To **connect to your prior knowledge**, compare what you are reading to
- things you have read before
- things you have experienced
- things you know about the topic

Reading TIP

A simple code can help you remember your reactions to what you are reading. You can use
- ! for "This is like something I have experienced"
- ? for "I don't understand this"
- ✓ for "This seems important"

4 MAKE PREDICTIONS. Before you read a nonfiction selection, use information about the author, the subject matter, and the title to guess what the selection will be about. Make predictions like the following:

- ❑ What will come next is . . .
- ❑ The author will support ideas by . . .
- ❑ I think the selection will end with . . .
- ❑ The title tells me that the selection will be about . . .

5 VISUALIZE. Visualizing, or allowing the words on the page to create images in your mind, helps you understand the author's message. In order to visualize what a selection is about, imagine that you are the narrator. Read the words in your head with the type of expression that the author means to put behind them. Make statements such as

- ❑ This parts helps me envision how . . .
- ❑ My sketch of this part would include . . .
- ❑ This part helps me see how . . .
- ❑ This part changes my views on . . .
- ❑ The author connects ideas by . . .

6 USE TEXT ORGANIZATION. When you read nonfiction, pay attention to the main idea and supporting details. Learn to stop occasionally and retell what you have read. Say to yourself

- ❑ The writer's main point is . . .
- ❑ The writer supports the main point by . . .
- ❑ In this section, the writer is saying that . . .
- ❑ I can summarize this section by . . .
- ❑ I can follow the events because . . .

7 TACKLE DIFFICULT VOCABULARY. Difficult words can hinder your ability to understand a writer's message. Use context, consult a dictionary, or ask someone about words you do not understand. When you come across a difficult word in nonfiction, say to yourself

- ❑ The lines near this word tell me that this word means . . .
- ❑ A dictionary definition shows that the word means . . .
- ❑ My work with the word before reading helps me know that the word means . . .
- ❑ A classmate said that the word means . . .

Reading **TIP**

Read nonfiction carefully the first time through. Take notes as you read. After you finish reading, reread your notes. Mark them up and make additions or corrections. Rereading your notes and clarifying them helps you remember what you've read.

Reading **TIP**

Skim a selection before you read it. Make a list of words that might slow you down, and write *synonyms*, words that have the same or nearly the same meaning, for each in the margins. As you read, use the synonyms in place of the words.

8 **MONITOR YOUR READING PROGRESS.** All readers encounter difficulty when they read, especially if the reading material is not self-selected. When you have to read something, take note of problems you are having and fix them. The key to reading success is knowing when you are having difficulty. To fix problems, say to yourself

- ❏ Because I don't understand this part, I will . . .
- ❏ Because I'm having trouble staying connected to the ideas in the selection, I will . . .
- ❏ Because the words in the selection are too hard, I will . . .
- ❏ Because the selection is long, I will . . .
- ❏ Because I can't retell what the selection was about, I will . . .

Become an Active Reader

The instruction with the nonfiction selections in this unit gives you an in-depth look at how to use one strategy. Learning how to use several strategies in combination will ensure your complete understanding of what you are reading. When you have difficulty, use fix-up ideas to correct the problem. For further information about the active reading strategies, see Unit 1, pages 4–15.

How to Use Reading Strategies with Nonfiction

Excerpt 1. Note how a reader uses active reading strategies while reading an excerpt from Abraham Lincoln's famous "House Divided" speech. Lincoln presented the speech at the closing of the Illinois Republican State Convention in 1858.

READ WITH A PURPOSE

I want to find out what the "house divided" speech is about.

CONNECT TO PRIOR KNOWLEDGE

I know Lincoln was elected president in 1860; this speech was presented two years before that.

"A house divided against itself cannot stand." I believe this government cannot endure permanently half slave and half free. I do not expect the Union to be dissolved—I do not expect the house to fall—but I do expect it will cease to be divided. It will become all one thing, or all the other. Either the opponents of slavery will arrest the further spread of it, and place it where the public mind shall rest in the belief that it is in the course of ultimate extinction; or its advocates will push it forward, till it shall become alike lawful in all the States, old as well as new—North as well as South.

VISUALIZE

I envision Lincoln saying these words loudly with great passion.

TACKLE DIFFICULT VOCABULARY

The context leads me to think that *arrest* must mean "stop."

Excerpt 2. Note how a reader uses active reading strategies while reading an excerpt from Christopher Reeve's speech to the Democratic National Convention in 1996.

WRITE THINGS DOWN

I will underline Reeve's idea of an "American motto."

MAKE PREDICTIONS

I predict that Reeve will talk about trying to walk again.

Now on the wall of my room while I was in rehab, there was a picture of the Space Shuttle blasting off, and it was autographed by every astronaut now at NASA, and on the top of that picture, it says, "We found nothing is impossible."

Now that, that should be our motto. It's not a Democratic motto, not a Republican motto, it's an American motto.

It's not something one Party can do alone. It's something we as a nation have to do together.

MONITOR YOUR READING PROGRESS

That first sentence is long. As I reread it, I'm going to add pauses.

USE TEXT ORGANIZATION

Location phrases like "on the wall" and "on the top of that picture" help me follow the description.

Reader's resource

Author Robert Silverberg is best known for his science fiction writing. However, his interest in archaeology, space exploration, and military history led him to write historical pieces, too. In **"Pompeii,"** Silverberg describes what happened when Mount Vesuvius erupted in Italy in AD 79. Ashes and lava covered people and animals and destroyed the city. Since AD 79, Mount Vesuvius has exploded many times, and it is still an active volcano. Its most recent eruption occurred in 1944.

Word watch

PREVIEW VOCABULARY

belch	monopoly
bewilder	oblige
catastrophe	ominous
critical	project
engulf	rutted
excavation	shrewdness
fruitless	shroud
gaudy	tranquility
haphazard	unruly
imposing	vitality
molten	

Reader's journal

Write about a natural disaster you have experienced or heard about.

"Pompeii"
by Robert Silverberg

Active READING STRATEGY

VISUALIZE

Before Reading ➤ PICTURE POMPEII

❑ Read the Reader's Resource and look over the photograph on page 237.
❑ Read the first four paragraphs on pages 237 and 238. Picture what Pompeii looks like today and what it looked like in AD 79. Add these images to your graphic organizer below.

Graphic Organizer: Image Chart

Images of Pompeii	
AD 79	**Today**

Pompeii

Robert Silverberg

During Reading

CONTINUE TO PICTURE WHAT HAPPENED IN POMPEII

❏ Continue reading the story. Mark words and phrases that help you imagine Pompeii in AD 79 and today.

❏ After you finish reading, you will come back to what you have marked and add some of it to your graphic organizer.

Not very far from Naples a strange city sleeps under the hot Italian sun. It is the city of Pompeii and there is no other city quite like it in all the world. No one lives in Pompeii but crickets and beetles and lizards, yet every year thousands of people travel from distant countries to visit it.

Pompeii is a dead city. No one has lived there for nearly two thousand years, not since the summer of the year AD 79, to be exact.

10 Until that year Pompeii was a prosperous city of twenty-five thousand people. Nearby was the Bay of Naples, an arm of the blue Mediterranean. Rich men came down from wealthy Rome, 125 miles to the north, to build luxurious seaside villas. Fertile farmlands occupied the fields surrounding Pompeii. Rising sharply behind the city was the four-thousand-foot bulk of Mount Vesuvius, a grass-covered slope where the shepherds of Pompeii took their goats to graze. Pompeii was a busy city and a happy one.

It died suddenly, in a terrible rain of fire and ashes.

The tragedy struck on the twenty-fourth of August, AD
20 79. Mount Vesuvius, which had slumbered quietly for centuries, exploded with savage violence. Death struck on a hot summer afternoon. Tons of hot ashes fell on Pompeii, smothering it, hiding it from sight. For three days the sun did not break through the cloud of volcanic ash that filled

NOTE THE FACTS

Why is Pompeii a unique city?

_____

_____

_____

Literary TOOLS

ESSAY. An **essay** is a short nonfiction work that expresses a writer's thoughts about a single subject. A good essay develops a single idea, or thesis, and is organized into an introduction, a body, and a conclusion. Underline a sentence in the first two paragraphs that is a good thesis for "Pompeii."

Tackle Difficult Vocabulary

Don't let difficult vocabulary halt your progress. When you come across a word you do not know, keep reading if you feel you understand enough. If you need the word for understanding, use the definition in the Words for Everyday Use at the bottom of the page, look up the word in a dictionary, or ask a friend or your teacher for help if the context does not help you. Write a synonym near the unknown word that helps you remember what it means. Then reread the sentence or section that contains the word. Learn to read for meaning, not for speed.

NOTE THE FACTS

In what way is the excavation of Pompeii different from other excavations?

_____

_____

_____

the sky. And when the eruption ended, Pompeii was buried deep. A thriving city had perished in a single day.

Centuries passed. Pompeii was forgotten. Then, fifteen hundred years later, it was discovered again. Beneath the protecting <u>shroud</u> of ashes, the city lay intact. Everything
30 was as it had been the day Vesuvius erupted. There were still loaves of bread in the ovens of the bakeries. In the wine shops, the wine jars were in place, and on one counter could be seen a stain where a customer had thrown down his glass and fled.

Modern archaeology began with the discovery of buried Pompeii. Before then, the digging of treasures from the ground had been a <u>haphazard</u> and unscholarly affair. But the <u>excavation</u> of Pompeii was done in a systematic, scientific manner, and so the science of serious archaeology
40 can be said to have begun there. Since the year 1748, generations of skilled Italian workmen have been carefully removing the ashes that buried Pompeii, until today almost four-fifths of the city has been uncovered.

Other Roman cities died more slowly. Wind and rain and fire wore them away. Later peoples tore down the ancient monuments, using the stone to build houses and churches. Over the centuries, the cities of the Caesars[1] vanished, and all that is left of them today are scattered fragments.

Not so with Pompeii. It was <u>engulfed</u> in an instant, and its
50 people's tragedy was our great gain. The buildings of Pompeii still stand as they stood two thousand years ago, and within the houses we can still see the pots and pans, the household tools, the hammers and nails. On the walls of the buildings are election slogans and the scrawlings of <u>unruly</u>

---

1. **Caesars.** Emperors of ancient Rome

words for everyday use

shroud (shroud') *n.*, something that covers or protects. *A <u>shroud</u> covered the body in the coffin.*

hap • haz • ard (hap' haz' ərd) *adj.*, not planned; casual. *<u>Haphazard</u> planning ensured that the wedding would be a disaster.*

ex • ca • va • tion (eks kə vā'shən) *n.*, something unearthed by digging. *<u>Excavation</u> for the new house uncovered pieces of old pottery.*

en • gulf (in gulf') *v.*, swallow up; overwhelm. *The huge waves threatened to <u>engulf</u> the small boat.*

un • rul • y (un roo' lē) *adj.*, hard to control. *Ralph's <u>unruly</u> hair always stuck up in the morning.*

boys. Pompeii is like a photograph in three dimensions. It shows us exactly what a city of the Roman Empire was like, down to the smallest detail of everyday life.

60 To go to Pompeii today is to take a trip backward in a time machine. The old city comes to vivid life all around you. You can almost hear the clatter of horses' hoofs on the narrow streets, the cries of children, the loud, hearty laughter of the shopkeepers. You can almost smell meat sizzling over a charcoal fire. The sky is cloudlessly blue, with the summer sun almost directly overhead. The grassy slopes of great Vesuvius pierce the heavens behind the city, and sunlight shimmers on the water of the bay a thousand yards from the city walls. Ships from every nation are in port, and the babble of strange languages can be heard in the streets.

70 Such was Pompeii on its last day. And so it is today, now that the volcanic ash has been cleared away. A good imagination is all you need to restore it to bustling vitality. . . .

At dawn on the twenty-fourth of August in the year 79, Pompeii's twenty-five thousand people awakened to another hot day in that hot summer. There was going to be a performance in the arena that night, and the whole town was looking forward to the bloody contests of the gladiators.[2] The rumble of heavy wooden wheels was heard as carts

80 loaded with grain entered the city from the farms outside the walls. Over the centuries the steady stream of carts had worn ruts deep into the pavement of Pompeii's narrow streets.

Wooden shutters were drawn back noisily. The grocers and sellers of fruit opened their shops, displaying their wares on trays set out on the sidewalk. In the wine shops, the girls who sold wine to the thirsty sailors got ready for another busy day. . . .

---

2. **gladiators.** In ancient Rome, men who fought other men or animals with weapons in an arena for the entertainment of spectators

words for everyday use

vi • tal • i • ty (vī tal´ə tē) n., energy; life. *Willa's health and vitality came back after her illness.*

MARK THE TEXT

Underline or highlight what we can learn from Pompeii that we can't learn from other ruins.

Use THE STRATEGY

VISUALIZE. Visualize what happened at dawn on the twenty-fourth of August in AD 79.

Reading TIP

Events arranged in order of the time in which they happened are said to be in **chronological order.** Starting with "At dawn on the twenty-fourth of August," the author uses chronological order to describe events in Pompeii in AD 79.

CONNECT TO PRIOR KNOWLEDGE.
Connect to what you already
know about children going
to school and businesses
opening up to envision what
the beginning of Pompeii's
last day was like.

FIX-UP IDEA

Reread
Quickly reread whenever
you do not understand a
line or two. Rereading
aloud is even more pow-
erful in unlocking
passages that are long or
difficult.

90   Outside, children headed toward school, carrying slates
and followed by their dogs. Nearly everyone in Pompeii
had a dog, and barking could be heard everywhere as the
Pompeiian pets greeted one another. A small boy who had
just learned the Greek alphabet stopped in front of a blank
wall and took a piece of charcoal from his tunic. Hastily he
scribbled the Greek letters: *alpha, beta, gamma.*

In the Forum, the town's important men had gathered
after breakfast to read the political signs that were posted
during the night. Elsewhere in the Forum, the wool
merchants talked business, and the men who owned the
100   vineyards were smiling to each other about the high quality
of this year's wine, which would fetch a good price in other
countries. . . .

The quiet morning moved slowly along. There was
nothing very unusual about Pompeii. . . .

But tragedy was on its way. Beneath Vesuvius' vine-
covered slopes, a mighty force was about to break loose.

No one in Pompeii knew the dangerous power
imprisoned in Vesuvius. For fifteen hundred years the
mountain had slept quietly, but far beneath the crest a
110   boiling fury of <u>molten</u> lava had gradually been gathering
strength. The solid rock of Vesuvius held the hidden forces
in check. An earthquake sixteen years before had been the
first sign that the trapped fury beneath the mountain was
struggling to break free. Pressure was building up. In the
city at the base of the mountain, life went on in complete
ignorance of the looming <u>catastrophe</u>.

At one o'clock in the afternoon on the twenty-fourth of
August, AD 79, the <u>critical</u> point was reached. The walls of
rock could hold no longer.

120   The mountain exploded, raining death on thousands.

Like many tragedies, this one was misunderstood at first.
Down in Pompeii, four miles from Vesuvius, a tremendous
explosion was heard, echoing ringingly off the mountains
on the far side of the city.

**words
for
everyday
use**

mol • ten (mōl´tən) *adj.,* melted or liquefied by heat. *The ironworker poured <u>molten</u> metal into the mold to harden.*
ca • tas • tro • phe (kə tas´ trə fē) *n.,* any great or sudden disaster or misfortune. *The flood was a huge <u>catastrophe</u> in this town.*
crit • i • cal (krit´i kəl) *adj.,* of or forming a crisis or turning point. *The final stretch of the race was <u>critical</u> in determining the winner.*

"What was that?" people cried from one end of town to another. They stared at each other, puzzled, troubled. Were the gods fighting in heaven? Is that what the loud explosion was?

"Look!" somebody shouted. "Look at Vesuvius!"

130 Thousands of eyes swiveled upward. Thousands of arms pointed. A black cloud was rising from the shattered crest of the mountain. Higher and higher it rose. An eyewitness, the Roman philosopher Pliny, described the cloud as he saw it from Misenum, twenty-two miles from Pompeii on the opposite side of the bay.

"Better than any other tree, the pine can give an idea of the shape and appearance of this cloud," Pliny wrote in his notebook later that day. "In fact it was <u>projected</u> into the air like an enormous trunk and then spread into many

140 branches, now white, now black, now spotted, according to whether earth or ashes were thrown up."

Minutes passed. The sound of the great explosion died away, but it still tingled in everyone's ears. The cloud over Vesuvius still rose, black as night, higher and higher.

"The cloud is blotting out the sun!" someone cried in terror.

Still no one in Pompeii had perished. The fragments of rock thrown up when the mountain exploded all fell

150 back on the volcano's slopes. Within the crater, sizzling masses of molten rock were rushing upward, and upwelling gas drove small blobs of liquefied stone thousands of feet into the air. They cooled high above the gaping mouth of the volcano and plummeted earthward.

A strange rain began to fall on Pompeii—a rain of stone. The stones were light. They were pumice stones, consisting mostly of air bubbles. They poured down as though there had been a sudden cloudburst. The pumice stones, or lapilli, did little damage. They clattered against

160 the wooden roofs of the Pompeiian houses. They fell by

DRAW A PICTURE

Draw of picture of what Pliny saw.

NOTE THE FACTS

Was the initial explosion very damaging? Why, or why not?

_____

_____

_____

words for everyday use

pro • ject (prō jekt´) v., throw or hurl forward. *The slingshot could project water balloons across the road.*

the hundreds in the streets. The people who had rushed out of houses and shops and thermopolia[3] to see what had caused the explosion now scrambled to take cover as the weird rain of lapilli continued.

"What is happening?" Pompeiians asked one another. They rushed to the temples—the Temple of Jupiter, the Temple of Apollo, the Temple of Isis. <u>Bewildered</u> priests tried to calm bewildered citizens. Darkness had come at midday, and a rain of small stones fell from the sky, and

170 who could explain it?

Some did not wait for explanation. In a tavern near the edge of the city, half a dozen gladiators who were scheduled to compete in that night's games decided to flee quickly. They had trumpets with them that were used to sound a fanfare at the amphitheater.[4] But they tossed the trumpets aside, leaving them to be found centuries later. Covering their heads with tiles and pieces of wood, the gladiators rushed out into the hail of lapilli and sprinted toward the open country beyond the walls, where they hoped they

180 would be safe.

Vesuvius was rumbling <u>ominously</u> now. The sky was dark. Lapilli continued to pour down, until the streets began to clog with them.

"The eruption will be over soon!" a hopeful voice exclaimed.

But it did not end. An hour went by, and darkness still shrouded everything; and still the lapilli fell. All was confusion now. Children struggled home from school, panicky in the midday darkness.

190 The people of Pompeii knew that doom was at hand now. Their fears were doubled when an enormous rain of hot ashes began to fall on them, along with more lapilli. Pelted with stones, half smothered by the ashes, the Pompeiians

MARK THE TEXT

Underline or highlight what added to the fear felt by the people of Pompeii.

---

3. **thermopolia.** Shops selling wine
4. **amphitheater.** Round building with an open space surrounded by rising rows of seats

---

words for everyday use

be • wil • der (bi wil´dər) v., confuse. *Cal's strange stories always seem to <u>bewilder</u> us.* bewildered, *adj.*
om • i • nous (äm´ə nəs) adj., threatening. *The <u>ominous</u> clouds brought rain to our picnic.* ominously, *adv.*

cried out to the gods for mercy. The wooden roofs of some of the houses began to catch fire as the heat of the ashes reached them. Other buildings were collapsing under the weight of the pumice stones that had fallen on them.

In those first few hours, only the quick-witted managed to escape. Vesonius Primnus, a wealthy wool merchant, called his family together and piled jewelry and money into a sack. Lighting a torch, Vesonius led his little band out into the nightmare of the streets. Overlooked in the confusion was Vesonius's black watchdog, chained in the courtyard. The terrified dog barked wildly as lapilli struck and drifting white ash settled around him. The animal struggled with his chain, battling fiercely to get free; but the chain held, and no one heard the dog's cries. The humans were too busy saving themselves.

Many hundreds of Pompeiians fled in those first few dark hours. Stumbling in the darkness, they made their way to the city gates, then out, down to the harbor. They boarded boats and got away, living to tell the tale of their city's destruction. Others preferred to remain within the city, huddling inside the temples or in the public baths or in the cellars of their homes. They still hoped that the nightmare would end—that the <u>tranquility</u> of a few hours ago would return. . . .

It was evening now, and new woe was in store for Pompeii. The earth trembled and quaked! Roofs that had somehow withstood the rain of lapilli went crashing in ruin, burying hundreds who had hoped to survive the eruption. In the Forum, tall columns toppled as they had in AD 63. Those who remembered that great earthquake screamed in new terror as the entire city seemed to shake in the grip of a giant fist.

Three feet of lapilli now covered the ground. Ash floated in the air. Gusts of poisonous gas came drifting from the <u>belching</u> crater, though people could still breathe. Roofs were collapsing everywhere. The cries of the dead and

200

210

220

Use THE STRATEGY

VISUALIZE. Visualize what is happening in the city. Mark the words that help you picture the events.

NOTE THE FACTS

How many people managed to get out of the city? How did they manage to get out?

_____

_____

_____

words for everyday use	**tran • quil • i • ty** (traŋ kwil´ə tē) _n._, quality or state of being calm. _Reading outside gives me a sense of <u>tranquility</u>._ **belch** (belch´) _v._, throw forth contents rapidly. _The smokestack <u>belched</u> black smoke into the sky._

MARK THE TEXT

Underline or highlight how the people of Pompeii behave once they sense the danger.

NOTE THE FACTS

What is Diomedes's plan? Why does it fail?

_____

_____

_____

230 dying filled the air. Rushing throngs, blinded by the darkness and the smoke, hurtled madly up one street and down the next, trampling the fallen in a crazy, <u>fruitless</u> dash toward safety. Dozens of people plunged into dead-end streets and found themselves trapped by crashing buildings. They waited there, too frightened to run farther, expecting the end.

The rich man Diomedes was another of those who decided not to flee at the first sign of alarm. Rather than risk being crushed by the screaming mobs, Diomedes
240 calmly led the members of his household into the solidly built basement of his villa. Sixteen people altogether, as well as his daughter's dog and her beloved little goat. They took enough food and water to last for several days.

But for all his <u>shrewdness</u> and foresight, Diomedes was undone anyway. Poison gas was creeping slowly into the underground shelter! He watched his daughter begin to cough and struggle for breath. Vesuvius was giving off vast quantities of deadly carbon monoxide that was now settling like a blanket over the dying city. . . .
250 The poison gas thickened as the terrible night continued. It was possible to hide from the lapilli but not from the gas, and Pompeiians died by the hundreds. Carbon monoxide gas keeps the body from absorbing oxygen. Victims of carbon monoxide poisoning get sleepier and sleepier until they lose consciousness, never to regain it. All over Pompeii, people lay down in the beds of lapilli, overwhelmed by the gas, and death came quietly to them. . . .

Two prisoners, left behind in the jail when their keepers
260 fled, pounded on the sturdy wooden doors. "Let us out!" they called. But no one heard, and the gas entered. They died, not knowing that the jailers outside were dying as well.

In a lane near the Forum, a hundred people were trapped by a blind-alley wall. Others hid in the stoutly built public bathhouses, protected against collapsing roofs but not

words for everyday use

fruit • less (frōōt ləs) adj., without results. _My search for the missing watch was_ <u>_fruitless_</u>.
shrewd • ness (shrōōd´nəs) n., cleverness. _Margie's_ <u>_shrewdness_</u> _as a pitcher led her to strike out many opponents._

against the deadly gas. Near the house of Diomedes, a beggar and his little goat sought shelter. The man fell dead a few feet from Diomedes' door; the faithful goat remained by his side, its silver bell tinkling, until its turn came.

270   All through the endless night, Pompeiians wandered about the streets or crouched in their ruined homes or clustered in the temples to pray. By morning, few remained alive. Not once had Vesuvius stopped hurling lapilli and ash into the air, and the streets of Pompeii were filling quickly. At midday on August 25, exactly twenty-four hours after the beginning of the holocaust,[5] a second eruption racked the volcano. A second cloud of ashes rose above Vesuvius' summit. The wind blew ash as far as Rome and Egypt. But most of the new ashes descended on Pompeii.

280   The deadly shower of stone and ashes went unslackening into its second day. But it no longer mattered to Pompeii whether the eruption continued another day or another year. For by midday on August 25, Pompeii was a city of the dead. . . .

    Arriving at Pompeii today, you leave your car outside and enter through an age-old gate. Just within the entrance is a museum that has been built in recent years to house many of the smaller antiquities found in the ruins.

290 Here are statuettes and toys, saucepans and loaves of bread. The account books of the banker Caecilius Jucundus are there, noting all the money he had lent at steep interest rates. Glass cups, coins, charred beans and peas and turnips, baskets of grapes and plums and figs, a box of chestnuts— the little things of Pompeii have all been miraculously preserved for your startled eyes.

    Then you enter the city proper. The streets are narrow and deeply <u>rutted</u> with the tracks of chariot wheels. Only special narrow Pompeiian chariots could travel inside the

300 town. Travelers from outside were <u>obliged</u> to change

---

5. **holocaust.** Great or total destruction of life

words for everyday use

rut • ted (rut´əd) *adj.,* grooved or carved out surface. *The <u>rutted</u> path cut through the trees.*

o • blige (ə blīj´) *v.,* compel or force. *My mother <u>obliged</u> me to do my homework.*

Use THE STRATEGY

VISUALIZE. Picture the shower of stone and ash that descended upon Pompeii.

Use THE STRATEGY

VISUALIZE. The words "Arriving at Pompeii today" direct you to shift your mind pictures to pictures of present-day Pompeii.

NOTE THE FACTS

Why were Pompeiian chariots narrower than other chariots?

_____

_____

_____

Use THE STRATEGY

VISUALIZE. Imagine that you are walking through present-day Pompeii.

MARK THE TEXT

Underline or highlight why it is difficult to tell what the Forum looked like.

vehicles when they reached the walls of the city. This provided a profitable <u>monopoly</u> for the Pompeiian equivalent of cab drivers twenty centuries ago!

At each intersection, blocks of stone several feet high are mounted in the roadway, so designed that chariot wheels could pass on either side of them.

"Those are steppingstones for the people of Pompeii," your guide tells you. "Pompeii had no sewers, and during heavy rainfalls the streets were flooded with many inches of
310   water. The Pompeiians could keep their feet dry by walking on those stones." . . .

The houses and shops are of stone. The upper stories, which were wooden, were burned away in the holocaust or simply crumbled with the centuries. The biggest of the shops are along the Street of Abundance, which must have been the Fifth Avenue of its day. Silversmiths, shoemakers, manufacturers of cloth—all had their shops here. And every few doors, there is another thermopolium, or wine shop. In many of these, the big jars of wine are still intact, standing
320   in holes in marble counters just the way bins of ice cream are stored in a soda fountain today. . . .

The center of the city's life was the Forum, a large square which you enter not far from the main gate of the city. Before the earthquake of AD 63, Pompeii's Forum must have been a truly <u>imposing</u> place, enclosed on three sides by a series of porticoes[6] supported by huge columns. At the north end, on the fourth side, stood the temple of Jupiter, Juno, and Minerva, raised on a podium ten feet high. But the earthquake toppled the temple and most of the
330   columns, and not much rebuilding had been done at the time of the eruption. Pompeii's slowness to rebuild was our eternal loss, for little remains of the Forum except the stumps of massive columns. . . .

Many public buildings were on the main square: the headquarters of the wool industry and several other

---

6. **porticoes.** Porch-like sheltered areas supported by roof-to-floor columns

words for everyday use

mo • nop • o • ly (mə näp´ə lē) *n.,* exclusive possession or control over something. *The company has a <u>monopoly</u> over the railroad business.*
im • pos • ing (im pō´ziŋ) *adj.,* making a strong impression because of great size or strength. *The <u>imposing</u> figure of the bear scared me silly.*

temples, including one dedicated to Vespasian (father of Titus), a Roman emperor who was worshiped as a deity.[7] Near the Forum was a macellum, or market, where

340 foodstuffs were sold and where beggars wandered.

Pompeii had many beggars. One of them was found in April 1957 at the gate of the road leading to the town of Nocera. A cast taken of him shows him to have been less than five feet tall and deformed by the bone disease known as rickets. On the last day of Pompeii's life, this beggar had gone about asking for alms,[8] and some generous citizen had given him a bone with a piece of meat still adhering to it. When the eruption came, the beggar tried to flee, jealously guarding his precious sack containing the cutlet and he was

350 found with it two thousand years later.

Pompeii was a city of many fine temples, both around the Forum and in the outlying streets. One of the most interesting is one dating from the sixth century BC, the oldest building in the city. Only the foundation and a few fragmented columns remain, but this temple was evidently regarded with great reverence, since it was located in the center of a fairly large triangular space adjoining the main theater. Nearby is the Temple of Isis, which was rebuilt after the earthquake and so is in fairly good preservation.

360 Isis, an Egyptian goddess, was one of the many foreign gods and goddesses who had come to be worshiped in the Roman Empire by the time of the destruction of Pompeii. Her gaudily decorated temple at Pompeii is the only European temple of Isis that has come down to us from the ancient world.

But many temples, bathhouses, amphitheaters, and government buildings have survived in other places. What makes Pompeii uniquely significant is the wealth of knowledge it gives us about the *private* lives of its people.

370 Nowhere else do we have such complete information about

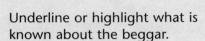

MARK THE TEXT

Underline or highlight what is known about the beggar.

MARK THE TEXT

Underline or highlight what is important about the Temple of Isis.

---

7. **deity.** God
8. **alms.** Money, food, or clothing given to poor people

words for everyday use

gau • dy (gäw' dē) *adj.,* tastelessly ornamented. *Aunt Penelope wore a gaudy orange, puce, and fuschia polyester gown to the zoo.* **gaudily,** *adv.*

the homes of the ancients, about their customs and living
habits, their humble pots and pans.

The houses in Pompeii show the evolution of styles over
a period of several centuries. Many of the houses are built
to the same simple plan: a central court, known as the
atrium, around which a living room, bedrooms, and a
garden are arrayed. This was the classic Roman style of
home. Some of the later and more impressive houses show
the influence of Greek styles, with paintings and mosaic[9]
380   decorations as well as baths, reception rooms, huge
gardens, and sometimes a second atrium.

The houses of Pompeii are known by name, and a good
deal is known of their occupants. One of the most famous is
the House of the Vetti Brothers, which is lavishly decorated
with paintings, mosaics, and sculptures. The inscriptions on
these houses are often amusing today. One businessman
had written on the walls of his villa WELCOME
PROFITS! Another greeted his visitors with the inscribed
words PROFITS MEAN JOY!

390   At the so-called House of the Tragic Poet, a mosaic shows
a barking dog, with the inscription *cave canem*— "Beware of
the dog." On the building known as the House of the
Lovers, which received its name because the newly married
Claudius Elogus lived there, someone had written a line of
verse, dedicated to the newlyweds, on the porch: *Amantes,
ut apes, vitam mellitem exigunt.* ("Lovers, like bees, desire a
life full of honey.")

One interesting house uncovered since World War II is
the Villa of Giulia Felix ("Happy Julia"), which was of
400   exceptional size. Apparently Giulia found the expense of
this elegant house too much for her budget because she had
opened her baths to the public and advertised the fact with
a sign on the gate. For a fee, Pompeiians who scorned the
crowds at the public baths could bathe at Giulia's in privacy
and comfort. Even this income does not seem to have been
enough, for another sign uncovered in 1953 announced
that the magnificent villa was for rent. . . .

One of the truly fascinating aspects of Pompeii is the
multitude of scribbled street signs. Notices were painted

---

9. **mosaic.** Design made by inlaying small bits of stone or glass to a surface

THINK AND REFLECT

How do the restored
buildings in Pompeii get
their names? (**Synthesize**)

_____

_____

_____

MARK THE TEXT

Underline or highlight facts
known about the Villa of
Giulia Felix.

410 directly on the stone and have come down to us. At the big amphitheater, an inscription tells us, "The troupe of gladiators owned by Suettius Centus will give a performance at Pompeii on May 31st. There will be an animal show. The awnings[10] will be used." And at the theater where plays were given, a message to a popular actor reads, "Actius, beloved of the people, come back soon; fare thee well!"

There are inscriptions at the taverns, too. "Romula loves Staphyclus" is on one wall. Elsewhere there is a poem that 420 sounds like one of today's hit tunes: "Anyone could as well stop the winds blowing, / And the waters from flowing, / As stop lovers from loving." . . .

Wherever you turn in Pompeii, echoes of the dead city strike you. In one rich house, a breakfast-set in silver, complete with two egg cups, was found. Shopping lists were discovered. Wall paintings show religious ceremonies, games, and everyday amusements. The vats used for bleaching cloth for togas still remain. In some of the twenty bakeries, newly baked loaves stand on the counters.

430 To enter Pompeii is to step into the Rome of the Caesars. An entire city, forever frozen in the last moment of its life by a terrible cataclysm,[11] awaits the visitor. Thanks to the painstaking work of generations of devoted Italian archaeologists, we can experience today the most minute details of life twenty centuries ago in a Roman city. So much do we know of the people of Pompeii that they take on vivid life for us—the banker Jucundus, the wool merchant Vesonius, the newlywed Claudius Elogus, the nobleman Diomedes. The dreadful eruption that snatched 440 the life of these people and this city in a single day also gave it a kind of immortality. Pompeii and its people live on today in timeless permanence, their city transformed by Vesuvius' fury into a miraculous survivor of the ancient world. ■

---

10. **awnings.** Structures of canvas or metal over doors to protect from rain or sun
11. **cataclysm.** Any great upheaval that causes sudden and violent changes

Use THE STRATEGY

VISUALIZE. Continue to picture what the restored buildings look like.

THINK AND REFLECT

What does visiting Pompeii allow us to do? (**Evaluate**)

_____

_____

_____

Reflect ON YOUR READING

After Reading ➤ SUMMARIZE STORY ELEMENTS

❑ Go back through the essay and add details about Pompeii in AD 79 and Pompeii today to your graphic organizer.
❑ Write a brief summary of the information you gathered.

_____

_____

_____

_____

Reading Skills and Test Practice

COMPARE AND CONTRAST STORY ELEMENTS

Discuss with a partner how to best answer these questions that ask you to compare and contrast story elements. Use the Think-Aloud Notes to write down your reasons for eliminating the incorrect answers.

_____1. How is Pompeii before AD 79 like Pompeii today?
    a. thousands of people live there
    b. Mount Vesuvius stands in the background
    c. guides lead visitors around
    d. there are no street signs

_____2. Compare people who escaped to people who didn't. The people who escaped
    a. left immediately.
    b. found shelter in their cellars.
    c. covered themselves in the baths at Giulia's.
    d. took refuge in the Forum.

How did the visualizations you made while reading help you to eliminate the incorrect answers?

_____

_____

_____

_____

Investigate, Inquire, and Imagine

RECALL: GATHER FACTS →
1a. Where is the city of Pompeii? How much time passed after Pompeii's destruction before the city was rediscovered?

INTERPRET: FIND MEANING
1b. Why do you think it took so long to rediscover the lost city?

ANALYZE: TAKE THINGS APART →
2a. List three different things archeologists have learned about Pompeii and its destruction.

SYNTHESIZE: BRING THINGS TOGETHER
2b. Why is the archeologists' information important? How can we use information about the way Pompeiians lived? How can we use information about the way the city was destroyed?

EVALUATE: MAKE JUDGMENTS →
3a. What do you think about how the people of Pompeii reacted to the initial explosion, the black cloud, and the falling stones? Why do you think more people didn't run away?

EXTEND: CONNECT IDEAS
3b. The people of Pompeii may have envisioned that the world as they knew it was ending. How do you envision the end of the world?

Literary Tools

ESSAY. An **essay** is a short nonfiction work that expresses a writer's thoughts about a single subject. A good essay develops a single idea, or *thesis*, and is organized into an introduction, a body, and a conclusion. As a narrative essay, "Pompeii" tells a true story to make a point.

1. Skim through the essay again. Identify the introduction, the body, and the conclusion.

Introduction	Body	Conclusion

2. What point is the author trying to make about the destruction of Pompeii? What details help make this point?

_____

_____

WordWorkshop

MATCHING. From the choices provided, identify the word or phrase that most closely matches the given term.

_____1. **ominous**
   a. high-flying kites
   b. dark sky

_____2. **shroud**
   a. cloth placed over a corpse
   b. folk costume

_____3. **engulf**
   a. rain shower
   b. tidal wave

_____4. **unruly**
   a. choir
   b. mob

_____5. **molten**
   a. water
   b. glass

_____6. **haphazard**
   a. branches fallen from a tree
   b. rows of desks in a classroom

_____7. **catastrophe**
   a. sunlight
   b. earthquake

_____8. **monopoly**
   a. retail clothing store
   b. the only taxi company in a city

_____9. **shrewdness**
   a. figuring out how to make money in the stock market
   b. failing an exam

_____10. **imposing**
   a. a leprechaun
   b. the Great Pyramid at Giza

Read-Write Connection

If you could go back in time, what place would you visit? Why?

Beyond the Reading

RESEARCH GHOST TOWNS. Use the library or the Internet to research a ghost town. Write a brief report on what you learn. Explain what happened to the town, and include a map that shows where the town is located.

GO ONLINE. To find links and additional activities for this selection, visit the EMC Internet Resource Center at **emcp.com/languagearts** and click on Write-In Reader.

"Satchel Paige"

by Bill Littlefield

Active READING STRATEGY

CONNECT TO PRIOR KNOWLEDGE

Before Reading ➤ **PREVIEW THE SELECTION**

❑ Read the Reader's Resource, and look at the photograph on page 254.

❑ Quickwrite what you know about baseball and baseball players.

_____

_____

_____

_____

❑ Use what you learn from the Reader's Resource and what you already know to fill in columns 1 and 2 in the K-W-L Chart below.

Graphic Organizer: K-W-L Chart

What I *Know*	What I *Want* to Learn	What I Have *Learned*

Reader's resource

With one exception, "Fleet" Walker in 1884, African-American baseball players were not allowed to play in the major leagues until 1947. Black players played on teams made up entirely of African-American players. These all-black teams played in the Negro National League and the Negro American league. Until 1950, the Negro leagues held an annual World Series. Jackie Robinson was the first African-American player in the major leagues when he joined the Brooklyn Dodgers in 1947. His success opened the door for others. In **"Satchel Paige,"** author Bill Littlefield describes how another famous player, 41-year-old Satchel Paige, finally got a chance to play in the major leagues.

Word watch

PREVIEW VOCABULARY

confrontation	prosper
dismay	rutted
exploit	taunt
flamboyant	waning

Reader's journal

Write about a person whose skills you admire.

_____

_____

_____

USE WHAT YOU KNOW

- ❑ Read the story about Satchel Paige.
- ❑ Underline or highlight things you learn about Paige. Respond in the margins to what you mark.

Literary TOOLS

BIOGRAPHY. A **biography** is the story of a person's life told by another person. As you read Bill Littlefield's account of Satchel Paige's life, think about how Littlefield feels about Satchel Paige.

NOTE THE FACTS

Who was luckier than Paige?

_____

_____

_____

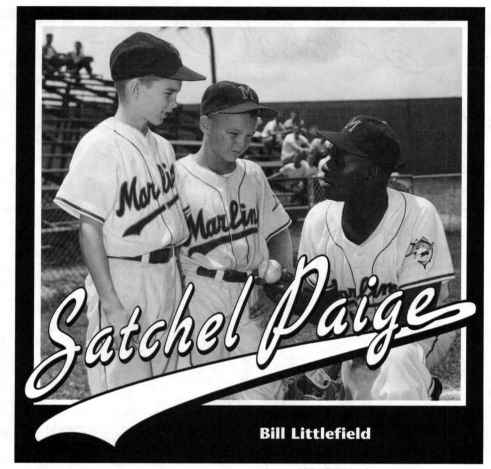

Satchel Paige

Bill Littlefield

Leroy "Satchel" Paige, perhaps the greatest pitcher ever, came out of the Negro leagues, where there'd been a Babe Ruth named Josh Gibson and a Rickey Henderson[1] named James "Cool Papa" Bell. By the time the major leagues finally allowed him to play, in 1948, Paige should have been too old, too slow, and too beat up to get anybody out. But for a few remarkable and <u>flamboyant</u> seasons with Cleveland and St. Louis, he showed folks what they'd been missing during all those years of segregated baseball. Maybe Satchel was lucky to finally have his chance, but the fans who saw him take advantage of it were luckier, and none of them ever forgot it.

10

---

1. **Babe Ruth . . . Rickey Henderson.** The author is comparing Negro League players to famous major league players to show the skill of the lesser-known Negro League players.

words for everyday use	**flam • boy • ant** (flam boi' ənt) *adj.*, showy, extravagant. *People stared at Nia's* <u>*flamboyant*</u> *outfit.*

Late in the afternoon of July 9, 1948, Leroy "Satchel" Paige began the long walk from the bullpen to the mound at Cleveland's Municipal Stadium. He didn't hurry. He *never* hurried. As he said himself, he "kept the juices flowing by jangling gently" as he moved. The crowd roared its appreciation. This was the fellow they'd come to see.

When Satchel finally reached the mound, Cleveland manager Lou Boudreau took the ball from starting pitcher Bob Lemon, who would eventually be voted into the Hall of Fame but had tired that day, and gave it to Paige. Probably he said something like, "Shut 'em down, Satchel." Whatever he said, Paige had no doubt heard the words a thousand times. Though he was a rookie with the Indians that year, no pitcher in the history of baseball had ever been more thoroughly prepared for a job. He kicked at the rubber, looked in for the sign, and got set to throw. In a moment, twenty-odd years later than it should have happened, Satchel Paige would deliver his first pitch in the big leagues.

The tall, skinny kid named Leroy Paige became Satchel Paige one day at the railroad station in Mobile, Alabama. He was carrying bags for the folks getting on and off the trains, earning all the nickels and dimes he could to help feed his ten brothers and sisters. Eventually it occurred to him that if he slung a pole across his narrow shoulders and hung the bags, or satchels, on the ends of the pole, he could carry for more people at once and collect more nickels and dimes. It worked, but it looked a little funny. "You look like some kind of ol' satchel tree," one of his friends told him, and the nickname stuck.

Even in those days, before he was a teenager, Satchel Paige could throw hard and accurately. Years later, Paige swore that when his mother would send him out into the yard to get a chicken for dinner, he would brain the bird with a rock. "I used to kill *flying* birds with rocks, too," he said. "Most people need shotguns to do what I did with rocks."

It was not a talent that would go unnoticed for long. He was pitching for the semipro Mobile Tigers before he was eighteen . . . or maybe before he was sixteen, or before he was twelve. There is some confusion about exactly when Satchel Paige was born, and Satchel never did much to clarify the

20
30
40
50

Reading STRATEGY
REVIEW

VISUALIZE. Picture Paige walking to the mound for his first pitch in the major leagues.

Reading TIP

Lines 1–29 summarize what happened on Paige's first day on a major league team. In line 30, the author starts using **chronological order** to share information about events in Paige's life. Events that are in chronological order are arranged in the order in which they happened.

NOTE THE FACTS

How did Satchel Paige get the nickname "Satchel"?

_____

_____

_____

matter. But there never has been any confusion about whether he could pitch. His first steady job in baseball was with the Chattanooga Black Lookouts. He was paid fifty dollars a month. In the seasons that followed he would also pitch for the Birmingham Black Barons, the Nashville Elite Giants, the Baltimore Black Sox, the Pittsburgh Crawfords, and the Kansas City Monarchs, among other teams.

60 If those names are not as familiar sounding as those of the New York Yankees, the Los Angeles Dodgers, or the Boston Red Sox, it's because they were all clubs in the Negro leagues, not the major leagues. Today the presence of black baseball players in the big leagues is taken for granted. Hank Aaron is the greatest of the home run hitters, and Rickey Henderson has stolen more bases than any other big leaguer. But before 1947, neither of them would have had the opportunity to do what they have done. Until Brooklyn Dodger general manager Branch Rickey signed Jackie Robinson, black players had no choice but to play for one of the all-black teams, and 70 making that choice, they faced hardships no major-leaguer today could imagine.

Players in the Negro leagues crowded into broken-down cars and bumped over <u>rutted</u> roads to makeshift ball fields with lights so bad that every pitch was a potential weapon. Then they drove all night for an afternoon game three hundred miles away. On good days they played before big, appreciative crowds in parks they'd rented from the major league teams in Chicago, New York, or Pittsburgh. On bad days they learned that the team they were playing for was too 80 broke to finish the season, and they would have to look for a healthier team that could use them, or else find a factory job.

It took talent, hard work, and a sense of humor to survive in the Negro leagues, and Satchel Paige had a lot of all three. But he didn't just survive. He <u>prospered</u>. Everybody knows about the fastball, the curve, and the slider. But Satchel threw a "bee" ball, which, he said, "would always *be* where I wanted it to *be*." He featured a trouble ball, which, of course, gave the

words for everyday use

rut • ted (rut′ əd) *adj.,* bumpy and marked by tracks made by wheels. *The car jolted over the <u>rutted</u> dirt road.*
pros • per (präs′ pər) *v.,* succeed, thrive. *The plant <u>prospered</u> in the sunny spot.*

hitters a lot of trouble. Even the few who could see it couldn't hit it. Sometimes he'd come at them with his hesitation pitch, a delivery so mysterious that the man at the plate would sometimes swing before the ball left Satchel's hand.

Nor was pitching his sole triumph. Early in his career Satchel Paige began building a reputation as a storyteller, a spinner of tall tales as well as shutouts. He particularly liked to recall an occasion upon which he was asked to come on in relief of a pitcher who'd left men on first and third with nobody out. "It was a tight situation," Satchel would say.

We only had a one-run lead, and that was looking mighty slim. But I had an idea. When I left the bench, I stuck a baseball in my pocket, so when the manager gave me the game ball on the mound, I had two. I went into my stretch just like usual. Then I threw one ball to first and the other to third. It was a good pickoff move, you see, and it fooled the batter, too. He swung, even though there was no ball to swing at. Those boys at first and third were both out, of course, and the umpire called strike three on the batter, so that was it for the inning. It's always good to save your strength when you can.

Major-leaguers today make enough money so that they don't have to work over the winter, but it hasn't always been so. Big-leaguers and Negro-leaguers alike used to make extra money after their regular seasons ended by putting together makeshift teams and playing each other wherever they could draw a paying crowd. This practice was called barnstorming, and Satchel Paige was the world champion at it. For thirty years, from 1929 to 1958, he played baseball summer and winter. When it was too cold to play in the Negro league cities, he played in Cuba, Mexico, and the Dominican Republic. In Venezuela he battled a boa constrictor in the outfield, or so he said, and in Ciudad Trujillo he dodged the machine-gun fire of fans who'd bet on the losing team.

Throughout the early years of these adventures, the years of Satchel's prime, he often barnstormed against the best white ballplayers of his day. St. Louis Cardinal great Dizzy Dean once told him, "You're a better pitcher than I ever hope to

FIX-UP IDEA

Reread
Quickly reread sections that are hard to follow.

NOTE THE FACTS

What is barnstorming?

_____

_____

_____

be." Paige beat Bob Feller and struck out Babe Ruth. And when Joe DiMaggio, considered by some the most multitalented ballplayer ever, beat out an infield hit against Paige in 1936, DiMaggio turned to his teammates and said, "Now I know I can make it with the Yankees. I finally got a hit off of ol' Satch."

Everywhere these <u>confrontations</u> took place, Satchel Paige would hear the same thing: "If only you were white, you'd be a star in the big leagues." The fault, of course, was not with Satchel. The fault and the shame were with major league baseball, which stubbornly, stupidly clung to the same prejudice that characterized many institutions in the United States besides baseball. Prejudice has not yet disappeared from the game. Black players are far less likely than their white counterparts to be hired as managers or general managers. But today's black players can thank Robinson, Paige, and a handful of other pioneers for the opportunities they enjoy.

Though the color line prevented Satchel Paige from pitching in the company his talent and hard work should have earned for him, he was not bitter or defeated. Ignorant white fans would sometimes <u>taunt</u> him, but he kept their insults in perspective. "Some of them would call you [names]," he said of his early years on the road, "but most of them would cheer you." Years later he worked to shrug off the pain caused by the restaurants that would not serve him, the hotels that would not rent him a room, the fans who would roar for his bee ball but would not acknowledge him on the street the next day. "Fans all holler the same at a ball game," he would say, as if the racists and the racist system had never touched him at all.

When he finally got the chance to become the first black pitcher in the American League at age forty-two (or forty-six, or forty-eight), he made the most of it. On that first day in Cleveland, Satchel Paige did the job he'd never

130

140

150

160

words for everyday use

con • fron • ta • tion (kän frun tā′ shən) n., heated opposition. *The <u>confrontation</u> might have led to a fight if Ms. Marquez hadn't stepped in.*
taunt (tônt) v., jeer, mock. *José ignored the <u>taunts</u> and the names Irwin called him.*

doubted he could do. First he smiled for all the photographers. Then he told the butterflies in his stomach to leave off their flapping around. Then he shut down the St. Louis Browns for two innings before being lifted for a pinch hitter. And still there were doubters. "Sure," they said to each other the next day when they read the sports section. "The old man could work two innings against the Browns. Who couldn't?"

170   But Satchel Paige fooled 'em, as he'd been fooling hitters for twenty-five years and more. He won a game in relief six days later, his first major league win. Then on August 3 he started a game against the Washington Senators before 72,000 people. Paige went seven innings and won. In his next two starts he threw shutouts against the Chicago White Sox, and through the <u>waning</u> months of that summer, his only complaint was that he was "a little tired from underwork." The routine on the major league level must have been pretty leisurely for a fellow who'd previously pitched four or five times a week.

180   Satchel Paige finished the 1948 season with six wins and only one loss. He'd allowed the opposing teams an average of just over two runs a game. Paige was named Rookie of the Year, an honor he might well have achieved twenty years earlier if he'd had the chance. The sportswriters of the day agreed that without Satchel's contribution, the Indians, who won the pennant, would have finished second at best. Many of the writers were <u>dismayed</u> when Satchel appeared for only two-thirds of an inning in the World Series that fall. Paige, too, was disappointed that the manager hadn't chosen to use

190   him more, but he was calm in the face of what others might have considered an insult. The writers told him, "You sure take things good." Satchel smiled and said, "Ain't no other way to take them."

Satchel Paige outlasted the rule that said he couldn't play in the big leagues because he was black. Then he made fools of the people who said he couldn't get major league hitters out because he was too old. But his big league numbers over

---

words for everyday use

wan • ing (wān' iŋ) *adj.,* approaching the end. *During the <u>waning</u> hours of the day, the setting sun turns the sky a rosy color.*
dis • may (dis mā') *v.,* afraid because of a fear of danger or trouble. *We were <u>dismayed</u> to see the team performing poorly at practice before the big game.*

WHAT DO YOU WONDER?

What do you wonder about Paige's abilities?

_____

_____

_____

Use THE STRATEGY

CONNECT TO PRIOR KNOWLEDGE. What do you think of Paige's being named Rookie of the Year twenty years after he could have been?

several years—twenty-eight wins and thirty-two saves—don't begin to tell the story of Paige's unparalleled career. Playing for teams that no longer exist in leagues that came and went with the seasons, Satchel Paige pitched in some 2,500 baseball games. Nobody has ever pitched in more. And he had such fun at it. Sometimes he'd accept offers to pitch in two cities on the same day. He'd strike out the side for three innings in one game, then fold his long legs into his car and race down the road toward the next ballpark. If the police could catch him, they would stop him for speeding. But when they recognized him, as often as not they'd escort him to the second game with sirens howling, well aware that there might be a riot in the park if Satchel Paige didn't show up as advertised. Once he'd arrived, he'd instruct his infielders and outfielders to sit down for an inning, then he'd strike out the side again.

For his talent, his energy, and his showmanship, Satchel Paige was the most famous of the Negro league players, but when he got some measure of recognition in the majors, he urged the writers to remember that there had been lots of other great ballplayers in those Negro league games. He named them, and he told their stories. He made their <u>exploits</u> alive and real for generations of fans who'd never have known.

In 1971, the Baseball Hall of Fame in Cooperstown, New York, inducted Satchel Paige. The action was part of the Hall's attempt to remedy baseball's shame, the color line. The idea was to honor Paige and some of the other great Negro league players like Josh Gibson and Cool Papa Bell, however late that honor might come. Satchel Paige could have rejected that gesture. He could have told the baseball establishment that what it was doing was too little, too late. But when the time came for Satchel Paige to speak to the crowd gathered in front of the Hall of Fame to celebrate his triumphs, he told the people, "I am the proudest man on the face of the earth today."

NOTE THE FACTS

How was Paige treated by the police?

_____

_____

_____

Use **THE STRATEGY**

CONNECT TO PRIOR KNOWLEDGE. What is your reaction to how Paige treated others?

NOTE THE FACTS

What could Paige have done upon being inducted into the Hall of Fame? What did he do instead?

_____

_____

_____

words for everyday use

ex • ploit (eks' ploit) *n.,* bold deed. *The crook's <u>exploits</u> made the front page of the newspaper.*

Satchel Paige, whose autobiography was entitled *Maybe I'll Pitch Forever*, died in Kansas City in 1982. He left behind a legend as large as that of anyone who ever played the game, as well as a long list of achievements celebrated in story and song—and in at least one fine poem, by Samuel Allen:

240   *To Satch*

Sometimes I feel like I will *never* stop
Just go on forever
Till one fine mornin'
I'm gonna reach up and grab me a handfulla stars
Swing out my long lean leg
And whip three hot strikes burnin' down the heavens
And look over at God and say
How about that!   ■

THINK AND REFLECT

What other people have some of Paige's qualities? **(Extend)**

_____

_____

_____

Reflect ON YOUR READING

After Reading ➤ **SUMMARIZE**

❏ When you finish reading, place numbers in front of items in the "What I Have Learned" column of your K-W-L Chart that indicate chronological order, or the order in which they happened in Paige's life.

❏ Summarize what you have learned about Satchel Paige. What are your feelings about him?

_____

_____

_____

_____

_____

THINK-ALOUD NOTES

_____

_____

_____

_____

_____

_____

_____

_____

_____

_____

_____

Reading Skills and Test Practice

FOLLOW THE SEQUENCE OF EVENTS

Discuss with your partner how to best answer the following questions about the sequence of events. Use the Think-Aloud Notes to write down your reasons for eliminating the incorrect answers.

_____1. Satchel Paige earned his nickname
   a. while he was carrying luggage to earn money as a child.
   b. while he was in the segregated Negro Leagues.
   c. after he began pitching for Cleveland and St. Louis.
   d. after he retired from baseball.

_____2. Which pair of events are in correct chronological order?
   a. Paige plays with the Chattanooga Black Lookouts. Paige pitches for the Mobile Tigers.
   b. Paige plays with the Cleveland Indians. Paige is inducted into the Baseball Hall of Fame.
   c. Paige plays with the Cleveland Indians. Paige works at a train station.
   d. Paige is inducted into the Baseball Hall of Fame. Paige joins the American League.

How did using the reading strategy help you to answer the questions?

_____

_____

Investigate, Inquire, and Imagine

RECALL: GATHER FACTS
1a. What do the numbers tell you about Paige? What don't they tell you?

→ INTERPRET: FIND MEANING
1b. What do Paige's actions suggest about his character?

ANALYZE: TAKE THINGS APART
2a. What difficulties did African-American players face during the years of segregation?

→ SYNTHESIZE: BRING THINGS TOGETHER
2b. How did Paige react in the face of these difficulties?

EVALUATE: MAKE JUDGMENTS
3a. What do you think are the main characteristics of Paige's personality?

→ EXTEND: CONNECT IDEAS
3b. How has Paige affected baseball?

Literary Tools

BIOGRAPHY. A **biography** is the story of a person's life told by another person. Look back to see how Bill Littlefield presents Satchel Paige.

1. Summarize three events that Littlefield describes.

_____

_____

_____

_____

_____

2. What type of writing style does Littlefield use to describe Paige—formal or informal? Include examples that support your answer.

_____

_____

_____

_____

WordWorkshop

USE VOCABULARY WORDS IN YOUR WRITING. Write a news story about a sports figure that uses all of the words below. You may change the form of the words when you use them in your story. On another sheet of paper, brainstorm ideas and write several rough drafts of your story. Write your final draft below. Use your own paper if your story is too long to fit below.

confrontation	flamboyant	taunt
dismay	prosper	wanting
expand	rutted	

_____

_____

_____

_____

_____

_____

_____

Read-Write Connection

What do you think of Satchel Paige as an athlete? as a person?

_____

_____

_____

_____

_____

Beyond the Reading

USE AN ALMANAC OR YEARBOOK. Use an almanac or yearbook to compile a list of information about another sports hero. Include major awards, titles, and achievements in your list.

GO ONLINE. To find links and additional activities for this selection, visit the EMC Internet Resource Center at **emcp.com/languagearts** and click on Write-In Reader.

FROM GERONIMO'S STORY OF HIS LIFE

by Geronimo

Active READING STRATEGY

WRITE THINGS DOWN

Before Reading ➤ **PREVIEW THE SELECTION**

❑ Read the Reader's Resource, and look over the photograph on page 266.

❑ Quickwrite what you know about Native American customs on the lines below.

_____

_____

_____

_____

❑ Preview the graphic organizer below. As you read, you will use a Cluster Chart to keep track of information you learn about Apache customs.

Graphic Organizer: Cluster Chart

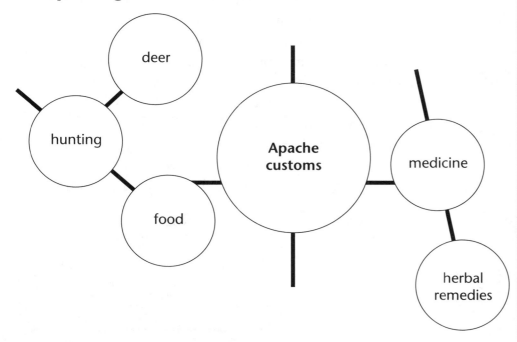

CONNECT

Reader's resource

Geronimo was an Apache. The name *Apache* comes from a Zuni word meaning "enemy." The Apaches call themselves N'de or Dineh, which means "the people." The Dineh were nomadic, that is, they traveled from place to place as they hunted. The Dineh shared their lands peacefully with white settlers at first. As the U.S. and Mexican armies took more and more of their land, the Dineh began to fight the settlers. In the 1870s, the U.S. government moved Dineh tribes from their homelands to reservations. Although Geronimo escaped many times, he and his followers were forced to make a final surrender to the government on September 4, 1886.

Word watch

PREVIEW VOCABULARY

abound	loiter
administer	profane
ascertain	prostrate
assemble	secluded
banish	suspend
consume	toil

Reader's journal

If you were writing the story of your life, what would you want people to understand about you?

GATHER INFORMATION

❏ Listen as your teacher or a classmate reads the first four paragraphs aloud. Highlight or underline what you learn about Apache customs. Add these details to your Cluster Chart.

❏ Continue reading the story silently on your own. Continue to highlight or underline information about Apache customs. When you finish, add the details to your chart. Add more circles as you need them.

Reading TIP

Geronimo gives you an inside view of tribal customs. He uses the first-person point of view to tell his story, that is, he takes part in the action and refers to himself using words such as *I* and *we*. As you read, pretend that you are with Geronimo in the situations he describes.

Literary TOOLS

AUTOBIOGRAPHY. An **autobiography** is the story of a person's life written by that person. As you read, think about why Geronimo may have written his life story.

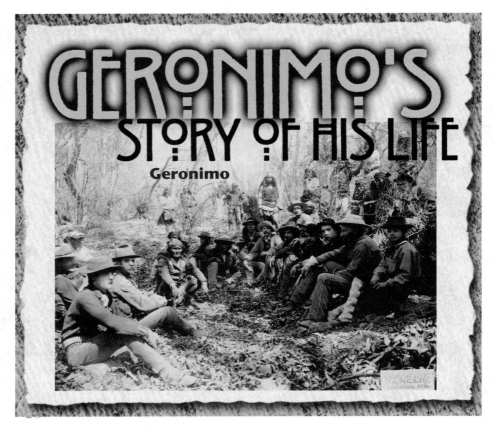

GERONIMO'S STORY OF HIS LIFE
Geronimo

I was born in No-doyohn Cañon, Arizona, June, 1829. In that country which lies around the headwaters of the Gila River I was reared. This range was our fatherland. Among these mountains our wigwams[1] were hidden. The scattered valleys contained our fields. The boundless prairies, stretching away on every side, were our pastures. The rocky caverns were our burying places.

I was fourth in a family of eight children—four boys and four girls. Of that family, only myself; my brother, Porico (White Horse); and my sister, Nah-da-ste, are yet alive. We are held as prisoners of war in this Military Reservation (Fort Sill).

As a babe, I rolled on the dirt floor of my father's tepee, hung in my *tsoch* (Apache name for *cradle*) at my mother's back, or <u>suspended</u> from the bough of a tree. I was warmed

30

---

1. **wigwams.** Traditional dwellings of Native American people of North America, consisting of a dome-shaped framework of poles covered with mats or sheets of bark

words for everyday use

sus • pend (sə spend') v., hang by or support from above. *The acrobat was <u>suspended</u> by the trapeze far above the heads of her audience.*

by the sun, rocked by the winds, and sheltered by the trees as other Indian babes.

When I was a child, my mother taught me the legends of our people; taught me of the sun and sky, the moon and stars, the clouds and storms. She also taught me to kneel and pray to Usen the spirit father, for strength, health, wisdom, and protection. We never prayed against any person; but if we had aught[2] against any individual, we ourselves took vengeance. We were taught that Usen does not care for the petty quarrels of men.

My father had often told me of the brave deeds of our warriors, of the pleasures of the chase, and the glories of the warpath.

With my brothers and sisters, I played about my father's home. Sometimes we played hide-and-seek among the rocks and pines; sometimes we <u>loitered</u> in the shade of the cottonwood trees or sought the *shudock* (a kind of wild cherry) while our parents worked in the field. Sometimes we played that we were warriors. We would practice stealing upon some object that represented an enemy, and in our childish imitation often performed the feats of war. Sometimes we would hide away from our mother to see if she could find us, and often when thus concealed go to sleep and perhaps remain hidden for many hours.

When we were old enough to be of real service, we went to the field with our parents, not to play, but to <u>toil</u>. When the crops were to be planted, we broke the ground with wooden hoes. We planted the corn in straight rows, the beans among the corn, and the melons and pumpkins in irregular order over the field. We cultivated these crops as there was need.

Our field usually contained about two acres of ground. The fields were never fenced. It was common for many families to cultivate land in the same valley and share the burden of protecting the growing crops from destruction

40

50

60

2. **aught.** Anything whatsoever

words for everyday use

loi • ter (loit' ər) v., spend time idly. *The convenience store put up a sign that warned people not to <u>loiter</u> in front of the store.*
toil (toil') v., work hard. *The farmer <u>toiled</u> in his fields.*

READ ALOUD

Pronouncing difficult vocabulary over and over can help you keep reading smoothly. Read the following words aloud several times.

Apache
Be-don-ko-he
Cho-ko-le
esadadedne
Gila
Kah
Nah-da-ste
No-doyohn Cañon
Porico
shudock
tiswin
tsoch
Usen

MARK THE TEXT

Underline or highlight games that Apache children play when they are young and what they do when they are older.

by the ponies of the tribe, or by deer and other wild animals.

Melons were gathered as they were <u>consumed</u>. In the autumn, pumpkins and beans were gathered and placed in bags or baskets; ears of corn were tied together by the husks, and then the harvest was carried on the backs of ponies up to our homes. Here the corn was shelled, and all the harvest stored away in caves or other <u>secluded</u> places to be used in winter.

We never fed corn to our ponies; but if we kept them up in the winter time, we gave them fodder[3] to eat. We had no cattle or other domestic animals except our dogs and ponies. . . .

Besides grinding the corn (by hand with stone mortars and pestles) for bread, we sometimes crushed it and soaked it; and . . . made from this juice a *tiswin*, which . . . was very highly prized by the Indians. This work was done by the squaws and children. When berries or nuts were to be gathered, the small children and the squaws would go in parties to hunt them, and sometimes stay all day. When they went any great distance from camp, they took ponies to carry the baskets.

I frequently went with these parties, and upon one of these excursions a woman named Cho-ko-le got lost from the party and was riding her pony through a thicket in search of her friends. Her little dog was following as she slowly made her way through the thick underbrush and pine trees. All at once a grizzly bear rose in her path and attacked the pony. She jumped off and her pony escaped, but the bear attacked her; so she fought him the best she could with her knife. Her little dog, by snapping at the bear's heels and distracting his attention from the woman, enabled her for some time to keep pretty well out of his reach. Finally the grizzly struck her over the head, tearing off almost her whole scalp. She fell, but did not lose

MARK THE TEXT

Underline or highlight how the Apache prepared corn.

---

3. **fodder.** Coarse food for cattle, horses, and sheep, such as hay, straw, and cornstalks

| words for everyday use | **con • sume** (kən sōom′) *v.*, eat or drink up. *The class <u>consumed</u> all of the party food.* |
| | **se • cluded** (si klōod′ ed) *adj.*, shut off or kept away from others. *Their cottage was in a <u>secluded</u> area of the woods, far away from any neighbors.* |

consciousness, and while <u>prostrate</u> struck him four good licks with her knife; and he retreated. After he had gone, she replaced her torn scalp and bound it up as best she could. Then she turned deathly sick and had to lie down. That night her pony came into camp with his load of nuts and berries, but no rider. The Indians hunted for her, but did not find her until the second day. They carried her home, and under the treatment of their medicine man all her wounds were healed.

The Indians knew what herbs to use for medicine, how to prepare them, and how to give the medicine. This they had been taught by Usen in the beginning, and each succeeding generation had people who were skilled in the art of healing.

In gathering the herbs, in preparing them, and in <u>administering</u> the medicine, as much faith was held in prayer as in the actual effect of the medicine. Usually about eight persons worked together in making medicine, and there were forms of prayer and incantations[4] to attend each stage of the process. Four attended to the incantations, and four to the preparation of the herbs.

Some of the Indians were skilled in cutting out bullets, arrowheads, and other missiles with which warriors were wounded. I myself have done much of this, using a common dirk or butcher knife.

Small children wore very little clothing in winter and none in summer. Women usually wore a primitive skirt, which consisted of a piece of cotton cloth fastened about the waist, and extending to the knees. Men wore breech cloths and moccasins. In winter they had shirts and leggings in addition.

Frequently when the tribe was in camp, a number of boys and girls, by agreement, would steal away and meet at a place several miles distant, where they could play all day free from tasks. They were never punished for these frolics;

110

120

130

ASK A QUESTION

Ask a question or respond to the story about Cho-ko-le.

_____

_____

_____

MARK THE TEXT

Underline or highlight how the Apache made medicine.

NOTE THE FACTS

What did the Apache wear?

_____

_____

_____

---

4. **incantations.** Verbal charms

words for everyday use

pro • strate (prä′ strāt′) *adj.,* lying face down. *After missing the hurdle, I landed <u>prostrate</u> on the track.*

ad • min • is • ter (əd mi′ nə stər) *v.,* dispense or give. *The nurse can <u>administer</u> aspirin to students.*

Use THE STRATEGY

WRITE THINGS DOWN. Continue to underline or highlight things about Apache customs that you can add to your graphic organizer later.

140 but if their hiding places were discovered, they were ridiculed. To celebrate each noted event, a feast and dance would be given. Perhaps only our own people, perhaps neighboring tribes, would be invited. These festivities usually lasted for about four days. By day we feasted; by night, under the direction of some chief, we danced. The music for our dance was singing led by the warriors, and accompanied by beating the *esadadedne* (buck-skin-on-a-hoop). No words were sung—only the tones. When the feasting and dancing were over, we would have horse races, foot races, wrestling, 150 jumping, and all sorts of games.

Among these games, the most noted was the tribal game of *Kah* (foot). It is played as follows: Four moccasins are placed about four feet apart in holes in the ground dug in a row on one side of the camp, and on the opposite side a similar parallel row. At night a camp fire is started between these two rows of moccasins; and the players are arranged on sides, one or any number on each side. The score is kept by a bundle of sticks, from which each side takes a stick for every point won. First one side takes the bone, puts up 160 blankets between the four moccasins and the fire so that the opposing team cannot observe their movements, and then begins to sing the legends of creation. The side having the bone represents the feathered tribe; the opposite side represents the beasts. The players representing the birds do all the singing, and while singing, hide the bone in one of the moccasins. Then the blankets are thrown down. They continue to sing; but as soon as the blankets are thrown down, the chosen player from the opposing team, armed with a war club, comes to their side of the camp fire and 170 with his club strikes the moccasin in which he thinks the bone is hidden. If he strikes the right moccasin, his side gets the bone, and in turn represents the birds, while the opposing team must keep quiet and guess in turn. There are only four plays: three that lose and one that wins. When all the sticks are gone from the bundle, the side having the largest number of sticks is counted winner.

This game is seldom played except as a gambling game, but for that purpose it is the most popular game known to the tribe. Usually the game lasts four or five hours. It is 180 never played in daytime.

After the games are all finished, the visitors say, "We are satisfied," and the camp is broken up. I was always glad when the dances and feasts were announced. So were all the other young people.

Our life also had a religious side. We had no churches, no religious organizations, no Sabbath day, no holidays, and yet we worshiped. Sometimes the whole tribe would <u>assemble</u> to sing and pray; sometimes a smaller number, perhaps only two or three. The songs had a few words, but

190 were not formal. The singer would occasionally put in such words as he wished instead of the usual tone sound. Sometimes we prayed in silence; sometimes each one prayed aloud; sometimes an aged person prayed for all of us. At other times, one would rise and speak to us of our duties to each other and to Usen. Our services were short.

When disease or pestilence <u>abounded</u>, we were assembled and questioned by our leaders to <u>ascertain</u> what evil we had done, and how Usen could be satisfied. Sometimes sacrifice was deemed necessary. Sometimes the offending one was

200 punished.

If an Apache had allowed his aging parents to suffer for food or shelter, if he had neglected or abused the sick, if he had <u>profaned</u> our religion, or had been unfaithful, he might be <u>banished</u> from the tribe.

The Apaches had no prisons as white men have. Instead of sending the criminals into prison, they sent them out of their tribe. These faithless, cruel, lazy, or cowardly members of the tribe were excluded in such a manner that they could not join any other tribe. Neither could they

210 have any protection from our unwritten tribal laws. Frequently these outlaw Indians banded together and

FIX-UP IDEA

Tackle Difficult Vocabulary
Use the Words for Everyday Use and the footnotes to help you understand difficult words. Try rephrasing a sentence with a challenging word by inserting words from the definition into the sentence. For instance, rephrase the sentence with *assemble* as "Sometimes the whole tribe would *gather in a group* to sing and pray."

MARK THE TEXT

Underline or highlight what crimes were considered punishable by the Apache people.

words for everyday use

as • sem • ble (ə sem′ bəl) v., gather in a group. *The students <u>assembled</u> in the gymnasium for a pep rally.*
a • bound (ə bound′) v., be plentiful. *The lake once <u>abounded</u> with fish, but now they are scarce.*
as • cer • tain (as′ ər tān′) v., find out with certainty. *Hank was unable to <u>ascertain</u> whether or not the famous basketball star had really been spotted in a local restaurant.*
pro • fane (prō fān′) v., show disrespect for sacred things. *One of the most terrible crimes to the Dineh was to <u>profane</u> their religion.*
ban • ish (ba′ nish) v., drive out or remove from a place. *We were <u>banished</u> from the kitchen while our parents wrapped Christmas gifts.*

WHAT DO YOU WONDER?

Ask a question or respond to how the Apache punish criminals.

_____

_____

_____

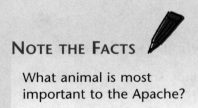

NOTE THE FACTS

What animal is most important to the Apache?

_____

committed depredations[5] which were charged against the regular tribe. However, the life of an outlaw Indian was a hard lot, and their bands never became very large. Besides, these bands frequently provoked the wrath of the tribe and secured their own destruction.

When I was about eight or ten years old, I began to follow the chase; and to me this was never work.

220 Out on the prairies, which ran up to our mountain homes, wandered herds of deer, antelope, elk, and buffalo, to be slaughtered when we needed them.

Usually we hunted buffalo on horseback, killing them with arrows and spears. Their skins were used to make tepees and bedding; their flesh, to eat.

It required more skill to hunt the deer than any other animal. We never tried to approach a deer except against the wind. Frequently we would spend hours in stealing upon grazing deer. If they were in the open, we would crawl long distances on the ground, keeping a weed or

230 brush before us, so that our approach would not be noticed. Often we could kill several out of one herd before the others would run away. Their flesh was dried and packed in vessels, and would keep in this condition for many months. The hide of the deer was soaked in water and ashes and the hair removed, and then the process of tanning continued until the buckskin was soft and pliable. Perhaps no other animal was more valuable to us than the deer.

In the forests and along the streams were many wild turkeys. These we would drive to the plains, then slowly

240 ride up toward them until they were almost tired out. When they began to drop and hide, we would ride in upon them and by swinging from the sides of our horses, catch them. If one started to fly, we would ride swiftly under him and kill him with a short stick, or hunting club. In this way we could usually get as many wild turkeys as we could carry home on a horse.

There were many rabbits in our range, and we also hunted them on horseback. Our horses were trained to follow the rabbit at full speed, and as they approached

___

5. **depredations.** Acts of robbing or plundering

250 them, we would swing from one side of the horse and strike the rabbit with our hunting club. If he was too far away, we would throw the stick and kill him. This was great sport when we were boys, but as warriors we seldom hunted small game.

There were many fish in the streams, but as we did not eat them, we did not try to catch or kill them. Small boys sometimes threw stones at them or shot at them for practice with their bows and arrows. Usen did not intend snakes, frogs, or fishes to be eaten. I have never eaten of
260 them.

There are many eagles in the mountains. These we hunted for their feathers. It required great skill to steal upon an eagle; for beside having sharp eyes, he is wise and never stops at any place where he does not have a good view of the surrounding country.

I have killed many bears with a spear, but was never injured in a fight with one. I have killed several mountain lions with arrows, and one with a spear. Both bears and mountain lions are good for food and valuable for their
270 skin. When we killed them, we carried them home on our horses. We often made quivers for our arrows from the skin of the mountain lion. These were very pretty and very durable.

During my minority,[6] we had never seen a missionary or a priest. We had never seen a white man. Thus quietly lived the Be-don-ko-he Apaches. ■

---

6. **minority.** Childhood years

MAKE A NOTE

Make a note about or respond to the Apache people's ideas about fishing.

_____

_____

_____

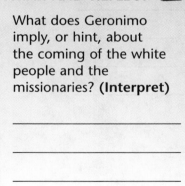

THINK AND REFLECT

What does Geronimo imply, or hint, about the coming of the white people and the missionaries? **(Interpret)**

_____

_____

_____

Reflect ON YOUR READING

After Reading ➤ ANALYZE INFORMATION YOU GATHER

❑ Look back through your notes and the information you underlined and highlighted. Add information about Apache customs to your Cluster Chart.
❑ Describe one of the customs you added to your chart, and discuss your reaction to the custom.

_____

_____

_____

_____

_____

_____

_____

_____

_____

_____

_____

_____

_____

_____

Reading Skills and Test Practice

MAKE INFERENCES

Discuss with your partner how best to answer the following questions that ask you to make inferences. Use the Think-Aloud Notes to write down your reasons for eliminating the incorrect answers.

_____1. What can you infer from the following statement, "I was warmed by the sun, rocked by the winds, and sheltered by the trees as other Indian babes"?
a. The legends of the Native American people feature nature.
b. Geronimo was outside a lot more than he should have been.
c. Nature is a vital part of Native American life.
d. Geronimo saw many animals.

_____2. When Geronimo says that before the white men arrived, "quietly lived the Be-don-ko-he Apaches," he means
a. white men were noisy.
b. life was hard after the white men arrived.
c. the Apaches were not busy before the white men arrived.
d. life was not changed when the white men arrived.

How did using the reading strategy help you to answer the questions?

_____

_____

_____

Investigate, Inquire, and Imagine

RECALL: GATHER FACTS
1a. What games did Geronimo play with his brothers and sisters?

→ INTERPRET: FIND MEANING
1b. Why were the games Geronimo played important?

ANALYZE: TAKE THINGS APART
2a. List some things that might cause someone to be banished from the tribe.

→ SYNTHESIZE: BRING THINGS TOGETHER
2b. Why was banishment an effective form of punishment? What effect did it have on the tribe?

EVALUATE: MAKE JUDGMENTS
3a. Judge the form of punishment used by Geronimo's people. Do you think it is fair to punish people this way?

→ EXTEND: CONNECT IDEAS
3b. What do you think of forms of punishment used in our society? Explain whether you think fines, prison, or the death penalty are good ways to punish people for crimes. Do you think our modern methods are honorable and effective?

Literary Tools

AUTOBIOGRAPHY. An **autobiography** is the story of a person's life written by that person. In this story, Geronimo writes about events in his life.

1. What did you learn about Geronimo's life that you didn't know before?

_____

_____

_____

_____

_____

2. How would the story of Geronimo's life differ if it were written by a government worker or a missionary? What details in the story might change?

_____

_____

_____

_____

_____

WordWorkshop

Word Race. Practice reading the words from this selection aloud. Have a classmate keep track of how many second it takes you to read the entire list. Have another person keep track of the words you mispronounce. Add notes near each word that help you pronounce them. For instance, you could add diacritical marks above *Apache* [ə paʹ chē], or write a note after the word: "rhymes with *scratchy*." Form teams to see which team can pronounce the same list of words the fastest with the fewest errors. Then see which team can *define* each word the fastest.

Words for Everyday Use	Apache Words
abound	Apache
administer	Be-don-ko-he
ascertain	Cho-ko-le
assemble	esadadedne
banish	Kah
loiter	No-doyohn Cañon
profane	shudock
secluded	tiswin
suspend	tsoch
toil	Usen

Read-Write Connection

How would you feel about living with Geronimo's people?

_____

_____

_____

_____

Beyond the Reading

Research Native American Culture. Working in a small group, research an aspect of Native American culture and society. You might focus on art, economics, history, the calendar, language, literature, clothing, medicine, religion, social issues, or warfare. Record information about this aspect as it applied to the Apache, or Dineh, and to two other groups. Compare and contrast the groups' beliefs about the subject you choose.

Go Online. To find links and additional activities for this selection, visit the EMC Internet Resource Center at **emcp.com/languagearts** and click on Write-In Reader.

from Gorillas in the Mist

by Dian Fossey

Active READING STRATEGY

READ WITH A PURPOSE

Before Reading ▶ **FIND A PURPOSE FOR READING**

❑ Read the title and look at the photograph on page 278.

❑ Fossey's purpose for writing is stated in the first sentence. She says she often is asked to talk about the most rewarding experience she has had with gorillas. This excerpt is her effort to answer that question. Put Fossey's purpose for writing—to describe her most rewarding experiences with gorillas—in the Before Reading section of the Author's Purpose Chart below.

Graphic Organizer: Author's Purpose Chart

Before Reading
Fossey's purpose for writing:

During Reading
Ideas Fossey communicates:

After Reading
How Fossey's ideas help fulfill her purpose for writing:

CONNECT

Reader's resource

Dian Fossey had a lifelong interest in animals. On a trip to Africa in 1963, she briefly met the famous anthropologist Louis Leakey and became interested in mountain gorillas. When Fossey returned to the United States, she raised money to start a research program. She established the Karisoke Research Centre in Rwanda in 1967. Intense observation over thousands of hours enabled Fossey to earn the trust of the wild gorilla groups she studied. Her research helped ensure their survival. Fossey's research was cut short when she was found murdered in her cabin at Karisoke on December 26, 1985. Her murder remains unsolved.

Word watch

PREVIEW VOCABULARY

foliage
intangible
meander
unfathomable

Reader's journal

What animal would you like to study? Why?

_____

_____

_____

GATHER INFORMATION
ABOUT FOSSEY'S
EXPERIENCES

❑ Read the selection.
❑ As you finish each
   paragraph, add details
   about Fossey's
   experiences with gorillas
   to your Author's Purpose
   Chart.

Literary TOOLS

DOCUMENTARY WRITING.
Documentary writing is
writing based on field notes.
Field notes are a person's
observations, reactions to, and
analysis of the subject matter
he or she is studying. *Fieldwork*
is work done in the native
environment of the subject—
for example, studying rain
forest insects in the Amazon or
studying ancient Asian herbal
remedies in Cambodia.
Ethology, the study of animal
behavior, is the scientific work
that Fossey undertook.
Ethology combines work in
laboratories and in the field.

MARK THE TEXT

Underline or highlight what
the cable to Dr. Leakey says.

Gorillas in the Mist
Dian Fossey

Often I am asked about the most rewarding experience I have
ever had with gorillas. The question is extremely difficult to
answer because each hour with the gorillas provides its own
return and satisfaction. The first occasion when I felt I might
have crossed an <u>intangible</u> barrier between human and ape
occurred about ten months after beginning the research at
Karisoke. Peanuts, Group 8's youngest male, was feeding
about fifteen feet away when he suddenly stopped and turned
to stare directly at me. The expression in his eyes was
10 <u>unfathomable</u>. Spellbound, I returned his gaze—a gaze that
seemed to combine elements of inquiry and of acceptance.
Peanuts ended this unforgettable moment by sighing deeply,
and slowly resumed feeding. Jubilant, I returned to camp and
cabled Dr. Leakey[1] I'VE FINALLY BEEN ACCEPTED BY
A GORILLA.*

   Two years after our exchange of glances, Peanuts became the
first gorilla ever to touch me. The day had started out as an
ordinary one, if any day working from Karisoke might be

---

1. **Dr. Leakey.** Scientist and colleague of Fossey's who encouraged her to
study gorillas

> **words for everyday use**
> **in • tan • gi • ble** (in tan′ jə bəl) *adj.,* not able to be seen or touched. *She awoke at that <u>intangible</u> moment between dark and dawn.*
> **un • fath • om • a • ble** (un fa′ thə mə bəl) *adj.,* impossible to comprehend. *The number of stars in the sky is <u>unfathomable</u>.*

considered ordinary. I felt unusually compelled to make this
20 particular day outstanding because the following morning I
had to leave for England for a seven-month period to work on
my doctorate. Bob Campbell and I had gone out to contact
Group 8 on the western-facing Visoke slopes. We found them
feeding in the middle of a shallow ravine of densely growing
herbaceous vegetation. Along the ridge leading into the ravine
grew large *Hagenia* trees that had always served as good
lookout spots for scanning the surrounding terrain. Bob and I
had just settled down on a comfortable moss-cushioned
Hagenia tree trunk when Peanuts, wearing his "I want to be
entertained" expression, left his feeding group to <u>meander</u>
30 toward us. Slowly I left the tree and pretended to munch on
vegetation to reassure Peanuts that I meant him no harm.

Peanuts' bright eyes peered at me through a latticework of
vegetation as he began his strutting, swaggering approach.
Suddenly he was at my side and sat down to watch my
"feeding" techniques as if it were my turn to entertain him.
When Peanuts seemed bored with the "feeding" routine, I
scratched my head, and almost immediately, he began
scratching his own. Since he appeared totally relaxed, I lay
back in the <u>foliage</u>, slowly extended my hand, palm upward,
40 then rested it on the leaves. After looking intently at my hand,
Peanuts stood up and extended his hand to touch his fingers
against my own for a brief instant. Thrilled at his own daring,
he gave vent to his excitement by a quick chestbeat before
going off to rejoin his group. Since that day, the spot has been
called *Fasi Ya Mkoni*, "the Place of the Hands." The contact
was among the most memorable of my life among the gorillas.

*Nine years after Dr. Leakey's death in 1972 I learned that
he had carried the cable in his pocket for months, even taking
it on a lecture tour to America. I was told that he read it
50 proudly, much as he once spoke to me of Jane Goodall's
outstanding success with chimpanzees. ■

words for everyday use	**me • an • der** (mē an' dər) *v.,* follow a winding course or wander. *The bubbly stream <u>meanders</u> through the hillside.* **fo • li • age** (fō' lē əj) *n.,* cluster of leaves, flowers, and branches. *Derek stared in awe at the dazzling emerald <u>foliage</u> in the park.*

Use THE STRATEGY

READ WITH A PURPOSE. What experience does Fossey describe in paragraph 2? Add this to your graphic organizer.

Reading STRATEGY
REVIEW

CONNECT TO PRIOR EXPERIENCE. What you have learned about Fossey's experiences?

_____

_____

_____

Reflect ON YOUR READING

After Reading ➤ SUMMARIZE WHAT YOU HAVE LEARNED

❑ Review your Author's Purpose Chart. How well did the author fulfill her purpose?

_____

_____

❑ Write a summary of Fossey's experiences with gorillas.

_____

_____

_____

_____

_____

_____

_____

_____

_____

_____

_____

_____

_____

_____

_____

Reading Skills and Test Practice

EVALUATE THE AUTHOR'S PURPOSE

With your partner, discuss how to answer the questions about an author's purpose. Use the Think-Aloud Notes to write down your reasons for eliminating the incorrect answers.

_____1. Which statement describes what Fossey wants readers to think about gorillas?
   a. They are wild.
   b. They are entertaining.
   c. They have to be taught to imitate humans.
   d. They can learn to trust humans.

_____2. Why does Fossey tell the story about Dr. Leakey keeping the cable she sent?
   a. to show surprise that Leakey kept it
   b. to be able use Leakey's name in her book
   c. to show how Leakey responded to her experience
   d. to give credit to Leakey for supporting her studies

How did using the reading strategy help you to answer the questions?

_____

_____

Investigate, Inquire, and Imagine

RECALL: GATHER FACTS
1a. What question do people frequently ask Fossey? Why is it difficult to answer?

→ INTERPRET: FIND MEANING
1b. Why do you think she follows this with the story about Peanuts?

ANALYZE: TAKE THINGS APART
2a. Make a list of the ways that Fossey and Peanuts demonstrate interest in one another.

→ SYNTHESIZE: BRING THINGS TOGETHER
2b. How does Fossey's observation describe a landmark event in the study of gorillas?

EVALUATE: MAKE JUDGMENTS
3a. Consider Fossey's techniques for fostering trust and friendship in Peanuts. How well do they work? What other techniques do you think she might have used?

→ EXTEND: CONNECT IDEAS
3b. Imagine you are able to observe some of Fossey's gorillas. What would you want to communicate to them or learn from them?

Literary Tools

DOCUMENTARY WRITING. **Documentary writing** is writing based on field notes. *Field notes* are a person's observations, reactions to, and analysis of the subject matter they are studying. *Fieldwork* is work done in the native environment of the subject—for example, studying rain forest insects in the Amazon, studying ice in Antarctica, or studying ancient Asian herbal remedies in Cambodia. *Ethology*, the study of animal behavior, is the scientific work that Fossey undertook. Ethology combines work in laboratories and in the field. Fossey used her field notes to write *Gorillas in the Mist*.

1. Why might Fossey have included the excerpt about Peanuts in her book?

   _____

   _____

2. What details about Peanuts help you understand mountain gorillas?

   _____

   _____

WordWorkshop

CROSSWORD PUZZLE. Use the following words from the selection in a crossword puzzle. Use the grid in Appendix A on page A-3 as a guide. Then create clues across and clues down for each word.

anecdote
Fossey
documentary writing
Leakey
foliage
intangible
Karisoke
meander
Peanuts
unfathomable

Read-Write Connection

Describe an interaction with an animal that you would find memorable.

_____

_____

_____

_____

_____

_____

_____

_____

Beyond the Reading

LEARN MORE ABOUT GORILLA RESEARCH. Use the Internet to find out more about gorilla research. Start at the Dian Fossey Gorilla Fund site at www.gorillafund.org. Use the site's links to find additional information. Then prepare a report on recent gorilla research.

GO ONLINE. To find links and additional activities for this selection, visit the EMC Internet Resource Center at **emcp.com/languagearts** and click on Write-In Reader.

"A Breath of Fresh Air?"

by Alexandra Hanson-Harding

Active READING STRATEGY

USE TEXT ORGANIZATION

Before Reading ➤ **PREVIEW THE SELECTION**

❑ Read the Reader's Resource and look at the photograph on page 284.

❑ Look over the organization of the article. Note how the headings help organize the article into sections.

❑ As you read, you will use the Outline below to record the main ideas of the article.

Graphic Organizer: Outline

"A Breath of Fresh Air?"	

I.   Introduction (first paragraph)
    A. Donora, PA—5,900 became ill, 20 died
    B.
    C.
	V. Are Changes Needed?
	    A.
	    B.
	    C.

II. Cleaning Up Our Act (1970 Clean Air Act)
    A. Business and government had to make changes
    B.
    C.
	VI. Too Strict?
	    A.
	    B.
	    C.

III. Not Clean Enough
    A.
    B.
    C.
	VII. Setting Tough Standards
	    A.
	    B.
	    C.

IV. The Culprits
    A.
    B.
    C.
	VIII. A Fierce Battle Ahead
	    A.
	    B.
	    C.

	IX. Conclusion (last paragraph)
	    A.
	    B.
	    C.

CONNECT

Reader's resource

The U.S. Environmental Protection Agency (EPA) was set up to protect not only the environment but also human life. People rely on air, water, and the land to live, so when these resources are threatened, human life is endangered. The EPA enforces federal laws designed to protect these natural resources. One of the events that led to the establishment of the EPA is described in "A Breath of Fresh Air?"

Word watch

PREVIEW VOCABULARY

aggravation
emission
provision

Reader's journal

How do you feel when you see signs of air pollution?

_____

_____

_____

_____

_____

ADD INFORMATION TO AN OUTLINE

❏ Read the introduction (the first two paragraphs) of "A Breath of Fresh Air?" Add two more sets of details from the paragraph to your Outline. (One set of details has been provided for you.)

❏ Continue reading the rest of the selection. Stop after each section to add details like those in II. A. to your Outline.

NOTE THE FACTS

What happened on a regular basis in 1950?

_____

_____

_____

Literary TOOLS

ARTICLE. An **article** is a brief nonfiction work on a specific topic. Encyclopedia entries, newspaper reports, and nonfiction magazine pieces are examples of articles. Hanson-Harding's article was published on the Junior Scholastic Online Internet site on April 11, 1997. What is the topic of her article? What is her main idea?

A Breath of Fresh Air?

Alexandra Hanson-Harding

It started with a dark, soupy haze that hung in the sky during the week of October 25, 1948. When it left, 5,900 people were seriously ill. Twenty more were dead.

It was not a horror movie. It really happened in Donora, Pennsylvania.[1] Back then, many people in the U.S. were struck down by polluted air. In New York City, smog caused 700 more deaths than normal in 1953, 1963, and 1966 combined. Throughout the 1950s, schools and
10   businesses in Los Angeles were closed on a regular basis because of Stage 3 "smog alerts." The air was so dirty, said Edward Camerena, a Los Angeles chemist, "You'd blow your nose and it would be black."

Cleaning Up Our Act
The U.S. has come a long way since then. In 1970, Congress passed the Clean Air Act. This law required private businesses and state and local governments to make changes to decrease air pollution. Carmakers had to build cars that leaked fewer harmful gases. Power plants were required to put special "scrubbers" in their smokestacks.
20   These changes—and those required by later laws—have made the air we breathe much cleaner.

---

1. **Donora, Pennsylvania.** A city 24 miles south of Pittsburgh on the Monongohela River

Not Clean Enough

Is the air today clean enough to protect people's health? The Environmental Protection Agency (EPA), the government agency that regulates air pollution, says no. Last November, Carol Browner, head of the EPA, announced that the EPA plans to set even tougher standards. After examining hundreds of studies, the EPA found that U.S. standards for two major pollutants were not tough enough. It also says that these two pollutants are costing the U.S. billions of dollars in hospital visits and days lost from work and school. Even worse, the EPA estimates that more than 40,000 people a year die prematurely (earlier than normal) because of dirty air.

The Culprits

What are the two pollutants? The first is ground-level ozone;[2] the second, something called fine particulates.

Ground-level ozone is an odorless, colorless gas that is formed when sulfates react with sunlight. (Sulfates are chemicals released when coal is burned.) Ozone that occurs naturally in the upper atmosphere helps to protect Earth, but ground-level ozone, which is worse on hot days, makes it harder for people to breathe. If people inhale too much of it over time, it can damage their lungs. Children are more likely to be harmed by ozone than adults, because their lungs are growing at a faster rate. People with lung problems also are at high risk.

The second pollutant, fine particulates,[3] are tiny particles that hang in the air. Some larger particulates are solid pieces of dust or soot. But the EPA is more concerned about the tiniest particulates, which can be inhaled more deeply into the lungs, damaging them. These particulates also contribute to haziness in the air. At some national parks, haze has decreased visibility by more than 77 percent on some days.

Together, ozone and fine particulates cause more than 1.5 million incidents of major breathing and lung problems a year, says the EPA. Such problems include the loss of lung

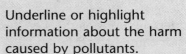

MARK THE TEXT

Underline or highlight information about the harm caused by pollutants.

NOTE THE FACTS

What problems does ground-level ozone cause? Who is especially at risk?

_____

_____

_____

---

2. **ground-level ozone.** A colorless gas just above the ground that is formed usually by a silent electrical discharge
3. **fine particulates.** Extremely small fragments or pieces

capacity and the <u>aggravation</u> of asthma in both adults and
children.

60

Adam Buchoff, 10, knows the problem first hand. He has
asthma, and has to use inhalers (devices used to convey
medicine to the lungs). "Sometimes it feels like a gorilla is
on your chest," he told *JS*.[4] "It can be tough."

Are Changes Needed?

The EPA has called for tougher standards for both
pollutants. Ozone comes mostly from car exhausts and
smokestack <u>emissions</u> on hot, sunny days. Particulate matter
is caused mostly by power plants and large incinerators.[5]

70

The EPA says that the proposed new standards would
reduce serious breathing problems in children by 250,000
cases per year. "The EPA proposal would give new
protection to nearly 133 million Americans, including 40
million children," says Carol Browner. "We will use the
very best science to do what is necessary to protect public
health in commonsense, cost-effective ways."

Too Strict?

However, more than 500 organizations are fighting the new
regulations, including many carmakers, oil companies, and

80

power-plant owners. More than a hundred members of
Congress are siding with them.

Why? Some opponents say that the new regulations will be
expensive, and that companies will pass the costs on to
consumers. The Automobile Manufacturers Group, for
instance, estimates that the price of putting additional air-
pollution controls on cars will be $2,000 per car. Low-pollutant
gasoline could cost an extra five to ten cents a gallon, according
to Al Mannato of the American Petroleum Institute (API).

Mannato says that we need to give the latest Clean Air

90

Act, passed in 1990, time to work. Some <u>provisions</u> of the

MARK THE TEXT

Underline or highlight the major causes of ozone and particulate matter.

NOTE THE FACTS

Who is fighting the EPA's measures?

_____

_____

_____

4. **JS.** Abbreviation for *Junior Scholastic Magazine*
5. **incinerators.** Furnaces or other devices for burning trash

words for everyday use

ag • gra • va • tion (ag rə vā′ shən) n., worsening. *The <u>aggravation</u> of Lindsay's allergies occurs in the summer when pollen counts are high.*
e • mis • sion (ē mish′ ən) n., gas or other substance that is let out. *Cars have to be tested to make sure their <u>emissions</u> are at acceptable levels.*
pro • vi • sion (prō vizh′ ən) n., condition. *The <u>provisions</u> of the law require businesses to make changes.*

law have not yet taken effect, such as new standards on diesel vehicles and reformulated gas. "Pollution will go down in the future because of regulations that are already in place," he told *JS*.

Most of all, he says that scientists do not agree on the effects of these pollutants. Also, says Mannato, there have not been enough studies of fine particulates to make a fair conclusion.

100   "The science isn't there, and air pollution will continue to go down in the future," Mannato says. "Therefore, the cost associated with these proposals is unjustified."

Setting Tough Standards

Dave Ryan of the EPA disagrees. He says that the vast majority of studies agree with the EPA's conclusions. "The weight of scientific evidence is with us," he says. "Science is always evolving. The EPA has a mandate [requirement] from Congress to make a decision every five years based on the best science available. That's what we've done."

110   Ryan says that the benefits of the new standards will drastically outweigh the costs. "In the year 2007," says Ryan, "the cost of implementing this for each American will be in a range from $26 to $34 per person. The total price tag will be between $6.5 and $8.8 billion a year. But the benefits per year will range from $70 to $120 billion. Obviously, that's an incredible payback."

A Fierce Battle Ahead

What will happen next? The EPA will complete its regulations in June. Then, Congress will review the new rules. If Congress decides that the plan is too expensive, it

120 can reject it. The battle between opponents and supporters of the new standards is expected to be fierce.

But it is not just up to Congress, says Ryan. Individuals also can make a difference. Turning down the thermostat[6] in cold weather, using cars less often, and recycling are just three ways people can use less energy and send fewer pollutants into the air. That will help kids like Adam Buchoff to breathe more easily. ∎

---

6. **thermostat.** An apparatus for regulating temperature

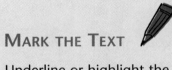

MARK THE TEXT

Underline or highlight the EPA's mandate.

WHAT DO YOU WONDER?

Ask a question or respond to ideas about how to make a difference.

_____

_____

_____

Reflect ON YOUR READING

❑ Use your outline to write a summary of the article.

_____

_____

_____

_____

_____

THINK-ALOUD NOTES

_____

_____

_____

_____

_____

_____

_____

_____

_____

_____

_____

Reading Skills and Test Practice

EVALUATE ARGUMENTS

READ, THINK, AND EXPLAIN. Discuss with a partner how to evaluate arguments. Use the Think-Aloud Notes to jot down your ideas before drafting your answers.

1. What are the advantages and disadvantages of passing the EPA's proposal?

    _____

    _____

    _____

    _____

2. What is your opinion of the proposal? Use details from the article to support your answer.

    _____

    _____

    _____

    _____

REFLECT ON YOUR RESPONSE. Compare your response with that of a partner. Were your responses similar? How did using the reading strategy help you answer the questions? What advice would you give to someone who wants to make a difference?

Investigate, Inquire, and Imagine

RECALL: GATHER FACTS
1a. What does the Clean Air Act require of businesses? What would new proposals require?

→ help reduce air pollution.

INTERPRET: FIND MEANING
1b. Why do many businesses oppose the EPA's proposal?

ANALYZE: TAKE THINGS APART
2a. Writers use many techniques to engage an audience. Some of these techniques include presenting statistics, sharing real-life stories, and including quotations or dialogue. Describe one method Hanson-Harding uses to get readers to accept her point of view. Give an example of the method.

→ SYNTHESIZE: BRING THINGS TOGETHER
2b. What is Hanson-Harding's main point?

→

PERSPECTIVE: LOOK AT OTHER VIEWS
3a. Evaluate whether industry and individuals will make changes that

EMPATHY: SEE FROM INSIDE
3b. What arguments are most likely to prompt a change in industry? in individuals?

WordWorkshop

WORD STUDY CHARTS. Use information provided in Words for Everyday Use and in a dictionary to complete a Word Study Chart for each of the following words: *aggravation, emission, provision.*

Word:	Word:	Word:
Pronunciation:	Pronunciation:	Pronunciation:
Origins:	Origins:	Origins:
Definition:	Definition:	Definition:
Sentence:	Sentence:	Sentence:
Drawing:	Drawing:	Drawing:

Literary Tools

ARTICLE. An **article** is a brief nonfiction work on a specific topic. Encyclopedia entries, newspaper reports, and nonfiction magazine pieces are examples of articles. What is "A Breath of Fresh Air?" trying to persuade readers to believe or do? Is the article successful? Why, or why not?

_____

_____

_____

_____

Read-Write Connection

Do you feel that you can make a difference in reducing pollution? Why, or why not?

_____

_____

_____

_____

_____

_____

_____

_____

_____

_____

Beyond the Reading

USE REFERENCE MATERIALS. At your school or local library, learn more about pollution by using the following reference materials: encyclopedias, almanacs, yearbooks, and atlases. What specific information about pollution can you find in each of these sources? Make a bibliography of the reference books you use. List information about specific kinds of pollution discussed in each one.

GO ONLINE. To find links and additional activities for this selection, visit the EMC Internet Resource Center at **emcp.com/languagearts** and click on Write-In Reader.

Unit 7  READING
Review

Choose and Use Reading Strategies

Before reading an excerpt from a speech, review and discuss with a partner how to use reading strategies with nonfiction.

1. Read with a Purpose
2. Connect to Prior Knowledge
3. Write Things Down
4. Make Predictions
5. Visualize
6. Use Text Organization
7. Tackle Difficult Vocabulary
8. Monitor Your Reading Progress

The excerpt below is from "Ain't I a Woman?", a speech presented by former slave Sojourner Truth to the Women's Convention in Akron, Ohio, in 1851. Use the margins and mark up the excerpt. Show how you use reading strategies to read actively. After you finish reading, summarize Truth's ideas in two or three sentences.

Well, children, where there is so much racket there must be something out of kilter. I think that 'twixt the negroes of the South and the women at the North, all talking about rights, the white men will be in a pretty fix soon. But what's all this here talking about?

That man over there says that women need to be helped into carriages, and lifted over ditches, and to have the best place everywhere. Nobody ever helps me into carriages, or over mud-puddles, or gives me any best place! And ain't I a woman? Look at me! Look at my arm! I have ploughed and planted, and gathered into barns, and no man could head me! And ain't I a woman? I could work as much and eat as much as a man—when I could get it—and bear the lash as well! And ain't I a woman? I have borne thirteen children, and seen most all sold off to slavery, and when I cried out with my mother's grief, none but Jesus heard me! And ain't I a woman?

Then they talk about this thing in the head; what's this they call it? [member of audience whispers, "intellect"] That's it, honey. What's that got to do with women's rights or negroes' rights? If my cup won't hold but a pint, and yours holds a quart, wouldn't you be mean not to let me have my little half-measure full?

Then that little man in black there, he says women can't have as much rights as men, 'cause Christ wasn't a woman! Where did your Christ come from? Where did your Christ come from? From God and a woman! Man had nothing to do with Him.

If the first woman God ever made was strong enough to turn the world upside down all alone, these women together ought to be able to turn it back, and get it right side up again! And now they is asking to do it, the men better let them.

Obliged to you for hearing me, and now old Sojourner ain't got nothing more to say.

Literary Tools

Select the best literary element on the right to complete each sentence on the left. Write the correct letter in the blank.

_____ 1. Dian Fossey's field notes are used as background information for a piece of _____.

_____ 2. Bill Littlefield's story about the life of Satchel Paige is a(n) _____.

_____ 3. Writer Alexandra Hanson-Harding's short informational work on air pollution is a scientific _____.

_____ 4. Geronimo's story of his own life is a(n) _____.

_____ 5. Robert Silverberg's views about the last days of Pompeii are expressed in a(n) _____.

a. essay, 237, 251

b. biography, 254, 263

c. autobiography, 266, 275

d. documentary writing, 278, 281

e. article, 284, 289

WordWorkshop

Game Show Network. In a small group, use the definitions of the words in this unit to create a game like one you might see on television. When you are finished, have other groups play your game.

1. You may create your own version of *Jeopardy* by adding definitions to a chart with five or six columns. Create a category for each of the columns that will fit definitions in the column, such as "Words Ending with *–ity or –ion*" or "Words You Might Find on a Cereal Box." Contestants who play your game would have to read the definition and ask a question that shows which word fits the definition—"What is the word *fruitless?*"

2. To play *Wheel of Fortune*, you may put up blanks for each letter in a word and its definition. Have contestants guess letters until they are able to recite the word and its definition: "Foliage is a cluster of leaves, flowers, and branches."

3. To play *Who Wants to Be a Millionaire*, you may create multiple-choice questions about the words. Your questions can start with easy words and then get more difficult.

On Your Own

Form a literature circle or book club that reads the same nonfiction article from a book or magazine. When you finish your discussions of the article, complete one of the following activities.

FLUENTLY SPEAKING. Rewrite a section of the article as a play and present the play to the class. Be sure to rehearse the play several times before you present it.

PICTURE THIS. Create a drawing or chart that communicates ideas from the article.

PUT IT IN WRITING. Create a newsletter or brochure that communicates ideas from the article.

Unit EIGHT

Reading Informational and Visual Media

INFORMATIONAL AND VISUAL MEDIA

Learning how to read online and print reference works, graphic aids, and other visuals will help you access, process, and think about the vast amount of information available to you.

Informational Media

Media are channels or systems of communication, information, or entertainment. *Mass media*, designed to reach the mass of the people, refers specifically to means of communication, such as newspapers, radio, or television. *Journalism* is the gathering, evaluating, and spreading, through various media, of news and facts of current interest. Journalism has expanded from printed matter (newspapers and periodicals) to include radio, television, documentary films, the Internet, and computer news services.

Newspapers, issued on a daily or weekly basis, report the news, provide commentary on the news, advocate various public policies, and furnish special information and advice to readers.

Periodicals, released at regular intervals, are publications that include journals, magazines, or newsletters. They feature material of special interest to particular audiences.

Technical writing refers to scientific or process-oriented instructional writing that is of a technical or mechanical nature, such as **instruction manuals**, **how-to instructional guides**, and **procedural memos**. In this unit, "Choosing a Dog" is an example of a how-to guide.

NOTE THE FACTS

How has journalism changed?

_____

_____

_____

Reading TIP

- In technical writing, look for words such as *first, second, then, next, before,* and *after.* These transitional words help you understand the sequence of steps.

- Technical writing may also include diagrams or pictures to help you.

- Icons may alert you to safety issues, optional steps, or other special features in the directions.

Elements of Informational Media

NEWS ARTICLES. **News articles** are informational pieces of writing about a particular topic, issue, event, or series of events. They can be found in newspapers, periodicals, and on Internet sites such as newsgroups or information services.

EDITORIALS AND COMMENTARIES. An **editorial** is an article in a newspaper or periodical that gives the opinions of the editors or publishers. A **commentary** expresses the opinion of a participant or observer of a particular event.

ESSAYS. An **essay** is a brief work of nonfiction that need not be a complete treatment of a subject.

INTERVIEWS. An **interview** is a question and answer exchange between a reporter who wants information and the person who has that information. "Contests!" in this unit is an example of an interview.

REVIEWS. A **review**, or *critique*, is a critical evaluation of a work, such as a book, play, movie, musical performance, or recording.

Electronic Media

Electronic media includes online magazines and journals, known as **webzines** or **e-zines**, **computer news services**, and many **web-based newspapers** that are available on the **Internet**. In addition to handling web documents, the Internet also allows people to send e-mail, access archives of files, and participate in discussion groups.

Multimedia is the presentation of information using the combination of text, sound, pictures, animation, and video. Common multimedia computer applications include **game**s, **learning software**, **presentation software**, **reference materials**, and **web pages**. Using multimedia can provide a varied and informative interactive experience.

Elements of Electronic Media

ELECTRONIC MAIL. **Electronic mail**, or **e-mail**, is used to send written messages between individuals or groups on the Internet. E-mail messages tend to be more informal and conversational in style than letters.

Reading STRATEGY REVIEW

CONNECT TO PRIOR KNOWLEDGE. What kinds of electronic media have you used? What do you like about using electronic media?

_____

_____

_____

WEB PAGES. A **web page** is an electronic "page" on the World Wide Web or Internet that may contain text, pictures, and sometimes animations related to a particular topic. A *website* is a collection of pages grouped together to organize the information offered by the person, company, or group that owns it.

NEWSGROUPS. Electronic discussions on a particular subject are grouped together into **newsgroups** on a wide range of subjects. Messages to a newsgroup are accessible in the form of a list on a local news server, or computer, that has a worldwide reach. Users can choose which messages they want to read and reply by posting messages to the newsgroup.

INFORMATION SERVICES. Information services, or *news services*, are providers of electronic news, information, and e-mail services.

BULLETIN BOARD SYSTEMS. A **bulletin board system**, or BBS, is an online service that allows users to post and read messages on a particular topic, converse in a *chat room*, play games with another person, and copy, or download, programs to their personal computers.

WEBZINES OR E-ZINES. Webzines or **e-zines** are periodicals that are available online. They may be available only online, or they may also be available in a magazine distributed by traditional methods.

ONLINE NEWSPAPERS. Major newspapers are now available online. Past editions of the paper are usually accessible through an online archive.

Visual Media

Many books and news media rely on **visual arts**, such as **fine art**, **illustrations**, and **photographs**, to convey ideas. Critically viewing a painting or photograph can add meaning to your understanding of a text.

Elements of Visual Media

GRAPHIC AIDS. Graphic aids are visual materials with information such as **drawings**, **illustrations**, **diagrams**, **charts**, **graphs**, **maps**, and **spreadsheets**.

PHOTOGRAPHS. Photographs can accompany news stories or documents, serve as scientific evidence or works of art, and record everyday life. New photographic technology allows for digital formats to be stored on disk and downloaded to computers.

THINK AND REFLECT

What do newsgroups and bulletin board systems have in common? **(Compare and Contrast)**

_____

_____

_____

THINK AND REFLECT

Give a situation in which a graphic aid would be helpful. **(Apply)**

_____

_____

_____

THINK AND REFLECT

Give an example of photojournalism and an example of visual art. (Apply)

_____

_____

_____

_____

DIGITAL PHOTOGRAPHY. With **digital photography**, images are converted into a code of ones and zeroes that a computer can read. Digital photographs can be manipulated into new images.

PHOTOJOURNALISM. Photojournalism is documentary photography that tells a particular story in visual terms. Photojournalists, who usually work for newspapers and periodicals, cover cultural and news events in areas such as politics, war, business, sports, and the arts.

VISUAL ARTS. The **visual arts** include painting, sculpture, drawing, printmaking, collage, photography, video, and computer-assisted art. With art, the artist tries to communicate with viewers, who may have different ideas about how to interpret the work. Learning about the location and time period of an artwork can contribute to a better understanding of it.

USING READING STRATEGIES WITH INFORMATIONAL AND VISUAL MEDIA

Active Reading Strategy Checklists

When reading informational and visual media, you will need to identify how the text is structured, or put together. Scan the material first. Headings, pictures, and directions will reveal what the selection wants to communicate. Use the following checklists when you read informational and visual media.

1 READ WITH A PURPOSE. Before reading informational and visual media, give yourself a purpose, or something to look for, as you read. Know why you are reading and what information you seek. Sometimes your teacher will give you a purpose: "Keep track of the steps in the process." Other times you can set your own purpose by previewing the title, the opening and closing paragraphs, and instructional information. Say to yourself

❑ I need to look for . . .
❑ I must keep track of . . .
❑ I need to understand the writer's views on . . .
❑ It is essential that I figure out how . . .
❑ I want to learn what happens when . . .

Reading TIP

Scan the first and last paragraphs, or any headings, pictures and graphs, before you read. This will give you a quick picture of what the writer wants you to understand.

2 CONNECT TO PRIOR KNOWLEDGE. Connect to information you already know about the writer's topic. As you read, build on what you know. Say to yourself

- ❏ I know this about the topic already . . .
- ❏ Other information I've read about this topic said . . .
- ❏ I've used similar visual aids by . . .
- ❏ I did something similar when . . .
- ❏ This information is like . . .

3 WRITE THINGS DOWN. As you read informational and visual media, write down or mark ideas that help you understand the writer's views. Possible ways to keep a written record include

- ❏ Underline information that answers a specific question.
- ❏ Write down steps in a process.
- ❏ Highlight conclusions the writer draws.
- ❏ Create a graphic organizer that shows how to do something.
- ❏ Use a code to respond to the writer's ideas.

4 MAKE PREDICTIONS. Before you read informational and visual media, use the title and subject matter to guess what the selection will be about. As you read, confirm or deny your predictions, and make new ones based on what you learn. Make predictions like the following:

- ❏ The title tells me that the selection will be about . . .
- ❏ Graphic aids show me that . . .
- ❏ I predict that the writer will want me to . . .
- ❏ This selection will help me . . .
- ❏ This writer will conclude by . . .

5 VISUALIZE. Visualizing, or allowing the words on the page to create images in your mind, helps you understand what informational and visual media is trying to communicate. In order to visualize what an informational and visual media selection is communicating, you need to picture the people, events, or procedure that a writer describes. Make statements such as

- ❏ I imagine these people will . . .
- ❏ A drawing of this part would include . . .
- ❏ I picture that this is happening in this section . . .
- ❏ I envision the situation as . . .

Reading **TIP**

Instead of writing down a short response, use a symbol or a short word to indicate your response.
+   I like this
–   I don't like this
√   This is important
Yes I agree with this
No I disagree with this
?   I don't understand this
!   This is like something I know
↶   I need to come back to this later

Use **THE STRATEGY**

VISUALIZE. Make a visual diagram of a procedure. You will remember the procedure longer and it will be easier to review.

6 USE TEXT ORGANIZATION. When you read informational and visual media, pay attention to the structure of the text. Learn to stop occasionally and retell what you have read. Say to yourself

- ❑ The title, headings, and pictures tell me this selection will be about . . .
- ❑ The writer's directions . . .
- ❑ There is a pattern to how the writer presents . . .
- ❑ The writer presents the information by . . .
- ❑ The writer includes helpful sections that . . .

7 TACKLE DIFFICULT VOCABULARY. Difficult words can hinder your ability to understand informational and visual media. Use context, consult a dictionary, or ask someone about words you do not understand. When you come across a difficult word in the selection, say to yourself

- ❑ Context makes me guess that this word means . . .
- ❑ A dictionary definition shows that the word means . . .
- ❑ My work with the word before reading helps me know that the word means . . .
- ❑ A classmate said that the word means . . .

8 MONITOR YOUR READING PROGRESS. All readers encounter difficulty when they read, especially if they haven't chosen the reading material. When you have to read something, note problems you are having and fix them. The key to reading success is knowing when you are having difficulty. To fix problems, say to yourself

- ❑ Because I don't understand this part, I will . . .
- ❑ Because I'm having trouble staying connected to the ideas in the selection, I will . . .
- ❑ Because the words in the selection are too hard, I will . . .
- ❑ Because the selection is long, I will . . .
- ❑ Because I can't retell what the selection was about, I will . . .

Become an Active Reader

Active reading strategy instruction in this unit gives you an in-depth look at how to use one active reading strategy with each selection. Learning how to use several strategies in combination increases your chances of success even more. For more information about the active reading strategies, see Unit 1, pages 4–15.

Reading **TIP**

Difficult words are usually crucial to understanding informational and visual media. If words are not defined in the text, look up the meanings in a dictionary, and write them down.

Fix-Up Ideas

- ■ Reread
- ■ Ask a question
- ■ Read in shorter chunks
- ■ Read aloud
- ■ Retell
- ■ Work with a partner
- ■ Unlock difficult words
- ■ Vary your reading rate
- ■ Choose a new reading strategy
- ■ Create a mnemonic device

How to Use Reading Strategies with Informational and Visual Media

To see how readers use active reading strategies, look over the responses one reader has while reading an excerpt from informational and visual media.

READ WITH A PURPOSE

I want to learn how to make a paper cup.

MAKE A PREDICTION

I predict I can make a cup that won't leak.

MONITOR YOUR READING PROGRESS

I'll review the process to make sure I didn't miss any steps.

WRITE THINGS DOWN

I'll underline key points.

CONNECT TO PRIOR KNOWLEDGE

I've made a paper airplane before. It's kind of like that—folding paper in a certain way to make something useful.

In Six Easy Steps, You Can Be Drinking Lemonade in a Paper Cup!

Step 1

All you have to do is fold your paper into a triangle like this. Mark the corners with Points A, C, and D as you see in the diagram.

Step 2

Next, you need to find Point B. To find Point B, just bring Point A down to the fold line C-D. Fold the edge at Point B to show the position. You can see how to do this in the diagram.

Step 3

This step is easy. All you have to do is open the paper back to the single diagonal fold. Then fold Point D over to Point B. Check this out in the diagram.

Step 4

The next step is to tuck the nearest flap with Point A into the pocket. Firm the edge. The diagram shows what the paper should look like now.

Step 5

For the next step, just turn the paper over. Fold Point C to the diagonally opposite corner. Tuck the remaining flap into this pocket. The diagram shows how it should look.

Step 6

All you have to do now is open up the cup by putting your finger into the space and opening it. You should have a cup that looks like the one in the diagram.

Voila! There's the paper cup. Now go find some ice-cold lemonade!

USE TEXT ORGANIZATION

The diagrams will help me follow the directions.

VISUALIZE

I can picture what it should look like at this stage.

TACKLE DIFFICULT VOCABULARY

The illustrations help me understand what the writer means by Point A, flap, and pocket.

"How to Eat Like a Child"

by Delia Ephron

People eat to fuel their bodies. They also eat to enjoy the tastes, smells, and textures of foods. Some people are picky eaters, meaning they eat only certain things. When eating with other people, there are certain rules people follow called table manners. Table manners include using silverware properly for most foods, not talking with your mouth full, and not playing with or spitting out foods. In "How to Eat Like a Child," Delia Ephron gives a different set of "rules" for eating.

Active READING STRATEGY

CONNECT TO PRIOR KNOWLEDGE

Before Reading ▶ THINK ABOUT WHAT YOU KNOW

❏ Think about how you ate when you were younger and about how younger children you know eat. Get together with a partner and compare ideas about what it's like to watch a young child eat.
❏ Skim the selection. Look at the headings. Choose two foods. Talk with your partner about how a child might eat these foods.
❏ Write the foods you chose in the left column of the Comparison Chart below. Write how you would eat each food in the center column. As you read, take notes about how the author says a child would eat it.

Graphic Organizer: Comparison Chart

Food	How I Would Eat It	Descriptions from Text

Reader's
journal

Write about an interesting eating habit you have now or had in the past.

_____

_____

_____

How to Eat Like a Child

Delia Ephron

 **Peas:** Mash and flatten into thin sheet on plate. Press the back of the fork into the peas. Hold fork vertically, prongs up, and lick off peas.

Mashed Potatoes: Pat mashed

potatoes flat on top. Dig several little depressions. Think of them as ponds or pools. Fill the pools with gravy. With your fork, sculpt rivers between pools and watch the gravy flow between them. Decorate with peas. Do not eat.

10   Alternative method: Make a large hole in center of mashed potatoes. Pour in ketchup. Stir until potatoes turn pink. Eat as you would peas.

 Animal Crackers:

Eat each in this order—legs, head, body.

Sandwich: Leave the crusts. If your

mother says you have to eat them because that's the best part, stuff the crusts into your pants pocket or between the cushions of the couch.

20 **Spaghetti:** Wind too many strands on the fork and make sure at least two strands dangle down. Open your mouth wide and stuff in spaghetti, suck noisily to inhale the dangling strands. Clean plate, ask for seconds, and eat only half. When carrying your plate to the kitchen, hold it tilted so that the remaining spaghetti slides off and onto the floor.

❏ Listen as your teacher reads aloud the section "Peas." As you listen, picture a child eating peas. Write the key points about peas in your Comparison Chart. Then write how you would eat peas. Are they similar?

❏ Read the rest of the selection on your own. Choose other foods to complete the chart. Try to include some foods that you eat in the same way described in the text and some foods that you eat differently.

MARK THE TEXT

Highlight or underline two references to peas in the "Mashed Potatoes" section.

Reading STRATEGY REVIEW

VISUALIZE. When you visualize, you use your imagination to experience something with all your senses. As you read, try to think about how each food would look, smell, taste, feel, and sound.

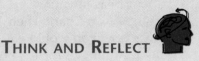

THINK AND REFLECT

Which is messier: eating ice cream in a cone or in a bowl? Which way would you get more ice cream? Why? **(Compare and Contrast)**

_____

_____

_____

_____

Fix-Up Idea

Try a Different Strategy If you are having trouble understanding what you read, you might want to use a different reading strategy. You could use text organization: look at the pictures and pay special attention to the headings. You could write things down: make notes in the margins about which ideas you like or underline things you have also done with food.

Ice-Cream Cone:

Ask for a double scoop. Knock the top scoop off while walking out the door of the ice-cream parlor. Cry. Lick the remaining scoop slowly so that ice cream melts down the outside of the cone and over your hand. Stop licking when the ice cream is even with the top of the cone. Be sure it is absolutely even. Eat a hole in the bottom of the cone and suck the rest of the ice cream out the bottom. When only the cone remains with ice cream coating the inside, leave on car dashboard.

Ice-Cream in Bowl:

40   Grip spoon upright in fist. Stir ice cream vigorously to make soup. Take a large helping on a spoon, place spoon in mouth, and slowly pull it out, sucking only the top layer of ice cream off. Wave spoon in air. Lick its back. Put in mouth again and suck off some more. Repeat until all ice cream is off spoon and begin again.

Cooked Carrots:

On way to mouth, drop in lap. Smuggle to garbage in napkin.

Spinach: Divide into little piles.

50   Rearrange into new piles. After five or six maneuvers, sit back and say you are full.

Chocolate-Chip Cookies:

Half-sit, half-lie on the bed, propped up by a pillow. Read a book. Place cookies next to you on the sheet so that crumbs get in the bed. As you eat the cookies, remove each chocolate chip and place it on your stomach.

60   When all the cookies are consumed, eat the chips one by one, allowing two per page.

Milk Shake:

Bite off one end of the paper covering the straw. Blow through straw to shoot paper across table. Place straw in shake and suck. When the shake just reaches your mouth, place a finger over the top of the straw—the pressure will keep the shake in the straw. Lift

70   straw out of shake, put bottom end in mouth, release finger, and swallow.

Do this until the straw is squished so that you can't suck through it. Ask for another. Open it the same way, but this time shoot the paper at the waitress when she isn't looking. Sip your shake casually—you are just minding your own business—until there is about an inch of shake remaining.

Then blow through the straw until bubbles rise to the

80   top of the glass. When your father says he's had just about enough, get a stomachache.

Chewing Gum:

Remove from mouth and stretch into spaghetti-like strand. Swing like a lasso. Put back in mouth. Pulling out one end and gripping the other end between teeth, have your gum meet your friend's gum and press them together. Think that you have just done something really disgusting.

NOTE THE FACTS

Why, according to the author, is a straw necessary for drinking a milk shake?

_____

_____

_____

_____

Use THE STRATEGY

CONNECT TO PRIOR KNOWLEDGE. How would you eat the foods on this page? Have you ever done any of the things the author mentions?

_____

_____

_____

_____

How would your mother react if you handed her a naked baked apple? **(Apply)**

_____

_____

_____

_____

Baked Apple: With your fingers,

peel skin off baked apple. Tell your mother you changed your mind, you don't want it. Later, when she is harassed and not paying attention to what she is doing, pick up the naked baked apple and hand it to her.

French Fries: Wave one French fry

in air for emphasis while you talk. Pretend to conduct orchestra. Then place four fries in your mouth at once and chew. Turn to your sister, open your mouth and stick out your tongue coated with potatoes. Close mouth and swallow. Smile. ■

Reflect ON YOUR READING

❏ Review your Comparison Chart. What were some foods you eat or have eaten in the way the author describes? What were some foods you have eaten differently?

❏ With your partner, talk about which descriptions you liked best and which you thought were most accurate.

❏ Write your own description of how to eat one of the foods the author mentions.

_____

_____

_____

_____

Reading Skills and Test Practice

RECOGNIZE TONE

Discuss with a group how best to answer questions that require you to recognize tone. Use the Think-Aloud Notes to write down your reasons for eliminating the incorrect answers.

_____1. The overall tone of "How to Eat Like a Child" is best described as
   a. smug.
   b. serious.
   c. annoyed.
   d. lighthearted.

_____2. Read the following passage:

   Stop playing with your food. Eat with your fork, and stop making a mess.

   What is the tone of this passage?
   a. smug
   b. serious
   c. annoyed
   d. lighthearted

How did using the reading strategy help you to answer the questions?

_____

_____

_____

THINK-ALOUD NOTES

_____

_____

_____

_____

_____

_____

_____

_____

_____

_____

_____

Investigate, Inquire, and Imagine

RECALL: GATHER FACTS
1a. According to the author, what should you do when you are done eating a sandwich, spaghetti, and an ice-cream cone?

→ INTERPRET: FIND MEANING
1b. What do these three descriptions have in common?

ANALYZE: TAKE THINGS APART
2a. List the ways the author suggests eating vegetables.

→ SYNTHESIZE: BRING THINGS TOGETHER
2b. After reading all the descriptions about vegetables, what conclusions might you draw about children and vegetables?

EVALUATE: MAKE JUDGMENTS
3a. How do you think parents would react to this selection? Why?

→ EXTEND: CONNECT IDEAS
3b. Explain whether this "how-to" essay is like other how-to essays you've read.

WordWorkshop

EPONYMS. An **eponym** is a word taken from a name, usually of a person or character. For example, the word *sandwich* comes from John Montagu, fourth Earl of Sandwich. He is said to have created the sandwich when too busy to stop for dinner. He ordered roast beef placed between two pieces of bread so he could continue playing cards while eating, and the sandwich was born. Use a dictionary to find the origin and meaning of each of the following words. Then use each word in a sentence.

boycott	Origin:
Sentence:	
cardigan	Origin:
Sentence:	
gargantuan	Origin:
Sentence:	
hooligan	Origin:
Sentence:	
pasteurize	Origin:
Sentence:	

Literary Tools

TONE. **Tone** is a writer's or speaker's attitude toward the subject or toward the reader. What is the tone of "How to Eat Like a Child"? Give three examples from the selection that support your answer.

_____

_____

_____

_____

_____

Read-Write Connection

Write your own humorous description of how to eat a certain food not mentioned in the selection.

_____

_____

_____

_____

_____

Beyond the Reading

MAKE A FAVORITE SNACKS BOOK. Take a poll of your class. Find out what each person's favorite healthy snack is and what each person's favorite sweet or junk food snack is. Each person should write how-to pieces saying how to make and eat their favorite snacks. Put all essays together to create a book of favorite snacks.

GO ONLINE. To find links and additional activities for this selection, visit the EMC Internet Resource Center at **emcp.com/languagearts** and click on Write-In Reader.

"Choosing a Dog"

Reader's resource

The Humane Society of the United States promotes humane treatment of animals and fosters respect, understanding, and compassion for all creatures. Many other organizations and shelters exist around the country to care for and protect animals. **"Choosing a Dog"** explains how to use these and other sources to pick the dog that will be right for you.

Reader's journal

If you could have any kind of pet, what would you choose? Why?

_____

_____

_____

_____

Active READING STRATEGY

WRITE THINGS DOWN

Before Reading ➤ START A **K-W-L** CHART

❏ Preview the selection. Look at the title and illustrations. Notice that the selection is broken into steps.
❏ Before you read, write down some things you know about choosing a dog. In the K-W-L Chart below, make notes in the "What I Know" column of the Before Reading row.
❏ Then jot down some things you want to know in the center column of the Before Reading row.

Graphic Organizer: K-W-L Chart

What I *Know*	What I *Want* to Know	What I Have *Learned*
Before Reading		
1		
2		
3		
4		
5		
6		

Choosing a DOG

During Reading

TAKE NOTES

❏ Listen as your teacher reads the introduction and the first line of step 1. What do you know about the kind of dog you want? What do you want to learn? Make a note in your K-W-L Chart. Listen as your teacher reads the rest of step 1. What did you learn? Make a note in the chart.

❏ Continue reading on your own. Stop at the end of the first sentence for each step. Write down what you know and/or what you want to learn about this step. Then read the rest of the step. Write down what you learned.

Choosing a dog can be challenging. It can also be one of the most rewarding experiences of your life if you know what steps to follow. Your choice—wise or unwise—will affect you, your family, and the dog for years to come, so choose wisely. Here are some tips:

1 Know what you want. Would you like a dog small enough to curl up in your lap? Do you prefer Labrador Retrievers that love retrieving Frisbees for hours? Do you want a dog that can keep up with you on long runs? Do you want a puppy or a grown dog? a purebred or a mixed breed? Remember that purebreds registered with the American Kennel Club can cost up to several hundred dollars. If owning a purebred isn't important to you, know what shelters and other sources charge for a dog.

NOTE THE FACTS

Why is choosing a dog an important decision?

_____

_____

10

READ ALOUD

Read aloud the highlighted text on this page. What decision do you need to make once you decide what kind of dog you want?

_____

_____

Literary TOOLS

CHRONOLOGICAL ORDER.
Chronological order is the arrangement of details in the order in which they occur. Writing that describes processes, events, and cause-and-effect relationships often uses chronological order. Why is chronological order important in this kind of writing?

_____

_____

2 Know what you can offer a dog. Do you have a large farm where a dog can run or a small apartment where
20 you will need to take it for several walks a day? Is someone home all day to give a dog attention, or will you only be home at night and on weekends? Some dogs don't mind a small space with enough exercise. Others, like Huskies, feel best when they can run for miles every day. Some dogs don't mind being left to themselves for large parts of the day, but others whine, bark, or shred everything in sight while they wait for their owner to come home.

3 Research. Read dog books. Talk to dog owners,
30 especially people who have dogs like the one you want. Find out what owning that particular dog has been like for them. What are the pros of having a dog like that? What are the cons?

4 Once you have decided on what kind of dog you are looking for, it's time to look for one that meets your requirements. Decide where you will and will not look in your search. Do you want to try animal shelters? Do you need to go through a breeder? Will a careful screening of the classified ads' pet section lead you to
40 some good choices? The more you have done your homework in steps 1–3, the more likely you will avoid wasting your time searching.

5 Once you go to the source that has the dog, interview the seller. Why is the dog for sale? How long has the owner had it? How does the owner describe the dog? Observe how the dog and owner get along. If there are children or other people in contact with the dog, watch how the dog and people interact. Any fear or hostility on the dog's part spells trouble.

50 **6** Mostly, see how the dog reacts around you. Here are several tests you should do:

a. The health test. Does the dog look healthy? Is its coat shiny and soft? Are its eyes bright? Is its nose free of discharge? Are the insides of its ears pink and healthy? Does the dog scratch excessively, cough, or show signs of diarrhea or other ill health?

b. The curiosity test. Stand behind the dog and drop a set of car keys. Does

60 the dog come over to see what you dropped? Does it run and hide? Does it ignore the sound? A dog that shows interest or curiosity is usually pretty smart. See if the dog comes when you call it. If it responds to your voice, you've got a great prospect. Walk away, still calling the dog. If the dog follows you, you've got an even better possibility.

c. The socializing test. Pet the dog and let it get

70 familiar with you. After a few minutes, gently have the dog lie down and turn it so it is belly up. A dog that cowers in this position may be too shy. A dog that fights you may be too aggressive. A dog that gently resists without fighting or cowering is a dog likely to listen to you since it is already showing trust.

If you've gotten this far and the dog you want has passed all of these tests, you're well on your

80 way to being a happy dog owner. Proceed with caution—and good luck! ∎

MARK THE TEXT

Highlight or underline the three tests you should do to see how the dog reacts.

Reflect ON YOUR READING

After Reading ➤ **REFLECT ON YOUR CHART**

❑ How did keeping a K-W-L Chart help your reading?
❑ Did you find answers to all the questions in your "What I Want to Learn" column? If not, how could you find answers to these questions?

_____

_____

_____

_____

THINK-ALOUD NOTES

_____

_____

_____

_____

_____

_____

_____

_____

_____

_____

_____

_____

Reading Skills and Test Practice

INTERPRET INFORMATION

Discuss with a partner how to answer questions that require you to interpret information. Use the Think-Aloud Notes to write down your reasons for eliminating the incorrect answers.

____1. Which would be the best dog to pick?
    a. one that is cute and melts your heart
    b. one that fits your lifestyle and reacts well around you
    c. a purebred with proper papers
    d. a dog that will play with you for hours

____2. The first illustration on page 303 helps highlight
    a. the fact that dogs need to be trained
    b. that you can train dogs to fetch things you need
    c. the test to see if a dog will eat your things
    d. the curiosity test

How did using the reading strategy help you to answer the questions?

_____

_____

_____

_____

Investigate, Inquire, and Imagine

RECALL: GATHER FACTS
1a. What two things do you need to assess about yourself when choosing a dog?

INTERPRET: FIND MEANING
1b. Why are these things important?

ANALYZE: TAKE THINGS APART
2a. Briefly outline the tests you should do once you find a dog that interests you.

SYNTHESIZE: BRING THINGS TOGETHER
2b. Summarize the aspects of choosing a dog that are most important. Comment on the things that are least important.

EVALUATE: MAKE JUDGMENTS
3a. How effective is this set of directions? Now that you have read this piece, do you feel qualified to choose a dog?

EXTEND: CONNECT IDEAS
3b. How could you adapt these tips to help people choose another kind of pet?

Literary Tools

CHRONOLOGICAL ORDER. **Chronological order** is the arrangement of details in the order in which they occur. Writing that describes processes, events, and cause-and-effect relationships often uses chronological order. Briefly list the steps of the process of choosing a dog.

1	
2	
3	
4	
5	
6	

WordWorkshop

ANIMAL WORDS. You may have heard the word *canine,* which refers to something related to dogs. Match the words below with the animals they refer to. Use a dictionary to check your responses.

feline	horse
ursine	cat
bovine	bear
porcine	cow
equine	pig

Then fill in the blanks with the correct words from the left column.

1. Hibernating is usually considered a(n) _____ behavior.

2. Chewing cud is a typical _____ activity.

3. With her long mane of hair, Tabitha has a(n) _____ look.

4. When I gained weight, Dirk told me I was looking a bit _____.

5. My aunt Helga is a(n) _____ lover; she has nine cats.

Read-Write Connection

What characteristics would you want in a dog or another animal? What do you have to offer this animal?

_____

_____

_____

_____

_____

_____

Beyond the Reading

RESEARCH ANIMAL LAWS. Research animal laws in your state. Use the Internet or use resources in the library. You may also be able to interview somebody who works at an animal shelter or in an animal control office. Find out what rules pet owners need to follow and what rules shelters must follow before releasing or putting an animal to sleep.

GO ONLINE. To find links and additional activities for this selection, visit the EMC Internet Resource Center at **emcp.com/languagearts** and click on Write-In Reader.

"CONTESTS!"

An Interview with David LaRochelle

Active READING STRATEGY

READ WITH A PURPOSE

Before Reading ➤ **SET A PURPOSE FOR READING**

❑ Read the Reader's Resource. Answer the Reader's Journal question. Discuss both with a few of your classmates.
❑ What do you want to learn from this interview?
❑ Preview the Connection Chart below. As you read, note David LaRochelle's reasons for entering contests and think about how they might apply to you. Try to decide if you would like to enter contests.

Graphic Organizer: Connection Chart

David LaRochelle's Reasons for Entering Contests	How the Reasons Apply to Me

CONNECT

Reader's resource

There are contests that challenge contestants to do all kinds of things, from eating as many hot dogs as possible in a short time to carving the best Halloween pumpkin. Contests are a fun way to be creative, do something fun, and maybe win a prize. David LaRochelle, an author and illustrator, has entered—and won—many contests. In the interview **"Contests!,"** LaRochelle talks about the kinds of contests he has entered, why he entered them, and what he has learned from them.

Reader's journal

Have you ever entered a contest? What kind of contest was it? How did you do? If you've never entered a contest, write about a contest you would like to enter.

_____

_____

_____

_____

_____

_____

READ TO FIND REASONS

❑ Listen as your teacher reads the first two questions and answers aloud. If you hear a reason why David LaRochelle enters contests, write it in your Connections Chart. Then think about whether this reason applies to you, and make a note in your chart.

❑ Continue reading the interview on your own. Keep noting LaRochelle's reasons for entering contests. For each reason you list, think about whether the reason would convince you to enter contests.

NOTE THE FACTS

What is the largest prize LaRochelle has won so far?

_____

_____

_____

_____

CONTESTS !

David LaRochelle

David LaRochelle is an author and illustrator who has a wide variety of hobbies. Over the years, LaRochelle has entered thousands of contests and has won a few. Here, he answers some questions about contests.

10 *When did you become interested in entering contests?*
The first contest I remember entering was a coloring contest in first grade. I won a transistor radio. I've been hooked on contests ever since.

What other types of contests have you entered—and what have been the results?
I've entered a wide variety of contests: building sandcastles, carving watermelons, taking photographs, inventing ice cream flavors, designing new shapes for pasta, identifying songs on the radio, and writing jingles, poetry, and essays.

20 The prizes I've won have been as varied as the contests. They range from T-shirts, CDs, and a Big Mac belt buckle to furniture, televisions, exercise equipment, and trips. My largest prize to date is $10,000 and a home entertainment center, which I won for creating a video praising the merits of a laxative!

Which contests have been your favorites?
I entered an essay competition in which the object was to nominate a worthy person who brings relief to others. My nominee was the founder of an organization that sends
30 upbeat mail to children with life-threatening diseases. When my essay was selected as the grand prize winner, I received $10,000, and the woman I nominated received

$25,000. It was a great feeling knowing that someone else also benefited from my good fortune.

Another favorite contest was one I entered when I was in seventh grade. Shasta soda pop sponsored a contest, asking entrants to describe in 30 words or less why their 14 flavors of pop were more fun than one. My entry was chosen as one of the first place winners and my prize was a seven-

40 minute shopping spree at a grocery store. I was able to keep all the food that I could get back to the checkout counter within the time limit. The fact that this was my first national win and the unusual nature of the prize made it one of my most memorable contests.

What was your entry for the Shasta contest, and why do you think it won?
I wrote: Shasta's fabulous fourteen flavors are far more fantastic than one flat, foul, fickle, flop of a flavor. They're freezy, frosty, fizzy, and far-out. Finally, they're fun. I'm

50 your fan forever.
The originality and humor of the alliteration probably made my entry stand out from the 75,000 other submissions. I used strong, descriptive language. Also, and very importantly, I followed the rules. I stayed within the 30-word limit and I answered the question of why I thought their fourteen flavors were more fun than one.

It sounds like you have been very successful with entering contests. Do you always win?
Heavens, no! Friends sometimes tell me, "David, you are so

60 lucky! I never win anything." Well, I am lucky, but part of the reason for my luck is that I enter many, many contests. Most of them I don't win, but friends only hear about my successes, not all the times that I lose.

Why do contests appeal to you?
Contests are a great place to take creative risks. I can experiment with something unusual and bizarre, and if it doesn't win, so what? I enjoy the challenge of trying to come up with a unique idea that no one else will submit. And of course, it's always nice to receive an unexpected

70 letter informing me that I've won a prize.

Literary TOOLS

INTERVIEW. An **interview** is a question and answer exchange between a reporter who wants information and the person who has that information. Read each question. Try to predict what LaRochelle's answer will be. After you read the answer, think about what follow-up questions you would ask if you were the interviewer.

Reading STRATEGY REVIEW

USE TEXT ORGANIZATION. Understanding how a text is organized can help you understand the selection. As you read the interview, use the interview format to help you. In this interview, the questions are in italics and the answers are in regular type.

NOTE THE FACTS

Why does LaRochelle like contests?

_____

_____

_____

_____

NOTE THE FACTS

What are two opportunities that LaRochelle has had as a result of contests?

_____

_____

_____

_____

What opportunities have contests given you?

The producer of a locally created gardening show heard about my successes in a pumpkin-carving contest. He asked me to carve a few pumpkins for his television program, which in turn, were seen by the producers of *Good Morning America*. Those producers flew me out to New York City to carve pumpkins live on their show. In preparation, I was up all night carving examples. I'm sure it was the first time anyone used the luxury hotel suite where I was staying as a place to carve pumpkins! At 5 o'clock the next morning I was escorted across the street to the studio. During the show, I was interviewed while carving an intricate jack-o'-lantern. It was very exciting to appear on national television. Later in the day, when I was walking down Broadway in Times Square, several New Yorkers stopped me and said, "I saw you on TV this morning—great pumpkins!" I felt like a celebrity, at least for the afternoon!

I also credit contests with the publication of my first book, *A Christmas Guest*. I originally wrote the story for a contest sponsored by a local writers' group. When the contest ended, a friend convinced me to send my manuscript to a publisher, where it was accepted as a children's story. That was the beginning of my career as a professional writer.

Is entering contests primarily something you do on your own, or does it involve teamwork?

Most of the contests I enter are solo affairs, but there have been some significant exceptions. For the sandcastle and video contests, I teamed up with a friend to create the winning entries.

Another favorite contest that required a great deal of teamwork was the National Scavenger Hunt sponsored by *GAMES* magazine. The object was to find as many of the thirty unusual objects as possible before the contest's deadline. My close friend Gary Nygaard and I worked together for several months trying to locate these items. I would have never been able to win on my own. Not only are two heads better than one when it comes to generating ideas, but when I was discouraged and ready to give up on ever finding a particular item, Gary's enthusiasm always got me interested again.

What sorts of things did you have to find for this contest?
A Boy Scout merit badge in atomic energy, a high school report card showing both an A and an F grade, a coupon that expired on February 29, a folding paper fan with a picture of a giraffe, the manual from a Betamax VCR, an American Express card that expired in the 1980s.

120 One of the most challenging things we had to locate was a St. Patrick's Day card printed in German. We tried Irish pubs, greeting card companies, ethnic restaurants, as well as writing letters to our friends all across the country. Eventually we contacted a foreign language camp where somebody there had a relative in Germany who found a card and mailed it to us just days before the deadline.

We ended up winning first place. Our prizes were deluxe editions of Monopoly, Scrabble, and Chinese checkers which we sold for enough money for a trip to Paris.

How have contests sharpened your writing skills? Have they sharpened other skills as well?
Entering jingle and essay contests has taught me the
130 importance of using strong, powerful language. When you are limited to 25 or 50 words, there is no room for any weak or unclear word choices. My editing skills have also improved. I often rewrite my entries many times before I am able to say what I want while staying within the word limit. These skills are particularly helpful in writing picture books, where the text is often sparse yet still needs to capture the reader's interest.

Contests have taught me other important skills too. Without a doubt the more contests I've entered, the more
140 creative I've become. The scavenger hunt taught me valuable research skills, as well as the importance of teamwork and persistence. I've also learned that it never hurts to try. More than once I've been disappointed with an entry and thought, "Why did I even bother entering? I'll never win." Months later I may be surprised to discover that this entry won an honorable mention, or even first prize.

THINK AND REFLECT

Would you find this kind of contest interesting? Why? **(Apply)**

_____

_____

_____

_____

READ ALOUD

Try reading the selection aloud with a partner. One person should read the questions and the other person should read the responses.

NOTE THE FACTS

What is a skill LaRochelle has developed from entering contests? What is something he has learned?

_____

_____

_____

_____

FIX-UP IDEA

Refocus

If you are having trouble with the selection, try setting a new purpose. Instead of focusing on LaRochelle's reasons for entering contests, try focusing on the main idea of each answer he gives. Read the question carefully. Then read his response. Try to summarize each answer in one or two sentences.

NOTE THE FACTS

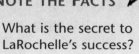

What is the secret to LaRochelle's success?

_____

_____

_____

_____

As you conduct writers' workshops for young authors, you encourage kids to enter contests. What advice do you give them?

150   These are my four tips for winning contests:
1. Enter. You'll never win unless you try.
2. Follow the rules. This includes paying attention to the deadline, word limit (if any), and judging criteria. It also means making sure your entry fits the contest's theme. If a contest asks you to tell how healthful a product is, for example, make sure that's the focus of your entry.
3. Be creative. Judges are often faced with thousands of entries. Unless your entry is somehow unique, it will be lost in the crowd. Creating an original contest entry

160   usually requires time. The first idea that pops into your head will probably pop into the heads of thousands of other people as well. Take the time to brainstorm other possibilities, and also take the time to create the best entry you can.
4. Don't get hung up on one contest. When you are finished with your entry, move on to the next contest. This also means not being discouraged if you don't win. I've lost hundreds of contests, but the reason I've been successful is that I've continued to enter.

170   *Explain your "55 words or less" contest that you conducted at a recent young authors conference for middle school students. Where did you get the idea? How many kids entered and what were the results?*

This contest was inspired by Steve Moss's "Fifty-Five Fiction" writing contest. I had just finished reading his book *The World's Shortest Stories*, which contains many of the winning entries from this contest.

I decided to have students try their hands at writing a complete story in 55 words or less. Although they had very little time to work—not much longer than ten

180   minutes—they came up with some impressive stories. About 40 students turned in finished entries, and these were the top three winners:

Writer's Block Battle • By Billy French • Wayzata Central Middle School

Lifting up my trusty pencil, I blocked my opponent's blow. A smirk of satisfaction crossed his face. Writer's Block was a deadly adversary, and was sure of uncreative victory. But as our swords clashed, words flew to the blank page. Before I knew it, I had a story! Author: 1, Writer's Block: 0.

190

Swimsuit • By Nellene Benhardus • St. Anthony Middle School

Brushing back my golden hair, I approach the beach. I notice eyes staring as I stride across the sand. Laying my towel out, I sit, absorbing the sun.
    "Alli?"
    "Yeah?"
    "Finished yet?"
    I step out of the dressing room and show Mom the suit I've selected.
    She sighs. "Man, you're slow!"

200

[no title] • By Michelle Reinke • Wayzata Central Middle School

"I'll be right back."
    The thought of fresh, chocolaty cookies filled my mind.
    Racing over across the kitchen, I grabbed a chair, dragging it along the floor. Clambering up, my arms reached for the lid. I could smell it. I peered inside.
    Empty?!?
    My mom came back and I spied the crumbs on her face.

210

These students were winners because they demonstrated the traits of a successful contestant: they entered, followed the rules, and had original, creative ideas. Not only are they successful contestants, they are successful authors as well. ■

THINK AND REFLECT

Which of these stories do you think is best? Why? **(Evaluate)**

_____

_____

_____

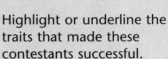

MARK THE TEXT

Highlight or underline the traits that made these contestants successful.

Reflect ON YOUR READING

REFLECT ON YOUR READING

After Reading ➤ **RESPOND TO THE INTERVIEW**

- ❑ Review the notes you made in your Connection Chart. Which reasons most make you want to enter a contest?
- ❑ Write a paragraph explaining why you would or would not want to enter a contest.
- ❑ Share your response with your group.

Reading Skills and Test Practice

FIND MAIN IDEAS

With a partner, discuss how to answer questions about main ideas. Use the Think-Aloud Notes to write down your reasons for eliminating the incorrect answers.

_____1. What is the most important information LaRochelle gives to future contestants?
   a. Get the judge's attention by bending the rules.
   b. If you don't win one of the first five contests you enter, contests may not be for you.
   c. Carefully choose the contests you enter based on your interests and skills.
   d. Have fun and be creative.

_____2. According to LaRochelle,
   a. the only reason he likes contests is the prizes he wins.
   b. contests are never fun if you lose.
   c. contests can offer surprising benefits beyond the prizes.
   d. people who win contests have too much time on their hands.

How did using the reading strategy help you to answer the questions?

_____

_____

_____

_____

THINK-ALOUD
NOTES

_____
_____
_____
_____
_____
_____
_____
_____
_____
_____
_____

Investigate, Inquire, and Imagine

RECALL: GATHER FACTS
1a. What was the first contest LaRochelle won? What was his first national win?

→ INTERPRET: FIND MEANING
1b. How might these experiences have affected his decision to enter other contests?

ANALYZE: TAKE THINGS APART
2a. Aside from prizes, list ways LaRochelle has benefited from entering contests.

→ SYNTHESIZE: BRING THINGS TOGETHER
2b. How important do you think prizes are in LaRochelle's decision to enter contests? How important would they be to you?

EVALUATE: MAKE JUDGMENTS
3a. Judge whether LaRochelle's tips for winning contests would prove successful for everybody.

→ EXTEND: CONNECT IDEAS
3b. How can these tips apply to other areas of life?

WordWorkshop

PREFIXES. The prefix *inter–* has several meanings. Most of them are related to "being between." *Inter–* can mean *between, carried on between, located between, carried on between,* and *occurring between.* Read each word in the chart below. Try to determine the meaning, keeping in mind the meaning of the prefix. Write your guess in the first column. Then use a dictionary to verify your response.

Word	My Guess	Verified Meaning
interscholastic		
international		
interject		
intervene		
interstate		

Literary Tools

INTERVIEW. An **interview** is a question and answer exchange between a reporter who wants precise information from a reliable source and the person who has that information. Why is LaRochelle an expert on contests?

_____

_____

Write a one sentence synopsis or summary of this interview.

_____

_____

Read-Write Connection

Write a complete story in 55 words or less. Take ten minutes or less to write your story.

_____

_____

_____

_____

_____

_____

_____

Beyond the Reading

ENTER CONTESTS. Research contests using the Internet. Find a contest that interests you. Pay special attention to the rules for submission, including the deadline. Complete an entry following the rules of the contest. Share your entry with your classmates before submitting it.

GO ONLINE. To find links and additional activities for this selection, visit the EMC Internet Resource Center at **emcp.com/languagearts** and click on Write-In Reader.

from *Dear Ms. Demeanor*

by Mary Mitchell

Active READING STRATEGY

USE TEXT ORGANIZATION

Before Reading ▶ **PREVIEW THE SELECTION**

❏ Read the Reader's Resource and the title. Look at the picture on page 328. Scan the rest of the selection and notice the subheads and the bold and regular text.
❏ Describe the format of the selection.
❏ Write the headings in the left column of the Text Organization Chart below.

Graphic Organizer: Text Organization Chart

Heading	Question	Answer

CONNECT

Reader's resource

Advice columnists Abigail Van Buren (Dear Abby) and Ann Landers are household names. Mary Mitchell is another advice columnist. Mitchell writes under the name Ms. Demeanor. The word *demeanor* means "way of behaving toward others" or "manners." A misdemeanor is a minor offense or act of misbehaving. Mitchell's column is an etiquette column, or one that deals with good manners, for young people. The questions and answers in this selection are from Mitchell's book *Dear Ms. Demeanor*, a collection of her advice columns for teens.

Reader's journal

Do you like to read advice columns in newspapers or magazines? Why, or why not?

_____

_____

_____

_____

_____

USE ORGANIZATIONAL FEATURES AS YOU READ

❏ With a partner, take turns reading the selection aloud. One person should read the question. The other person should read the answer. How do you know which is which?

❏ Write the main idea of each question in the center of your Text Organization Chart. Write the main idea of each answer in the right column.

❏ Stop at the end of each question to answer the margin questions.

NOTE THE FACTS

What does Ms. Demeanor suggest?

_____

_____

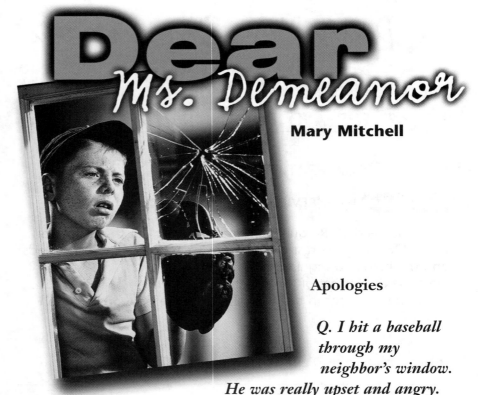

Dear Ms. Demeanor

Mary Mitchell

Apologies

Q. I hit a baseball through my neighbor's window. He was really upset and angry. He's really old, too, and when I tried to apologize, he just grumbled. What should I do?

A. Oops. Poor guy can hardly be blamed for being upset, can he? Sometimes older folks find communicating with young people frustrating because their hearing isn't sharp or the person they're trying to communicate with doesn't speak clearly. Since the personal approach wasn't successful, try writing.

   You must apologize and make amends. Send a letter and apologize again for the trouble you caused. It might read something like this:

Dear Mr. Smith:
   Please accept my apology for breaking your window the other day. It was careless of me, and I feel bad about it. I know all the trouble it has caused you. If you would like, I will repair the window myself. If you have made other arrangements, please send me the bill so that I can pay for the damage.
         Sincerely,
         Bobby Jones

10

20

Remember that there is more to a letter than just words. Be sure that you use clean stationery. Write in ink, not pencil. Make a scratch copy first if you feel clumsy about writing.

30 The date should be at the top, on the right side of the paper. Start the "Dear Mr. Smith" below the date and at the left, a little in from the edge of the paper. Indent the first word of each paragraph about one inch. The all-purpose closing for just about any kind of letter is, *Sincerely.* It is especially appropriate for a letter of apology to someone older than you, or in a formal letter such as a business letter.

You'll probably want to deliver your letter by hand, since he is a neighbor. Even so, write your name, street address, and city and state with zip code at the top left corner on

40 the front of the envelope. Your neighbor's full name, such as Mr. John Smith, goes in the center of the front of the envelope with your city and state underneath. Don't abbreviate the state name.

Properly addressing anything you send is a way to show respect for the person who will receive it. Never omit honorifics—*Mr.*, *Mrs.*, *Ms.*, or *Miss*—from an envelope. The only other word which can be abbreviated on an address is *Dr.* for *Doctor.* Write everything else out in full.

Condolences

50 *Q. My friend's father died. I went to the funeral, but now I want to send her a letter, too. How should I do it and what should I say?*

A. Regardless of whatever else you have done—attended the funeral, sent flowers, paid a visit to your friend's home, telephoned—the condolence letter is a must. You should be congratulated for thinking of it. Such letters are comforting and diverting for those who have suffered a loss. Some even become part of a family history to be passed down to future generations. Forget about buying sympathy cards or

60 condolence cards. They are impersonal and the easy way out.

MARK THE TEXT

Highlight or underline the all-purpose closing for any letter.

THINK AND REFLECT

What does Ms. Demeanor say about sympathy cards? What do you think her opinion of other greeting cards would be? **(Infer)**

_____

_____

_____

_____

Write your letter in ink. Use a fountain pen if you have one. A ballpoint will do if you don't, but it isn't very refined. Try to use black ink. If you own personal note paper, use it. If not, ask your parents for some good stationery. If your handwriting is hard to read, go ahead and type the letter or have someone type it for you. Sign it in ink.

70   What you write depends on how you feel. Write from the heart. Don't try to be formal; it comes out wooden and impersonal. At the very least, acknowledge your friend's loss. Say how sad you are about it. If you and your friend's father shared time together, mention that and any special memories of it. Say how much he will be missed. Offer your friend your help. The condolence letter is the place to recall in more detail the special characteristics of the deceased, visits to your home, lessons learned from that person, good times shared, etc. Such reminiscences celebrate the life of the deceased rather than being morbid and depressing about the loss. The shared memories of that life and times become

80   treasured by the family of the person who has died.

Pen Pals

Q. I have a pen pal in Australia who lives on a vineyard. He writes the greatest letters. They are so good, I read them to my parents and friends. But I live in Raleigh, North Carolina, and I think my letters are boring. How can I make my letters more interesting?

A. First of all, Raleigh probably sounds pretty interesting to your pen pal because it is so far away. Don't give yourself a bad rap that you don't deserve. America is probably as

90   interesting to him as Australia is to you. Also, the very fact that you have a pen pal indicates you probably are an interesting and curious individual. You probably communicate that about yourself without being aware of it. The funny thing about letter writing is that we all love to receive them, but we all think they're a chore to write. The easiest way to get started is to write the way you talk. Think of a letter as a one-sided conversation. Write the things you would say or ask your pen pal if you were together in person.

FIX-UP IDEA

Reread
If you have trouble understanding any of the questions and answers, reread them, switching roles with your partner. If you were reading the questions earlier, now read the answers and have your partner read the questions.

MARK THE TEXT

Highlight or underline Ms. Demeanor's advice to get started writing a letter.

100   I think the surest way to make a reader yawn from the start is to write "How are you? I am fine." There are many interesting ways to start a letter. You might want to begin with something like "Last night I saw a television program about vineyards, and you came to mind. Your letters make me feel like I have real inside information." The goal of letter writing is to draw the reader into your written conversation as quickly as you can. You can tell your friend something you did that was exciting, fun, or wonderful; for example, "Today I went to Sea World and petted a dolphin

110 for the first time. It would have been great if you could have been there, too. Do they have a Sea World where you live?"

    It is much more interesting to write specific questions. They make the reader feel part of your conversation. Think about how you would feel if someone wrote to you and asked, "Have you recovered from the flu yet? What did you do when you had to stay in? Did you see anything special on TV? Read anything great?"

    By comparison, think about how you would respond to

120 "How are you? I'm fine." Both are basically the same questions. The difference is in how you ask.

    Go ahead and use exclamation points to underline sentences or phrases if you want. In a personal letter these devices convey your enthusiasm. Steer clear of apologies for not writing sooner. They only make your letter sound like you're writing to fulfill an obligation rather than writing for the fun of it. Make your letter enthusiastic and full of your own personality. That will make your pen pal feel your letter was worth waiting for.

130 **RSVP**

Q. I got an invitation to a party. At the bottom of the invitation it said, "regrets only." What does that mean, and what should I do about it?

A. *Regrets only* written at the bottom of an invitation means (strictly speaking) that if you cannot attend, you are expected to tell the host in advance. If you plan to attend, you don't have to call to accept the invitation.

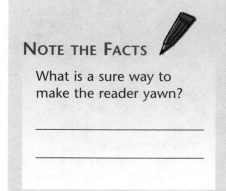

NOTE THE FACTS

What is a sure way to make the reader yawn?

_____

_____

Literary **TOOLS**

TONE AND REGISTER. Tone is a writer's or speaker's attitude toward the subject or toward the reader. A writer or speaker shapes the tone of a message by carefully choosing words and phrases that express his or her feelings about a topic. **Register** refers to language appropriate for a specific relationship between people. For example, when talking with a friend, you speak in a register that is warm, open, and informal. When speaking to a young child, you speak in a register that is non-threatening and simple to understand. As you read, determine the register the author is using and look for clues about the author's tone.

NOTE THE FACTS

What should you do if you receive an invitation that says *Regrets only?*

_____

_____

THINK AND REFLECT

How is Ms. Demeanor's comment about responding to an invitation similar to her response about condolence letters and pen pal letters? **(Compare and Contrast)**

_____

_____

_____

MARK THE TEXT

Highlight or underline what _RSVP_ means.

However, if you were a host planning a party, wouldn't you want your guests to let you know one way or the
140   other? Wouldn't you like to know that they were pleased to be invited and looking forward to coming? I know I would, so go ahead and do it.

Call the host and tell him or her that you received the invitation, how excited you are about the party, and that you plan to attend. If you cannot attend, do the same thing. Explain that you won't be there. Respond immediately to any invitation and be sure to stick to your commitment. Nothing is worse than holding out until the last possible moment in case you receive a "better offer."

150   _RSVP_ is used most often on invitations. It is a request for a reply. It means "Respond if you please" in French (not, "Roast skunk very possible," as in the comic strip "L'il Abner"). If the RSVP is followed by a telephone number, just call the host. Sometimes the letters are followed by the host's address. In that case, send the host a short note right away. Indicate whether you'll be able to attend.

These guidelines will serve you well for most informal invitations sent today, the kind with casual wording on colorful, printed, fill-in-the-blank cards. Formal invitations
160   are a different story. They require a bit more homework. ∎

Reflect ON YOUR READING

After Reading ➤ DISCUSS HOW TEXT IS ORGANIZED

❑ With a partner, discuss your opinions about the advice Ms. Demeanor gives. If you need to, review the advice by rereading the answer sections of the text.

❑ Talk about how text in an advice column differs from other newspaper columns and articles.

Reading Skills and Test Practice

DRAW CONCLUSIONS

Discuss with a partner how best to answer questions about drawing conclusions. Use the Think-Aloud Notes to write down your reasons for eliminating the incorrect answers.

_____1. Ms. Demeanor's replies can best be summarized as falling within what kind of register?
  a. humorous
  b. sarcastic
  c. patronizing
  d. formal

_____2. Why is the title *Dear Ms. Demeanor* a good one?
  a. The title is a play on the words *demeanor* and *misdemeanor*.
  b. The title is a short way to say she's the meanest one.
  c. The title shows that the columnist is a feminist.
  d. The title is a play on the word *demure*.

How did using the reading strategy help you to answer the questions?

_____

_____

_____

_____

Investigate, Inquire, and Imagine

RECALL: GATHER FACTS
1a. When the person who broke the window tried to apologize, how did the neighbor respond?

INTERPRET: FIND MEANING
1b. What are some of the advantages of writing an apology instead of trying to apologize in person?

ANALYZE: TAKE THINGS APART
2a. List the different suggestions and tips Ms. Demeanor offers to letter writers. Which seem most important?

SYNTHESIZE: BRING THINGS TOGETHER
2b. In general, what do these tips and suggestions mean? Summarize Ms. Demeanor's ideas about letter writing.

EVALUATE: MAKE JUDGMENTS
3a. How is Ms. Demeanor's use of language different from that of most adults? Why do you think she writes this way?

EXTEND: CONNECT IDEAS
3b. Compare Ms. Demeanor's advice with advice you have gotten from a parent or another adult. How is it similar? How is it different?

Literary Tools

TONE AND REGISTER. **Tone** is a writer's or speaker's attitude toward the subject or toward the reader. **Register** refers to language appropriate for a specific relationship between people. An author chooses a register, such as formal, informal, polite, firm, or humorous. Tone is reflected in word choices and in more subtle ways to create a piece that is friendly, enthusiastic, helpful, remorseful, or that reveals another tone. In deciding on a level of formality, a writer needs to consider both the subject and the audience.

For each of the following forms of writing, write an *F* if it requires the use of formal language, or an *I* if informal language is acceptable.

Personal narrative
Book review for *The New York Times*
Thank-you note to a neighbor
Letter of condolence to a friend
Paper on nuclear war
Step-by-step procedures to a chemistry experiment
Résumé
Obituary for the newspaper
Journal entry in a diary
Testament in a will

WordWorkshop

Mnemonic Devices. Mnemonic devices help you remember things. For example, you may have heard the spelling rule "*i* before *e* except after *c* and when it sounds like an *a* as in *neighbor* and *weigh*." Mnemonic devices may be rhymes, acronyms, or striking or silly images. For example, the mnemonic device "'A d-dress,' I stuttered" might help you remember that *address* has two *d*s.

Make up mnemonic devices to help you remember the following words and their meanings.

salutation

correspondence

The following words are commonly misspelled. Make up a mnemonic device to help your remember the spelling of these words.

sincerely

stationery

Read-Write Connection

Which advice from Ms. Demeanor do you agree with? Which do you disagree with? Why? Do you think Ms. Demeanor gives good advice? Why, or why not?

_____

_____

_____

_____

_____

Beyond the Reading

Give Advice. Write your own etiquette advice column. Work with a group of your classmates. Each person should write a "problem" letter. Switch letters. Each person should write an advice response. Then discuss the questions and responses. What are other solutions?

Go Online. To find links and additional activities for this selection, visit the EMC Internet Resource Center at **emcp.com/languagearts** and click on Write-In Reader.

BEADS & BANGLES

In Africa, beads have played an integral role in daily life for years. Beads are worn for protection, identification, and to indicate status, wealth, power, and age. Before the 1400s, beads were crafted from berries, animal teeth, stones, shells, and bone. Then traders brought in multicolored glass beads. Native American artisans are also known for their traditional beadwork, with beads made from bone, shells, stone, turquoise, and other semi-precious stones. Today beads of all shapes, sizes, and materials are popular. You'll see some examples in the **Beads & Bangles** catalog.

Reader's
journal

If you could make beaded jewelry, what would you make?

_____

_____

_____

_____

_____

_____

Active READING STRATEGY

USE TEXT ORGANIZATION

Before Reading ➤ PREVIEW TEXT

❏ Look at the catalog page and order form on pages 337–338. On page 337, notice the way the text is organized. Notice how different headings and pictures are used to help you understand the information on the page.

❏ Preview the form on page 338. What kind of form is it? What is it used for?

❏ Pick out three different kinds of beads from the catalog and fill in the information in the chart below.

Graphic Organizer: Information Chart

Name/Description of Item	Style #	Color	Quantity	Price
1.				
2.				
3.				

BEADS & BANGLES

Summer Catalog

Page 73

BEADS and CORDING

Red Horn Bead

#25-171   Irregular 4mm Red Horn Bead
2.50/strand   20.00/10 strand

1mm Lace Adjuster

#25-001   Porcelain 1mm Double Lace Adjustor
Designed to make adjustable or double strand
necklaces or bracelets, using 1mm cord.

White or Brown   3.00/doz   15.00/100

Turquoise Nuggets
with Extra Large Hole

At the time we sent this to the printer,
we didn't have these in yet, so we couldn't
price them . . . By the time you see this,
however, they will be in stock and priced.
If interested, please call for prices.

#20-486   9-15mm Blue (with Matrix) Turquoise Nuggets
1/8" Hole; easily fits 2mm cord.

NYMO BEAD CORD
size "B" (medium weight)

#61-129   Size "B" Nymo Bead Cord
A bit thicker than "A" and "O" listed in our
Spring catalog.
See Brass Wire Needle or Big Eye Needle,
page 15, Spring catalog, or use
"Sharps," found in most craft or fabric stores.
.60/each   6.00/doz   24.50box (80 bobbins)

Bone Bead Sample Assortment

NEW!

#45-390   1 pair of *each* of the new Carved Bone
Tubes, Donuts, Horns, and *Claws.*
30 beads total. These bone beads are all hand carved,
so will vary slightly in size and pattern. Assortments
are made with colors currently in stock. Some pairs
may be antiqued, others will be natural bone color.

$16.00/per assortment pack
(Average cost per bead: 53¢)

Imitation Sinew

- New stock numbers
- New quantity and price
- Flat 1/8" (2.5mm) sturdy light
  brown cord
- Great for heavy ceramic
  beads, trade beads, and
  "mountain man" designs
- When twisted, will fit beads
  with 1mm hole

#61-600   60 foot bobbin   1.25
#61-604   4 oz (150 yard spool)   4.50
#61-608   8 oz (300 yard spool)   7.00

BASIC GLASS BEADS and NEW COLORS

AB and Iris Round Glass Beads

#23-244   4mm Round Glass Beads, Fancy Colors
1.75/100   15.00/Mass

Ruby AB
Sapphire AB
Blue Iris

Colors Available
Emerald AB

Crystal AB
Amethyst AB
Purple Iris

#23-246   6mm Round Glass Beads, Fancy Colors
2.75/100   25.00/Mass

Emerald AB
Crystal AB

Colors Available

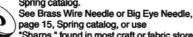

Sapphire AB
Amethyst AB

Cobalt Blue and Ruby Islamic Beads

#22-860   Islamic Glass Beads
with embossed Gold Moon and Stars.
The new ruby and dark cobalt
are beautiful in sunlight!

Cobalt or Ruby   9.00/50   16.00/100

We're still out of the original black (which was on
page 76 in the Spring catalog), but we'll keep you
updated on in-stock colors.

During Reading

ANALYZE THE TEXT'S ORGANIZATIONAL FEATURES

❑ Scan the Beads & Bangles Summer Catalog page and read items of interest. Try to make sense of the page. Which items are new? What choices do you have for different items? Notice how information on each item is organized.

❑ With a partner, discuss the following questions about the form on page 338: What kind of information does the form provide? What information does it ask for?

FIX-UP IDEA

Connect to What You Know
Have you ever looked at a catalog before? Have you ever ordered from one? Think about what kinds of information you would need to place such an order. Look for this kind of information on the catalog page.

ILLUSTRATION AND ORDER FORM. An **illustration** is a photograph, drawing, or diagram that makes a concept clearer by giving a visual example. An **order form** is a printed document with blank spaces for required or requested information, used by consumers to buy merchandise or services. How might illustrations help you place an order from a catalog?

BEADS & BANGLES

200 N. Front - Suite 6
P.O. Box 410
Spokane, WA 99210-00450

FAX 509 555 2602
℗ Phone (509) 555-8565

Toll Free Order Line
1 (800) 555-2156

| LEAVE THIS BLANK | T | P | Rcvd |
| | | | Pmt |

Name of Business _The Bead Corner_
Name of Individual _Frances Graceful Bear_
Street _3100 Euclid Avenue_
City _Cleveland_   State _OH_   Zip _44115_
Phone Number (_800_) _555-3460_   Date _10/19/xx_

❑ Is this your first order?
❑ Is this a change of address?

❑ COD ☒ Open Acct. ❑ Prepaid ❑ VISA ❑ MasterCard ❑ Other

SHIP VIA
☒ UPS   ❑ Parcel Post
❑ UPS 2nd Day Air   ❑ 1st Class Mail
❑ Other _____

Bankcard # _____ Exp. Date _____
Signature _____

Quantity	Unit	Style Number	Color	Description of Item	Unit Price	Total
2	doz	61-129	——	Nymo bead cord	6.00	
1	50	22-860	Ruby	Islamic glass beads	9.00	
3	mass	23-246	Crystal	6mm round glass beads	25.00	
4	strand	25-171	——	Red horn bead	2.50	

Critical Thinking

- What would you do if you wanted to buy turquoise nuggets? Why?

_____

- In which colors are the Islamic glass beads available?

_____

- How many ounces of sinew are in a 150-yard spool?

_____

- How could you order from Beads & Bangles if you did not have an open account? What are the other payment options?

_____

- How many bobbins of Nymo bead cord is Frances Graceful Bear ordering for The Bead Corner?

_____

Reflect ON YOUR READING

❑ Imagine you are ordering from the Beads & Bangles Summer Catalog. Order enough beads and cord to make a choker or necklace for a friend. Fill out the order form below as accurately as you can, providing all required information. Check your math.

❑ Exchange your order form with your partner. Check your partner's order form and be sure that it is filled out completely and correctly.

BEADS & BANGLES 200 N. Front - Suite 6 P.O. Box 410 Spokane, WA 99210-00450	Name _____ Street _____ City _____ State _____ Zip _____ Phone Number_____ Date _____ Is this a first order?___ Is this a new address?___
__COD__Open Account__Prepaid__Visa__Mastercard__Other Bankcard # _____Exp. Date _____ Signature_____	**SHIP VIA** ❑ UPS ❑ Parcel Post ❑ Other

Quantity	Unit	Style #	Color	Description of Item	Unit Price	Total
				Total Price	**$**	

Reading Skills and Test Practice

ANALYZE THE AUTHOR'S PURPOSE

READ, THINK, AND EXPLAIN. Discuss with your group how to answer the following question that asks you to analyze the author's purpose. Use the Think-Aloud Notes to jot down ideas.

What tells you that more than one version of this catalog is printed each year? Why might there be several versions of the catalog? Use details and information in the catalog to answer the question on your own paper.

THINK-ALOUD NOTES

_____
_____
_____
_____
_____
_____
_____
_____
_____
_____

Investigate, Inquire, and Imagine

RECALL: GATHER FACTS
1a. What are the different quantities of Nymo bead cord you can order?

→ INTERPRET: FIND MEANING
1b. Why do you think that three different quantities are listed?

ANALYZE: TAKE THINGS APART
2a. List the information you would need to fill out the order form.

→ SYNTHESIZE: BRING THINGS TOGETHER
2b. Summarize the steps you would take to place an order.

EVALUATE: MAKE JUDGMENTS
3a. Is the catalog appealing to you? Does it make you want to buy the company's products? Why, or why not?

→ EXTEND: CONNECT IDEAS
3b. If you were employed in the marketing department for Beads & Bangles, what changes would you make to the catalog layout? Would you change the illustrations, the headings, or the overall organization?

WordWorkshop

COLOR WORDS. The catalog describes the colors of the beads. Beads are available in cobalt, ruby, sapphire, emerald, and amethyst. First identify the basic color for each color listed. For example, cobalt is a shade of blue. Then brainstorm a list of other shades of each color. When you are done brainstorming, use a thesaurus to help you find other color words.

Catalog Color	Base Color	Other Shades
cobalt	blue	navy
ruby		
sapphire		
emerald		
amethyst		

Choose three shades for one color and explain the differences among them.

_____

_____

_____

Literary Tools

ILLUSTRATION AND ORDER FORM. An **illustration** is a photograph, drawing, or diagram that makes a concept clearer by giving a visual example. An **order form** is a printed document with blank spaces for required or requested information, used by consumers to buy merchandise or services. Describe the cobalt blue and ruby Islamic beads based on the text description. What additional information do you learn from the illustration?

_____

_____

What information would you need for the order form on page 339 if you wanted to buy cobalt blue and ruby Islamic beads?

_____

_____

Read-Write Connection

If you were going to order from this catalog, which beads would you choose? What type of cording would you select? Why?

_____

_____

_____

_____

Beyond the Reading

CREATE AN ORDER FORM. Work in a small group to design your own imaginary mail-order business. Decide what products to offer, how much they would cost, what forms of payment your business would accept, and how you would ship items. Then create a one-page sales brochure that includes product information and an order form. Exchange your order sheets with one person from another group and see how easy it is to find needed information and place an order.

GO ONLINE. To find links and additional activities for this selection, visit the EMC Internet Resource Center at **emcp.com/languagearts** and click on Write-In Reader.

Unit 8 **READING** Review

Choose and Use Reading Strategies

Before reading the passage below, review with a partner how to use each of these reading strategies with informational and visual media.

1. Read with a Purpose
2. Connect to Prior Knowledge
3. Write Things Down
4. Make Predictions
5. Visualize
6. Use Text Organization
7. Tackle Difficult Vocabulary
8. Monitor Your Reading Progress

Now apply at least two of these reading strategies as you read "How Hail Is Formed." Use the margins and mark up the text to show how you are using the reading strategies to read actively.

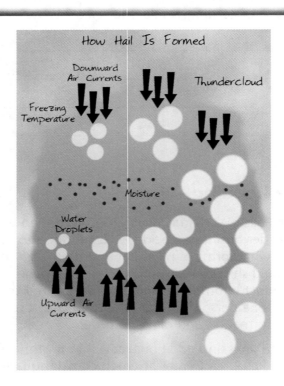

Hail . . . is formed when summer clouds become saturated and the water falls. But now, instead of falling to the ground as rain, something different happens. Strong winds, called updrafts, force the water drops up into the top of the cloud. The air is colder at the top of the cloud. It's freezing, in fact. The water drop therefore becomes covered in ice.

Other strong winds, called downdrafts, cause the water, now an ice drop, to fall. Another updraft will take it to the top again. As a result, it becomes bigger and bigger with another ice coating. The water drop, now an ice ball, is tossed up and down from air current to air current. As the water is sent up and down, it freezes and gathers more and more water that also freezes. Eventually, the stone gets too heavy to get tossed up and down any longer. It then falls to the ground as hail.

WordWorkshop

WORD STUDY. What words did you have trouble with while reading? Did you underline them or write them in a word study notebook? If not, review the selections and the WordWorkshop activities and choose five to ten words you would like to study. For each word, create an entry like the one below. Each entry should include the word, the definition, a synonym, and a contextual sentence. It may also contain a picture or other mnemonic to help you remember the word.

Definition: outward manner	Synonym: bearing

demeanor

Even a dog with a calm <u>demeanor</u> may snap at you if it is hurt.

Literary Tools

Select the best literary element on the right to complete each sentence on the left. Write the correct letter in the blank.

_____1. A(n) _____ may be a drawing, photograph, or diagram.

_____2. "Contests!" is an example of a(n) _____.

_____3. The _____ of *Dear Ms. Demeanor* is more serious than "How to Eat Like a Child."

_____4. Most catalogs contain a(n)_____ to allow consumers to buy products.

_____5. Directions often use _____ to help reader's understand the steps of the process.

a. chronological order, 312, 315

b. illustration, 338, 341

c. interview, 319, 326

d. order form, 338, 341

e. register, 331, 334

f. tone, 331, 334

On Your Own

FLUENTLY SPEAKING. Practice placing and taking telephone orders. You can use the Beads & Bangles order form on page 339 or use another catalog that is available to you. When placing an order, make sure you have all the information you need. Speak clearly. When taking an order, help the person you're speaking with to find the necessary information, offer options, and ask for clarification if necessary.

PICTURE THIS. Find an art contest. Try looking online or in magazines for young people. Following the rules of the contest, create an artwork to submit.

PUT IT IN WRITING. Write a set of directions for something you know how to do well. Think about features, such as headings, diagrams, illustrations, and icons that may make your directions clearer. After you finish, ask a classmate to try to follow your directions. If he or she has trouble, revise the difficult spots or add more direction.

Unit NINE

Developing Vocabulary Skills

TACKLING DIFFICULT VOCABULARY AS YOU READ

To understand what you read, you need a set of tools for dealing with words you don't know. Glossaries and footnotes, context clues, prior knowledge of word parts and word families, and dictionaries are tools that can help you unlock the meaning of unfamiliar words.

Using Definitions, Footnotes, Endnotes, and Glossaries

Some textbooks, like this one, provide **definitions** of selected words on the page on which the word is used. **Footnotes**, like definitions, also appear on the same page as the words to which they refer. Specifically, footnotes appear at the foot, or bottom, of a page and are numbered to correspond to the words or phrases they explain. Sometimes footnotes cite a source of information. Other times they define uncommon words and phrases. If you see a superscripted number next to a word in the text you are reading (palmer[1]), but can't find the footnote at the foot of the page, check the end of the article, chapter, or book. A footnote that comes at the end of a document is called an **endnote**. A **glossary** is an alphabetized list of important words and their definitions. Glossaries usually appear at the end of an article, a chapter, or a book.

To use definitions, footnotes, endnotes, and glossaries, follow these steps:

❶ Read the paragraph or short section containing the unfamiliar word to get a sense of the meaning.

❷ Check the definition, footnote, endnote, or glossary entry for the word.

❸ Reread the paragraph or section, this time keeping in mind the definition of the new word.

NOTE THE FACTS

How can you use definitions to improve your reading comprehension?

_____

_____

_____

_____

Using Context Clues

You can often figure out the meaning of an unfamiliar word by using context clues. **Context clues**, or hints you gather from the words and sentences around the unfamiliar word, prevent you from having to look up every unknown word in the dictionary. The chart below defines the types of context clues and gives you an example of each. It also lists words that signal each type of clue.

THINK AND REFLECT

If someone says, "Justin and Jordan are opposites in many ways; for example, Justin is very shy, but Jordan is gregarious," what do you think *gregarious* means? (Apply)

Context Clues

comparison clue	shows a comparison, or how the unfamiliar word is like something that might be familiar to you
signal words	*and, like, as, just as, as if, as though*

EXAMPLE

The physical education teacher was as <u>strident</u> in her commands as a military officer training new recruits. (Military officers in boot camps are known to be harsh and insistent, which must be the meaning of *strident*.)

contrast clue	shows that something contrasts, or differs in meaning, from something else
signal words	*but, nevertheless, on the other hand, however, although, though, in spite of*

EXAMPLE

When our parents demanded that my sister and I apologize to one another, my sister obeyed; I, on the other hand, stood in <u>defiance</u>. (The words *on the other hand* signal a contrast between the speaker and her obedient sister. *Defiance* must mean "disobedience.")

restatement clue	uses different words to express the same idea
signal words	*that is, in other words, or*

EXAMPLE

I was <u>mortified</u> when I forgot my lines during the performance; I've never felt so ashamed! (As the second sentence suggests, *mortified* means "extremely ashamed or embarrassed.")

examples clue	gives examples of other items to illustrate the meaning of something
signal words	*including, such as, for example, for instance, especially, particularly*

EXAMPLE

The <u>dilapidated</u> house, with its chipped paint, broken windows, and collapsed roof, was an eyesore in a block full of expensive houses and manicured lawns. (Details about chipped paint, broken windows, and a collapsed roof suggest that *dilapidated* means "decayed or deteriorated through neglect.")

CONTINUED

cause-and-effect clue	tells you that something happened as a result of something else
signal words	*if/then, when/then, thus, therefore, because, so, as a result of, consequently*

EXAMPLE

The stray dog was <u>emaciated</u> because it had not eaten for more than a week. (If not eating caused the dog to be emaciated, *emaciated* must mean "extremely thin.")

Using Your Prior Knowledge

You can often use your knowledge of word parts and other words to help you figure out the meaning of a new word.

BREAKING WORDS INTO BASE WORDS, WORD ROOTS, PREFIXES, AND SUFFIXES

Many words are formed by adding prefixes and suffixes to main word parts called **base words** (if they can stand alone) or **word roots** (if they can't). A **prefix** is a letter or group of letters added to the beginning of a word to change its meaning. A **suffix** is a letter or group of letters added to the end of a word to change its meaning.

Word Part	Definition	Example
base word	main word part that can stand alone	firm
word root	main word part that can't stand alone	cred
prefix	letter or group of letters added to the beginning of the word	bi–
suffix	letter or group of letters added to the end of the word	–tion

When you encounter an unfamiliar word, check to see if you recognize the meaning of the prefix, suffix, base word, or word root. In combination with context clues, these meanings can help you unlock the meaning of the entire word. On the following pages are charts listing the meanings of the most common prefixes, suffixes, and word roots.

Reading STRATEGY
REVIEW

READ WITH A PURPOSE. Rather than read the charts on the following pages all the way through from beginning to end, set a purpose for reading, and then let that purpose guide how you read the charts. For example, if you just want to become familiar with what prefixes, suffixes, and word roots are, read only a few lines from each chart, but read them carefully, studying how each word part contributes to the meaning of the words in the Examples column. Your teacher might set a purpose for you, too. If so, approach the charts as your teacher directs.

Common Prefixes		
Prefix	**Meaning**	**Examples**
ambi–/amphi–	both	ambidextrous, amphibian
anti–/ant–	against; opposite	antibody, antacid
bi–	two	bicycle, biped
circum–	around; about	circumnavigate, circumstance
co–/col–/com–/con–/cor–	together	cooperate, collaborate, commingle, concentrate, correlate
counter–	contrary; complementary	counteract, counterpart
de–	opposite; remove; reduce	decipher, defrost, devalue
dia–	through; apart	dialogue, diaphanous
dis–	not; opposite of	dislike, disguise
dys–	abnormal; difficult; bad	dysfunctional, dystopia
em–/en–	into or onto; cover with; cause to be; provide with	embark, empower, enslave, enfeeble
ex–	out of; from	explode, export, extend
extra–/extro–	outward; outside; beyond	extraordinary, extrovert
hyper–	too much, too many, or extreme	hyperbole, hyperactive
hypo–	under	hypodermic
il–, im–, in–, ir–	not	illogical, impossible, inoperable, irrational
	in; within; toward; on	illuminate, imperil, infiltrate, irrigate
inter–	among or between	international, intersect
intra–/intro–	into; within; inward	introvert, intramural
meta–	after; changed	metamorphosis, metaphor
mis–	wrongly	mistake, misfire
non–	not	nonsense, nonsmoker
out–	in a manner that goes beyond	outrun, outmuscle
over–	excessive	overdone, overkill
per–	through, throughout	permeate, permanent
peri–	all around	perimeter, periscope
post–	after; later	postgame, postpone
pre–	before	prefix, premature *CONTINUED*

Common Prefixes (continued)

Prefix	Meaning	Examples
pro–	before; forward	proceed, prologue
re–	again; back	redo, recall
retro–	back	retrospect, retroactive
semi–	half; partly	semicircle, semidry
sub–/sup–	under	substandard, subfloor, support
super–	above; over; exceeding	superstar, superfluous
sym–/syn–	with; together	sympathy, synonym, synergy
trans–	across; beyond	transatlantic, transfer, transcend
ultra–	too much, too many, extreme	ultraviolet, ultrasound
un–	not	unethical, unhappy
under–	below or short of a quantity or limit	underestimate, understaffed
uni–	one	unicorn, universe

Common Suffixes

Noun Suffix	Meaning	Examples
–ance/–ancy/–ence/–ency	quality or state	defiance, independence, emergency
–age	action or process	marriage, voyage
–ant/–ent	one who	defendant, assistant, resident
–ar/–er/–or	one who	lawyer, survivor, liar
–dom	state or quality of	freedom, boredom
–es/–s	plural form of noun	siblings, trees
–ion/–tion	action or process	revolution, occasion
–ism	act; state; or system of belief	plagiarism, barbarism, Buddhism
–ist	one who does or believes something	ventriloquist, idealist
–itude, –tude	quality of, state of	multitude, magnitude
–ity/–ty	state of	longevity, infinity
–ment	action or process; state or quality; product or thing	development, government, amusement, amazement, ointment, fragment
–ness	state of	kindness, happiness

CONTINUED

Common Suffixes (continued)

Adjective Suffix	Meaning	Examples
–able/–ible	capable of	attainable, possible
–al	having characteristics of	personal, governmental
–er	more	higher, calmer, shorter
–est	most	lowest, craziest, tallest
–ful	full of	helpful, gleeful, woeful
–ic	having characteristics of	scientific, chronic
–ish	like	childish, reddish
–ive	performs or tends toward	creative, pensive
–less	without	hapless, careless
–ous	possessing the qualities of	generous, joyous
–y	indicates description	happy, dirty, flowery

Adverb Suffix	Meaning	Examples
–ly	in such a way	quickly, studiously, invisibly
–ward, –ways, –wise	in such a direction	toward, sideways, crosswise

Verb Suffix	Meaning	Examples
–ate	make or cause to be	fixate, activate
–ed	past tense of verb	walked, acted, fixed
–ify/–fy	make or cause to be	vilify, magnify, glorify
–ing	indicates action in progress (present participle); can also be a noun (gerund)	running, thinking, being
–ize	bring about; cause to be	colonize, legalize

Common Word Roots

Word Root	Meaning	Examples
acr	highest point	acrobat
act	do	actor, reaction
ann/annu/enni	year	annual, bicentennial
aqu	water	aquarium, aquatic
aster, astr	star	asteroid, disastrous
aud	hear	audition, auditorium

CONTINUED

Common Word Roots (continued)		
Word Root	**Meaning**	**Examples**
bene	good	beneficial, benefactor
bibl, bibli	book	Bible
chron	time	chronic
cosm	universe; order	cosmic, cosmos
cred	believe; trust	credit, credible
cycl	circle	bicycle, cyclone
dem/demo	people	democracy
derm	skin	dermatologist
dic/dict	say	dictate, dictionary
duc/duct	lead; pull	conduct, reproduction
dyn	force, power	dynamic, dynamite
equ/equi/iqui	equal	equidistant, equitable, iniquity
fer	carry	transfer, refer
fin	end	finish, infinite
firm	firm, strong	confirm, reaffirm
flect/flex	bend	deflect, reflex, flexible
fort	strong	fortify, comfort
ge	earth	geode, geography
gress	go	progress, regress
hydr	water	hydrate
ign	fire	ignite, ignition, igneous
ject	throw	projector, eject
judic	judgment	prejudice, judicial
lect/leg	read; choose	lecture, election, collect
liber	free	liberate, liberal
loc	place	location, relocate
locut/loqu	speak	elocution, loquacious, colloquial
log/logue	word, speech, discourse	logic, dialogue
luc/lumin	shine; light	translucent, illuminate
mal	bad	malevolent
man/manu	hand	manufacture, manual *CONTINUED*

Common Word Roots (continued)		
Word Root	**Meaning**	**Examples**
metr	measure	metric
morph	form	morpheme, metamorphosis
mot	move	motor, emotion
mut	change	mutation, transmutable
nov	new	novelty, renovate
onym	name	synonym, antonym
path	feel; suffer; disease	sympathy, pathology
ped	foot, child	pedal, pediatrics
phon/phony	sound; voice; speech	symphony
phot	light	photography
physi	nature	physical, physics
pop	people	popular, populate
port	carry	transport, portable
psych	mind; soul	psychology, psychic
reg	rule	register, regulate
rupt	break	disrupt, interruption, rupture
scrib/script	write	describe, prescription
son	sound	sonic
spec/spect/spic	look	speculate, inspect, despicable
spir	breathe	spirit, inspiration
ter/terr	earth	inter, extraterrestrial, terrain
therm	heat	thermal
top	place	topography, topical
tract	draw; drag	retract, tractor, contract
typ	stamp; model	typical, type
ver	truth	veracity, verifiable
vert	turn	divert, introvert, extrovert
vid/vis	see	video, visual
viv	alive	vivacious, vivid
vol/volv	turn	evolution, revolve

The more meanings of prefixes, suffixes, and word roots you know, the better equipped you are to tackle difficult vocabulary words.

Even if you don't know the meaning of a word part, however, you can often figure out the meaning of a word using word parts. To do this, think of as many familiar words as you can that contain each part of the word.

For example, if you were tackling the word *biosphere*, you might first think of words beginning with the prefix *bio–*: *biography* and *biology*. You know that a biography is a book about someone's life and that biology is the study of living things, so you're pretty sure that *bio–* has something to do with life. You know that the word *atmosphere* is the whole mass of air surrounding the earth, and you've heard the word *sphere* used to refer to a realm. From this information, you might guess (correctly) that a *biosphere* is a realm in which life can exist.

This process is even easier when you work with a partner. Think aloud with your partner about how to break apart a word. Then discuss the meanings of each part and a possible meaning for the entire word.

RECOGNIZING COMBINING FORMS

Some word roots have become very common in English and are used all the time in combination with each other and with base words to create new scientific, medical, and technical terms. These combining forms can look like prefixes and suffixes, but contain more core meaning. The chart on the next page defines and gives examples of some common combining forms that will help you tackle new words.

THINK AND REFLECT

Think aloud about how you would use word parts to figure out the meaning of the word *inordinate*. Record notes from your think aloud here. **(Apply)**

_____

_____

_____

_____

_____

Combining Forms		
Word Part	**Meaning**	**Examples**
acro–	heights	acrophobia
anthropo–	human being	anthropologist
archaeo–/arche–	old	archeology
astr–/astro–	star	astronaut, astrology
audio–	hear	audiovisual
auto–	self	autobiography, automatic
bi–/bio–	life	biography, biosphere
bibl–/biblio–	book	bibliography
–centric	having such a center	egocentric
chron–/chrono–	time	chronology
–cracy	form of government; social or political class	aristocracy, democracy
ethno–	race; people; cultural group	ethnography
ge–/geo–	earth; soil	geography, geology
–graph/–graphy	something written, drawn, or represented by graphics	telegraph, photography
hydr–/hydro–	water	hydroelectric, hydrometer
–logy/–ology	study of	geology, biology
mal–	bad	malfunction, malnutrition
–mania	madness	kleptomania, megalomania
–metry	having to do with measure	geometry, symmetry
micro–	small; minute	microscope, microcosm
omni–	all	omnipresent, omnibus
–onym	name	synonym, antonym
–phile	one who loves	bibliophile
–phobe	one who has an irrational fear	arachnophobe, acrophobe
–phobia	exaggerated fear of	claustrophobia, photophobia
phon–/–phone/phono–	sound; voice; speech	telephone, phonograph
phot–/–photo–	light	photograph, telephoto
physi–/physio–	nature; physical	physiological
pseud–/pseudo–	false	pseudonym, pseudointellectual
psych–/psycho–	mind	psychiatrist, psychology
–scope/–scopy	view	telescope, microscopy
–ster	one who does or is	mobster, spinster
therm–/thermo–	heat	thermometer, thermodynamics
tel–/tele–	distant	telegram, telephone

Exploring Word Origins and Word Families

The English language expands constantly and gathers new words from many different sources. Understanding the source of a word can help you unlock its meaning.

One source of new words is the names of people and places associated with the thing being named. Words named for people and places are called **eponyms**.

THINK AND REFLECT

List five ways that new words come into the English language. **(Analyze)**

_____

_____

_____

_____

_____

_____

> **EXAMPLES**
> **graham crackers**   These sweet crackers are named after Sylvester Graham, an American reformer in dietary sciences.
> **watt**   This unit that measures power is named after James Watt, a Scottish engineer and inventor.

Another source for new words is **acronyms**. Acronyms are words formed from the first letter or letters of the major parts of terms.

> **EXAMPLES**
> **NASA,** from _National Aeronautic and Space Administration_
> **NATO,** from _North Atlantic Treaty Organization_

Some words in the English language are borrowed from other languages.

> **EXAMPLES**
> **coyote** (Spanish), **cavalier** (French), **karate** (Japanese)

Many words are formed by shortening longer words.

> **EXAMPLES**
> **flu,** from _influenza_
> **fridge,** from _refrigerator_
> **memo,** from _memorandum_

Brand names are often taken into the English language. People begin to use these words as common nouns, even though most of them are still brand names.

> **EXAMPLES**
> Walkman   Q-tip   Band-Aid

Using a Dictionary

When you can't figure out a word using the strategies already described, or when the word is important to the meaning of the text and you want to make sure you have it right, use a dictionary.

There are many parts to a dictionary entry. Study the following sample. Then read the explanations of each part of an entry below.

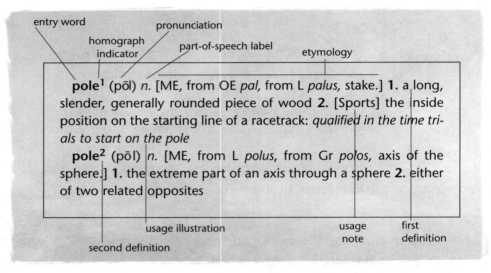

The **pronunciation** is given immediately after the entry word. The dictionary's table of contents will tell you where you can find a complete key to pronunciation symbols. In some dictionaries, a simplified pronunciation key is provided at the bottom of each page.

An abbreviation of the **part of speech** usually follows the pronunciation. This label tells how the word can be used. If a word can be used as more than one part of speech, a separate entry is provided for each part of speech.

An **etymology** is the history of the word. In the first entry, the word *pole* can be traced back through Middle English (ME) and Old English (OE) to the Latin (L) word *palus*, which means "stake." In the second entry, the word *pole* can be traced back through Middle English to the Latin word *polus*, which comes from the Greek (Gr) word *polos*, meaning "axis of the sphere."

Sometimes the entry will include a list of **synonyms**, or words that have the same or very similar meanings. The entry may also include a **usage illustration**, which is an example of how the word is used in context.

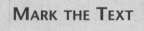

MARK THE TEXT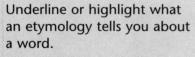

Underline or highlight what an etymology tells you about a word.

Understanding Multiple Meanings

Each definition in the entry gives a different meaning of the word. When a word has more than one meaning, the different definitions are numbered. The first definition in an entry is the most common meaning of the word, but you will have to choose the meaning that fits the context in which you have found the word. Try substituting each definition for the word until you find the one that makes the most sense.

If you come across a word that doesn't seem to make sense in context, consider whether that word might have another, lesser known meaning. Can the word be used as more than one part of speech, for example, as either a noun or a verb? Does it have a broader meaning than the one that comes to your mind? For example, in the story "Ta-Na-E-Ka" (Unit 3, page 50), Ernie offers to keep Mary's five dollars "in trust" for her. The most common meaning of the word *trust* involves a feeling that you can rely on someone, but that meaning doesn't quite make sense here. If you check the footnote at the bottom of the page, you will find that *trust* can also mean "account of money for future use."

Keep in mind that some words not only have multiple meanings but also different pronunciations. Words that are spelled the same but are pronounced differently are called **homographs**.

Understanding Denotation and Connotation

The **denotation** of a word is its dictionary definition. Sometimes, in order to understand a passage fully, it is helpful to know the connotations of the words as well. A **connotation** of a word is an emotional association the word has in addition to its literal meaning. For example, the words *slender* and *scrawny* both denote "thin," but *scrawny* has a negative connotation of weakness whereas *slender* has a positive connotation of attractiveness. The best way to learn the connotation of a word is to pay attention to the context in which the word appears or to ask someone more familiar with the word.

NOTE THE FACTS

What is the difference between a *denotation* and a *connotation?*

_____

_____

THINK AND REFLECT

Imagine that you have injured your hand, and you call your mother at work to tell her. How would her reaction be different if you described the injury as a *gash* instead of a *cut?* If a character in a story described a tiny paper cut as a *gash*, what might that tell you about the character? **(Apply)**

_____

_____

_____

_____

Reading **TIP**

In your word study notebook, record for each word:

- definition
- pronunciation
- etymology
- sample sentence or illustration

Keeping a Word Study Notebook

Keeping a **word study notebook** is a convenient way to log new words, their meanings, and their spellings, as well as prefixes, suffixes, word roots, and other concepts. In addition, you can use your word study notebook to write down words that you have trouble remembering how to spell. You may even want to set aside a section of your notebook for word play. You can use this area to create jokes, silly rhymes, jingles, skits, acrostics, and games using the words you have logged.

When you record a new word in your notebook, include its definition, pronunciation, and origins, along with an example sentence or drawing to help you remember it.

Here is a sample page from a word study notebook.

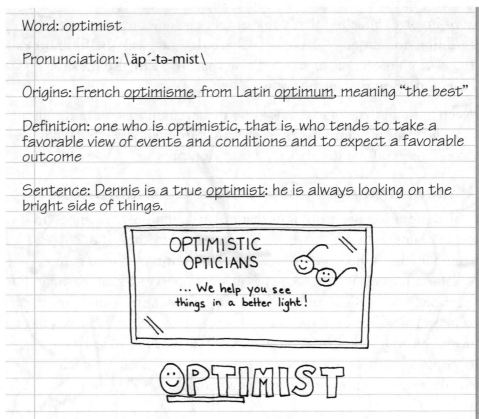

Word: optimist

Pronunciation: \äp´-tə-mist\

Origins: French *optimisme*, from Latin *optimum*, meaning "the best"

Definition: one who is optimistic, that is, who tends to take a favorable view of events and conditions and to expect a favorable outcome

Sentence: Dennis is a true *optimist*: he is always looking on the bright side of things.

OPTIMISTIC OPTICIANS

... We help you see things in a better light!

OPTIMIST

Review the words in your word study notebook and practice using the words in your speech and writing. Also, look for the words from your notebook as you read and listen. The more associations you develop and the more encounters you have with a word, the more likely you are to remember it.

Using Mnemonic Devices

A **mnemonic** (ni mä′ nik) **device** is a catchy phrase or striking image that helps you remember information. For example, you might have heard the phrase "the princiPAL is your PAL" as a trick for remembering the difference between *principal*, the person, and *principle*, the idea. The rhyme "*I* before *E* except after *C*" is a mnemonic for a spelling pattern.

Mnemonic devices are effective in learning new vocabulary words because you learn new information by linking it to words, images, and concepts that are already familiar to you. Vocabulary mnemonics can be sayings, drawings, jingles, or whatever works for you. To remember the definition of *neophyte*, you could say, "A neophyte fighter is new to fighting." To remember how to spell *museum*, you could associate the word with others like it: we are a<u>muse</u>d at the <u>museum</u>. A mental picture can also help you remember meaning and spelling.

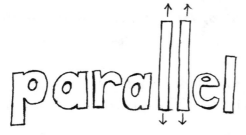

Categorizing and Classifying Words

Another technique for learning vocabulary words is categorizing and classifying the words. To categorize or classify a list of vocabulary words, sort them into groups that share a theme, topic, or characteristic. Then label each group. Like mnemonic devices, this technique works because it helps you create associations with and among new words.

For example, imagine that you need to learn the meanings of the following vocabulary words from "The Twelve Labors of Hercules" (Unit 5, page 163).

assent	expiate	remorse
composure	foliage	semblance
dank	iridescent	serene
derange	lair	
divert	protrude	

NOTE THE FACTS

What is a mnemonic device?

_____

_____

_____

THINK AND REFLECT

Why is the graphic to the left an effective mnemonic for remembering the meaning of *parallel*? (Interpret)

_____

_____

_____

THINK AND REFLECT

Explain how each of these words fits in the category to which it has been assigned. **(Interpret)**

_____

_____

_____

_____

_____

_____

_____

Here is how one student classified these words.

"The Twelve Labors of Hercules" Vocabulary	
Words about unpleasant states	dank, derange, remorse
Words about change	divert, expiate
"Agreeable" words	assent, composure, serene
Words about something you can see	foliage, iridescent, lair, protrude, semblance

Learning Synonyms, Antonyms, and Homonyms

A good way to expand your vocabulary is to learn synonyms, antonyms, and homonyms. As with using mnemonic devices and classifying or categorizing words, working with synonyms, antonyms, and homonyms will help you build associations for new words.

synonym	same (or nearly the same) meaning	smooth, even
antonym	opposite meaning	happy, sad
homonym	same pronunciation but different meaning	right, write, rite

One way of using synonyms and antonyms to make many connections to a new word is to create a **concept map**. In a concept map, you list synonyms, antonyms, examples, nonexamples, and a contextual sentence for the word you are studying. The best way to use a concept map is to fill it out with a small group or as a whole class. That way, you get to hear everyone else's associations with the word, too. Look at the concept map for _wretched_ on the next page.

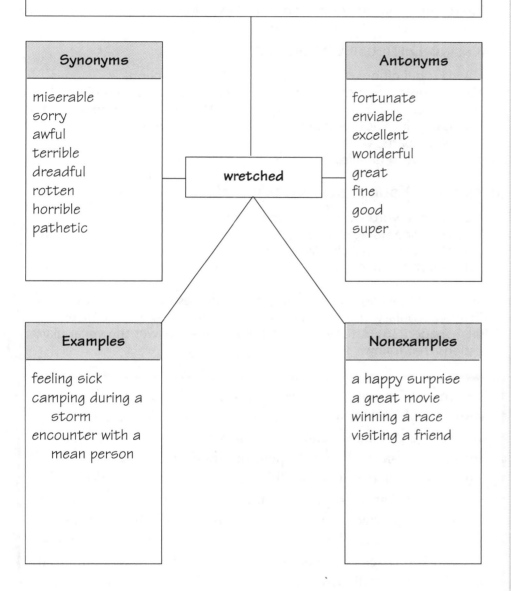

Real-Life Contexts

On the day of the big test, I felt <u>wretched</u>; my stomach was queasy, I had a headache, and I was nervous and sweaty.

The weather Tuesday made for a <u>wretched</u> picnic; it was hot, humid, and overcast, and the rain started to fall about midafternoon.

Synonyms

miserable
sorry
awful
terrible
dreadful
rotten
horrible
pathetic

wretched

Antonyms

fortunate
enviable
excellent
wonderful
great
fine
good
super

Examples

feeling sick
camping during a
    storm
encounter with a
    mean person

Nonexamples

a happy surprise
a great movie
winning a race
visiting a friend

THINK AND REFLECT

Add one more synonym, antonym, example, and nonexample to the boxes in the chart. **(Apply)**

_____

_____

_____

_____

Unit 9 **VOCABULARY** Review

Choose and Use Vocabulary Strategies

Before completing the vocabulary activities below, review with a partner how to use each of these vocabulary strategies.

TACKLING DIFFICULT VOCABULARY

- ❑ Use definitions, footnotes, endnotes, and glossaries
- ❑ Use context clues
- ❑ Use prior knowledge of word parts, word origins, and word families

- ❑ Use a dictionary
- ❑ Understand multiple meanings
- ❑ Understand connotation and denotation

IMPROVING YOUR ACTIVE VOCABULARY

- ❑ Keep a word study notebook
- ❑ Use mnemonic devices
- ❑ Categorize and classify words
- ❑ Learn synonyms, antonyms, and homonyms

Now read the passage below using the strategies from this unit to tackle difficult vocabulary in this excerpt from "Pompeii" by Robert Silverberg (Unit 7, page 236). After you finish the passage, answer the vocabulary questions that follow.

> The tragedy struck on the twenty-fourth of August, AD 79. Mount Vesuvius, which had slumbered quietly for centuries, exploded with savage violence. Death struck on a hot summer afternoon. Tons of hot ashes fell on Pompeii, smothering it, hiding it from sight. For three days the sun did not break through the cloud of volcanic ash that filled the sky. And when the eruption ended, Pompeii was buried deep. A thriving city had perished in a single day.
>
> Centuries passed. Pompeii was forgotten. Then, fifteen hundred years later, it was discovered again. Beneath the protecting shroud of ashes, the city lay intact. Everything was as it had been the day Vesuvius erupted. There were still loaves of bread in the ovens of the bakeries. In the wine shops, the wine jars were in place, and on one counter could be seen a stain where a customer had thrown down his glass and fled.

Modern archaeology began with the discovery of buried Pompeii. Before then, the digging of treasures from the ground had been a haphazard and unscholarly affair. But the excavation of Pompeii was done in a systematic, scientific manner, and so the science of serious archaeology can be said to have begun there.

1. The word *perished* most likely means
   a. plummeted.
   b. died.
   c. peaked.
   d. covered.

2. Which of the following words in paragraph 3 offers the best context clue for unlocking the meaning of the word *haphazard?*
   a. treasures
   b. excavation
   c. archaeology
   d. systematic

3. The best synonym for *slumbered* would be
   a. slept.
   b. lived.
   c. snored.
   d. existed.

4. An antonym for *unscholarly* is
   a. haphazard.
   b. serious.
   c. random.
   d. intact.

5. Imagine that your teacher has given you the following list of vocabulary words.

belch	gaudy	project
bewilder	haphazard	rutted
catastrophe	imposing	shrewdness
critical	molten	shroud
engulf	monopoly	tranquility
excavation	oblige	unruly
fruitless	ominous	vitality

Use a dictionary and your knowledge of word parts to determine the meaning of each of these words. Then, on your own paper, do the following activities:

   a. Create a word study notebook entry for one of the words.
   b. Create a mnemonic device for one of the words.
   c. Categorize the words.

On Your Own

FLUENTLY SPEAKING. Learn the pronunciations of each of the vocabulary words from the previous activity. Then practice reading the words aloud until you can read the entire list without stumbling. Use the Word Recognition Skills: Word Race form in Appendix A, page A-4. Record your personal best time.

PICTURE THIS. Read a story, article, or poem that contains words that are new to you. Pick a particularly interesting word, and create a collage of images, other words, and small objects that have something to do with the word. Be prepared to explain to the class why you chose the things you did.

PUT IT IN WRITING. Find and read a book, story, article, or poem that interests you. Make a photocopy of the text, and cut out interesting or unfamiliar words. Also cut out some common words like *the, and, my,* and so on. Cut out at least thirty words. Then arrange at least fifteen of the words into a poem. Glue the poem into your notebook.

Unit TEN

TEST-TAKING
Strategies

PREPARING FOR TESTS IN YOUR CLASSES

Tests are a common part of school life. You take tests in your classes
to show what you have learned in each class. In addition, you might
have to take one or more standardized tests each year. Standardized
tests measure your skills against local, state, or national standards and
may determine whether you graduate, what kind of job you can get,
or which college you can attend. Learning test-taking strategies will
help you succeed on the tests you are required to take.

These guidelines will help you to prepare for and take tests on the
material you have covered in class.

Preparing for a Test

- ❑ **Know what will be covered on the test.** If you have questions
  about what will be covered, ask your teacher.

- ❑ **Make a study plan** to allow yourself time to go over the material.
  Avoid last-minute cramming.

- ❑ **Review the subject matter.** Use the graphic organizers and notes
  you made as you read as well as notes you took in class. Review
  any study questions given by your teacher.

- ❑ **Make lists** of important names, dates, definitions, or events. Ask a
  friend or family member to quiz you on them.

- ❑ **Try to predict questions** that may be on the test. Make sure you
  can answer them.

- ❑ **Get plenty of sleep** the night before the test. Eat a nutritious
  breakfast on the morning of the test.

Reading STRATEGY
REVIEW

**CONNECT TO PRIOR
KNOWLEDGE.** Which of
these test strategies do
you already use? Which
might help you on your
next test?

_____

_____

_____

_____

_____

_____

_____

_____

_____

Taking a Test

- ❏ **Survey the test** to see how long it is and what types of questions are included.
- ❏ **Read all directions and questions carefully.** Make sure you know exactly what to do.
- ❏ **Plan your time.** Answer easy questions first. Allow extra time for complicated questions. If a question seems too difficult, skip it and go back to it later. Work quickly, but do not rush.
- ❏ **Save time for review.** Once you have finished, look back over the test. Double-check your answers, but do not change answers too readily. Your first ideas are often correct.

Answering Objective Questions

An **objective question** has a single correct answer. This chart describes the kinds of questions you may see on objective tests. It also gives you strategies for tackling each kind of question.

MARK THE TEXT

Underline or highlight the guidelines in the chart that you want to try next time you take a test.

Questions Found on Objective Tests	
Description	**Guidelines**
True/False. You are given a statement and asked to tell whether the statement is true or false.	■ If any part of a statement is false, then the statement is false. ■ Words like *all, always, never,* and *every* often appear in false statements. ■ Words like *some, usually, often,* and *most* often appear in true statements. ■ If you do not know the answer, guess. You have a 50/50 chance of being right.
Matching. You are asked to match items in one column with items in another column.	■ Check the directions. See if each item is used only once. Also check to see if some are not used at all. ■ Read all items before starting. ■ Match those items you know first. ■ Cross out items as you match them.
Multiple Choice. You are asked to choose the best answer from a group of answers given.	■ Read *all* choices first. ■ Rule out incorrect answers. ■ Choose the answer that is most complete or accurate. ■ Pay particular attention to choices such as *none of the above* or *all of the above.*

Short Answer. You are asked to answer the question with a word, phrase, or sentence.	■ Read the directions to find out if you are required to answer in complete sentences. ■ Use correct spelling, grammar, punctuation, and capitalization. ■ If you cannot think of the answer, move on. Something in another question might remind you of the answer.

Answering Essay Questions

An essay question asks you to write an answer that shows what you know about a particular subject. Read the following essay question prompt on "The Cow of No Color" (Unit 5, page 175).

> Evaluate the chief's wisdom. Is he a wise leader? Why, or why not?

A simplified writing process will help you tackle questions like this. Follow these steps:

1 ANALYZE THE QUESTION. Essay questions contain clues about what is expected of you. Sometimes you will find key words that will help you determine exactly what is being asked. See the list below for some typical key words and their meanings.

Key Words for Essay Questions

analyze; identify	break into parts, and describe the parts and how they are related
compare	tell how two or more subjects are similar; in some cases, also mention how they are different
contrast	tell how two or more subjects are different from each other
describe	give enough facts about or qualities of a subject to make it clear to someone who is unfamiliar with it
discuss	provide an overview and analysis; use details for support
evaluate; argue	judge an idea or concept, telling whether you think it is good or bad, or whether you agree or disagree with it
explain	make a subject clearer, providing supporting details and examples
interpret	tell the meaning and importance of an event or concept
justify	explain or give reasons for decisions; be persuasive
prove	provide factual evidence or reasons for a statement
summarize	state only the main points of an event, concept, or debate

THINK AND REFLECT

Using the information in the chart, explain in your own words what the prompt above about "The Cow of No Color" is asking you to do. **(Apply)**

_____

_____

_____

Reading TIP

Steps for answering essay questions:
1 Analyze the question
2 Plan your answer
3 Draft your answer
4 Revise your answer

2 PLAN YOUR ANSWER. As soon as the essay prompt is clear to you, collect and organize your thoughts about it. First, gather ideas using whatever method is most comfortable for you. If you don't immediately have ideas, try freewriting for five minutes. When you **freewrite**, you write whatever comes into your head without letting your hand stop moving. You might also gather ideas in a **cluster chart**. (See Appendix B, page B-7, for an example of this kind of chart.) Then, organize the ideas you came up with. A simple outline or chart can help. For example, the following graphic organizer might help you organize an essay for the prompt on "The Cow of No Color" on the previous page.

Thesis Statement:	The chief in "The Cow of No Color" is not a wise leader.
Main Points	**Supporting Details**
1. The chief allows his emotions to control his behavior.	He becomes very jealous of the wise woman and sets out to trick her.
2. The chief is easily tricked.	He is speechless when the old woman uses a riddle just like the one he gave

Get to know other graphic organizers that might help you by reviewing those on the before-reading pages and in Appendix B of this book.

3 WRITE YOUR ANSWER. Start with a clear thesis statement in your opening paragraph. Your **thesis statement** is a single sentence that sums up your answer to the essay question. Then follow your organizational plan to provide support for your thesis. Devote one paragraph to each major point of support for your thesis. Use plenty of details as evidence for each point. Write quickly and keep moving. Don't spend too much time on any single paragraph, but try to make your answer as complete as possible. End your essay with a concluding sentence that sums up your major points.

4 REVISE YOUR ANSWER. Make sure you have answered all parts of the question and included everything you were asked to include. Check to see that you have supplied enough details to support your thesis. Check for errors in grammar, spelling, punctuation, and paragraph breaks. Make corrections to your answer.

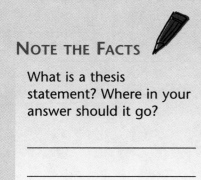

NOTE THE FACTS

What is a thesis statement? Where in your answer should it go?

_____

_____

_____

TAKING STANDARDIZED TESTS

Standardized tests are given to large groups of students in a school district, a state, or a country. Statewide tests measure how well students are meeting the learning standards the state has set. Other tests, such as the Scholastic Aptitude Test, or SAT, are used to help determine admission to colleges and universities. Others must be taken to enter certain careers. These tests are designed to measure overall ability or skills acquired so far. Learning how to take standardized tests will help you to achieve your goals.

You can get better at answering standardized test questions by practicing the types of questions that will be on the test. Use the Reading Skills and Test Practice questions in this book and other sample questions your teacher gives you to practice. Think aloud with a partner or small group about how you would answer each question. Notice how other students tackle the questions and learn from what they do.

In addition, remember these points:

NOTE THE FACTS

What can you do if you encounter a question that is too difficult?

_____

_____

_____

_____

❑ **Rule out some choices** when you are not sure of the answer. Then guess from the remaining possibilities.

❑ **Skip questions that seem too difficult** and go back to them later. Be aware, however, that most tests allow you to go back only within a section.

❑ **Follow instructions exactly.** The test monitor will read instructions to you, and instructions may also be printed in your test booklet. Make sure you know what to do.

Answering Multiple-Choice Questions

On many standardized tests, questions are multiple choice and have a single correct answer. The guidelines below will help you answer these kinds of questions effectively.

❑ **Read each question carefully.** Pay special attention to any words that are bolded, italicized, written in all capital letters, or otherwise emphasized.

❑ **Read all choices** before selecting an answer.

❑ **Eliminate** any answers that do not make sense, that disagree with what you remember from reading a passage, or that seem too extreme. Also, if two answers have exactly the same meaning, you can eliminate both.

MARK THE TEXT

Underline or highlight the suggestions in this list that are new to you.

NOTE THE FACTS

What is a think aloud? What should you include in a think aloud?

_____

_____

_____

_____

_____

❑ **Beware of distractors.** These are incorrect answers that look attractive because they are partially correct. They might contain a common misunderstanding, or they might apply the right information in the wrong way. Distractors are based on common mistakes students make.

❑ **Fill in circles completely** on your answer sheet when you have selected your answer.

Answering Reading Comprehension Questions

Reading comprehension questions ask you to read a passage and answer questions about it. These questions measure how well you perform the essential reading skills covered in Unit 2 of this book.

The Reading Skills and Test Practice questions that follow each literature selection in this book are reading comprehension questions. Use them to help you learn how to answer these types of questions correctly. Work through each question with a partner using a **think aloud**. Say out loud how you are figuring out the answer. Talk about how you can eliminate incorrect answers and determine the correct choice. You may want to make notes as you eliminate answers. By practicing this thinking process with a partner, you will be more prepared to use it silently when you have to take a standardized test.

The following steps will help you answer the reading comprehension questions on standardized tests.

❑ **Preview the passage and questions** and predict what the text will be about.

❑ **Use the reading strategies** you have learned to read the passage. Mark the text and make notes in the margins.

❑ **Reread the first question carefully.** Make sure you know exactly what it is asking.

❑ **Read the answers.** If you are sure of the answer, select it and move on. If not, go on to the next step.

❑ **Scan the passage** to look for key words related to the question. When you find a key word, slow down and read carefully.

❑ **Answer the question** and go on to the next one. Answer each question in this way.

Answering Analogy Questions

Analogy questions ask you to find the relationship between two words and then to recognize a similar relationship in another pair of words. In an analogy question, the symbol : means "is to" and the symbol :: means "as." For instance, the following analogy:

WARM : HOT :: ODD : BIZARRE

is read as

WARM IS TO HOT AS ODD IS TO BIZARRE.

Look at the example below.

PORK : PIG ::

a. VEAL : CALF

b. DOE : DEER

c. BACON : FISH

d. FUR COAT : MINK

The example above would be read aloud as "*Pork* is to *pig* as. . . ." Follow these guidelines for answering analogy questions:

❑ Think of a sentence that relates the two words. For the example above, you might think "Pork is meat from a pig."

❑ Try substituting the words from each answer pair in the sentence.

"Veal is meat from a calf."

"Doe is meat from a deer."

"Bacon is meat from a fish."

"A fur coat is meat from a mink."

❑ Decide which sentence makes the most sense.

❑ If none of the options makes sense, try to think of a different sentence that relates the words, and work through the same process with the new sentence.

The chart on the following page lists some common relationships used in analogy questions.

THINK AND REFLECT

Using the process described here, how would you answer the analogy question above? **(Apply)**

_____

_____

_____

Common Analogy Relationships

Relationship	Example
synonyms	strong : powerful
antonyms	chaotic : calm
cause and effect	smoking : lung cancer
effect and cause	lung cancer : smoking
general and specific	dog : Saint Bernard
less intense and more intense	happy : overjoyed
part to whole	lettuce : salad
whole to part	salad : lettuce
age	colt : stallion
gender	actress : actor
worker and tool	plumber : wrench
worker and product created	carpenter : house
tool and associated action	hammer : pound
scientist and object of study	geologist : rocks
raw material and end product	wood : cabin
person and associated quality	judge : wise
symbol and what it stands for	heart : love

Answering Synonym and Antonym Questions

Synonym or antonym questions give you a word and ask you to select the word that has the same meaning (for a **synonym**) or the opposite meaning (for an **antonym**). You must select the best answer even if none is exactly correct. For this type of question, you should consider all the choices to see which is best. Always notice whether you are looking for a synonym or an antonym. You will usually find both among the answers. Think aloud with a partner about how to answer the following question:

Mark the letter of the word that is most nearly the OPPOSITE in meaning to the word in capital letters.

1. SUPPLE
    a. colorful
    b. smooth
    c. stiff
    d. humorous

Answering Sentence Completion Questions

Sentence completion questions present you with a sentence that has two words missing. You must select the pair of words that best completes the sentence. The key to this kind of question is to make sure that both parts of the answer you have selected work well in the sentence. Think aloud with a partner about how to complete the following sentence.

> 2. Prior to going on stage, Emilia felt _____; however, after a successful performance, she felt _____.
>
> a. calm . . . worried
> b. timid . . . arrogant
> c. anxious . . . confident
> d. nervous . . . distressed

THINK AND REFLECT

How would you select the correct answer to the sentence completion question? **(Apply)**

_____

_____

_____

_____

_____

Answering Constructed-Response Questions

In addition to multiple-choice questions, many standardized tests include **constructed-response questions** that require you to write essay answers in the test booklet. Constructed-response questions might ask you to identify key ideas or examples from the text by writing a sentence about each. In other cases, you will be asked to write a paragraph in response to a question about the selection and to use specific details from the passage to support your answer. For example, the following prompt might occur after William Stafford's poem "One Time," Unit 4, page 130.

> **Essay prompt:** How do the images in this poem show the passing of time?
>
> **Short response:** The images in "One Time" focus on the passing of day into night. The speaker describes evening flowing "between houses" and pausing near the school. The railing that Tina is holding is "still warm from the sun," and Tina is enjoying the "last light" on her face. The speaker imagines that the pigeons are discussing dreams, which are associated with night. Then, he or she mentions that they are "deep in the well of shadow," indicating that night has finally come.

NOTE THE FACTS

What must you include in your answers to constructed-response questions?

_____

_____

_____

_____

Other constructed-response questions ask you to apply information or ideas from a text in a new way. Imagine that you have just read the story "Zlateh the Goat" (Unit 3, page 72) on a standardized test. This story tells about how a boy and goat grow closer after surviving a terrible storm together. One question might ask you to imagine that you are Zlateh the goat and that you were suddenly given the ability to speak. How would you describe the storm from your perspective? Another question might ask you to write a news story about what happened to the two main characters, Zlateh and Aaron. As you answer these questions, remember that you are being evaluated based on your understanding of the text. Although these questions offer opportunities to be creative, you should still include ideas, details, and examples from the passage you have just read.

The following tips will help you answer constructed-response questions effectively.

Reading STRATEGY REVIEW

CONNECT TO PRIOR KNOWLEDGE. Compare the Tips for Answering Constructed-Response Questions to what you already do. Which tips will you use next time you have to respond to a constructed-response question?

_____

_____

_____

_____

Tips for Answering Constructed-Response Questions

❑ **Skim the questions first.** Predict what the passage will be about.

❑ **Use reading strategies** as you read. Underline information that relates to the questions and make notes. After you have finished reading, you can decide which of the details you have gathered to use in your answers.

❑ **List the most important points** to include in each answer. Use the margins of your test booklet or a piece of scrap paper.

❑ **Number the points** you have listed to show the order in which they should be included.

❑ **Draft your answer to fit** in the space provided. Include as much detail as possible in the space you have.

❑ **Revise and proofread** your answers as you have time.

Unit 10 TEST-TAKING Review

Choose and Use Test-Taking Strategies

Before answering the sample test questions below, review with a partner how to use each of these test-taking strategies.

GENERAL STRATEGIES

- ❑ Know what will be on the test
- ❑ Make a study plan
- ❑ Review the subject matter
- ❑ Make lists
- ❑ Try to predict questions
- ❑ Preview the passage and questions
- ❑ Plan your time
- ❑ Use reading strategies to read the passage
- ❑ Come back later to questions that seem too difficult
- ❑ Save time for reviewing answers

STRATEGIES FOR OBJECTIVE TESTS

- ❑ Read each question carefully
- ❑ Read all answer choices before selecting one
- ❑ Scan the passage again if you are uncertain of the answer
- ❑ Rule out some choices
- ❑ Beware of distractors
- ❑ Understand how to answer analogy questions
- ❑ Understand how to answer synonym and antonym questions
- ❑ Understand how to answer sentence completion questions
- ❑ Fill in circles completely

STRATEGIES FOR ESSAY TESTS

- ❑ Understand how to answer constructed-response questions
- ❑ Analyze the question
- ❑ Plan your answer
- ❑ Write your answer
- ❑ Revise your answer

Now read "Mount Vesuvius" below and answer the questions that follow. Use the strategies from this unit to complete this practice test.

Mount Vesuvius is a volcano located in the southern part of Italy near a city called Naples. It stands at the center of a larger, older volcano called Mount Somma, which is more than 300,000 years old. Like the large volcanoes of the Hawaiian islands, Mount Vesuvius began as an underwater volcano.

A volcano is a large hill or a mountain that has been formed around a crack, or vent, in the earth's crust where heat, gas, and molten rock can escape. Far below this vent, the center of the earth is extremely hot. At a depth of fifty to sixty miles below the earth's surface, the temperature is hot enough to melt rock and form lava, which gradually rises toward the earth's surface. This lava collects in underground pools. It is highly charged with steam and other gases, such as carbon dioxide, hydrogen, carbon monoxide, and sulfur dioxide, which cause the pressure to build.

Finally, the steam and gases escape from the surface of the lava with violent explosions. Lava shoots up and forms a fiery fountain. As the first visible effect of an eruption, rock, dust, and ash from the explosion rocket into the air and spread in a cloud over the surrounding landscape. Next molten lava flows out of the vent, mixes with the ash to form mud, and rolls down the mountain. In cone-shaped volcanoes like Mount Vesuvius, the lava and other materials harden into a cone that slopes outward away from the vent.

Volcanoes are classified as active or inactive depending on whether or not they have erupted within recorded history. Mount Vesuvius is the only active volcano on the European continent. A particularly significant eruption occurred in AD 79, when a violent explosion blew the top off the mountain. At times over the next twenty-four hours, the column of ash above Vesuvius's vent was twenty miles high. Molten lava traveled approximately sixty miles an hour. More than 3,000 people are believed to have died in the eruption. The cities of Pompeii and Herculaneum were buried in ash and debris. Pompeii was engulfed up to the rooftops in ten feet of volcanic material. Herculaneum was buried under seventy-five feet of ash. This eruption became the first ever to be witnessed and recorded. A man named Pliny described the event in two letters to a Roman historian.

Often, after an explosive eruption, a volcano will become dormant for a period of hundreds of years. Mount Vesuvius, however, has erupted dozens of times since AD 79. In 1637, its eruption killed about 3,500 people. Its most recent eruption occurred in 1944.

Today, about three million people live in the area around Mount Vesuvius. Orchards and vineyards have been planted on its slopes, and a train carries people from the base of the mountain up to an observatory near the vent itself.

1. What would you expect to find in the next paragraph of this article?

   a. a description of tube-shaped volcanoes
   b. a report of the current risks that the volcano will erupt
   c. an explanation of what lava is made of
   d. a humorous anecdote about the author's trip to see Mount Vesuvius

2. Which of these sentences is the best summary of the passage?

   a. Volcanoes are violent eruptions of lava.
   b. Volcanoes take many shapes.
   c. Mount Vesuvius is a cone-shaped volcano, born underwater, that continues to erupt periodically.
   d. Mount Vesuvius erupted, burying Pompeii, Italy, in AD 79.

3. What makes the eruption of Mount Vesuvius in AD 79 significant?

   a. It killed more people than any other eruption of Mount Vesuvius.
   b. It was the first volcanic eruption to be recorded by a firsthand observer.
   c. It formed Mount Vesuvius from Mount Somma.
   d. It sent Mount Vesuvius into a dormant state.

4. Imagine that you were present for the eruption of Mount Vesuvius in AD 79. Describe what you see as the volcano erupts. Use details from the text to help you with your answer.

   _____

   _____

   _____

   _____

   _____

   _____

   _____

   _____

   _____

5. ROCK : LAVA ::

   a. RAIN : FOG
   b. ICE : WATER
   c. DIRT : WORMS
   d. ASH : FIRE

On Your Own

Fluently Speaking. Use "Mount Vesuvius" on pages 375–376- to perform a repeated reading exercise. Read the passage aloud to a partner. Have your partner record the time it takes you to read the passage and the number of errors you make. Then have your partner read the passage to you with your record time and number of errors. On your second reading, see if you both can improve your initial time and error rate and include more vocal expression. Reread the passage a third time, once again improving your time and error rate and increasing your vocal expression.

Picture This. Find an informational article on a topic that interests you. After reading the article, come up with two essay questions. Practice planning answers for essay questions by constructing a graphic organizer that will help you organize your answer for each question. For more practice on planning responses to essay questions, exchange essay questions with a partner, and plan your answer for your partner's questions.

Put It in Writing. Find and read an informational article on any topic that interests you. After you have read the article, write three multiple-choice and two constructed-response questions that test reading comprehension. As models, use the sample questions in this unit as well as those in the Reading Skills and Test Practice section that follows every literature selection in this book. Finally, exchange your passage and questions with a partner, and take one another's tests.

Appendix A:
Building Reading Fluency

WORD RECOGNITION SKILLS: INCREASE YOUR AUTOMATICITY

WHAT ARE WORD RECOGNITION SKILLS? Word recognition skills are skills that help you recognize and decipher words. Learning how to read increasingly more words with faster recognition leads to **automaticity,** the ability to recognize words quickly and automatically. The activities below develop word recognition skills.

1 **CREATE A CROSSWORD PUZZLE.** Put together a crossword puzzle that includes clues for words you are studying and clues for facts everyone should know. Look at puzzles in the newspaper or a puzzle book to learn how to number your clues and add blank spaces. Here is how you might set up a puzzle.

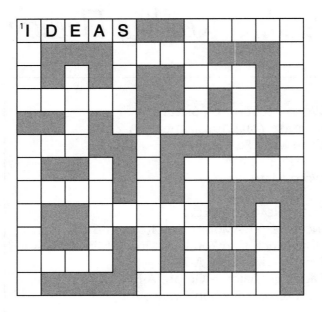

2 **CREATE A WORD RACE.** Make a list of 20 words you have studied. Practice reading the words aloud. Have a classmate keep track of how many seconds it takes you to read the entire list. Have another person keep track of the words you mispronounce. Have teams compete to see which team pronounces the same list of words the fastest with the fewest errors.

3 **CREATE A WORD MATRIX.** Choose vocabulary words that you find difficult to pronounce and place them in a chart. Add the same words to each row of your chart, but add the words to each row in a different order. Practice reading the words until you are comfortable pronouncing them. Have a partner time how many words in your chart you can read in 1 minute.

WORD RECOGNITION SKILLS: WORD MATRIX

Choose 5 words that you find difficult to pronounce, and place them in the matrix below. Add the same words to each row, but use the words in a different order in each row. After a brief practice run-through, have a classmate use a clock or timer to see how many times you can make it through the chart in 1 minute. Have another classmate circle or check words you pronounce correctly. Use the second matrix below to run through your words a second time. Try to increase the number of words spoken correctly on your second reading.

Number of words correct in 1 minute: _____

Number of words correct in 1 minute: _____

SILENT READING SKILLS: INCREASE THE AMOUNT YOU READ

WHAT ARE SILENT READING SKILLS? **Silent reading skills** are skills you use as you read a text to yourself. Fluent silent readers can read a text quickly, easily, and smoothly. To build **silent reading fluency**, set aside time each day to read parts of a long selection or book. Most often, choose selections you consider easy and interesting. Vary the subject matter of selections you choose and, over time, include selections from several different genres—fiction, nonfiction, drama, short stories, poems, and informational and visual media. Use the charts below to keep track of your silent reading activity.

1 **FILL IN A FREE READING LOG.** Read silently for a sustained period several times a week. Write down what you read, the number of minutes you read, the number of pages you read, and your thoughts and reactions. Selections you read may be easy, moderate, or challenging.

2 **USE A PAGES-PER-MINUTE GRAPH.** Chart the number of pages you read in a 30-minute reading session. Try to increase the number of pages you read in each session. Be sure the selections you use for this activity are easy to read.

3 **USE A MINUTES-PER-SECTION GRAPH.** Each reading session, chart the time it takes you to read 5 pages of a selection. Try to decrease the number of minutes it takes to read 5 pages. Be sure the selections you use for this activity are easy to read.

SILENT READING SKILLS: HOW MUCH CAN YOU LEARN IN 10 MINUTES?

READING RATE. Pay attention to your silent reading rate. Do you vary your rate as you read? Do you slow down for difficult vocabulary and long sentences? Do you speed up when the ideas are easy to understand? Learn to use different reading rates with different tasks. Here are three methods to try.

Scan	Skim	Read Closely
To locate particular information (to find a quotation, verify a statement, locate a word, or answer a question)	To get the overall picture (to preview or to review)	To absorb the meaning of a book you're reading for fun or a textbook on which you'll be tested (to read with understanding the first time)

Practice using different reading rates as you read silently for 10 minutes. How much can you learn in 10 minutes? Write what you learn below.

SILENT READING SKILLS: FREE READING LOG

Develop your silent reading fluency by reading silently for a sustained period several times a week. Keep track of what you read each day. List your reactions and thoughts about what you read.

Week of _____

Date/ Minutes Read	Title/Author	Pages Read From/To	Reactions/Thoughts

Total number of pages read this week:

Total number of minutes read this week:

Genres read this week: (circle)
Fiction   Nonfiction   Poetry   Drama   Informational or Visual Media   Other _____

SILENT READING SKILLS: PAGES-PER-MINUTE GRAPH

Choose an easy and interesting book. Read for 30 minutes, and count the number of pages you read. Record the number in the chart below. Try to read more pages in each practice session.

Over 10 pages										
9 pages										
8 pages										
7 pages										
6 pages										
5 pages										
4 pages										
3 pages										
2 pages										
1 page										
Practice Number	1	2	3	4	5	6	7	8	9	10
Number of Pages Read										

SILENT READING SKILLS: MINUTES-PER-SECTION GRAPH

Choose an easy and interesting book. Record in the chart below the time it takes you to read 5 pages of the book. Try to decrease the time it takes you to read 5 pages each time you read. You can time several 5-page sections in one reading by placing paper clips at 5-page intervals. Each time you reach a paper-clipped page, stop to record the time it took you to reach that page.

10 minutes										
9 minutes										
8 minutes										
7 minutes										
6 minutes										
5 minutes										
4 minutes										
3 minutes										
2 minutes										
1 minute										
Practice Number	1	2	3	4	5	6	7	8	9	10
Number of Minutes Read										

Oral Reading Skills: Perform Rereading Activities

WHAT ARE ORAL READING SKILLS? **Oral reading skills** are skills you use when you read aloud. Have you ever noticed how radio and television reporters read a news report? They do not read every word at the same speed and volume. They emphasize important points by putting more stress on some words. They use facial expressions and the tone of their voice to convey what words mean. They add pauses to give listeners time to think about what is being said. These news reporters exhibit **oral reading fluency**, the ability to read aloud smoothly and easily.

HOW CAN YOU BUILD ORAL READING SKILLS? To demonstrate that you are a fluent oral reader, you do not have to read fast without mistakes. Even the best news reporters mispronounce words or stumble over unfamiliar phrases. Good news reporters, however, use strategies that make the oral reading task easier. They read and reread material before they go on the air, and they vary their speed and vocal expression. The rereading activities below build oral reading skills.

1. **PREPARE A REPEATED READING EXERCISE.** Choose a 100–150-word passage that you consider difficult to read. With a partner, use the passage to prepare a repeated reading exercise. Read the passage aloud to your partner. Have your partner record the time it takes you to read the passage and the number of errors you make. Then have your partner read the passage to you while you record the time and number of errors. On your second reading see if you both can improve your initial time and error rate, and include more vocal expression. Reread the passage a third time, working to decrease your time and error rate and trying to increase your vocal expression.

2. **PERFORM A CHORAL READING.** Find a poem, song, or part of a story that would be fun for a group to read aloud. Practice reading the piece aloud. Everyone in the group should use the same phrasing and speed. Have group members add notes to the text that help them pronounce the words and pause at appropriate times. Poems such as "Jabberwocky" on page 117 and "Life Doesn't Frighten Me" on page 125 work well as choral readings.

3. **THINK ALOUD.** Read a selection aloud with a partner. As you read, discuss thoughts you have about what you are reading. Ask questions, make connections and predictions, and respond to the ideas in the selection. When you are finished with your oral reading, reread the selection again, either orally or silently.

4. **PERFORM A PLAY.** Read aloud a play you have previously read silently. Assign parts. In small groups, have each speaker rehearse his/her part several times. Present the play to an audience. Use props and costumes, if possible.

5. **WRITE YOUR OWN PLAY.** Rewrite a prose selection, or a part of a prose selection, as a play. Assign parts. In small groups, have each speaker rehearse his/her part several times. Present the play to an audience. Use props and costumes, if possible.

6. **MAKE A RECORDING.** Read a 100–150-word passage into a tape recorder or DVD player. Listen to your recording. Keep track of errors you make: mispronouncing a word, leaving a word out, or adding a word that is not there. Rerecord the passage. Try to decrease the number of errors you make, and increase the smoothness with which you read the passage. Rerecord the passage until you can read it smoothly without error.

7 **MEMORIZE A PASSAGE.** Memorize a 100–150-word passage from a selection you have read. Have a partner help you memorize the passage by chunking it. Memorize short sections at a time, and work up to repeating the entire passage from memory. Possible passages to memorize include lines from a speech, poem, or song, such as Peggy Seeger's ballad "The Springhill Disaster" on page 105 or scenes from a short story or play such as *The Ugly Duckling* by A. H. Milne on page 199.

8 **MAKE A VIDEO.** Reread a selection with a partner. Prepare a video script that retells the selection. Record the retelling. Show the video retelling to an audience.

9 **EXPERIMENT WITH SPEED AND EXPRESSION.** Read a section of a selection silently. Reread the section aloud to a partner. Experiment with your speed and expression by rereading the section aloud in several different ways. Discuss which speed and means of expression work best.

10 **READ WITH A MASK.** Read silently, pretending that you are a character or the speaker in a selection. Reread aloud using a character or speaker mask that you hold in front of your face or wearing a costume that the character or speaker might wear.

11 **VIEW AND REENACT.** Watch a dramatic version of a selection on video. Read the print version, and reenact part of the selection.

ORAL READING SKILLS: REPEATED READING EXERCISE

❑ Choose a 100–150-word passage that you consider difficult to read. With a partner, use the passage to prepare a repeated reading exercise.

❑ Use a computer or a copier to make 6 copies of the passage: 3 for yourself and 3 for your partner.

❑ Read the passage aloud to your partner. Have your partner record the time you start reading, errors you make while reading, and the time you stop reading. Add this information to your Repeated Reading Record on page A-12.

❑ Have your partner read the passage to you. As your partner reads, record the time he/she starts reading, errors he/she makes, and the time he/she stops reading. See if your partner can improve your time and error rate. Record this information in your partner's Repeated Reading Record.

❑ Read the passage again. This time, work on varying your speed and vocal expression. Record the start/stop times and the number of errors you make, but this time your partner should listen for the meaning your words communicate. Have your partner comment on your speed and expression. For instance, your partner might note that "you read the first line too slow," "you had excellent pauses in the 2nd paragraph," or that you should "show more anger in the last line."

❑ Have your partner read the passage again. Record your partner's start/stop times and errors. Write down ways that your partner can vary his/her speed and vocal expression.

❑ You and your partner should reread the passage one more time. Continue to work on varying your speed and expression, and try to decrease your time and your number of errors. Record the information in your Repeated Reading Record.

ORAL READING SKILLS: REPEATED READING RECORD

Name: _____

Text Read: _____

Date	Evaluator	Errors	Time	Speed/Expression

ORAL READING SKILLS: REPEATED READING RECORD

Name: _____

Text Read: _____

Date	Evaluator	Errors	Time	Speed/Expression

ORAL READING SKILLS: PASSAGE FOR FLUENCY PRACTICE

from "Dragon, Dragon" by John Gardner, page 151.

There was once a king whose kingdom was plagued by a dragon. The king did not know which way to turn. The king's knights were all cowards who hid under their beds whenever the dragon came in sight, so they were of no use to the king at all. And the king's wizard could not help either because, being old, he had forgotten his magic spells. Nor could the wizard look up the spells that had slipped his mind, for he had unfortunately misplaced his wizard's book many years before. The king was at his wit's end.

Every time there was a full moon the dragon came out of his lair and ravaged the countryside. He frightened maidens and stopped up chimneys and broke store windows and set people's clocks back and made dogs bark until no one could hear himself think.

Time started:_____ Number of errors:_____ Time stopped:_____
Comments about speed and expression:

There was once a king whose kingdom was plagued by a dragon. The king did not know which way to turn. The king's knights were all cowards who hid under their beds whenever the dragon came in sight, so they were of no use to the king at all. And the king's wizard could not help either because, being old, he had forgotten his magic spells. Nor could the wizard look up the spells that had slipped his mind, for he had unfortunately misplaced his wizard's book many years before. The king was at his wit's end.

Every time there was a full moon the dragon came out of his lair and ravaged the countryside. He frightened maidens and stopped up chimneys and broke store windows and set people's clocks back and made dogs bark until no one could hear himself think.

Time started:_____ Number of errors:_____ Time stopped:_____
Comments about speed and expression:

ORAL READING SKILLS: PASSAGE FOR FLUENCY PRACTICE

from "Pompeii" by Robert Silverberg, page 237

Not very far from Naples a strange city sleeps under the hot Italian sun. It is the city of Pompeii and there is no other city quite like it in all the world. No one lives in Pompeii but crickets and beetles and lizards, yet every year thousands of people travel from distant countries to visit it.

Pompeii is a dead city. No one has lived there for nearly two thousand years, not since the summer of the year AD 79, to be exact.

Until that year Pompeii was a prosperous city of twenty-five thousand people. Nearby was the Bay of Naples, an arm of the blue Mediterranean. Rich men came down from wealthy Rome, 125 miles to the north, to build luxurious seaside villas. Fertile farmlands occupied the fields surrounding Pompeii. Rising sharply behind the city was the four-thousand-foot bulk of Mount Vesuvius, a grass-covered slope where the shepherds of Pompeii took their goats to graze. Pompeii was a busy city and a happy one.

Time started:_____   Number of errors:_____   Time stopped:_____
Comments about speed and expression:

Not very far from Naples a strange city sleeps under the hot Italian sun. It is the city of Pompeii and there is no other city quite like it in all the world. No one lives in Pompeii but crickets and beetles and lizards, yet every year thousands of people travel from distant countries to visit it.

Pompeii is a dead city. No one has lived there for nearly two thousand years, not since the summer of the year AD 79, to be exact.

Until that year Pompeii was a prosperous city of twenty-five thousand people. Nearby was the Bay of Naples, an arm of the blue Mediterranean. Rich men came down from wealthy Rome, 125 miles to the north, to build luxurious seaside villas. Fertile farmlands occupied the fields surrounding Pompeii. Rising sharply behind the city was the four-thousand-foot bulk of Mount Vesuvius, a grass-covered slope where the shepherds of Pompeii took their goats to graze. Pompeii was a busy city and a happy one.

Time started:_____   Number of errors:_____   Time stopped:_____
Comments about speed and expression:

Appendix B:
Graphic Organizers for Reading Strategies

READING STRATEGIES CHECKLIST

Use at least one before-, during-, or after-reading strategy listed below.

Reading Strategy	Before Reading	During Reading	After Reading
READ WITH A PURPOSE	____ I write down my reason for reading. ____ I write down the author's purpose for writing.	____ I read with a purpose in mind.	____ I reflect upon my purpose for reading.
CONNECT TO PRIOR KNOWLEDGE	____ I write down what I know about a topic.	____ I use what I know. ____ I add to what I know.	____ I think about what I learned.
WRITE THINGS DOWN	____ I have the materials I need for writing things down.	____ I mark key points. ____ I use sticky notes. ____ I take notes. ____ I highlight. ____ I react to text.	____ I summarize.
MAKE PREDICTIONS	____ I preview. ____ I guess.	____ I gather more information. ____ I guess again.	____ I analyze my predictions.
VISUALIZE	____ I picture the topic.	____ I make a mind movie. ____ I continue my mind movie.	____ I sketch or summarize my mind movie.
USE TEXT ORGANIZATION	____ I skim the text.	____ I read sections or stanzas. ____ I pay attention to introductions and conclusions. ____ I use headings and signal words. ____ I read charts and graphic aids. ____ I study the pictures. ____ I follow familiar plot, themes, and hidden outlines.	____ I use the organization to review the text.
TACKLE DIFFICULT WORDS	____ I study words beforehand.	____ I use context clues. ____ I look at prefixes and suffixes. ____ I consult a dictionary. ____ I ask a teacher or friend for help.	____ I use the words and add them to my working vocabulary.
MONITOR YOUR READING PROGRESS		**Fix-Up Ideas** ____ I reread. ____ I ask questions. ____ I read in shorter chunks. ____ I read aloud. ____ I take time to refocus. ____ I unlock difficult words. ____ I change my reading rate. ____ I create a mnemonic device.	

READ WITH A PURPOSE: AUTHOR'S PURPOSE CHART

An author may write with the following purposes in mind:

- ❑ to inform (expository/informative writing)
- ❑ to entertain, enrich, enlighten, and/or use an artistic medium such as fiction or poetry to share a perspective (imaginative/descriptive writing)
- ❑ to make a point by sharing a story about an event (narrative writing)
- ❑ to reflect (personal/expressive writing)
- ❑ to persuade readers or listeners to respond in some way, such as to agree with a position, change a view on an issue, reach an agreement, or perform an action (persuasive/argumentative writing)

The following types of writing reflect these purposes:

- ❑ Expository/informative: news article, research report
- ❑ Imaginative/descriptive: poem, short story
- ❑ Narrative: biography, family history
- ❑ Personal/expressive: diary entry, personal letter
- ❑ Persuasive/argumentative: editorial, petition

Before Reading
Identify the author's purpose, the type of writing he or she uses, and the ideas he or she wants to communicate.

During Reading
Gather ideas that the author communicates to readers.

After Reading
Summarize the ideas the author communicates. Explain how these ideas help fulfill the author's purpose.

READ WITH A PURPOSE: READER'S PURPOSE CHART

Fill in the Reader's Purpose Chart at each stage of reading to set a purpose for reading and to help you attain it.

Before Reading
Set a purpose for reading. *(Example: I am going to determine the overall mood of this poem.)*

During Reading
Take notes on what you learn. *(Example: mournful owl—sounds sad)*

After Reading
Reflect on your purpose and what you learned. *(Example: I wanted to find the overall mood of this poem. From the notes that I took, I believe the mood is melancholy and sad.)*

CONNECT TO PRIOR KNOWLEDGE: K-W-L CHART

Connect to what you know and what you want to know by filling in the first two columns before you read. Fill in the last column after you read.

What I *Know*	What I *Want* to Learn	What I Have *Learned*

CONNECT TO PRIOR KNOWLEDGE: REACTIONS CHART

Since you cannot write in, mark up, or highlight text in a textbook or library book, use this chart to record your thoughts and reactions. As you read, ask yourself questions, make predictions, react to ideas, identify key points, and/or write down unfamiliar words.

Page #	Questions, Predictions, Reactions, Key Points, and Unfamiliar Words

WRITE THINGS DOWN: NOTE TAKING CHART

Take notes in the chart below as you read nonfiction or informational selections.

Section or Page	Main Ideas	My Reactions

Summary of My Notes

WRITE THINGS DOWN: PRO AND CON CHART

As you read a persuasive or argumentative selection, take notes on both sides of each argument.

Arguments in Favor (Pro)	Arguments Against (Con)
Argument 1: Support:	Argument 1: Support:
Argument 2: Support:	Argument 2: Support:

WRITE THINGS DOWN: VENN DIAGRAM

Use a Venn diagram to compare and contrast ideas in one selection or to compare two selections.

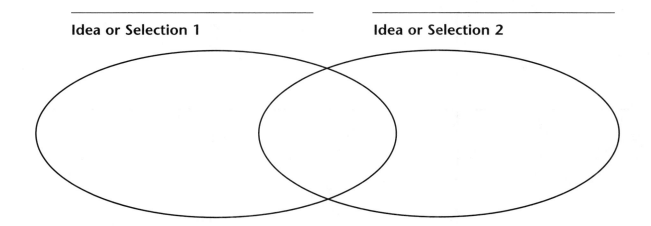

Idea or Selection 1　　　　**Idea or Selection 2**

WRITE THINGS DOWN: CLUSTER CHART

Fill in the cluster chart below to keep track of character traits or main ideas. In the center circle, write the name of the character or topic. In the circles branching out from the center, write details about the character or topic.

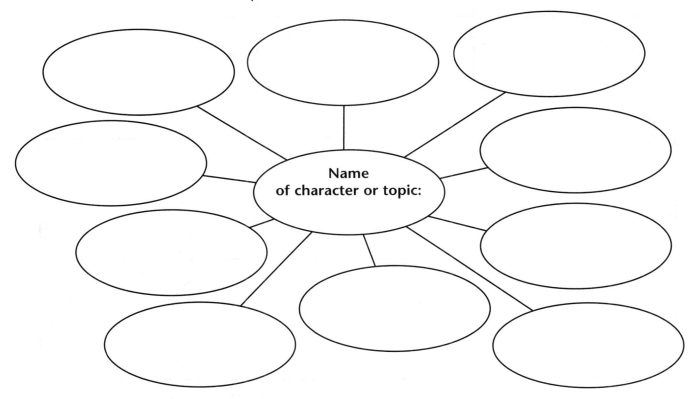

Name of character or topic:

WRITE THINGS DOWN: WRITING IDEAS LOG

Keep track of writing ideas inspired by what you read. Draw pictures or write brief notes that you can use later in a writing assignment.

Date	Idea	Inspired By

MAKE PREDICTIONS: PREDICTION CHART

Gather information before and during reading that helps you make predictions about a literature selection. Write your predictions in the "Guesses" column. Write reasons for your guesses in the "Reasons" column. As you read, gather evidence that either supports or disproves your predictions. Change your predictions and add new ones as you learn more about the selection.

Guesses	Reasons	Evidence

MAKE PREDICTIONS: CHARACTER CHART

A **character** is a person (or sometimes an animal) who figures in the action of a literary work. Choose one character from the selection and fill in the chart below based on what you learn about the character as you read.

Character's Name:	Physical Appearance	Habits/ Mannerisms/ Behaviors	Relationships with Other People	Other Characteristics
Your description of the character at the beginning of the story				
Your predictions for this character				
Your analysis of the character at the end of the story				

VISUALIZE: SENSORY DETAILS CHART

As you read, identify images or words and phrases that contain sensory details. Write each sensory detail beneath the sense to which it appeals.

Sight	Sound	Touch	Taste	Smell

VISUALIZE: FIGURATIVE LANGUAGE CHART

As you read, identify examples of figurative language. Write down examples of figurative language in the first column below. In the second column, write down the comparison being made by the figurative language, and in the third column, describe what the figurative language makes you envision.

Example of Figurative Language	What Is Compared	What You Envision

USE TEXT ORGANIZATION: STORY STRIP

Draw pictures that represent key events in a selection. Then write a caption under each box that explains each event. Draw the events in the order in which they occurred.

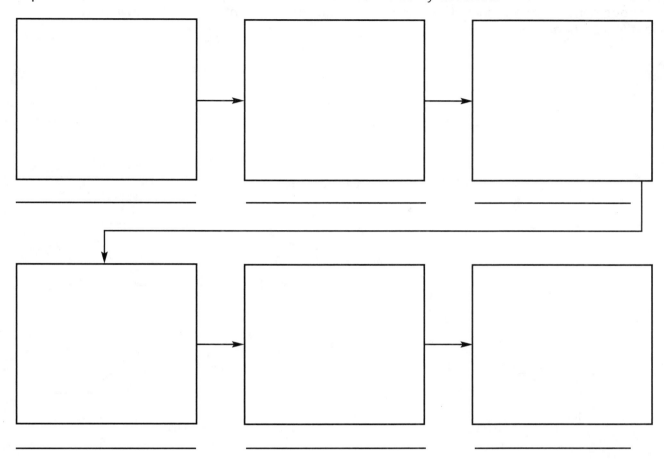

USE TEXT ORGANIZATION: TIME LINE

Use a time line to keep track of important events in a literature selection.

Dates:

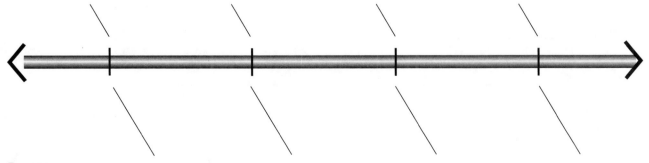

Events:

Use Text Organization: Plot Diagram

Use the plot diagram below to chart the plot of a literature selection. In the spaces provided, describe the exposition, inciting incident, rising and falling action, climax, resolution, and dénouement. Be sure to include in the rising action the key events that build toward the climax of the selection.

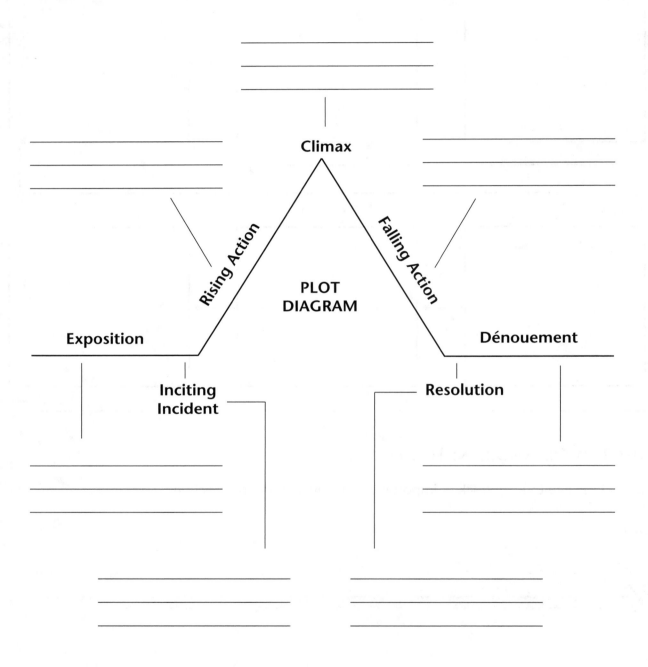

USE TEXT ORGANIZATION: CAUSE-AND-EFFECT CHART

Keep track of what happens in a story and why in the chart below. Use cause-and-effect signal words to help you identify causes and their effects. (Examples of cause-and-effect words: *as a result, because, if/then, since, therefore, this led to.*)

Cause → → → → → → → → → → → Effect

_____   _____

_____   _____

↓
↓

**Summary statement of what happened
in the selection and why:**

_____

_____

USE TEXT ORGANIZATION: SUMMARY CHART

Read and summarize short sections of a selection at a time. Then write a summary of the entire work.

Summary of Section 1:
Summary of Section 2:
Summary of Section 3:
Summary of the Selection:

USE TEXT ORGANIZATION: DRAWING CONCLUSIONS LOG

Draw conclusions about a selection by gathering supporting points for key ideas. Reread the supporting points and key ideas and draw a conclusion about the main or overall message of the selection.

Key Idea:	Key Idea:	Key Idea:
Supporting Points:	Supporting Points:	Supporting Points:

Conclusion about Overall Message:

USE TEXT ORGANIZATION: MAIN IDEA MAP

To find the main or overall message of a whole selection or a part of the selection, gather important details into a Main Idea Map. Use the details to determine the main or overall message. Note: In fiction, the main idea is also known as the theme.

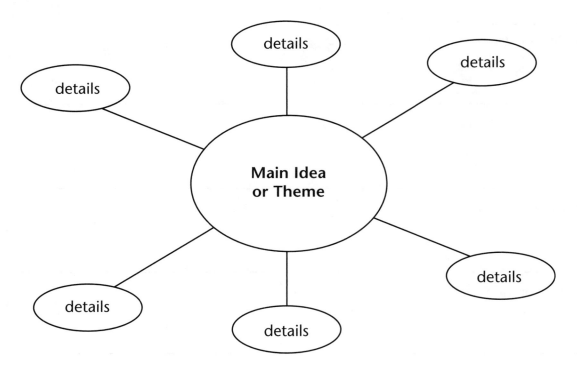

TACKLE DIFFICULT VOCABULARY: WORD SORT

Write one challenging word or phrase in each of the boxes below, along with its definition and part of speech. Cut the boxes apart. Then sort the words using one of the following methods.

- Same parts of speech
- Words with similar or opposite meanings
- Words with prefixes and suffixes
- Words that relate to each other or that can be used together
- My own sorting method: _____

Word: **Definition:** **Part of Speech:**	**Word:** **Definition:** **Part of Speech:**	**Word:** **Definition:** **Part of Speech:**
Word: **Definition:** **Part of Speech:**	**Word:** **Definition:** **Part of Speech:**	**Word:** **Definition:** **Part of Speech:**

TACKLE DIFFICULT VOCABULARY: WORD STUDY NOTEBOOK

Keeping a word study notebook is a convenient way to log new words, their meanings and their spelling, as well as prefixes, suffixes, word roots, and other concepts. When you record a new word, include its definition, pronunciation, and origins, along with an example sentence and a drawing to help you remember it.

Word: _____

Pronunciation: _____

Origins: _____

_____

Definition: _____

Sentence: _____

Drawing:

Tackle Difficult Vocabulary: Word Study Log

Keep track of the words you gather in your word study notebook in the log below.

100								
95								
90								
85								
80								
75								
70								
65								
60								
55								
50								
45								
40								
35								
30								
25								
20								
15								
10								
5								
Total Number of Words in My Word Study Notebook	Week of	Week of	Week of	Week of	Week of	Week of	Week of	Week of

TACKLE DIFFICULT VOCABULARY: WORD MAP

Write a challenging word or phrase in the first box below. Beneath the word or phrase, include its definition, word parts you recognize, and several synonyms. In the two boxes at the bottom, write a sentence that uses the word or phrase and create a drawing that helps you remember it.

A Challenging Word or Phrase

Definition

Word Parts I Recognize

Synonyms

A Sentence That Contains the Word or Phrase

A Picture That Illustrates the Word or Phrase

MONITOR YOUR READING PROCESS: FIX-UP IDEAS LOG

Recognizing that you don't understand something is as important as knowing that you do understand it. Sometimes you may find yourself just reading the words but not actually comprehending or getting the meaning of what you are reading. If you are having trouble comprehending something you are reading, try using some of the fix-up ideas listed below to get back on track.

- Reread
- Ask a question
- Read in shorter chunks
- Read aloud
- Retell

- Work with a partner
- Unlock difficult words
- Change your reading rate
- Choose a new strategy
- Create a mnemonic device

Problems I Encountered while Reading	Fix-Up-Ideas I Used

MONITOR YOUR READING PROGRESS: YOUR OWN GRAPHIC ORGANIZER

Graphic organizers help you understand and remember information. Use your imagination to modify a graphic organizer in this appendix, or invent a new one. Use your graphic organizer to arrange ideas as you read and to guide your discussion and writing actions after you read. Graphic organizer possibilities are endless!

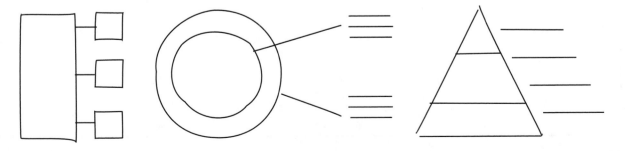

MONITOR YOUR READING PROGRESS: READING STRATEGIES EVALUATION CHART

My Evaluation of My Progress	My Teacher's Evaluation of My Progress
Things I Do Before Reading	My Actions Taken Before Reading
Things I Do During Reading	My Actions Taken During Reading
Things I Do After Reading	My Actions Taken After Reading

MONITOR YOUR READING PROGRESS: BOOKS I WANT TO READ

Keep track of books you want to read in the chart below. Whenever you read a book on your list, add a checkmark to the first column to indicate that you have read the book.

✔	Title	Author	Genre	Notes

Appendix C: *Acknowledgments*

LITERARY ACKNOWLEDGMENTS

Susan Bergholz Literary Services. "Eleven" by Sandra Cisneros from *Woman Hollering Creek*. Copyright © 1991 by Sandra Cisneros. Published by Vintage Books, a division of Random House, Inc., and originally in hardcover by Random House, Inc. Reprinted by permission of Susan Bergholz Literary Services, New York. All rights reserved.

Georges Borchardt, Inc. "Dragon, Dragon" by John Gardner from *Dragon, Dragon and Other Tales*. Copyright © 1975 by Boskydell Artists, Ltd. Reprinted by permission of Georges Borchardt, Inc.

Walker Brents. "The Twelve Labors of Hercules" retold by Walker Brents. Copyright © 2000 by Walker Brents.

Curtis Brown Ltd. *The Ugly Duckling* by A. A. Milne. Copyright © 1941 by A. A. Milne. Reproduced by permission of Curtis Brown Ltd., London.

Don Congdon Associates, Inc. "All Summer in a Day" by Ray Bradbury from *Magazine of Fantasy and Science Fiction*, March 1954. Copyright © 1954, renewed 1982 by Ray Bradbury. Reprinted by permission of Don Congdon Associates, Inc.

Graywolf Press. "One Time" by William Stafford from *The Way It Is: New & Selected Poems*. Copyright © 1982, 1998 by the Estate of William Stafford. Reprinted with the permission of Graywolf Press, Saint Paul, Minnesota.

HarperCollins Publishers, Inc. "Zlateh the Goat" by Isaac Bashevis Singer from *Zlateh the Goat and Other Stories*. Text copyright © 1966 by Isaac Bashevis Singer. Used by permission of HarperCollins Publishers, Inc.

Henry Holt and Company, LLC. "The Cow of No Color" by Nina Jaffe and Steve Zeitlin from *The Cow of No Color: Riddle Stories and Justice Tales from Around the World.* Copyright © 1998 by Nina Jaffe and Steve Zeitlin. Reprinted by permission of Henry Holt and Company, LLC.

Houghton Mifflin Company. "Don't Step on a Crack" by Lila Perl from *Don't Sing Before Breakfast, Don't Sleep in the Moonlight: Everyday Superstitions and How They Began*. Text copyright © 1988 by Lila Perl. Reprinted by permission of Clarion Books/Houghton Mifflin Company. All rights reserved. From *Gorillas in the Mist* by Dian Fossey. Copyright © 1983 by Dian Fossey. Reprinted by permission of Houghton Mifflin Company. All rights reserved.

International Creative Management, Inc. "How to Eat Like a Child" by Delia Ephron from *How to Eat Like a Child*. Copyright © 1977, 1978 by Delia Ephron. Reprinted by permission of International Creative Management, Inc.

David LaRochelle. "Contests!". Copyright © 2000 by David LaRochelle.

Little, Brown and Company, (Inc.). "Satchel Paige" by Bill Littlefield from *Champions: Stories of Ten Remarkable Athletes*. Text copyright © 1993 by Bill Littlefield; illustrations copyright © 1993 by Bernie Fuchs. By permission of Little, Brown and Company (Inc.).

Nancy Love Literary Agency. From *Dear Ms. Demeanor* by Mary Mitchell. Copyright © 1995. Published by McGraw-Hill Companies. Reprinted by permission of the author.

Random House, Inc. "Priscilla and the Wimps" by Richard Peck from *Sixteen: Short Stories by Outstanding Writers for Young Adults* by Donald R. Gallo, ed. Copyright © 1984 by Richard Peck. Used by permission of Random House Children's Books, a division of Random House, Inc. "Life Doesn't Frighten Me" by Maya Angelou from *And Still I Rise*. Copyright © 1978 by Maya Angelou. Reprinted by permission of Random House, Inc.

Marian Reiner. "The Sidewalk Racer, or On the Skateboard" by Lillian Morrison from *The Sidewalk Racer and Other Poems of Sports and Motion*. Copyright © 1965, 1967, 1968, 1977 by Lillian Morrison. Used by permission of Marian Reiner for the author.

Scholastic, Inc. From "Ta-Na-E-Ka" by Mary Whitebird. Published in *Scholastic Voice,* December 13, 1973. Copyright © 1973 by Scholastic, Inc. Reprinted by permission. From "A Breath of Fresh Air?" by Alexandra Hanson-Harding published in *Junior Scholastic*, April 11, 1997. Copyright © 1997 by Scholastic Inc. Reprinted by permission.

Stormking Music, Inc. "The Springhill Disaster" by Peggy Seeger and Ewan MacColl. Copyright © 1960 (renewed) by Stormking Music, Inc. All rights reserved. Used by permission.

Ralph M. Vicinanza Ltd. "Pompeii" by Robert Silverberg from *Lost Cities and Vanished Civilizations*. Copyright © 1962 by Robert Silverberg. Published by permission of Robert Silverberg c/o Ralph M. Vicinanza, Ltd.

ART ACKNOWLEDGMENTS

Cover Illustration Works; **65** © Ed Eckstein/CORBIS; **112** © Karl Weatherly/CORBIS; **131** © Owen Franken/CORBIS; **417** © Archivo Iconografico, S.A./CORBIS; **201** Paul Almasy/CORBIS; **237** © Jennifer Wreisner; **254** © Bettmann/CORBIS; **278** © Yann Arthus-Bertrand/CORBIS; **311** Roger Ressmeyer/CORBIS; **328** SuperStock.